GIVING MUSIC its DUE

THE MUSIC ALLIANCE

musi©publishersassociation

Giving Music Its Due

by Terri Anderson

The history and work of the UK organisations for composers, authors and publishers of music, the Music Publishers' Association, the Mechanical Copyright Protection Society, and the Performing Right Society.

Published in 2004 by The MCPS-PRS Alliance Limited, Copyright House, 29-33 Berners Street, London W1T 3AB.

© The MCPS-PRS Alliance Limited

ISBN 0 9547105 1 7

The Mechanical Copyright Protection Society
The Performing Right Society
The MCPS-PRS Alliance
Copyright House, 29-33 Berners Street, London W1T 3AB

The Music Publishers Association
Strandgate, 18-20 York Bldgs, London WC2N 6JU

Designed by WPA London Ltd
Printed by Ashford Colour Press Ltd

Contents Page

Acknowledgments

For his PRS history up to 1988 *Harmonious Alliance*, which he kindly agreed should be a key source of historical information for the Author – Professor Cyril Ehrlich. For his enthusiastic and guiding involvement from germ of idea to final printed work – Chief Executive of MCPS, PRS and the Music Alliance John Hutchinson, who on behalf of those companies commissioned this first combined history all the UK music rights organisations. For their support of the project and their thoughtful input at various stages, PRS Chairman David Bedford, MCPS Chairman Jonathan Simon, MPA Chairman Andrew Potter and British Music Rights Chairman Sir Alistair Hunter. For their support, advice, interest and generous provision of information from their personal recollections or archive resources throughout this project – former PRS CEO Michael Freegard, former MCPS MD Robert Montgomery and MPA CEO Sarah Faulder.

For their unstinting willingness to supply ideas and information, check work in progress and kindly point out errors and potential political disasters, members of the former or current top management of MCPS, PRS and the Alliance – Executive Director PRS John Axon, Executive Director MCPS Sandra Cox, former New Technology Director Mark Isherwood, Chief Legal Counsel David Lester, former Executive Director MCPS Chris Martin, Chief Operating Officer Steve Porter and Chief Information Officer John Rathbone; also Company Secretary Amanda Arnold.

Appreciative thanks also to all other interviewees and contributors of text and pictures who gave their time to this project – including CISAC Secretary General Eric Baptiste, former PRS Chairmen Wayne Bickerton and Roger Greenaway, Chris Butler, Director and General Manager of Music Sales Ltd, former Director General of the BPI John Deacon, Chief Executive of PPL Fran Nevrkla, former MCPS Chairman Bob Kingston, former MCPS Deputy MD Keith Lowde, former MCPS Data Services Controller Godfrey Rust, former MCPS MD Frans de Wit, former MPA Chairman Stephen James, Universal Music Group Senior Vice President International, Legal and Business Affairs Crispin Evans, former MCPS Commercial Operations Controller Graham Churchill, former Director General of British Music Rights Frances Lowe, British Music Rights General Manager Henrietta Yoxall, PRS and Alliance External Director Malcolm Coster, British Academy of Composers and Songwriters Chairman David Ferguson and CEO Chris Green, PRS Members Fund General Secretary John Logan; also other former colleagues of the Author during her 12 years with PRS and the Alliance, who in this history project not only helped but found time in their demanding schedules to give that help at the moment it was most needed – Sue Booth, Adrian Crookes, Graham Davies, Diana Derrick, Rob Ferrari, David Francis, Chris Gardner, Jonathan Hodgetts, Ray Luker, Peter Nottingham, Simi Obra, Mike Orchard, Mike Palmer, Sue Roberts, Andy Rock, John Rowe, Clive Thomas, Ed Williamson, and Karen Fishman for legal expertise.

Thanks also to contributors Paul Brindley of MusicAlly and journalists Nigel Hunter and David Laing for editorial assistance, and Tony Collins for permission to use an extract from his book *Crash*. Final and particular mention, for their uncritical confidence in the Author's abilities and for their unflagging practical help and general good humour at every stage in the work – Senior PA Maureen Bowtell, Alliance Planning and Research Manager Jeremy Mortimer, and Alliance Publications and Design Manager Paul Nichols.

Preface

It is widely accepted that companies and organisations need to be aware of their history just as much as individuals or civilisations do. In corporate histories are all the elements to be found in the stories of peoples and their governments, their wars , their inventions, their greatness and their pettiness – just on a smaller and faster scale and without most of the colourful epic language. There are also lessons to be learnt for the future.

This book tells the story of four UK organisations which serve the very particular interests of a particular group of people. These people are as individually unalike as the rest of the human race, but they have one very special thing in common: they are music creators. The intrinsic value of what they create might be the subject of endless debate, often vociferous (one of the best ways to start a heated argument is to start a nice civilised discussion about musical taste), but thanks to hard-won protection under Copyright Law, the monetary value of their works can be established. This monetary value can also, in countries with good law and the means to enforce it, be realised. But to achieve that it has proved sensible and necessary all over the world for music creators to resort to collective administration of their rights. And since businesses have been built on the commercial exploitation of those rights, alongside the collecting societies which licence users and pay royalties to creators there are trade associations for music businesses, and professional associations for composers and songwriters.

The stories of the Mechanical-Copyright Protection Society Limited (MCPS) and the Performing Right Society Limited (PRS) as collecting societies; of the Music Publishers' Association (MPA) as a trade body; and of The MCPS-PRS Alliance Limited as the joint operating company which brought their activities together, are set out in this book, which is prefaced with some personal thoughts and stories from the Chairmen who were at the head of each organisation at the time this account was written, and from the Chief Executive of PRS, MCPS and the Alliance.

John Hutchinson
Chief Executive

As Chief Executive of PRS, MCPS and their operational Alliance John Hutchinson is one person who certainly subscribes to the idea that a company should know its own history; he is also able to reflect on the organisations he runs from a vantage point which is rare in the music business – that of the outsider who joined that rather strange business quite late and from an apparently very different profession.

Just nine years ago I was busy working away in an entirely different world as Managing Director of VISA UK. I had spent just over 34 years in the world of banking and, although quite late in my career I had broken out from my first job with Lloyds Bank and gained experience with Nationwide Building Society and VISA, I was still very much a financial services man.

Because the banking world had been going through profound changes, many of my contemporaries had already retired by the age of 51 when I was first approached about a job with PRS.

Many people within the music industry have suggested that I must have been surprised at how different this business is when compared to where I worked before. Well – Yes and No.

Yes – this is a much less predictable and more exciting business but, No – the same business rules apply; you just have to find out how to apply them. Early in my time as Chief Executive of MCPS and PRS, I defined how I saw our responsibilities as collecting societies as being to collect as much money as possible and distribute it as quickly, fairly and accurately as possible and at the least possible cost.

I think what did come as somewhat of a surprise to me was how many of the various skills that I had gained in all those 34 years would be required just a very few months into the new job. It required no more than commonsense to recognise that PRS and MCPS belonged together but it required all the experience I had gained in people management and in mergers and acquisitions to make an Alliance happen.

The Alliance is, for me, the biggest thing to happen during my tenure as Chief Executive; but probably the most important developments for members of both PRS and MCPS are that the business has continued to grow, each year's results has been better than the last and we have never missed a distribution deadline. We should never underestimate people's desire for unexciting routine when it relates to their personal finances!

David Bedford
Chairman of the
Performing Right Society

My involvement in PRS goes back a long way and is actually a part of my family history. My paternal grandmother, Liza Lehmann, a distinguished composer, mainly of songs, became the first writer member of PRS in 1914. I grew up, therefore, with a full knowledge of, and sympathy for, the rights of creators. This was reinforced by frequent meetings with my cousin, writer Rosamund Lehmann.

A more personal professional involvement came with my admission as a writer member in December 1967. Later, I became Chairman of the Association of Professional Composers, one of the three composers' organisations which now make up the British Academy of Composers and Songwriters. In this capacity, my involvement became more critical, sometimes even confrontational. Like many of my classical colleagues, I couldn't fully understand the rationale behind sampling [meaning in this case the sampling of performances for the purposes of royalty distribution, as opposed to full census] and believed that I should be paid for all my performances.

However, having got a taste for the politics of music, and being determined to continue to help creative colleagues in some way, I stood for election to the PRS General Council (as the Board was then called) at the 1994 AGM, and was elected. Since then I've served as Deputy Chair Writer for a period, before being elected to the Chair.

Thus I've seen PRS both as a customer and as an insider, have complained to PRS in the past, and listened to complaints in the present.

I've seen PRS grow from a membership of 199 when my grandmother joined (198 publishers, 1 writer!), to 4000 when I joined, to today's 38,000. There's no question that PRS has improved out of all recognition over the last 36 years since I was admitted. We distribute more money, faster, more transparently and more accurately than ever before. That is the thread running through PRS history, as is the greater management efficiency, which has led to an administration rate of 43.5% in 1928 being reduced to today's 14.5%.

There's still a big difference between PRS and the Alliance. PRS is member facing, we cover the country with Open Meetings, our M magazine has been an enormous success, our new distribution system will be giving far greater choice to members as to the way in which they receive their money, and more and more members are registering works online.

It is true that there are governance differences between PRS and MCPS, particularly in the way the Boards are set up: elected by the members in the case of PRS and appointed by the MPA in the case of MCPS. The way the money is distributed differs in that many writers are not paid directly by MCPS, with the money going first to the publishers so that advances can be recouped. Nevertheless, at the moment roughly 50% of collecting societies embody the mechanical right as well as the performing right with or without two separate names, and the number is increasing. It's very important, therefore, that the Alliance succeeds. We are in the business of collecting and giving out money to our creators and their publishers, and there is no room for squabbling.

"Without music, life is a journey through a desert" (Pat Conroy).

And unless our creators receive a just reward for their work, whatever the means of its propagation – live concert, broadcast, online – we may end up with a desert.

Jonathan Simon
Chairman of the Mechanical-
Copyright Protection Society

It was a wise man who observed that the only thing that was new was the history yet to be written. Having worked in our industry for almost two generations, I welcome this enterprise, believing that careful reflection upon things past can so often unearth the key to how we should approach some seemingly impossible situation in the immediate future. The advent of the printing press might arguably be bracketed with the emergence of the photocopier and the development of the tape cassette as the potential devaluation – if not the total destruction – of the creator's art. Though such innovations have, in truth, often provided more and greater opportunities for creators than the problems heralded by the doomsayers at the time of their coming.

In collection society terms, MCPS remained coloured for many years by its somewhat humble origins. Like its counterparts in the USA, Australia and South Africa, where the amount of direct collection by copyright owners was material, it fed off the scraps which were left behind. These included minor record companies, production music and, where such existed, broadcast mechanicals. The advent of the new UK Copyright Act of 1988 and the achievement of virtually a total mandate represented a quantum leap for the Society. This position of strength has since made its bargaining position of a far greater superiority when negotiating industry wide licences.

Despite these rather uncertain times, I now see a society which shares much of the potency of its sister society, the PRS, and is a natural partner in the Alliance. There seems to have been a misplaced perception that the rationale and *modus operandi* of each of the two societies are at loggerheads. They are not and probably never have been. Aside from the difference, albeit fundamental of agent versus assignee, their aims are identical. As a consequence, I have never felt any discomfort in sitting on both Boards.

Over recent years the Alliance has demonstrated ably that, aside from the obvious saving of costs, there are many other advantages. Rationalisation of information systems to achieve clean, common data is a long sought and welcome goal; in the digital age, the ability to issue joint licences and to address the scary prospect of "bundling rights", are scenarios which were unforeseen at the start of my tenure. As to the future, while there may be more of the problems faced in the past, surely they must continue to be outweighed by the opportunities.

Andrew Potter

Chairman of the
Music Publishers' Association

The phrase "writers and their children" resonates on the earliest pages of this history. Songs and symphonies are the offspring of writers and composers, who appoint music publishers as guardians. Publishers, many of whom are themselves creative musicians, help nurture the music and guard its well-being. Although this history shows how British publishers have played a leading part in forming and developing main music collecting societies, it also reflects their acute awareness of their responsibilities to the music – to protect as well as realise its value. By licensing a right through a collecting society, it is as though we are sending the child away to school – placing it in the hands of another authority, often far from home. Publishers are therefore "critical friends" of societies – and so of course are the writers with whom they govern the societies. Although we express unease when our own company interests are threatened, publishers are also among the strongest and most willing contributors to the collective strength.

Within the wealth of information in this book can be found the reasons why collective administration is important to publishers. Commissioned by a dynamic Chief Executive as a record of many crucial changes, and written by a leading player at the heart of the alliance process, it provides an expert view of the operation of two distinct organisms seeking clear progress within a complex environment. This complexity embraces the economics and behaviour of the creative and customer markets, the value that society places on music, the law of copyright, and the shifting uses of music, as well as the handling of data about multi-owned songs across many different territories. There is an obvious logic for publishers actively to share the addressing of these issues in order to save cost and enhance value.

As PRS Chair for the crucial six years in the wake of the Monopolies and Mergers Commission report and as one of the first joint Chair of the Alliance, I felt very keenly the determination of publishers and writers alike to work together to improve and strengthen the value, recognition and operation of music rights. The Alliance was a firm token of this determination. May it continue from strength to strength!

The Boards

Throughout the history of all three organisations many individual members, both writers and publishers, have contributed their time and attention to being a Board Director for one or more of these organisations.

All are Directors within the meaning of the Companies Act, but that says little about the people themselves. From the owners, heads and senior managers of publishing companies (and publishers were the founders of all these organisations at different points in history), to the many composers and songwriters who in time joined them in the work of directing the organisations, a great variety of interesting, talented, strong-minded, sometimes trenchant, and committed individuals have represented and served the interests of many thousands of their UK peers in the sphere of music creation and commercial exploitation.

They directed often embattled companies as they tried to improve copyright law and apply it, to fight piracy, to provide member services, to communicate and gain understanding for the complicated business of rights licensing and collection which drew little natural sympathy from governments, users, press or public. They brought to the job their knowledge of their own areas of interest, their hopes, expectations and demands for themselves and all others in their professions, their opinions and arguments. While the role of Board Director for PRS, MCPS or the MPA was often in past times relatively undemanding, those who have served in the past decade have faced calls on time and attention which reflect the huge increase in volume and pace of work the organisations have shouldered: work requiring ever more complex strategic thinking and decision-taking from the Boards, preceded by the necessity to accept and absorb levels of business information which their predecessors would have found daunting.

So there is some flavour of a roll of honour in this list of Board Directors who were in place at the time this history was published, some of them having been elected or appointed many times over many years and some of them fairly new to the task. Because the membership of the four Boards overlaps, the Directors are listed here in a table indicating their span of directorships.

Board Directors		Representing	MPA	MCPS	PRS	MCPS-PRS Alliance
Elected or appointed Directors						
Mark Anders	publisher	Bug Music	•			
Peter Barnes	publisher	Pink Floyd Music Publishers Ltd	•			
Nigel Beaham Powell	writer				•	•
David Bedford (Chairman, PRS)	writer				•	•
Catherine Bell	publisher	Chrysalis Music Ltd	•		•	
William Booth	publisher	EMI Music Publishing Ltd	•	•		
Tom Bradley	publisher	Quiet Man Music	•	•		•
Chris Butler	publisher	Music Sales Limited			•	
Peter Callander	writer			•	•	•
Jonathan Channon	publisher	EMI Music Publishing Ltd			•	
Peter Cornish	publisher	Fairwood Music Ltd		•		•
Malcolm Coster	external				•	•
Paul Curran	publisher	BMG Music Publishing Ltd	•	•	•	
Leslie East	publihser	Assoc. Board Royal Schools of Music (Publishing) Ltd	•			
Jane Dyball	publisher	Warner/Chappell Music Publishing Ltd	•	•	•	
Nigel Elderton	publisher	Peermusic (UK) Ltd			•	•
Crispin Evans	publisher	Universal Music Publishing Int. Limited	•	•	•	•
David Ferguson	writer			•		
Guy Fletcher	writer				•	
Wanda Goldwag	external				•	
Nicky Graham	writer				•	
Edward Gregson	composer				•	
Barrie Guard	writer			•		•
Christopher Gunning	composer				•	
Andy Heath	publisher	4AD Music Ltd	•	•	•	
Stuart Hornall	publisher	Hornall Bros Music Ltd	•	•		
Stephen James	publisher	Dejamus Ltd	•			
David Japp	publisher	Carlin Music Corporation	•			

Board Directors		Representing	MPA	MCPS	PRS	MCPS-PRS Alliance
David Kassner	publisher	Kassner Associated Publishers Ltd	•			
David Kee	external					•
Andrew King	publisher	Mute Songs			•	
Richard King	publihser	Faber Music Ltd	•			
Mick Leeson	writer				•	•
John McLeod	writer				•	
John Minch	publisher	Boosey & Hawkes Music Publishing Ltd	•			
Mitch Murray	writer				•	
Andrew Neve	writer				•	
Ben Newing	publisher	Schott/Universal Edition		•		
Simon Platz	publisher	Bucks Music Group Ltd	•			
Andrew Potter (Chairman, MPA)	publisher	Oxford University Press	•	•	•	
Ellis Rich	publisher	Independent Music Group	•	•	•	•
Shirley Ranger	publisher	United Music Publishers Ltd	•			
Nicholas Riddle	publisher	Peters Edition Ltd	•			
Sarah Rodgers	writer			•		•
James Rushton	publisher	Chester Music Ltd	•			
John Schofield	publisher	Josef Weinberger Ltd	•			
Jonathan Simon (Chairman, MCPS)	publisher	Moncur Street Music Ltd		•		•

Executive Directors

			MPA	MCPS	PRS	MCPS-PRS Alliance
John Axon					•	
Sandra Cox				•		
Sarah Faulder		Chief Executive MPA	•			
John Hutchinson		Chief Executive the Alliance, MCPS and PRS		•	•	•
David Lester						•
Steve Porter						•
John Rathbone						•
John Sweeney					•	

A number of the Directors listed as current members of one or more of the Boards are pictured here among the PRS Directors of 1996. This was the Board at the time that John Hutchinson joined PRS as Chief Executive. The picture also includes several very well-known and greatly respected Directors who served one, two or all the organisations, but who are no longer on any of the Boards and so are not named in the table of current Directors.

Pictured – *left to right, standing*: Tony Pool (Boosey & Hawkes Music Publishing), writer Andrew Neve, Maggie Rodford (Air-Edel Associates), Jonathan Simon (Really Useful Group, later Moncur Street Music), writers Joseph Horovitz, Nigel Beaham-Powell, Nicholas Graham, Bruce Welch, Stephen James (Dejamus), David Hockman (PolyGram International Music), writer Chris Gunning, Barry Hitchens (Warner Chappell Music), Nigel Elderton (peermusic (UK)), Pete Waterman (Consultant Director), writer Mick Leeson, Deborah Harris (EMI Music Publishing), writers David Bedford and Mitch Murray. *Left to right, seated*: Malcolm Coster (External Director), Paul Curran (BMG Music Publishing), writer Peter Callander, Chief Executive John Hutchinson, Chairman Andrew Potter (Oxford University Press), writer Professor Edward Gregson, Ellis Rich (Supreme Songs, later Independent Music Group), Richard Toeman (Josef Weinberger).

INTRODUCTION AND THREE BEGINNINGS

Introduction

Giving music to the world, and giving music its due

"Music is a part of moral education"
Aristotle

"Music is the product of a man's brain, and
...should be treated as the most sacred of all property."

MP and author T P O'Connor

"Music, of all the liberal arts, has the greatest influence
over the passions and is that to which the legislator
ought to give the greatest encouragement."
Napoleon Bonaparte

"Music is spiritual. The music business is not."

Van Morrison, songwriter and performer
(in an interview with *The Times*)

"Songs are, and always have been, the currency of
this business. The song stays around longer than the
bands, the record companies and the radio stations.
It stays there forever. We use songs to tell us where we
are – to navigate through the mad thing we call life."

Fran Healy, songwriter and performer
(when accepting his Ivor Novello Songwriter of the Year Award in 2000)

Writers and their children

There is a connection between plagiarism and kidnap in the origin of those two words, presumably because creators have always had an emotional attachment to their creations which is something like an attachment of a parent to a child.

The right of a creator to control the use of his creations and to be paid fairly for that use has enjoyed great moments in history. The first and for many years the strongest music authors' society was set up in 1851 in France[1]. As Napoleon's words indicate, post-revolutionary ideals embraced creators of intellectual property and their rights, and supported moves to help them. Creators' rights have always had eloquent support from great individuals: politicians, authors, performers and business leaders. O'Connor was speaking in a 1924 debate in the UK Parliament on music copyright. That these rights have also frequently been attacked is evidenced by the fact that he was defending PRS in what was actually the second of three attempts to abolish the organisation by Act of Parliament.

So, while copyright has through its history been strongly supported, it has also been consistently opposed, undermined and flouted. Although good law and efficient administration are in place in many countries of the world today, that conflict is as evident now as it ever was. In the UK, collecting societies are the target of regular criticism from various directions, but PRS and MCPS are probably safe from any further outright abolition attempts in Parliament – although (perhaps because) both are subject to rigorous scrutiny by various powers from the Office of Fair Trading and the Copyright Tribunal to the media and groupings of their own members.

At the annual Ivor Novello Awards, organised by the British Academy of Composers and Songwriters (BACS) and sponsored by PRS, writers regularly and feelingly make the point that "what really matters is the song" as Fran Healy's words express. And they mean not only the original creative work but also the intellectual property rights which automatically came into existence as soon as that song was composed; rights which belong without question to the creator.

The song – the musical creation – is the constant. Live performance, recordings in a variety of analogue or digital and real or virtual configurations, and dissemination via retail, broadcast or internet are just manifestations of the song. Without the song, these manifestations could not exist, and so the musical creation has a real, realisable, value to all individuals and commercial enterprises which make use of it; and it therefore has a monetary value to the creator which fairly deserves to be linked as closely as possible to the benefit it brings to the user.

This strong conviction is fundamental to the attitudes and expectations which music creators and copyright owners hold in relation to their rights administration societies. It is also a powerful element in the societies' attitudes and ways of working. It is the foundation on which the licensing theory and practice of collecting societies is built, often in the teeth of opposition from music users who hold the widespread view that music use should be cheaper. That may be understandable: more puzzling is the apparent belief, now rife, that where music on the internet is concerned it should actually be free.

The deep-seated sense of the value of creativity and the strong personal and emotional attachment of the creator to the works lead to a kind of paradox, characteristically condensed into a couple of terse sentences by Van Morrison. He might at that moment have been thinking specifically of the record business, but collecting societies are part of the music business as a whole. These organisations undoubtedly bring great benefit to creators, protecting and administering their rights so that they can earn money from them. But the nature and proper function of collecting societies *as businesses* can engender an impression that

---

1 The first collecting society in the world was also founded in France, the dramatic writers' society SACD, in 1791

"it's all about money". At that point the attitudes of the creator and the society can diverge.

In the case of the performing right one example is the wish to receive "recognition" that a work has been performed, even if the payment involved is vanishingly small. Particularly true where writers in less commercially popular musical genres such as contemporary classical, jazz and folk are concerned, this translates as a wish to see every possible effort made by PRS to obtain performance information, even at a high administration cost that considerably reduces total royalties which can be distributed. This is of course at odds with the basic business principle, also the collecting societies' purpose and mission, which is to collect and distribute as much money as possible, to as many members as possible, as quickly as possible, at the lowest possible administrative cost. As the PRS chapter records, these ideas have been at the heart of many issues, activities, conflicts and developments over the years.

In the area of mechanical rights just one illustration would be the first piece of legal work, in the mid-70s, handled by a lawyer whose firm worked for MCPS. David Lester, now the Chief Legal Counsel for the MCPS-PRS Alliance, dealt with the case which ranged the recording artist Tomita and his record label RCA against Imogen Holst, the successor copyright owner to her father Gustav Holst.

In response to a standard application and under the Statutory Licence terms of that time, MCPS had cleared a request for a Tomita recording of the *Planets Suite*. However, it became clear that the recording was in fact an adaptation of the work. Imogen Holst was adamant in her refusal to have her father's works adapted in any way. MCPS does not have a mandate to authorise adaptations:

Gustav Holst, composer of *The Planets*, and an early PRS member.

because it had (as it turned out) been misled into granting a licence, it took action on her behalf and sought an injunction to prevent the recording being made or issued. Tomita was a very commercially successful artist at the time and neither he nor his record company could understand why a copyright owner would wish to forego the kind of income which one of his hit recordings could engender. But the potential income was irrelevant to Ms Holst, whilst the integrity of her father's music as he originally intended it to be heard was of the greatest importance and value.

This case established the precedent that a music creator's wishes could not be overridden in exchange for monetary value. That precedent continues to be invoked by writers who refuse to permit their works to be licensed for any usage connected with certain negative images, practices, activities etc (most common examples are TV ads featuring alcohol or cigarettes, or drama involving drugs, sex or violence or, latterly more likely, all three).

A simple concept but a complicated history

Development of the concept, and then the legal protection, of copyright applies to many forms of creative and artistic works, but this history focuses specifically on music copyright, more specifically on the collective administration of that right, and most specifically on the two UK collecting societies.

Some interesting ironies figured in the history of these organisations. The performing right, now and for some decades past seen by UK writers and music publishers as a cornerstone of their livelihood, was a largely unheeded provision of the Copyright Acts of 1882 and 1888. Even at the time of the 1911 Act, enforcement of the right and establishment of a performing right society was vehemently opposed by publishers as an obstacle in the road to ever-greater sheet music sales. One of the leading, most vocal and vitriolic opponents to the founding of PRS was the MPA Chairman of the time, William Boosey; but his attitude would eventually undergo such a dramatic conversion that he became the first Chairman of PRS.

So the MPA had a powerful hand in the creation of PRS, which it never sought to own or directly control. It had no involvement in the founding of any of the three UK mechanical rights organisation which, in the early 20s, would amalgamate as MCPS. Yet it was MCPS which was bought by the MPA over 60 years later. The Association holds the vast majority of the shares, with a few being held by individuals who were at one time required to hold *a share* while a Board Director .

The stories of both collecting societies are interesting and complicated. One aspect of that is illustrated in persistently conflicting views about similarities and differences between them; the view that they are similar enough to run their operations through one company was the basis for the (many say long overdue) alliance between them in the late 90s, and the benefits which arise from that. Others are adamant that a democratically-run membership organisation is so strikingly different to a commission-based agency (owned by the trade association of the commercial companies within its membership) that the two must always and inevitably be seeking different objectives and following different policies

Themes

Similarities and differences between PRS and MCPS – in their function, history, style and governance – form one theme in the book. Others which developed of their own accord during the writing of this book include the never entirely comfortable, though now seemingly much better than it used to be, relationship between publisher and writer (a major theme in the PRS history *Harmonious Alliance*, published in 1988); tension between rights owners and rights users (and beside that the conflict between creators' exclusive rights in law and the "fair dealing" exceptions to copyright law which have in recent years been won by users); Anglo-American versus European approaches to rights administration (copyright as a property right or as an inalienable author's right – *droit d'auteur*); tension between the intangible and tangible – the musical work on one hand and its material recorded form on the other ("creators and derivatives" in occasional official parlance) and the way all that has affected the attitudes in the record and publishing sides of the music business.

Less a theme, more a conclusion and pointer to the future, is the strong evidence that sectors of the music industry which used to be able to ignore each other ("creators and derivatives") have found it decreasingly possible to do so in the past 10 years – and now find it impossible. Technology and the consumer are forcing rights owners to converge in their thinking and administration just as usage of all kinds of rights converges in an electronic, digitised world. But those rights are as yet distinct and separate, and that was the basis on which the organisations whose stories are told here were founded.

GIVING MUSIC ITS DUE

MECHANICAL-COPYRIGHT PROTECTION SOCIETY LIMITED
(ESTABLISHED OVER A QUARTER OF A CENTURY)

9A, SACKVILLE STREET,
PICCADILLY,
LONDON, W.1

THE MUSIC PUBLISHERS'
ASSOCIATION LIMITED
73-75 MORTIMER STREET · LONDON WIN 7TB
TELEPHONE: 01-580 3399 · 01-636 6027
SECRETARY: DAVID TOFF

musi©publishersassociation

Terminology

Any attempt to tell these stories demands some simplification of terminology. In this book, the elected or appointed directors of all the organisations are referred to as "Boards" throughout (with a few exceptions where an old document or an individual is being quoted directly). To refer to all the titles of Committee, Council, General Council etc which have been in use at different times would be tedious and confusing. For the same reason managers' titles used throughout are, as a rule, those the individuals held at the time this history was completed. Similarly, although the titles President and Chairman have been used at different times to describe the same position within these organisations, in this book the title Chairman is generally used to indicate the head of the elected or appointed board, and president is used to refer to the honorary position holding that title (which has only, as far as can be discovered, applied to PRS). It should be mentioned here however, that the person at head of the MPA Board was until recently always given the title President. Within the music and collecting society business the word "author" is widely used to mean the creator, sometimes more specifically the lyricist as opposed to the composer as a song, though the general public would tend to assume that an author writes literature. In this book it always means "creator of a musical work" – composer, songwriter or lyricist.

Beginnings

The beginnings of all three UK organisations serving those who write and publish music were understandably a response to the need to make money legitimately from musical creativity, and to prevent money being made illegitimately. Both purposes could be pursued because they were supported by copyright law, and so the third core purpose of these organisations was, and still is, lobbying for improved copyright legislation which keeps up with the technology aimed at evading it.

The Music Publishers' Association

Managing somehow to evoke a combination of the coffee house beginnings of Lloyds of London and the New Testament description of the Last Supper, the first brief written history of the MPA notes that "it had been the custom of a few music publishers to meet in a room situated in Bond Street" in the late 1870s. The meetings were mainly social ("games of cards were indulged in amongst other amenities") but then, as now, a group of any two or more music business people will inevitably talk shop. And then, as now, the shop talk was predominantly focused on making money out of their business and defending its earning power from marauders.

To quote again from the short history written in 1945 by retiring MPA Secretary Charles Dixey, who had succeeded his father George in that role and so ensured that the Dixey family had served for an unbroken 60 years: "Gradually it became apparent that if their property was to be preserved, joint action should be taken to stop the misuse of their copyrights. Therefore in 1881 the Association came into existence. It was a small band and for many years it struggled on, doing most useful work but always handicapped by lack of the financial support necessary to meet the expenses, which were mainly legal".

The small band of MPA founders who first formally met at Messrs Collards in London's Grosvenor Street "to discuss how to combat increasing threats and ensure fair wages for fair work" represented publishers including Chappell, Hopwood & Crew, Novello, Patey & Willis and Lafleur. Their intention was to protect the rights of authors, composers and publishers, and at that time one of the major increasing threats was piracy of copyright printed music, sold by hawkers on the streets; and another was illegally imported printed music (for example, at one time the ancestors of the late 20th century butter and beef runners across the border between the Irish Republic and Northern Ireland were the Irish print entrepreneurs of the late 19th and early 20th centuries who exploited a legal loophole by printing copies of UK copyright sheet music and bringing the printed copies into the English market via Liverpool docks).

So fighting piracy was the task for which the MPA was primarily formed. As early as 1884 it was offering the very large sum of £10 to anyone who assisted with the conviction of an importer of "pirated copyrights"; in 1905 it orchestrated a "publishing ban" to draw attention to still-widespread illegal importation and to the lack of legislative support for copyright issues. It would be good to be able to look back 122 years later and record that this task was successfully completed; that the MPA had comprehensively seen off the copyright buccaneers, scuttled their ships and strung every man-jack of 'em from the yardarms of Tin Pan Alley[2] leaving music copyright unmolested for all succeeding generations of composers, songwriters and publishers.

The facts, of course, are nothing like that. Anyone reading the Minutes of MPA Board meetings from any of those 122 years would experience a permanent sense of *déjà vu*. The main issues which preoccupied the founders of the MPA continue to do so today. It would not be too difficult to quote fairly extensively from randomly-chosen Minutes in any of 12 decades and match the subject matter to accounts of recent meetings.

What has changed is the nature of the piracy, the range of organisations involved in fighting it, and hard-won progressive improvement in protection under the law which helped anti-piracy activity by the music business to be more effective (but, of course, the pirates became more effective too). Much later the record industry would take on its share of the anti-piracy battle, through its own trade association: the BPI – British Phonographic Industry – was incorporated in 1973. Later still, and into the present, all these rights-related organisations came to work together, with BPI and MCPS leading the action, in fighting copyright infringement from the blatant large-scale manufacture of counterfeit recordings (possibly now decreasing in developed countries) to several varieties of electronic piracy via the internet (increasing everywhere).

In the early years the issue of copyright infringement was a complicated one in some ways, particularly where the MPA was concerned just before and for some time after PRS was formed, with publishers at one time effectively inviting music users to infringe the right PRS was trying to license. The strands of that story are followed in more detail in other chapters, but they were part of the weave from the outset.

---

2 It can be safely assumed that there were yardarms in Tin Pan Alley because it has always been essential for everyone in the music business to know when the sun was over one.

So was "new technology". The arrival of the Aeolian Organ was a notable early issue which would have qualified under that heading. At a meeting of the MPA Board in September 1898 it was resolved to take legal advice on whether the sale of perforated music rolls for the purpose of reproducing copyright tunes by mechanical means should be deemed an infringement of copyright; also whether that would be affected by the country in which the instruments and music rolls were manufactured. It was decided to litigate against one company for infringement of three copyrights owned by Boosey & Co. The judgement in April 1899 puzzlingly had the judge making no comment on whether the perforation of the paper representing the music notes was an infringement, but deciding that the copying of words specifying time and key from the copyright owners' printed music was an infringement. He granted an injunction against the defendant, which was promptly overturned on appeal, at a cost to the MPA of the huge sum of £908. It took the MPA until 1903 to finish paying the bill, but eight years later it had the satisfaction of knowing that its lobbying had contributed to the provisions of the 1911 Copyright Act. This introduced the mechanical right into UK law for the first time (typically a little behind some other European countries and the US).

As Dixey recorded, the first task of the MPA was to tackle infringement of copyright "in this Country and in the Dominions". With the polite understatement of his day he noted: "The Law was not helpful and all endeavours to get the Government to make necessary amendments were postponed year after year. Despite these difficulties the Association was able to do good work. Many actions and prosecutions, both here and in the Dominions, were successful."

The infringements being tackled by the MPA in its early years related to illicit printing and sale of sheet music (in fact an infringement both of the copyright in the creative musical work itself and the copyright in the printed page). Contemporary accounts of litigation and early "anti piracy raids" undertaken by MPA publisher members are fascinating not only for their witness to the seriousness of the problem for copyright owners, but also for the social history embedded in the titles of the songs which were pirated, and in the wording and content of the court decisions. Just one example is that of a meeting of publishers in December 1887 called to discuss "the best means of effectually stamping out the sale in the streets of London and other important cities of cheap unauthorised editions of copyright works [which] threatens to assume alarming proportions". Successful detective work in tracking down the illicit printer of copies of the popular title *Whistle And I Shall Hear* and getting an injunction against him is recorded, and a call for concerted action by publishers to "give this illegal traffic a severe check until a short Act of Parliament can be passed giving publishers the same rights as are given to the owners of prints, photos etc." meaning the right to seize all illegal prints from the vendor.

Lags in legislation in different countries, as always, hampered the copyright owners and helped the pirates. For example, British musical works had no protection in the USA until 1891 (protection eventually being conferred by the Chase Act) and so American sheet music pirates in 1870s and 1880s were busily depriving British writers and publishers of their income by flooding a British Dominion, Canada, with illegal music reprints.

It was not until 1909 that the USA passed a Copyright Act which could be extended in certain circumstances to foreign countries, granting similar protection to that enjoyed by US citizens. It stipulated that, to gain protection, books had to be printed from type which had been set in America. The implications of this on UK printed music were in doubt. A test case was arranged, *Littleton et al v Oliver Ditson Co.*, and a ruling obtained that it was not necessary for music to be printed in the USA for it to be protected. The £1,000 cost of this action – a very large sum at the time – was shared by several publisher members of the MPA, who considered the satisfactory result both important and worth the money.

These examples of the continual watchfulness of the MPA on two fronts – fierce and often litigious action against all kinds of piracy, and lobbying governments for stronger copyright law –encapsulate the story of the organisation for most of its existence.

It was set up to give a collective voice and co-operative muscle to the originally numerous and small companies in a rapidly growing business sector, and that is what it did. As time went on the increasing sophistication and broader preoccupations of the Association reflected the developments of the businesses it served; but it began with the clear aim of being a good trade association, and the relatively even tenor of its history is evidence that it concentrated on fulfilling that aim in a pragmatic way.

The Mechanical-Copyright Protection Society

It really began with musical boxes – or should have done. It would be difficult to disagree with the proposal that these fall squarely within the concept of reproduction of music by mechanical means. However, in 1896 the Swiss, who surely could not have been thinking about their pre-eminence in the musical box business sector, did disagree, and no mechanical right for music copyright owners was defined or established within the Berne Convention of that time.

However, what amounted to a mechanical right was in existence in Germany some time before 1905, and in Article 13 of the 1908 Berne Convention, mechanical rights are proclaimed. The 1988 Copyright, Designs and Patents Act in the UK gives copyright owners exclusive rights of which those comprising mechanical rights are to copy the work and to issue copies of the work. This means recording in any mechanical or electronic way, manufacturing copies and including audio copies of the work in goods and programmes, including computer software, made available to the public.

America was quick to embody the mechanical right in its law. The speed may have had something to do with the perceived need to ensure that this exclusive right was restrained in a way that would prevent music copyright owners from frustrating the record industry's wish to make discs of music which could generate commercial wealth for the whole US music industry. So the 1909 US Copyright Act imposed a compulsory licence.

The first UK law making it clear that reproduction of copyright music in the form of a record was protected was the 1911 Copyright Act. The reason why this Act also embodied a Statutory Licence[3] (a compulsory licence after the first recording of any copyright music) was that the British Government shared the US Government's fear that the then all-powerful music

---

3 Music copyright owners were obliged to give a licence for the recording of their works (ie they had no right to refuse a licence) provided that the necessary fee was paid: that fee was originally 5% percent of retail price, rising to 6.25% in 1928 and remaining at that level until the statutory licence was removed in the 1988 Act.

publishers would want to strangle the infant record industry at birth, and the best way to do this would have been to deprive it of any worthwhile copyright music to record. Whether or not that was the formed intention is not set down in history, and it is arguable that as a strategy it would have been a Canute-like failure quite quickly. But there are certainly interesting comparisons to be made with the successful pleas by the record industry itself many years later which resulted in the granting of an exclusive right in the UK 1988 Copyright Act for record companies to control the rental of recordings: few if any rental licences were ever issued and no significant record rental business ever developed in the UK.

The publishers who anticipated that the statutory recording licence would kill the sheet music market were right. That is only a small overstatement: the sheet music market, which for so long represented almost 100% of publishers' revenue, fell off quite rapidly as the record industry burgeoned and today it accounts for about 1%.

The 1911 Act also underscored the fact that the mechanical right (in the early days often referred to as "the musical instrument right") began with the writer: it stated that publishing agreements which had been entered into before 1911 could not be assumed to include mechanical rights unless these were specifically referred to. This allowed composers to retain these rights and administer them themselves if they wished, and a few did – and still do. The 1911 Act ruled that there should be a fee for the compulsory licence and this was set at 5% of the retail price of the record with a minimum fee per track of a halfpenny but works published before the 1911 Act came into force only received half the statutory fee. This made life easy for all parties in one sense, but having availed themselves of the compulsory licence, record companies could be very remiss about paying.

The compulsory licence made it easy for most publishers to deal directly with record companies of any reasonable size and turnover. But there was a role for collective administration and in 1910, anticipating the 1911 Act, the Mechanical-Copyright Licenses[4] Company, abbreviated to Mecolico, was formed; and the competing Copyright Protection Society (Mechanical Rights) Ltd was founded very soon afterwards. Copyright owners joined one or the other, and a few joined both.

Little can be easily discovered about either of these two organisations, although the Mecolico sticker which was put on records to show that the copyright owners' licence fee had been paid survived for many decades of use by MCPS (notably in later years to indicate that a record was a legally imported pressing) and so this name is familiar to many in the UK music industry even now.

The origins of MCPS are still more obscure. It is mentioned in documents dating back to 1923, but its certain existence can only be pinned to 1924. It seems likely that the Mechanical-Copyright Licenses Company became insolvent: for whatever reason, in 1924 it merged with MCPS, and in 1925 the Copyright Protection Society (which incidentally appears to have paid composers and publishers their shares of mechanical licence fees directly – as most continental European societies still do but as the publisher owned MCPS never has done) transferred all its members into MCPS, granting them shares in the company in return. MCPS has a poorly documented early history, although it is clear that it always operated as an agency and was never a "collective" or true "membership society" as was PRS. It did not have the resources to create and maintain a solid archive, possibly because for most of its life MCPS remained a very small organisation, joined by the great majority of music publishers but little used by them in their preference to license direct and avoid agency fees.

---

4 UK English spelling rules that the noun is *licence* while the verb is license, which infuriates and confuses Americans, who only have the latter spelling for both usages, and everyone translating into UK English from any other language, and many UK English as well, yet if some existing documents are assumed to be correct, MCL (Mecolico) used the "wrong" spelling in its name.

MCPS was responsible for the licensing of record companies to record, and manufacture records of, copyrights owned by publishers and writers. Originally a new record company, until it had demonstrated its solvency plus a good bill paying and accounting record and some solidity in its business, was required to buy Mecolico stamps from MCPS which were applied to each disc put on sale (without which a record dealer could not offer it for sale). MCPS paid the music copyright owners with the money from the stamps.

The Performing Right Society

The early years of PRS have a hint of grainy, black and white, silent comedy film. The weedy juvenile hero in the ill-fitting jacket, horn-rimmed spectacles and dingy straw boater runs the gauntlet of melodramatic life-threatening disasters, with everyone out to get him, but somehow sleepwalks through it all and survives every catastrophe, including the ones he innocently brings on himself.

The UK performing right society is certainly younger than the MPA and the original mechanical rights agencies, and "weedy" is not an unfair description of its youth, although it was tenacious and intelligent where it lacked strength

In fact, among all the countries in the world with well-developed music industries around the start of the 20th century, Britain and America were the slowest in establishing such rights societies. Once they *were* set up, although success hardly came overnight in true showbiz fashion, the trend throughout most of the century for American and British repertoire to dominate the international music market would ensure that the music rights societies in both nations moved into the society "premier league", and stayed there.

PRS was a late starter largely because its formation was initially very effectively resisted by powerful music users and producers in the UK, and by many music publishers. With the record industry little more than a novelty before the First World War, this was a music market in which the sale of printed music was a hugely successful business. The sale of pianos into British homes was the highest in Europe – an almost unbelievable total of two million were reportedly sold in 1910 to a population of about 32 million – and was matched only in the US: so the voracious appetite for song sheets was expected to grow indefinitely. Performance of music in concerts and the music halls, tea dances and theatres was the vital marketing of those days. The idea of charging performing licence fees for such self-propelled free advertising for printed music was as unpopular with publishers and many writers as it was with the impresarios and venue owners, who had no wish to share their profit with the creators of the music they used.

In Britain's commercial and social life unchanging good order in everything was expected, wanted and taken for granted. The assertion of intellectual property rights, strengthened and updated in the 1911 Copyright Act, was an idea so new that the struggling PRS would be well over 10 years old before a leading publisher would publicly acknowledge that the performing right was the single most important means by which the economic status of composers and songwriters had been significantly improved.

There was a performing right in UK law from 1843. It was poorly framed and rather weak, although it was enough to empower the later much reviled Harry Wall[5], who was the first person recorded as attempting to license this right, but went about it in a solo entrepreneurial way which damaged the credibility of the right and rights owners generally. The 1911 Act sorted the situation out, and should have resulted in the immediate, or even anticipatory, formation of a UK performing right collecting society. This did not happen because of external opposition from users and because of equally powerful "internal" opposition from publishers and writers.

5 see PRS chapter for details

But whatever the strength and high public profile of the opposition to the exploitation of the performing right and the establishment of a collective administration society devoted to it, there were always supporters for the cause.

In 1912 voices in favour included a few influential publishers who took a positive view. They rejected the idea that the existing publishing business was threatened by the performing right and believed it would bring additional income, pointing to the French performing right society SACEM's impressive revenues from concerts and the novel but growing entertainment of "picture shows" (which must also have become the largest employment sector for versatile pianists whose egos could stand the anonymity, often invisibility, of cinema work; who in turn must collectively have contributed mightily to the sales of sheet music).

Even then, those in favour of a performing right society were thinking about constituting it on principles which persist today and are still generally accepted, though regularly if informally debated by publishers. It was broadly accepted that success required that publishers should include *all* their works in the care of a society, not just a selection; and that a UK society founded by publishers (as against the successful SACEM and other European societies, which were founded by writers who then admitted publishers) must give full benefits to composers and authors from the outset.

Over a year later, through advance and retreat and pleas for exemptions for some users such as religious charities and military events[6] a set of draft rules for a performing right society was put in front of the MPA. The initial reaction was what Groucho Marx might have described as "nice try, but no cigar". Sensitive issues inevitably included the royalty split between writers and publishers, provoking prolonged argument. As stagnation loomed, the now zealously pro-PRS William Boosey told the MPA Board that he was going to move ahead pre-emptively, leaving behind those who were "too nervous or not sufficiently interested".

Just before Christmas 1913 the representatives of 10 important publishers signed an agreement which led to the formal registration early the following year of the Performing Right Society Ltd, then as now a company limited by guarantee and having no share capital. Boosey chaired a meeting at Chappell Music at which a Committee of eight writers and eight publishers (one of these to be the Society Chairman, with a composer as Vice-Chairman) was set up. Funding was a loan of £50 from each publisher, repayable at 4% interest.

So on 6th March 1914 PRS was founded on the initiative of leading publishers in the MPA who had come to realise the potential earnings from a performing right. Then, belatedly and initially very weakly, PRS set out to administer the performing right. It was still largely opposed by the copyright owners themselves, who originally seemed to see the PRS as a similar threat to their livelihood as the pirates of the day (for entirely different reasons).

The first PRS Committee comprised representatives of publishers Ascherberg, Augener, Bosworth, Chappell (in the person of William Boosey as the Society Chairman), Feldman, Francis, Day & Hunter, Hawkes, Lafleur, Lengnick and Schott. This list emphasises the small, family-run nature of the business then; and the complete subsequent change in the publishing business is highlighted by the fact that every one of these companies has been acquired or otherwise absorbed by larger publishers in a process which has led to market domination by a handful of publishing operations. These are almost all now divisions of multinational entertainment companies which often include record companies as well as music publishing. The founding writers were musical show writers Vice-Chairman Lionel Monckton (*The Arcadians* and *The Quaker Girl*) and Paul Rubens; popular songwriters Hermann Lohr, Bennett Scott, Worton David and Henry Pether (a "major member" at the outset as writer of big hits for music hall stars Vesta Victoria, Harry Lauder and George Robey); and lyricists Arthur Ropes (as Adrian Ross) and Harold Simpson.

---

6 The "religious charities" argument has little meaning today, but music used in religious services has always been exempt from licensing by PRS (though that is not the case in some other countries); music performance at military events was not exempted. For many years music events which were organised solely to raise money for charity were able to apply for licence exemption which was usually granted by PRS, but the Board decided to end this practice in the mid-90s, on the grounds that PRS should not deny their members any legitimate income, and members concerned could decide for themselves whether to donate their royalties to support the nominated charity on any occasion.

The Music Alliance of MCPS and PRS

Although performing and mechanical rights societies in Europe had always been predominantly operated either as single organisations or as separate societies which shared all their operational resources, MCPS and PRS remained entirely separate through most of their history. The reasons for this are mentioned here and in the main MCPS history section, having much to do with British as against Continental European culture, and consequent big differences in writer/publisher attitudes and relationships (these relationships, many writers would claim even today, being rather more acidic and competitive in the UK than elsewhere).

So it is not surprising that it would be almost 80 years after PRS was formed and 70 years after the formation of MCPS that the two UK societies would first attempt to bring together all their overlapping and duplicating activities into one operating company. That attempt, which had the working title ServiceCo, was dropped. It was another two years before their second attempt was successful, when the Music Copyright Operational Services Limited was incorporated in 1998. It was to be known generally by the more descriptive title of the MCPS-PRS Alliance, and in 2001 the jointly owned operating company's name was officially changed to The MCPS-PRS Alliance Limited. By late 2003 it was likely that a further step would be taken to allow the Music Alliance to be officially used as the day-to-day name for the operating company, thus returning to the name it popularly acquired almost by accident soon after it was formed, the use of which was at that time firmly rejected by the MCPS and PRS Boards.

The Music Publishers' Association

The MPA is a trade association, with the traditional role of promoting and protecting the commercial interests of its members, allied to providing services such as business sector information, training, and a range of practical advice. Its role as a lobbyist in the cause of copyright protection and enforcement has always been an important part of the MPA's work, with the "enforcement" issue well to the fore from the founding of the Association. Today, however, it sees its role very much as that of explaining and promoting the business of music publishing – which the MPA members themselves admit has previously been "shrouded in mystery". Although it is the senior of the two main businesses in the music industry, it has never been as well understood by the public as, for example, literary publishing and since the rise of generations of consumers whose focus is firmly on recorded music it is far less well known and understood than its counterpart record business.

In one of its own publications the MPA offers a description of music publishing. As defined by the MPA, music publishing is about investing in and managing the rights in music to enable it to reach its many audiences and ensure that the writer – the creator behind every song or symphony – is adequately remunerated. Music publishers are concerned with the development, promotion and protection of the interests and rights of songwriters and composers. Music publishing is reliant upon a partnership between the writer and publisher, the latter supporting the creativity of the former through business administration. The publishers' business is diverse and international, demanding a range of business and creative skills relating to:

• finding, developing and supporting writing talent, and offering guidance on matters such as record deals and commissions

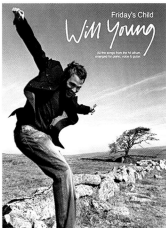

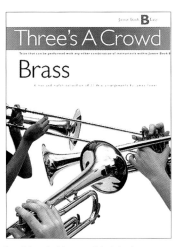

Where printed music is concerned publishers "have to take a long view" as explained by Music Sales Director and UK General Manager Chris Butler. Although this part of their business now represents only a tiny part of overall revenue, publishers welcome the income and know that many items in the print catalogue, especially those of entire classical works, will continue to sell steadily for decades – over a century in a few cases. Although a top selling printed item may only reach sales of 10,000 copies a year, those sales can continue annually for a long time. Music education requires a steady supply of printed music for teaching and examination pieces, and there is a reliable market for printed popular music – in versions which cater for "different levels of musical literacy" - where the printed book is often a matching folio to the recorded album release.

• editing and producing performance materials and printed music

• promoting and marketing the writer's music, and ensuring that it is registered with the appropriate collecting societies

• licensing and monitoring music use; tracking, collecting and distributing royalties

• safeguarding the music copyright against unauthorised use

Printed music and fighting piracy

The publishers' task of safeguarding their writers' copyrights was one impetus for the setting up of their own trade association. From 1881, the earliest Minutes of the MPA Board record the music publishers' concern about the piracy of sheet music and the action needed to combat it, thereby underlining the overriding importance which sale of printed music had for the business in its first half century and more. Printed music was as important, and as attractive to the public, as records later became, and the MPA used to run sheet music "charts" which listed the highest-selling hits. These were in fact the only measure of the market success of music until the record sales charts started to be compiled in the late 50s.

Although the industry has changed greatly, and income from mechanical rights has for many decades been far more commercially important to publishers, in 2003 sheet music is still a concern of the MPA. Today sheet music piracy is seldom if ever the work of illicit copyists and printers; the photocopier provides the means for cheap and instant mass copying. Dealing with this is largely through efforts to inform would-be music copiers about the illegality of what they are doing, and to ensure that they obtain permission where appropriate from the publisher to photocopy.

Since 1979 the MPA has published a *Code of Fair Practice* which not only helps to clarify the (confusing to many) issues relating to photocopying but also grants concessions to would-be copiers over and above those allowed by law, so recognising the practical difficulties often faced by performing musicians. The Code is currently undergoing its fifth revision.

Another important service is the publication, currently on CD ROM, of a Catalogue of Printed Music, which lists up-to-date information on who owns the copyright and who distributes the sheet music, as well as information on the composer, publisher, arranger etc. The MPA is also the UK agency administering the systematic unique numbering of printed music editions: the ISMN is similar to the ISBN unique identification scheme for books.

The MPA publishes guidelines to good practice in the hire of music in consultation with the bodies representing the professional and amateur orchestras, the Association of British Orchestras and Making Music, as well as the BBC. The MPA's traditional role in negotiating hire fees, primarily for orchestral parts, has been curtailed by competition rules which demand that such fees are negotiated directly between the hirer and each individual music publisher. The MPA oversees and works to promote its members' interests in other uses of printed music including the sending and downloading of files containing music notation via the internet; and the less obvious – the administration of publishers' graphic rights on TV, for example when during the broadcast of an orchestral concert the camera shows the pages of printed music being used by the musicians.

While the concern with printed music can be traced in an unbroken line back to the formation of the MPA, as can the Association's efforts as a lobbyist in the cause of music copyright protection, the role of information provider and communicator with a wide membership developed relatively recently. And the activity of offering training for publishers and their staff did not begin until more recently still.

Training people to work in music publishing

Traditionally publishers trained their own managers and staff in-house. For what still counts as much the major part of its history music publishing was a business of small, independent, mostly family-owned and run companies. The provision of informal on-the-job training was the only option for them. Later the bigger, but still independent, publishers developed better devised and more formalised training, but it was still in-house. In some companies the training was widely recognised as excellent. Today's music publishing business is still to a significant extent managed by professionals who at some point in their early careers went through the Chappell Music training system. Similarly many record business managers still active today were originally trained by EMI Records in a system which was closely akin to that of the British Civil and Colonial Services; and there may even be some owners and managers in record retailing who went through the courses organised by the Training Officer of the Gramophone Record Retailers Association. The myriad vocational full and part time music industry Further and Higher Education courses available today (of uneven usefulness to the business sectors at which they aim) were a long way in the future, and while City and Guilds was a familiar term the initials NVQ (National Vocational Qualification) had yet to enter education jargon.

A number of factors contributed to the decline of structured in-house training schemes in many businesses, including music publishing. Business competition demanded leaner company administration budgets; waves of mergers and takeovers formed large companies owned by much larger entertainment multinationals; and successive generations of (often transient) independent and sole-trader publishing enterprises all contributed

to the waning of such in-house training. This meant the demise of much of the structured training of any kind (though Warner/Chappell and EMI amongst others still provide more generic business training), because there have never been any kind of accredited external education or training courses aimed at producing "qualified music publishers".[1] The MPA was a natural agency to pick up the role of providing and facilitating training for the benefit of all publishers.

MPA currently offers

• an Induction Day – run three times a year this offers a "big picture" of what music publishing is all about including its creative, legal and business aspects, and explains the key organisations with which it is involved on a daily basis, including particularly the collecting societies, for the benefit of new and would-be entrants into the business as independents or as employees.

• seminars on specific topics and issues, such as copyright, contracts in music publishing, access to finance (for business set-up or development), royalties and tracking, negotiating skills and contracts. One of the biggest ever attendances at an MPA seminar was for a session on "The Global Business of Music Publishing" – a recognition that publishers cannot think nationally any longer and must be able to function in a truly international market.

• links exist with other organisations to develop specific courses of which publishers can take advantage for themselves or their employees, such as the course run by the London College of Printing (obviously focused mainly on printed music); and the current co-operation with the Music Managers Forum on the delivery of a continuing professional development course in music publishing, designed to bridge the gap between MPA Induction Days and the specialist seminars.

---

1 MPA training events which include legal content can earn Continuing Professional Development points for legal professionals. The broad nature of music publishing – that is, the creative/copyright administration side of it – is too broad and varied to make it easy to provide a single all encompassing course, and the need is not acute (and again the situation is the same in the record industry). Many Further and Higher Education colleges, including the BRIT performing arts school supported by the British Record Industry Trust, offer

courses aimed at preparing students to work in some aspect of the music business, but no single recognised form of accreditation has as yet been developed.

While not directly linked with the MPA's training activitities, its Jobseekers' service is another excellent example of the way that the Association works to assist publishing companies and the existing and would-be professionals who work in those companies.

Serving a large but changing business

Today the MPA serves a business which is huge, but shrinking in terms of the number of companies involved. As recently as 1977 the Association had around 500 individual member companies; currently the number is around 200, although these embrace over 3000 affiliated and administered companies. Acquisitions and mergers have been the main thread of the global music business story for about three decades, and the deals are becoming bigger, more intensely competed for, and more frequent. It is unlikely that the music publishing business landscape will look the same at the end of 2004 as it did at the end of 2003, and how it will look in 2010, or 2020, is open to the kind of fanciful speculation on which the founding fathers of the MPA would never have wasted their time because they *knew* that nothing was going to change quickly (and many were comfortably certain that nothing was ever going to change).

The shape and character of the music publishing business has indeed changed enormously, but the MPA's role is as it was originally, that of promoting the business interests of its members, lobbying in the cause of copyright protection and enforcement and giving a collective voice to UK publishers and encouraging them to work together on matters of mutual concern and benefit.

Development of the association

Having set up as a society to address issues affecting publishers and the authors and composers whose works they published, the MPA's 1881 Rules included among the Association's Objects that it would "watch over the general interests of the Music Publishing trade"; communicate with the proper authorities on all matters connected with copyright; endeavour to settle disputes, by arbitration, on Trade Questions submitted to the Society; and, in a intriguingly specific reference, "consider the best means for the more economical winding up of insolvent estates". Interestingly the draft Rules had included as potential members "Manufacturers or Dealers in Musical Instruments" but this was deleted and the word Authors substituted.

Representation of its members' interests included communication with the press as well as with "Authorities", and there are many instances in the Minute books of cuttings from papers (particularly the *Musical Herald*) where music publishing and copyright issues are addressed. As early as 1881, a letter to that magazine from a choirmaster naively reported that he kept a manuscript book "into which we copy any new tune which takes our fancy" believing it to be "a practice very extensively adopted". He asked whether this was infringement of copyright. The Editor rather mysteriously replied "We would rather say nothing on this point", so the MPA took up the correspondence in very firm terms.

With or without the MPA's efforts, knowledge of copyright and the need for licences spread. Minutes of the MPA Committee meeting of July 1884 recorded that the sum of £5 had been sent to the Association by an Oxford Street retailer who, at the time "being ignorant of the law of Copyright", had illegally imported from America sheet music for various compositions. The illegal importation of sheet music is an ongoing problem for publishers to this day.

Expanding activity

MPA activities grew through its first three decades and included, inevitably and expensively, litigation against infringers. More positively there was also participation in events, such as the International Exhibition of 1885 and the 1910 International

Congress of Music Publishers; active lobbying during the Berne Convention discussions in 1905, and rightly much prior and post consideration of the 1911 UK Copyright Act; involvement in music education via the Schools and Associated Board syllabuses; consideration of price discounting; meetings and AGMs for MPA members. The MPA had a hand in the creation of various societies such as the Musical Defence League (1905 Minute entry), the British Composers' Society (several mentions during 1910), and of greatest significance in the context of this history, the Performing Right Society, the founding of which was the subject of various heated discussions minuted in 1913, before its incorporation was achieved in 1914. The incorporation of MCPS in 1924 was also, of course, a significant event in the publishing business.

The fortunes of the British music publishing business in the first half of the 20th century were inevitably greatly affected by the two World Wars. There were major fluctuations in the national economy and people's earnings, with drops in disposable income, most dramatically during the Depression years, affecting the sale of such expensive luxuries as sheet music. The industry had to cope in World War I with the enforced release of music printers plates for making munitions; and in both wars with rationed availability (combined with low quality and high cost) of printing paper, and the conscription of so many skilled tradesmen. However, the attitude of the MPA and its members could be as tough as the times, as indicated by a 1929 refusal to allow troops to have their sheet music free.

The music business survived and even prospered, despite everything, and publishing began to boom after the end of Word War II, but the influence of the US was then the chief characteristic of the business. This was the heyday of the original Tin Pan Alley, and American music became increasingly accessible through sub-publishing deals. The market for jazz grew, as did that for songs recorded by the big US stars such as Glenn Miller, Frank Sinatra, Bing Crosby and Judy Garland. This was all boosted by the cinema and record industry. Alongside the growth

in market size and economic value (despite the fact that the publishing business had to drop printed music prices in response to the effect the movies and records were having on sales) there was increasing variety. The market for standard (classical) music vied with that for popular ballads, songs from musicals, jazz, swing and bebop. Then came R&B, rock'n'roll and pop. Now there is a rich choice of music influenced by ethnic styles from all over the world, which have too many different genre names to list here. Some of these are so specific, particularly in dance music, that only small bands of creators, DJs and adherents would know what exactly they referred to; and many are of very short duration of popularity.

Expanding concerns

The MPA's original focused concerns about printed music properly and necessarily broadened into a concern about its members' whole range of intellectual property rights. In the 40s and 50s the invention of the concept of the teenager as a definable target market, especially for music, led to a rise in demand for merchandise linked to their idols. This trend expanded hugely in the 60s with The Beatles' world domination of teen style. It was a new and lucrative business alongside the unprecedented levels of income from Beatles records and song copyrights – and in their wake from those of many other "British invasion" bands who conquered the American market. Publishers looked to their rights in the increasing variety of music usage driven by the youth market. The emphasis on ensuring that all the uses of the rights were properly licensed and paid for paved the way for dealing with new usage in the post 60s "electronic age" – which included everything from the arrival of the cassette recorder and the tidal wave of private piracy/home taping, to the music file sharing of the internet. Licensing these uses is very much the concern of the publishers, who of course still own the mechanical rights; hence their (and the MPA's) vested interest in MCPS and the way it handles such licensing. The practical aspects of licensing are handled by MCPS and PRS and so are dealt with in the appropriate chapters.

However, the impact of post 60s market and usage developments on the administration of mechanical rights (assigned traditionally in the UK to the publisher and not, as with the performing right, to the collecting society) played a part in the MPA's determination to take the private company MCPS into its own hands, thereby ensuring that control over the administration of mechanical rights remained with publishers. The details of this important episode in the histories both of MCPS and the MPA are covered in the MCPS Chapter.

The close relationship between the MPA and MCPS after 1976 - with the former owning the latter; with the publisher membership of both overlapping to an appreciable extent; and with MCPS as source of mechanical rights revenue – inevitably means that the histories of the two organisations overlap considerably in terms of issues and events. For this reason the MPA chapter here is quite short while the MCPS chapter frequently mentions the MPA. What often differs (sometimes considerably) is the two organisations' points of view on matters which concern them both. The records of both organisations reflect the inevitable tensions between the two bodies arising from the fact that the MPA represents the publisher owners of the mechanical rights, giving them a vested interest in how their rights are administered by MCPS, whose role is to license those rights and collect and distribute the royalties. The MPA is a trade body and MCPS is an operational company, and have different roles.

The MPA and the record business

However, the MPA has always been an authoritative voice on major policy matters affecting music publishers, and as such it is the direct counterpart of the record industry trade organisation the BPI, with which it has had both to fight and to co-operate at different times. One example was the abolition of RRP (recommended retail price) in the late 70s and early 80s. Following

the abolition of statutory Resale Price Maintenance, the record companies' RRP had been the basis on which the then still statutory mechanical licence rate of 6.25% was calculated. The alternatives appeared to be to base MCPS licence fees on the trade price (lower than RRP) or possibly on the realised retail price, with the very real prospect that the end of RRP would lead to price cutting by retailers, often to below previous RRP levels.

At the 1980 AGM of the Music Publishers' Association the Chairman Ron White signalled the start of battle. He cited as a major issue the MPA Board's support for an MCPS fight (fronted

Ron White of EMI Music Publishing, who was Chairman of the MPA from 1978 to 1985, and later served as PRS Chairman from 1987 until his death in 1990.

by the negotiating arm the Mechanical Rights Society) against the record companies' threatened abolition of RRP; he called it "the most serious threat to music publishers" since the 1956 Copyright Act. As *Music Week* reported in December 1980: "A hint of the extent of the acrimony surrounding the negotiations between the BPI and the MRS [came when] MRS general administrator [also MCPS MD] Bob Montgomery disclosed that a meeting the previous week between the two bodies had polarised into 'two separate camps' with Montgomery 'bearing white flags' between them". And this was after the two sides had already been in negotiations for two years.

As the dispute had begun so it had continued and so it would end, with no negotiated settlement: while the BPI and MRS engaged in sporadic and apparently futile talks, the record companies one by one took unilateral action through 1980 and 1981.Successive issues of *MW* reported RRP abolition by Phonogram (January), Virgin (March), Polydor and EMI (May) with that company introducing what it called "list price" – to which many dealers took exception. Then came CBS (August), Chrysalis and RCA (November). A replacement for the "lost" RRP had to be found, and for over 12 months the attempts continued, via surveys of actual retail prices being charged and the results of those surveys being challenged and rejected. Agreement finally came in 1982, with a "notional" retail price on which mechanical licence fees could be calculated. Then the 1988 Copyright Act abolished the statutory mechanical licence and changed the landscape entirely – a business change which is again detailed in the MCPS chapter, and one which precipitated yet another tussle with the record business, in the continuing lively, increasingly communicative but inevitably frequently fractious relationship between the two sides of the music industry.

Today's MPA

Originally a defensively British organisation beset by mostly foreign copyright infringers, although from the outset its membership was open to "all Music Publishers, Music Sellers, Authors and Composers, whether English, Foreign or Colonial", the MPA today is aware that its UK members are part of an international publishing business (domestic and international revenues are about equal), and so the Association is actively involved in global ideas and initiatives.

MPA Chief Executive since 1997 and a copyright lawyer whose firm worked for MPA and MCPS long before that, Sarah Faulder runs a small but very active organisation. In 1996, before she joined, British Music Rights was established as the lobbying vehicle on behalf of music publishers, composers and songwriters and their collecting societies. Accordingly, the MPA's lobbying is largely run through British Music Rights in close liaison with each of its members, including the MPA. The MPA continues to play a part in addressing printed music piracy on behalf of its members, but MCPS handles most other piracy issues.

The appointment of Faulder in succession to the long-serving Secretary-General Peter Dadswell marked, as intended by the Board, a change in pace, style and level of activity for the MPA office. This is recalled by publisher Andrew Heath, who was in the chair from 1993 to 1997, during four very important years of change and development at the MPA. His extra year in office was served in order to help the Association to weather a period in which ill health led to extended absences by Dadswell, who nevertheless continued his excellent service whenever he was well enough. Heath recalled: "After Peter retired we brought in Sarah Faulder to move the association forward. It was significant and indicative of our intentions that we changed the role to that of CEO."

Change and forward motion at the MPA was part of the rolling change in all the writer and publisher organisations. On Heath's watch there had been the beginning, and end, of the ServiceCo ideas of a joint "back office" for MCPS and PRS (*see Alliance chapter*) and then a second successful application of the idea in the formation of the Alliance. Heath reflected that around that time "there must have been a fortunate alignment of the stars" which facilitated great and much-needed change. "I was one of several relatively fresh faces in positions at the head of key organisations: people who did not have the baggage of the past". He identifies songwriter Guy Fletcher, Chairman of BASCA – the largest of the writers' Guilds – as "approachable and ready to work together"; to Andrew Potter, who took over the Chairmanship of PRS at a point when it was emerging from a series of major difficulties and who was ready to lead his Board through change in attitude and activity; and John Hutchinson, who came from an entirely different business to take the CEO's seat at PRS in late 1995, and soon made it clear he was ready to take forward many new ways of working and developmental ideas.

Heath was particularly keen to build better, closer and friendlier relations with the writers, through their Guilds. "I spent a lot of time and effort talking to the Guilds, because I knew that without common understanding of where we all needed to go, nothing would happen." He is clear that a fruit of that understanding, on which he worked closely with Fletcher, was the MCPS-PRS Alliance. "That could not have gone forward without the support of all the writers' constituencies, and we worked to ensure that they knew about and understood and supported it – not just at the level of the Guilds' Boards but within the membership." Although he was no longer in the MPA chair when the Alliance officially came into existence, he had remained part of a process he described as "difficult, a nightmare at times, but a very exciting time". Towards the end of his four year tenure Heath led the MPA into playing a key part in the first steps toward setting up a new lobbying and information organisation which would later become British Music Rights.

A gathering of writer/publisher rights people at the music industry international convention Midem in 1999 (*left to right*) Kim Howells, then Trade and Industry Minister; then MPA Chairman Tom Bradley; then British Academy of Composers and Songwriters Chairman Guy Fletcher; current MPA Chairman Andrew Potter, with MCPS Chairman Jonathan Simon behind him; composer David Stoll; former MPA Chairman Andrew Heath; MPA CEO Sarah Faulder; and BACS CEO Chris Green.

He would, in fact, describe his entire period at the head of the MPA Board as exciting, and stressed that the MPA continues to "take a very close interest in the workings of the Alliance and British Music Rights, on behalf of MPA members".

Chairman from July 1997 for a year, Stephen James recalled that the Association and its CEO continued to move through a time of transition. "There were a lot of changes taking place within the MPA office due to the fact that Peter Dadswell was retiring and a new Chief Executive had been sought and was starting in January 1997. This was to prove to be an important move in expanding and setting up the organisation to handle several other issues that were about to beset the music publishing industry. I am thinking mainly of the new European Union Copyright Directive. The draft Copyright Directive served to underline the need for an active lobbying presence in Brussels for the British music publishers and accordingly the MPA rejoined the International Confederation of Music Publishers (ICMP)".

Sarah Faulder added that through this membership the interests of British publishers could be represented internationally through ICMP's membership of the Rightholders Coalition which proved to be an important lobbying force in the shaping of the Copyright Directive. ICMP, the MPA and British Music Rights worked very effectively together on the Copyright Directive.

The MPA needs to serve the differing expectations of different sections of a broad membership. That breadth is illustrated by the sector identifications in its membership list, namely advertising, ballet, brass/military/wind band, chamber, children's, choral/vocal, country, dance/electronic, early music, educational, folk, hip-hop/rap, indie, jazz/blues/big band, latin, light, metal, MOR, musicals, new age, opera/operettas, orchestral, organ, pop music, punk, reggae, religious, R'n'B/soul, rock, television/film, urban and world music.

Classical publishers rely heavily on the MPA for its negotiation of the BBC printed music hire fees (a major source of income) and to oversee their interests in PRS. The MPA also represents classical publishers' interests in music in education. Three MPA committees discuss and make decisions at a quite detailed level in this area; the Classical Publishers Committee, the Printed Music Publishers Committee and the Hire Librarians Committee.

Pop publishers look to the MPA to oversee their interests vis-à-vis MCPS and PRS. The Pop Publishers Committee concerns itself very largely with the licensing of their rights including issues relating to the activity, administration and processes of the two collecting societies, and their delivery of service.

The MPA was the first music industry body, some 30 years ago, to be appointed sponsor for Government grant schemes for British

exports. The grants have been variously offered by the British Overseas Trade Board, the DTI and currently UK Trade & Investment. Limited grants are available for companies taking stands at trade shows and, outside Europe, for travel and accommodation for export purposes. The MPA only recently ceased to be a sponsor due to the fact that most music publishers prefer to be flexible to meet with trading partners at trade shows rather than to be tied to a stand and therefore the MPA found itself operating this scheme for companies that were not its members. Publishers still come in droves to Cannes during Midem (the annual international music industry convention). Inside the cavernous Palais de Festivals on the world-famous Croisette their traditional place has been increasingly filled for many years by record companies, and now annually-more-numerous audio-visual and multi-media producers, technology hardware and systems companies, DRM (digital rights management) companies and ISPs (internet service providers). However, the MPA continues to take

Composer Peter Lawlor and Katherine Mearman of Orange receive the Award for the Best Use of Specially-Commissioned Music at the first MPA Music in Advertising Awards in 2003. Photo by Alan McAteer

its place every year on the British at Midem stand. The MPA was the only trade body to take a stand in the early days but the stand today embraces all the industry's trade bodies– the BPI, AIM and PPL[2] on the record industry side and British Music Rights and its component elements (PRS. MCPS, MPA, the British Academy of Composers and Songwriters) on the authors' and publishers' side and has become a joint showcase and meeting place for all members of the UK music industry. A recent feature of this combined presence of UK music business organisations is hosting a visit by a British politician which has helped to raise the profile of the British music industry in the eyes of Government.

Organising, or co-organising/sponsoring events of interest to publishers has been an increasing part of the MPA's activity, particularly networking events for members to meet each other and contacts from elsewhere in the industry until recently the MPA administered the annual BBC televised song competition A Song for Europe, where the UK public votes for the British entry to the Eurovision Song Contest. In latter years it did this in association with the British Academy of Composers and Songwriters.

Very recently the Association launched the Music in Advertising Awards supported by the Institute for Practitioners in Advertising (IPA) and MusicWorks. These judge and then publicly recognise the most creative and effective use of music in advertising. And this is another sign of the times, in that it emphasises the increasing dependence of advertisers on copyright music to promote products and services.

Advertising agencies had long tended to commission specially-composed music and words for ad jingles. These sometimes did little more than set the product name to a potentially irritatingly memorable sequence of a few musical notes – the apex of the art surely being the same three notes repeated for the words Esso Blue in an ad for paraffin, in the years when vast amounts of this fuel were in use in domestic heaters. Anyone over 40 who ever watched ITV can probably still sing several versions of Esso

jingles, including those three notes. Music publishers, who handle their own synchronisation rights, were over two decades ago quick to recognise the potential of linking popular songs with ads which were seen repeatedly by many-million-strong audiences. A symbiotic relationship was encouraged between publishers with hit song copyrights and advertisers looking for an already hugely well-known song. The song enhanced the recognition and consumer recollection of the product being advertised, and the ad reinforced the popularity of the song (and the commercial recording, once the record industry caught up with the idea)[3]. The outstanding example was the international revival as a result of a TV commercial for Levi jeans of the song Heard It Through the Grapevine written by Norman Whitfield and Barrett Strong, and recorded first by Gladys Knight and the Pips and then by Marvin Gaye for Motown Records.

This use of copyright music in ads became a significant source of income to the music business. However, as with most things in most businesses, but strikingly so in the music industry, there is now evidence of this marketing phenomenon going in a circle. Much as they appreciate the contribution a great pop song can make to their product promotion, advertisers have come to realise the value to the publisher and record company of having their song on a TV commercial. So they are setting up their own publishing companies, and commissioning original works again, but only if they can publish them.

In the UK the MPA, particularly certain Board members and Sarah Faulder herself, participates actively in the lobbying and "public education" work of British Music Rights. This is entirely in line with the MPA's earliest objectives: one of its founding Rules was "to communicate with the proper authorities on all matters concerning copyright", and from the start its Committee Minutes contain regular accounts of contact with and appeals to MPs, Government lawyers and top civil servants on music rights protection issues. The MPA lobbied in its members' cause before the 1911, 1956 and 1988 Copyright Acts (the last as a very active

---

2 British Phonographic Industry, Association of Independent Music and Phonographic Performance Ltd

3 Writers and some recording artists can, and some do, refuse to allow their music to be used in ads for certain types of product – or at all; for example, the Beatles never permitted their recordings to be used on ads, but relatively recently their songs began to be used – recorded by other artists – when their publishing company ATV Music (owned by writer and recording artist Michael Jackson) gave permission for their use.

The MPA members' magazine has in recent years developed into a source of information about national and international issues of general interest to music copyright owners

A well-recognised indication that a business sector has taken root, can be expected to have a future and now wants recognition, is the point when it starts collecting and publishing statistics about itself. The music industry was unusually slow to do this, perhaps because its self image was one of a "free spirit" concerned with the excitement and immediacy of creating wonderful music rather than peering with collective short-sightedness at columns of figures.

Although there were for many years figures collected by the Board of Trade on record sales, it was only after the incorporation of the BPI in the early 70s that annual statistics on sales and values began to be collected and published. These, of course, focus on manufacturing, trade and retail information relating to recordings in the UK, while the IFPI (International Federation of the Phonographic Industry) produces international statistics. On the publishing side the collection and publication of statistics were even slower to develop. A regular report on the size and value of music publishing worldwide has for many years been produced by the NMPA (National Music Publishers Association in the US) and the Annual Reports and Accounts from PRS, MCPS and the MPA have always told a useful story about the value of copyright to anyone who went to the trouble to deduce the overall picture from several different sources.

Statistics on the sale of sheet music have been collected since 1978. In 1994 the various music industry bodies first got together in the cause of all-industry statistics, with the then MPA Chairman Andy Heath as one of the main motive forces behind the project to commission and contribute to a statistical review. In association with British Invisibles the Overseas Earnings of the UK Music Industry report was produced in 1995, which proved to be very useful, revealing and influential (with Government and the media). The first joint industry report focused on the invisible earnings abroad of the UK music industry. It was followed by a second, *The Value of Music*, which looked at broader statistics on the value of the domestic market (this time produced by the National Music Council in collaboration with Westminster University and

partner in the Music Copyright Reform Group with PRS and MCPS). Music publishing is, however, a truly international business, and the MPA is very much part of the global network of the ICMP; this body is concerned mainly with lobbying at an international level, at the European Commission or WIPO (World Intellectual Property Organisation), and with international business issues often relating to the work of collecting societies. In the UK another important development was the establishment in 2002 of the Music Business Forum, which is mentioned in the British Music Rights chapter.

published in 1996). There followed *A Sound Performance* (National Music Council 1999) covering both domestic and overseas earnings, and its update (2002) the *Counting the Notes* report. It seems obvious that the UK industry has now established itself as provider of statistics and is expected to go on doing so, which points to the need for a more settled and organised approach to who does this and how the reports are to be regularly organised and funded – instead of the pass-the-parcel approach taken so far.

The MPA and the UK collecting societies

The MPA is highly supportive of the MCPS-PRS Alliance, and Sarah Faulder sums up the general view in the simple statement "It's a very good thing" which is striving to increase efficiency, reduce costs to writers and publishers, and has to an as yet limited but increasingly useful extent facilitated an improvement in understanding of writer and publisher issues across the Boards, management and staff of all three organisations. It is important to note, however, that the MPA deals directly but separately with the MCPS and PRS Boards, while its relationship with the Alliance as an operating company is strictly at arm's length.

So the MPA cannot directly impose policy decisions on PRS or MCPS. However, its choice of MCPS directors does inevitably have some influence on the latter's thinking and direction. But the MPA can and does voice its members' views as strongly as it feels necessary. For example it did so recently on behalf of its standard (classical) publisher members in the case of the referral to the Copyright Tribunal of PRS' Tariff LC.

The MPA's relationship with MCPS as the licensing and collecting agency it owns remains as it has been since 1976: the MPA appoints the MCPS Board, but does not dictate its agenda. Funding of the MPA by MCPS, via a management charge, has changed to a large extent, and the MPA is primarily funded by

subscriptions from its publishing company members (the reduced proportion of funding via management charge now amounting to two fifths). However, the relationship between the parent and wholly-owned subsidiary is such that there can never be any doubt that the music publishers have a very big vested interest in how that licensing and collecting and royalty distribution operation is handled. MCPS is accountable to the MPA, a fact recognised in the regular reports to the MPA Board by senior MCPS executives. Accountability to the full membership of the MPA has been improved with the recent introduction of Open Meetings at which MCPS is able to update publishers on all its activities and answer questions.

Further information about the MPA can be found on its website www.mpaonline.org.uk

Two generatons of the James music publishing family have headed the MPA Board. Pictured together at an industry event are Dick James and his son Stephen.

The Association's Board (which until recently was called Council) has provided stability and continuity over the years, and in particular its Chairs (previously Presidents) have generally served the Association and its members for considerable periods of time. The MPA Articles now stipulate a maximum term of office for the Chair of three years. Recent Presidents/Chairs include:

1963 – 1965	J J Phillips	KPM Music Ltd
1965 – 1970	C R L (Leslie) Avenell	Alfred Lengnick & Co Ltd
1970 – 1972	David Toff [1]	David Toff Music Publishing Co Ltd
1972 – 1974	J J Phillips	EMI Music Publishing Ltd
1974 – 1977	Dick James	Dick James Music Ltd
1977 – 1978	O M J (Jonson) Dyer	Peters Edition Ltd
1978 – 1985	R N (Ron) White	EMI Music Publishing Ltd
1985 – 1989	A P (Tony) Pool	Boosey & Hawkes Music Publishers Ltd
1989 – 1993	Jonathan Simon	The Really Useful Group plc
1993 – 1997	Andy Heath	Momentum Music Ltd
1997 – 1998	Stephen James	Dejamus Ltd
1998 – 2001	Tom Bradley	EMI Music Publishing Ltd
2001 –	Andrew Potter	Oxford University Press

[1] David Toff was in the unique position of having also acted as caretaker Secretary during his Presidency from 1971 until the EGM of April 1972, when his appointment as full-time Secretary to the Association was approved.

The MeCHANiCaL-COPYRIGHT PrOtEctiON SOCIETY

Introduction

The MCPS offices at Elgar House in Streatham, London – which became one of the two main offices of the MCPS-PRS Alliance from 1997.

Unlike PRS, MCPS does not appear to have worried about its name, possibly because it was always a business-to-business organisation, dealing with commercial companies which operated in the same industry as its copyright owning members; so it was not burdened with the need to be recognisable to a huge number of diverse licensees who were members of the general public. But like PRS it sees no need to incorporate its nationality in its name, which reflects the terminology of the Copyright Acts which have over the years empowered the copyright owners to issue and be paid for the licences which MCPS as their agent administers.

Today the *mechanical right* is really a misnomer. At the time the right was defined in the 1911 Copyright Act the only application of this right was via the use of mechanical contrivances to make copies of records and so the "mechanical right" term was coined as a kind of verbal shorthand for the Act's wording, which refers to the "restricted act" being that of "copying" a work and making copies of it. A range of alternative means of copying a work

within the meaning of the Act have developed over the years. MCPS licenses all users of the right to make copies of copyright music in any medium other than print, and so licenses both material and intangible, permanent and transient copies – from nostalgic vinyl analogue discs to an increasingly sophisticated range of digital copies including CDs, audiovisual products, and downloads onto computers and mobile phones.

For the purpose of administering these rights the copyright holders, essentially the music publishers in the MCPS context, have created distinctions between the various types of use of their rights. In simple terms there are three: audio products (records); synchronisation (originally literally the synchronised addition of a soundtrack including music to a film, and now applying to all kinds of audiovisual works); and video products (the direct audiovisual counterparts to records). The distinctions are aligned with differences in the terms under which these usages are licensed: these respectively are via licence fees based on reported sales; via lump sum fees; and via a combination of these two.

MCPS is mandated as an agency to license all audio product, and to administer the "sync right" in terms of blanket licences for television (though that usage is usually licensed directly by the publisher where feature films are concerned). MCPS is also mandated to issue blanket licences to radio and television broadcasters for their use of the mechanical right. All other usages – which can be quite varied these days – are subject to optional mandates from publishers, subject in some cases to decision by the MCPS Board. Licensing is dealt with in more detail at various appropriate points later in this chapter. The use of music on the internet is obviously an increasingly important issue, and the mechanical right is involved in the uploading of copyright music files onto servers, and again if these are downloaded; the performing right is also involved in music distribution via the internet, and the joint licensing of these rights by PRS and MCPS is detailed in the Alliance chapter.

In complete contrast to the performing right, mechanical rights administration in the UK has, as stated, always been dealt with on an agency basis, and this is still the case within the MCPS-PRS operational alliance.

MCPS refers to itself as a collecting society, and that term is used in this history, but it is not and never was a membership society in the strict and generally accepted sense. The mechanical rights organisations in the UK were formed and owned by music publishers as companies which were a combination of co-operative and agency. There was never any question of an assignment of their mechanical rights (originally assigned to the publishers by their contracted writers) to the body administering those rights. In this, MCPS and its US counterpart the Harry Fox Agency are entirely different to the European collecting societies. The Anglo American approach is that copyright is a property right and as such can be sold or assigned as the owner wishes. In contrast, a writer cannot under European interpretation of the authors' right, *droit d'auteur*, be completely "alienated" from his rights; so both mechanical and performing rights are assigned to collecting societies. These then pay writers and publishers their respective shares of licence income directly, in accordance with the terms of the writer/publisher contracts. In the UK publishers may therefore choose to allow MCPS to license on their behalf, or may license directly themselves. They mandate MCPS to administer the mechanical rights in their repertoire only in respect of stated users and particular kinds of use. Traditionally, publishers dealt directly with the major record companies, and a universal mandate for MCPS to license all record companies was not forthcoming until fairly recently in the society's history.

The agency function of MCPS, the fact that the rights were not assigned, the ability of publishers to "cherry pick" the best deals for themselves and bypass MCPS, and a society business agenda which was often subordinate to the publishers' agenda, all led to a distinctive culture and practice. These are viewed and summed up from different perspectives by two people eminently associated

MCPS MD Bob Montgomery (*seated left*) with a group including his head of licensing Graham Chhurchill (*standing left*) and – some years before they were appointed to their current eminent positions in the UK record industry – Fran Nevrkla , now CEO of PPL (*standing third from left*) and current BPI Executive Chairman Peter Jamieson (*seated right*).

with MCPS, and with the Mechanical Rights Society which for a number of years existed to negotiate the licences which MCPS then operationally administered.

Former MCPS Managing Director Bob Montgomery states simply: "Publishers always wanted to operate MCPS to their individual advantage, with no priority given to the common good." MCPS Board Director Crispin Evans characterises MCPS as "an organisation which has to exist to do for publishers collectively what they would far rather do for themselves, but cannot". The fact is that in the UK (as in the US) publishers wish as far as possible to make their own deals with users, and to use whatever commercial edge their particular size and strength of repertoire brings them.

In 1976 MCPS was bought by the MPA. PRS was interested in buying it – which would have given the UK merged or allied organisations for the administration of the performing and mechanical rights similar to those in most other European countries. However, there was determination among publishers that it would remain under their control: it did and it does, although much else has changed and developed over the past 28 years.

This purchase of MCPS by the MPA was the first major turning point in a largely uneventful and workmanlike MCPS history, and one major outcome was that the MPA-appointed MCPS Board took charge of licensing policy. The next business-changing event was the 1988 Copyright Act. The effects of this propelled MCPS into a much higher level of activity and income, coincidentally giving it presence and profile in the music industry which it had never previously warranted. The third transforming development for MCPS was the long-signalled operational alliance with PRS in1997 (considered at least twice before).

There were also events which significantly altered the market in which the society operates. These included various changes in the types of product which the record companies made from shellac and then vinyl analogue discs and later analogue cassettes and analogue music videos, through digital CDs to combined video and audio in DVD. There was also gradual change in the way that broadcasters operated which led to an increase in the amount of mechanical licence income from that sector. Other factors were the rise of commercial piracy via manufacture of counterfeit music products; the proliferation of uses of the mechanical right in consumer novelties from greetings cards and toys to clothing (MCPS has in its time licensed recordings on sound chips which were then sewn into knickers, socks and T-shirts); the explosion in the legitimate and pirated use of copyright music on the internet; music in computer games and, most recently, the unexpectedly big market for copyright music as ring tones on mobile phones.

These events are covered in more detail in the MCPS chapter which follows. As with the story of PRS, the intention is to navigate an interesting route at the surface rather than diving to great depths of detail.

Trying to do for publishers what they would far rather do for themselves

MCPS appears not to have been highly regarded or strongly supported by publishers during its first seven decades in business. It remained a small organisation while the statutory licence fee (enshrined in successive Copyright Acts) was in place. That statutory provision made it simple for publishers to license record companies directly, and thereby avoid any fees to an agent such as MCPS. Until that statutory provision was removed, publishers tended to use MCPS to license a variety of small uses and users of the rights, and to deal with the difficult time and labour-intensive end of licensing work which they did not want to undertake directly, and from which publishers were content to receive small amounts of revenue. MCPS also acted as a useful "back-stop" for overseas mechanical income: overseas societies which might not have mechanisms for distributing on an individual basis to UK rights owners' local sub-publishers might well be willing simply to send the lump sum to MCPS and leave it to the UK organisation to work out how to distribute it.

One MCPS area of activity did ensure that all publishers became members, but although it was seen as an essential service it meant little in terms of revenue or agency commission for many years. This was the MCPS blanket fee for the use of mechanical rights by broadcasters when they made recordings of copyright music for use in radio or TV programmes or when they copied or "dubbed" commercial recordings embodying copyright musical works onto tape for use in pre-recorded programming. Revenue from these licences was for many years very small. It was not until the late 70s that the then Managing Director Bob Montgomery successfully undertook a series of tough negotiations with broadcasters to raise the value of the blanket licence considerably.

For a relatively short period there existed another kind of MCPS licence. This was a kind of wild card in the organisation's small pack, which might have been played high for potentially large stakes but which was used– puzzlingly and frustratingly to some, understandably to others – with such caution that it never came close to winning a trick. The MCPS home recording licence cost £1.50 and was available to members of the public who wanted to make legal home recordings of commercial recordings. It was withdrawn by MCPS in September 1980 after the BPI ceased to support it – and of course such a licence needed joint support from both sets of copyright owners, the writers/publishers and the record companies. The record industry decided the licence "was neither economic nor practical"; only 10,000 had been issued in the previous year, barely covering administration costs. Another reason that the scheme was withdrawn was to clear the way for a joint industry campaign for a royalty on blank tape: the scheme was not restored when that campaign failed.

Since record industry research repeatedly reinforced the blindingly obvious view that the public was largely impervious to the fact that such "home taping" was illegal under the Copyright Act, and most of the tiny proportion of those who *did* know did not care, the licence was doomed to obscurity without some kind of heavy public information and marketing or PR push behind it. The fact that this was never done indicates the music industry's mixed feelings about it. On one hand, it was seen as a good idea, since it was thought that legislators would be more ready to help rights owners to stamp out commercial piracy and demand a levy on private copying if there was a legitimate way for the public to make their own recordings. On the other, a home taping licence (especially if it were widely used and bringing in decent revenue) might tempt Government to reject any idea of a levy in new legislation on the grounds that the rights owners didn't need one. The licence was left to sink or swim, and quietly sank. However, the idea of this kind of licence is reinvented occasionally by those who are not aware that it once existed, and as recently as the summer of 2003 there was some correspondence in the UK press which raised it again, but this won little attention at official or public level.

Fighting for the value of the rights and revenue growth

So MCPS was still small and not particularly strong or united when in 1928 the specially-formed Music Copyright Defence Association appealed to the Board of Trade for an increase in the statutory mechanical licence rate of 5% of the retail price of a record, as set down in the 1911 Act.

The situation was then (until 1988) quite different for mechanical and performing rights arbitration/adjudication. PRS was subject to the Performing Right Tribunal, to which only the users, not the society, might appeal. For mechanical rights there was no Tribunal, and the Board of Trade was responsible for deciding whether a licence rate or tariff should be changed; in this case if appealed to by the licensor rather than the user.

The 1928 MCPS appeal to the BoT was on the grounds that records were by the mid-20s increasingly being manufactured double sided, with two recordings on them rather than just one. This of course halved the amount a publisher could earn from each song which was recorded, because the 5% royalty was for the whole record. Having several songs on one record was not unheard-of at that time, and the Act provided for a minimum royalty per work of a halfpenny (0.2p). This protected rights owners from manufacturers who might want to win a particular part of the market by putting several songs on a disc and selling it at a very low price while still only paying MCPS 5% of the very low retail price. The MCPS appeal had some success. There was no question of doubling the statutory licence fee, but the BoT did award an increase from 5% to 6.25% of retail, and raised the per track minimum to three farthings (0.3p). There was no further attempt to have the statutory royalty raised until the Record Royalty Review of 1976 (*see below*) but revenue from the record industry to the publishers increased from 1941 to 1988 via an arrangement related to the use of commercial recordings by broadcasters. Because the MCPS licence to record companies only entitled them to make records for retail, and did not thereby also license the broadcast of the recording, a payment was made by Phonographic Performance Ltd (PPL) .This was a percentage of PPL income from licensing the record companies' performing right in commercial recordings for broadcast and public performance. In 1987, just before it ceased, this PPL payment was £900,000 out of total PPL royalty revenues of £14.1m.

PPL also made a voluntary payment to the Musicians' Union for the benefit of musicians who played on the recordings. This is worth explaining here because it eventually led to a development in MCPS business in the mid-90s.

Under an international agreement between the international record industry body IFPI and FIM (International Federation of Musicians, PPL agreed in the 40s to set aside 32.5% of its revenue for recording artists. Of this, 20% was retained by PPL to pay to individual acts (little is know about how distributions were calculated, and anecdotal evidence indicated that artists had to request the money, and many never found out they were entitled to it). The other 12.5% was given to the MU in respect of "unidentified" session players. As the MU had no information on which to base distributions, this income was ring-fenced in a Special Fund to benefit musicians generally, notably giving financial support for festivals and other performances and activities such as workshops for young musicians.

This practice was abandoned following the 1988 MMC report which recommended that all performers on recordings should receive "equitable remuneration". PPL and MU started to try to identify session players after this but the process did not gain momentum until the UK Government ratified the European Rental Directive in 1996, making such equitable remuneration binding for performers. Prior to this, PPL unilaterally offered 50% to performers.

It was at this point that the two performers' societies were formed. One is the Association of United Recording Artists (AURA), which seeks only featured, relatively high-earning recording artists (the "stars") as members and concentrates on distributing money to them. The other is the Performing Artists Media Rights Association (PAMRA), which accepts for membership any musician who played or plays on records. AURA was supported by the Music Managers' Forum (MMF), while PAMRA was supported by the unions MU and Equity. Both were independent from PPL itself. Non-AURA and PAMRA musicians are paid directly by PPL. However, both PAMRA and AURA were limited to receiving monies from PPL; under the UK law PPL remains the sole collection body. While AURA receives lump sums and then administers its own distributions, the distribution calculations for PAMRA are undertaken by PPL.This fact was always very likely to lead to some form of merger or alliance between the two organisations, and in December 2003 a joint press release from AURA, the actors' union Equity, the Music Producers Guild (MPG), the Musicians Union (MU), PAMRA and PPL announced that following two years of working together AURA, MPG, the MU and PAMRA had signed "a significant collaborative deal" with PPL, and that Equity was expected also to sign up in early 2004. The outcome would be a "single service" for performers via PPL's handling of administration, while the performer organisations "remain at the forefront of negotiations with overseas societies". This development was another example of the clear trend towards cost-reducing operational collaboration in the "rights business" which has been so noticeable in the past few years, and is strongly predicted to continue and increase.

Well before this, in anticipation of the provisions of the 1996 change in UK law, PPL had turned to MCPS to help it assemble data about recordings and make distributions, and for several years MCPS revenue benefited from the contract with PPL, as described later in this chapter.

Returning to the MCPS success in wringing a better statutory mechanical rate from the BoT in 1928, it can be said that this helped music publishers to weather the years of the Depression and World War II when, like PRS, MCPS found that the rights business was sustained and grew as a result of the wartime boom in demand for entertainment, including recorded music.

Peace returned, and MCPS appears to have continued, still in quite a small way, to do what it had been set up to do. But expectation of more marked business growth was sparked in music publishers by the 1956 Copyright Act, which would require broadcasters to have mechanical licences. The value of these was not set out and so would have to be negotiated, and this led publishers to tighten control on the licensing of their rights. So in 1955 the UK music publishers founded another organisation, the Mechanical Rights Society, with an elected ruling Council of publishers (writers were not brought in until the 80s). This was a negotiating body, formed in preparation for the new Act. All the UK publishing companies became MRS members in order to benefit from the forthcoming deal for the new revenue stream. MCPS also became a member, and the memberships of the two organisations were identical, or virtually so.

The importance of the way MCPS had to deal with broadcasters should be stressed. Without an arbitrating Tribunal, the mechanical rights holders had to exert their rights entirely through negotiation, working with the broadcasters to do a deal that everyone could live with. What was learnt at the time proved very useful when new broadcasters came into the market, one of the biggest of such licence agreements eventually being with BSkyB satellite television. MCPS' ability to distribute lump sums for blanket broadcast deals had, of course, originally been usefully honed by 40 years of dealing with the lump sum PPL payments.

The relationship between MRS and MCPS was that the commercial policy of MCPS towards users was dictated by the former, rather than by the MPA. It was the job of MCPS to administer the terms of any MRS agreements with users. This arrangement persisted even after the MPA bought MCPS in 1976.

A very significant tactical move

Early in the 70s the issue of PRS possibly taking over or at least having a hand in running MCPS was raised. The trigger was a proposal that PRS might assist MCPS in programming its computers (this technical and operational trigger for co-operation recurred twice in the 90s, the second time being one key factor in the creation of the MCPS-PRS Alliance). PRS CEO Michael Freegard was not prepared to have this idea go forward without having PRS management involved in running the MCPS operation; that was resisted by MCPS and the idea stalled. Those involved at the time are also now willing to admit that there was strong resistance to the possibility of a joint performing and mechanical right organisation which would want to pay both kinds of royalties directly to interested parties: the publishers had no wish to relinquish their position as the recipients of the gross mechanical rights payments which they could hold before paying on the writers' share. This is anecdotally supported by Bob Montgomery's recollection that at the first MPA Board meeting he attended in June 1976 the Chairman Dick James complained that Montgomery had been "seen coming out of the PRS building" a few days before, and demanded an explanation for this.

The story of the MPA takeover of MCPS in 1976 is told in different sets of available records. It had been mooted, to approval, at the MPA AGM in June 1975. The Minutes of the MPA Board meeting in September record that the Chairman Dick James "gave a detailed report of a special but unofficial meeting with MCPS representatives earlier that month, at which the situation concerning the acquisition of MCPS by the MPA was clarified". Negotiations were expected to be concluded by the end of the year. In December James reported that MCPS now had a schedule for taking the matter forward, based on a plan proposed by the MPA, and he himself had in mind "a very efficient man who would be available in time to help organise the details and future operations of MCPS". In January 1976 the MPA Purchasing Committee recommended that the association should make a formal bid to MCPS shareholders of about £12 a share (a total of £230,400); that the price should be raised through bank loans; that after the purchase the legal status of MCPS should be changed to that of a company limited by guarantee, like PRS. The Board heard that the unofficial reaction from MCPS had been that the offer was "a bit on the low side" but they were seriously interested. After detailed discussion the Chairman summed up by saying that it was ultimately to the music publishing industry's benefit to have its own collecting society and in any case the present arrangement was so unsatisfactory as to make it likely that some publishers would prefer to break away from MCPS. Regarding bank financing, he had been given assurance that the MCPS assets were good security and the loan was a certainty (even without the available guarantees from individual members of MPA). Purchase proposals were agreed unanimously, and James announced that the "very efficient man" he had in mind was Bob Montgomery, then heading Chappell Music.

As traced in the UK music industry business paper *Music Week*, the story contains much detail and additional information which is not reflected in the MPA Board Minutes, but much of which clearly came from interviews with the MPA Chairman and probably other directors, and other industry figures. The *MW* coverage began in January 1976 with a news story announcing that Bob Montgomery, MD of the UK's leading music publisher Chappell, had resigned with immediate effect because he had been invited by MPA President Dick James and his Board to "become involved in their plans for the collection of mechanical royalties". This move, the story added, came after a year of deliberations by an MPA working party, including Montgomery himself, on the future for mechanical rights administration.

Reportedly one source of discontent for publishers was that MCPS at that point was profit-making, paying dividends to its shareholders (though admittedly less than 1% of total collections); another was the cost of collection, then about 12%.

In February, at the international music convention Midem, Dick James was reported as hinting strongly to a meeting of the International Publishers Association that the MPA would be taking over MCPS. Responding to a reference to "the desirability of publishers controlling their own mechanicals income", he said that "momentous happenings" were imminent, and would lead to the MPA being responsible for mechanical rights collection. This would align the UK with the USA, where the mechanical collection agency Harry Fox had long since been taken over by the National Music Publishers Association (NMPA). Simultaneously it would sharpen contrast with the European situation, where performing and mechanical rights were frequently administered by a single society or by closely allied societies using the same operating company.

It was suggested in the *MW* reporting that following the American pattern was more logical for the UK because both favoured a royalty distribution method which paid mechanicals to the music publishers who then passed the due shares to their contracted writers. In Europe the mechanical rights societies distribute royalties directly to writers as well as publishers. *MW* reported that although the takeover had been contemplated for some years, MPA's interest had quickened when in about 1974 PRS began to intensify its interest in the collection of mechanicals. The prospect of the UK moving towards the European model did not appeal to most publishers, and this led to the takeover proposals being formulated by a special committee. MPA Minutes show that the official offer went to MCPS shareholders "after a slight delay at the Department of Trade" on 1 March. A meeting was arranged between loan guarantors and the National Westminster Bank.

Pictured at a BASCA Gold Badge Awards - sponsored by MCPS - in the early 90s are (*left to right*) MCPS MD Frans de Wit, with famous entertainers Norman Wisdom and Roy Castle who were Badge recipients, flanking Guy Fletcher, Chairman of the then still separate writers' guild, the British Academy of Songwriters, Composers and Authors.

One hundred and seven publishing companies, alphabetically from AIR Music to Virgin Music, attended an EGM (Extraordinary General Meeting) of the MPA on 31 March, at which the proposed MCPS purchase was put before them in detail. James' opening statement set the scene: "It is no secret that the MPA Council has been considering the possibility of the purchase of MCPS for some time. As many people here will know, some 18 months ago the PRS showed interest in expanding their interest in mechanical collection. Many of the major publishers at the time expressed severe reservations about this [believing that] the collection of performance and mechanical income should not be in the same hands." He added that it had been necessary to proceed initially in "some secrecy", both because of Government takeover rules and because bringing plans into the open would "jeopardise the success of the operation". He was also able to

reveal that there had been a 100% acceptance of the offer by MCPS shareholders: the stated price per share in the final offer had risen to £17.50. The financing of the deal was explained (as stated earlier). However, it was pointed out that any takeover bid had to be approved by the Department of Trade. Also this was a situation where a company without profits or assets was taking over a profitable organisation. The bank would require "an obvious outside source of repayment should anything go wrong". Some 14 publishing companies had come forward as guarantors.

The April 1976 MPA Board meeting learned that there was no further obstacle and the takeover would become unconditional on 22 April; National Westminster Bank would pay the shareholders; share transfers would be stamped and new share certificates would be issued to MPA. Directors elected to the interim Board of MCPS were David Adams, Leslie Avenell, Jonson Dyer, Dick James, Bob Kingston (Chairman) Derek Knibb and Bob Montgomery (MD). In June Kingston reported to the MPA on the state of MCPS affairs; he compared it to the Harry Fox Agency in the US and reported the "main shortcomings" as lack of budgetary control and overstaffing. Arthur Young consultants were called in to report. Computerisation and methods of distribution were also big issues; there was "need for improvements without (so far as is possible) capital investment".

In August Montgomery reported to the MPA Board that the loan from National Westminster (originally anticipated to be repaid over five years) had been repaid in full via an interest-free loan from MCPS to the MPA. He also reported that preliminary Arthur Young recommendations included staff training and re-siting under one roof, and stressed the "new MCPS approach" with more meetings with publishers and better issue of information.

Further information comes from those who were personally involved in the deal. Bob Kingston was managing director of Southern Music London from 1959 to 1977, and in 1976 was vice-chairman of MRS, the mechanical rights licence negotiating body which decided on the rates MCPS would charge: "I was asked by the MRS Board to begin negotiations with the shareholders of MCPS, the majority shareholder being EMI. But Dick James informed me that its members, music publishers, felt that it was more fitting that Music Publishers Association should acquire ownership of MCPS. This was agreed by MRS and LG (Len) Wood, then EMI MD, agreed to sell its shareholding to MPA. His only request was that MPA, as soon as possible, would find a place on its board for Ron White who headed the EMI publishing activities. This was eventually achieved."

As the MCPS purchase deal had begun rolling, James had been quoted in *MW*: "This could be one of the most exciting times in the UK music industry in years. Should the expected bid be successful it would provide the MPA with a real opportunity to gain teeth. The MCPS has done an excellent job but it could well be that this is the time for copyright owners to take control." The background to such an emphatic statement, and to the deal itself, was as stated above – that publishers did not universally support the creation of a monopoly agency and the major publishers at that time in general did a better job on their own. The acquisition of MCPS by MPA was arguably defensive, but it was also a pointer to further changes down the road.

Some questions hung over circumstances of the purchase at the time, and are still occasionally mentioned today, relating to the fact that the MPA did not have the ready funds to make the purchase and the funding was ultimately achieved through MCPS itself. Bob Montgomery's view is firmly positive. Confirming in passing that it would undoubtedly have been easier for PRS to buy MCPS ("They actually had the money, and MPA as a trade association didn't") he reiterates that the original bank loan was repaid, via the interest free loan from the collecting society to the MPA – that loan being out of money which had come in to MCPS after the purchase by the MPA.

The deal was finalised on 22 March 1976. MPA then owned MCPS, and the publishers controlled their rights while the agency did the administration. Over the following months MCPS won agreement from the MPA that the former would strengthen its remit and be given more room to manoeuvre.

The re-making of MCPS from the inside – with a few external battles along the way

Bob Kingston was chairman of MCPS with Bob Montgomery as MD. Those involved at the time recall that they retained some of the MCPS staff, but dispensed with the services of those hostile to any change in operating methods. In truth, Montgomery says now, there was very little management to get rid of or retain.
The management team had to be built. Montgomery found an organisation, which was functioning, but rather in the manner of a three-wheeled wagon. It had approximately 100 staff, who were spread around four office sites in Streatham, with the majority in the original Elgar House at 380 Streatham High Road.

The computer system was superannuated. There was no royalty accounting system; this work was done by Barric, a Barclays Bank subsidiary, which was by then making it clear that they were not going to be able to support this work much longer. Office accommodation was poor. A former manager recalls her office (one of the desks propped up on a large pile of directories) in which seven staff attempted to share one telephone with the flex stretched across the room several feet off the floor. It was frequently necessary to climb over the directories, and in doing so to risk being garrotted by the phone wire at neck height.

Montgomery's first tasks were urgent and pragmatic. He needed to replace the computer system, improve working conditions, review and improve the organisation's future staff needs and the morale and working practices of the existing staff, and reinvigorate the best of existing managers while also bringing in new managers to take MCPS forward faster and more efficiently.

MCPS at that time was handling less than 10% of UK recording right revenue. The resulting level of fixed-in-advance commission earned, on which the company had to run, was low; life was a budgetary struggle and staff wages were correspondingly depressed. MCPS employees regarded with some envy the generally higher levels of remuneration for managers and staff at PRS, which was not under the same financial pressure as MCPS because it retrospectively recouped its full administrative costs from revenue before distribution of royalties.

One of the managers Montgomery worked with in his first year as MD was Ray Ellis. He had started at MCPS in 1956 and left as deputy general manager in 1977 to join the fledgling Leosong Copyright Bureau (retiring as MD in 1998 but still a part-time consultant). He had not particularly welcomed the MPA takeover. "Up until then, MCPS had operated in a gentlemanly, family atmosphere which always tried to be as co-operative as possible where new clients were concerned, negotiating in a commercial but helpful way. We would often offer a lower royalty rate to a newcomer, with built-in provisions for increases as they grew and established their business. Royalties can kill a project before it gets off the ground." However, he like most others then – and certainly now when constant change is endemic in the UK collecting society operation, as it is in other business sectors – accepted that things could not go on as they were. "I could see that the society had to be put on firmer ground. I was seconded some time before the takeover to the PRS to look at their systems. We were all for modernising our methods but wanted to make quite sure that it would work. We had already started on a system for broadcast royalties, but up to 1977 things were mostly done by a laborious manual procedure at the MCPS. Bob Montgomery had his ideas and they were mostly good ones, but in 1977 I thought it was time for me to look at other opportunities. Thereafter, looking at the MCPS from outside, I could see the process of change

accelerating. The family atmosphere went and more legal people came in." As if the first year of major change at MCPS was not enough to cope with, 1976 also brought a serious public tussle with the BPI over the statutory mechanical licence fee.

It was not initiated by MCPS or MPA, but by PRS which then managed Britico, to which most overseas societies belonged in order to receive UK mechanical rights income. The rights holders in the musical works – writers and publishers – wanted the statutory rate of 6.25% of retail price raised: the record industry as licensees unsurprisingly did not– and in fact retaliated by counterclaiming that it should be reduced.

A public hearing was necessary. In November a panel headed by Hugh Francis QC began a hearing which over three months accumulated 27 days of evidence from 20 witnesses and a mountain of paper information. On one side was the Record Royalty Revision Association comprising the various writers' and publishers' organisations including MRS and the MPA, which claimed that the 1928 royalty rate and per track minimum "has ceased to be equitable". They asked for the rate to rise to 8% in line with the BIEM[1] European rate; and they wanted the minimum "now worth less than the smallest coin of the realm" to be raised to at least 1p. Initially the BPI had just resisted the call for a rise, but it actually pressed for a reduction after a statistical report showed that record price rises and the very great increase in volume of record sales since 1928 had resulted in a substantial rise in the real value of revenue to the writers and publishers. This report carried much weight with the Panel in the end. As reported in *Music Week* the Panel's attitude was "that the superstars already made fortunes on their writing; successful and moderately successful composers made a good living; and the unsuccessful whose songs did not sell would not be helped by a rise to 8% or even 10% – nor would classical composers". The RRRA submission that a higher rate of licence fee would put the two sides on a footing to negotiate a "fair" rate between them was rejected as impossible within the law. The Panel added that such

1 International bureau for mechanical rights administration organisations (Bureau International des Sociétés de Musique gerant les Droits d'Enregistrement et de Reproduction Mécanique). Founded in 1929 to set a common tariff across Continental) Europe. Individual record companies had to apply for a BIEM licence. The need to confront BIEM was the main reason for the founding of IFPI as the international federation of record industry trade organisations in 1933. An *ad hoc* contract between BIEM and IFPI was in existence from 1930 but the first Standard Contract was signed in 1947. It has been revised at regular intervals ever since – last revision was 1997 when the headline rate was reduced from 9.306% of PPD to 9.009%. MCPS is a member of BIEM although it has not elected to try bringing the UK market within the scope of the Standard Contract.

collective bargaining could also not be fair "since the public that pay the pipers could not be parties to the agreement."

The ruling was that the *status quo* would remain. Speaking on behalf of the BPI, its Copyright Committee Chairman Robert Abrahams (later to be the External Affairs Director for PRS) said that the decision would save the record industry some £2.5m annually against the cost of an 8% rate. Conversely, this meant that the writers and publishers were denied £2.5m a year, but the point was not made by *MW*, underlining the persistent tendency of press, public and Government to equate the entire music industry with the record industry (an issue which MCPS, PRS, the MPA and the writers' organisations would tackle with some success when they formed British Music Rights in the mid-90s).[2]

During 1977 there was considerable change in MCPS staff and in staff attitude. A refreshed and externally reinforced senior management – all called controllers, as was also the style then at PRS and other organisations of similar perceived "civil service" character– was fairly quickly put in place. MCPS was reorganised into departments which were focused on and tasked with specific, existing and new areas of activity, and Bob Montgomery rebriefed or recruited controllers appropriately. As Montgomery's lieutenant from 1981 Keith Lowde necessarily played a major part in defining changes and carrying them through. He recalls that a definable problem in the early years after the takeover had been "lack of clarity and purpose" among managers, linked to unprofitable use of their time in endless meetings, a problem which was, of course, hardly unique to MCPS and which is still a staple ingredient of management theory text books. His early move was to ban all meetings (more than two managers in discussion constituted a meeting). Such changes, combined with a consolidation of differently-located offices into one, and the practice of setting firm business objectives for managers and expecting them to deliver, gave impetus to positive internal structural change and increased professionalism. Although music publishers then tended to exclude from their mandates to MCPS

most or all of the most lucrative licensing work which they could easily do themselves directly, they had no option but to use MCPS to license broadcasters. This was because the blanket licence agreements allowing broadcasters to record copyright music for use in programmes existed between organisations, not individuals; between MCPS and the Independent Television Companies Association (ITCA) for independent television, the Association of Independent Radio Contractors (AIRC) for the infant independent local radio, and the BBC for publicly-funded national TV broadcasting and for UK network radio broadcasting – of which it was then still the monopoly provider.

As pointed out earlier, these blanket licence agreements were in fact the reason why most publishers became MCPS members, even if they put little or no other licensing business through the agency of that society. But these broadcasting agreements had rolled on for many years without review, and by 1977 were bringing in a pittance: a total of about £120,000 annually. Renegotiation of these licences was one of the first objectives in Montgomery's sights. Understandably stiff resistance from the broadcasters eventually subsided in repeated rounds of talks, and by the end of 1977 Montgomery had increased total revenue to nearly £900,000 per annum. Probably more importantly he had established the basis for regular licence fee reviews from then on. In due course, when independent local radio (ILR) stations started to proliferate in the 80s this proved very valuable.

The publishers certainly appreciated the great improvement in this revenue stream, but were not noticeably more inclined to increase MCPS' mandate to administer other income streams for them. To increase efficiency and thereby hope to attract more licensing work in order to earn higher commission income MCPS needed to modernise. That needed investment, which could only be funded from commissions. "We were way behind with distributions," Montgomery remembers. "Dick James had assumed that the purchase of MCPS by the MPA could be used to force MCPS commission down to the 3% charged by Harry Fox.

2 See British Music Rights chapter

That was a fallacy. MCPS had to do far more analysis of returns from record companies, and it was expected to distribute 'line by line' and not just hand over lumps sums as Harry Fox did. We had hundreds of distributions every quarter for very small sums on which commission could not possibly cover administrative cost". The problem appeared intractable; the business equivalent of an Escher drawing in which perspective has to be radically shifted in order to achieve a believable picture.

Finance Controller Norman Robinson and a "think tank" meeting of managers achieved the perspective shift. Looking at income streams and distribution records and noting how many distributions amounted to less than £1 (collectively impacting adversely on administrative time and cost while delivering totally insignificant benefit to the individual recipients) the proposal arose that all such royalty sums should be put into MCPS "profit" rather than being distributed. The *quid pro quo* for members was that commission rates could drop, from 15% to 8%. All this was embodied in a revised membership agreement. But getting acceptance from the MPA Board was a battle. Montgomery recalls with relish: "The MPA was furious – but what else could we do? The MCPS Accounts were qualified because we had all this money awaiting distribution. Eventually it was accepted as a practical, even a good, idea".

"Eventually" is a mild understatement. The MPA Minutes record the fairly brief but furious skirmish which preceded the acceptance report by Montgomery. The April 1978 special meeting of the MPA Board discussed the new MCPS commission tariff and membership agreement. Chairman Jonson Dyer reported: "The MCPS Board has worked very hard and conscientiously to rescue MCPS from an extremely weak position", but several publishers made it clear that they saw the new terms as "interfering with publishers' business" and in their view MCPS had no right to present the MPA with a *fait accompli*. The MCPS move was plainly no PR coup with many of the MPA members (who were also its own members, of course).

Montgomery reiterated the pragmatic reasons behind the changes; not only would there be the benefit of greater future efficiency, but the immediate need was for drastic measures to assure a further 1978 royalty distribution, including replacement of the computer system. Dyer agreed that the true position of MCPS had not been known until after the MPA takeover and that the current management had to work against time "to stop it grinding to a halt". He wisely advised that compromise was needed, and the new membership agreement and tariff were a workable compromise. The Board resolved to ask the MCPS Board to "take note" of these discussions, but "meanwhile expressed confidence in the Board of MCPS and its direction of the society".

This proved to be equivalent to the World War I Christmas Day football match in no-man's-land. Hostilities resumed. An open forum for publishers in June brought an overwhelming vote against the new MCPS agreement and tariff; a vote of no confidence in the MCPS Board was passed (although the Minutes record that there were more abstentions than votes cast). The meeting resolved that MCPS should withdraw and cancel the new membership agreement; must propose an alternative; in future must send MCPS Board Minutes to all MPA Board members and the MPA must immediately draw up new terms of reference for MCPS. A motion calling for the MCPS Board to resign was, however, defeated.

At the end of that month the MPA Board meeting received the MCPS reply. This was firm rejection of the first three demands and comment reserved on the fourth. The obvious choices for the MPA were either to rescind the publishers' resolutions and accept the new MCPS agreement, or to demand *en bloc* MCPS Board resignation and appoint replacement directors. As the Minutes stated "much discussion followed". The decision was that "in the light of explanations offered" resolutions one to three would be abrogated. The new agreement was accepted, with undertakings including the ultimate reinstatement of distribution of royalty amounts under £1. The MPA noted also that the premature publicity about the new MCPS terms was regretted (but with a calmer eye to its PR, the MPA in November 1978 approved a new logo and went about refreshing its image in print).

The problems with the MCPS Accounts had been serious for more than one year and things had to be put right, in order not only to make proper and full distributions, but to establish a full audit trail. This related both to money and to the paperwork relating to usage reports and royalty payments. Implementation of a complex tracking system starting with a credit control function was the route to solving the problem. No further sets of accounts needed to be qualified after 1978.

During late 1977 and mid-1978 MCPS had worked furiously on its systems, going 10 months without making a distribution. With a theatrical flourish, the distributions were ready for the day of the 1978 MPA AGM (with Montgomery and his Commercial Operations Controller Graham Churchill handing cheques to members at the door of the meeting). A piece of possibly-not-merely-coincidental timing meant that MCPS announced it would be able offer monthly distributions, and these have been delivered without interruption since the introduction of a new Membership Agreement in 1978. They crowned this by introducing interest payments on late distribution, which was the first time such an offer had been made to members by any collecting organisation. Predictably, these developments ruffled the feathers of rights societies abroad, since it diverged from their own broadly established practices and threatened to spark demands for similar treatment from their own members.

Progress was also achieved in terms of how rigorously MCPS could audit licensees. Fronted by the Mechanical Rights Society (MRS), an agreement had been established in 1973 with the BPI (known simply as The MRS, MCPS, BPI Agreement). It specified the exact conditions under which record companies would comply with the terms of the 1956 Act and make their licence payments. Renegotiations of this agreement by MRS on behalf of publishers

Keith Lowde, former Finance Director and Deputy MD of MCPS

Robert Abrahams, who as a legal expert with the record industry helped the BPI to win its case in the Record Royalty Review of the former statutory mechanical licence fee, and later served as Director of External Affairs within the PRS top mangement team
.

and MCPS began in 1978, though they were only concluded in 1982. Out of the tough talking MCPS activated the existing but dormant audit rights. This led, as MCPS intended, to the righting of many long-standing wrongs in terms of inaccurate reporting by licensees of the number of records actually being shipped for distribution as against the declarations made.

MCPS improved its accounting times in 1978, as a result of the new Membership Agreement. This included monthly distributions. For all the progress in 1978 and MPA acceptance of some controversial management decisions, peace did not reign for very long. 1979 saw another MCPS/MPA clash when the latter decided that the former needed heavier restraint and more critical oversight. As Montgomery recalled events, the intention was for

MPA to place on the MCPS Board two publishers chosen specifically for their critical stance towards MCPS. The MCPS Executive resisted. Although parent company MPA had the right to appoint MCPS Directors, Montgomery and MCPS legal advisor Colin Fraser (of the then Joynson Hicks legal firm, which did great work for MCPS over many years and through several of changes of its own name) decided to find out whether they could get sufficient support from MPA member publishers to call an EGM to vote on a blocking resolution. Quiet canvassing showed that they could count on enough support. The MPA's coincidental failure to notify MCPS formally of its intention to appoint the two new publisher Directors, within the necessary 48 hours before the relevant Board meeting, allowed MCPS to refuse to have them appointed that day. And as MPA adverse reaction started to mount, presentation of the prospect of an EGM, at which an MCPS resolution would almost certainly be won, settled the issue. Needless to say, none of these backstage dramas were reflected in the next Annual Report which merely made diplomatic reference to two MCPS Board places remaining unfilled.

There was a modest amount of drama in late 1983 and into January 1984 when, against some lively but eventually unsuccessful rearguard actions, MPA succeeded in giving the MRS licence negotiating functions, assets and liabilities to MCPS – which was also given an enlarged Board. It was around that time that writers began to make it clear that they thought there was far too much control in the hands of the MPA publishers. They demanded more seats for writers on the enlarged MCPS Board. The MPA agreed, because it had no wish to turn back on its decision to enlarge the MCPS Board, and it took the "tactical view that it was vital not to antagonise the writer element and crucial that they should be educated as to how MCPS worked".

MCPS needed to attract membership and persuade its members to put more of their licensing business its way. Increased efficiencies and innovations in its offerings to publishers were a bid for both, and it enjoyed some success; the society started to obtain

new mandates, and income started to climb from the 1977 total of £5m. Growth and improving efficiency were helped when in 1981 MCPS moved its office from 380 Streatham High Road to 41 Streatham High Road, taking the Elgar House name with it. At that point it had about 180 staff, five regional managers and five staff at MCPS' Irish office in Dublin. But the real leap forward would come after the 1988 Copyright Act, which would see MCPS income rise greatly and rapidly over a few years.

But until then publishers continued largely to license directly the recording and manufacture of audio products by the record companies. There was no incentive to give this licensing work to MCPS, because Section 8 of the 1956 Copyright Act laid down a statutory licence fee of 6.25% – which in the days of Resale Price Maintenance (RPM) was based on the dictated retail price for a record. After the abolition of RPM, it was calculated on a formula agreed with the record industry and called RRP (Recommended Retail Price) which in turn was abolished in 1980 (*see MPA chapter*). Royalty calculations from 1982 were then based on ex VAT trade prices with an agreed mark-up variable depending upon the category of product. For example 7-inch and 12-inch singles were given a 25% mark-up for the purposes of calculating mechanicals.

That did not change until the 1988 Copyright, Design and Patents Act came into force, sweeping away the statutory fee. In the discussions with the Department of Trade and Industry that preceded first the Copyright Bill and then the Act itself, MCPS realised that Section 8 (the statutory fee) would be abolished, leaving publishers vulnerable to the greater power of record companies. MCPS persuaded the membership that strength lay in collective bargaining; the alternative being each track individually licensed at varying rates, which would have been an administrative nightmare.

David Lester, Chief Legal Counsel for the MCPS - PRS Alliance, and formerly Director of Legal Affairs for MCPS

The 1988 Copyright Act and another new membership agreement.

The 1988 Copyright, Designs and Patents Act was certainly one if not the single most important external event in MCPS history, causing a transformation at least equal to that in Disney's Cinderella. However, the changes in the CDPA having been clearly signalled in advance, preparations were well in hand for a second revision and update of the MCPS Membership Agreement in the same year. The mood among members was very different this time, partly because the need for change was obvious with the imminent disappearance of the Statutory Licence and all that implied, and partly because there was time and impetus for MCPS to seek to take the publishers with them as they developed the detail of the new agreement.

David Lester, who was charged with constructing the new agreement and liaising with the publishers, was determined to achieve consensus. MCPS management made it clear that the abolition of the statutory level of mechanical royalty presented an opportunity for MCPS to join the BIEM/IFPI agreement and raise the UK rate to the European one; and that MCPS needed collective strength on licensing phonomechanicals (generally referred to as audio products) because it was certain that a rise in the rate would be collectively opposed by the UK record industry.

Publishers were therefore asked to take a huge step in accepting that MCPS should be granted complete exclusivity in licensing audio products. After a careful process of refinement of the draft new Membership Agreement, to incorporate every legitimate demur and call for further detail (Lester remembered without checking any files that it ran to 48 drafts[3]), the major MCPS members agreed to this historic and progressive change.

Other aspects of the new Agreement included publishers' retention of complete choice as to whether they mandated MCPS to license music for TV commercials and film soundtracks; and placed decision-making power in the hands of the MCPS Board with regard to all other mechanical rights, whereby if the Board decided MCPS would license a usage they could bind MCPS members to blanket agreements issued for that usage, and if the Board decided MCPS would not assume the mandate to license a usage, the members could choose whether or not to grant that mandate on an individual basis.

This agreement has so far stood the test of time, and of continuing change in the business environment in which the mechanical right is invoked and administered.

The 1991 Copyright Tribunal: win, lose or draw for the publishers?

Having abolished the statutory mechanical licence rate, the 1988 Act also meant that MCPS, in having the authority under the new Act to lay down a licensing scheme, was brought under the jurisdiction of the Copyright Tribunal (previously the Performing Right Tribunal). The changes in the law set in train a process which, many would say inevitably, led to the Tribunal settling the issue of a new negotiated mechanical royalty rate. The Tribunal decision was, in the manner of local government election results,

---

3 Lester recalls that the process was lengthy but calm. He had vowed to achieve total consensus without losing his temper but was eventually driven into confrontation by a senior executive in one major publishing company. Lester called the man later to apologise for breaking his promise to himself, and was told his opponent had understood his position but had been interested to see just how far he could be pushed before he exploded.

announced by both sides to be victory for each. In truth, it was probably best described as "a draw". The 1991 battle between the record industry and the publishers regarding the new mechanical royalty rate to replace the now-abolished statutory 6.25% was played out in a music industry atmosphere that acknowledged that there was only one way to resolve the issue conclusively and irrefutably, and the sooner that was faced and dealt with the better for everyone.

One reason why judgement in a public forum, the Copyright Tribunal, was thought necessary – and therefore a reason why private negotiations were never going to be more that a precursor to a formal fight – went back several years to the purchase of Chappell Music by Warners in 1987/88. This created a market share giant; it was also a then-unfamiliar instance of a music user buying a music copyright owner. The size of the deal led to a referral to the Monopolies and Mergers Commission (MMC), but no enquiry resulted. However the user/copyright owner takeover aspect led to fears about the likelihood of cosy cut-price deals being struck for the use of a publishing company's copyrights by the record company which owned it. Happily, no such cosy dealing took place, but it was generally felt in 1991 that there had to be a Copyright Tribunal hearing and independent judgement, to demonstrate very publicly that the two sides of the music industry were not compromising on this vital central issue.

The result of the Tribunal was an improvement on the existing mechanical royalty rate, but (as has consistently proved to be the case in Copyright Tribunals) the reference to European rates was dismissed; so the only chance which MCPS had to establish the BIEM/IFPI rate in the UK was lost. From the society's point of view, the result could accurately be described as mixed, but in the opinion of some it was really a failure. One of the protagonists on the MCPS side goes so far as to label it "MCPS' Calais"[4], even though it brought the benefit of having the MCPS rate supersede controlled composition clauses, and indeed in

subsequent years the Tribunal-imposed MCPS rate stayed steady while the BIEM rate fell.

The Tribunal had not, however, exclusively dealt with the licence rate. It also looked at and ruled on the terms and conditions of the MCPS licence, and the result of this was that MCPS effectively changed from what has been described as a "post box" – accepting record companies' own calculations of publishing royalties and simply generating royalty statements for MCPS members – to a fully functioning royalty calculation and distribution organisation, because record companies began to provide sales accounting information. By late 1992 MCPS had developed its Audio Products and RDS (royalty distribution) systems which, in current Executive Director MCPS Sandra Cox's estimation "made a huge difference to the way we did business, and was a platform from which were launched many other changes and developments". As was often the case with the Tribunal, some elements of its decision on this issue gave with one hand and took with the other, effectively maintaining the *status quo* under another guise. MCPS had before the Tribunal been able to place a limit on the number of promotional copies of a product which could be made by the licensed record company "free of charge". The record companies, for reasons not too difficult to deduce, wanted the right to make unlimited quantities of promo copies. The Tribunal granted that right, but on condition that every promo copy was "indelibly stamped" to indicate that it was for promotion and not for sale. Record companies claimed they would not abide by this ruling, and MCPS reintroduced as an option a limit on the number of promotional copies, so in practice there was no noticeable change.

What was particularly interesting and highly significant to the Society, in the wake of the Tribunal, was that in one important respect nothing happened. Many had predicted that since the chance of achieving the BIEM rate had been one of the main inducements for MCPS publisher members to sign the new membership agreement, a failure to achieve that goal would result

---

4 This is in the historical context of the loss of Calais by Mary Tudor, though others have suggested that "Dunkirk" would be as good an analogy from more recent history.

in some disintegration of membership. It didn't. That was a clear signal that the UK publishers had decided that they wanted collective administration for what was now their core business, together with the protection which a stronger rights organisation could offer. That fact was probably a stepping stone towards the attempts to bring MCPS closer in terms of organisational structure to PRS. Although the early 90s attempt to set up what was called ServiceCo[5] failed, that proved a temporary halt on the road to the setting up of the MCPS-PRS Alliance in 1997.

A change at the top and contentious business change

While the Tribunal was in imminent prospect, to the surprise of the industry in general and many MCPS members in particular in terms both of fact and timing, the MCPS Board removed Bob Montgomery from his Managing Director role. Several of those closest to the action at the time say on reflection that the respective stances and characters of the MD and the Board were then such that the town was not big enough for both of them and it was inevitable that it would be the MD who took the departing stagecoach. Montgomery did, however, play his part as a very active consultant to the MCPS side during the Tribunal itself.

Montgomery's successor was Frans de Wit, a music publisher rather than a career administrator, who had been brought in from the Netherlands to head EMI Music Publishing He regarded his first task to be "to settle the staff down and get everyone pointing in the same direction" after a period of disruption. Other priorities were encouraging members to come on board with the new Membership Agreement; convincing members of the advantages of the administrative changes arising from the Tribunal while dealing with disappointment that the rate decided on had been 1% less than the hoped-for BIEM rate; and generally rebuilding management and membership confidence in MCPS

and future prospects. The major practical preoccupation at that point was obviously to deal with the impact of the Tribunal's detailed decisions. One was to repay the BPI the difference between the higher intended rate and the lower imposed one; higher rate payments from the record industry having been put into an escrow account pending the decision. There was work to be done also on rebuilding and improving the MCPS relationship with the BPI, in pursuit of which regular meetings with the BPI Director General and Legal Director were established.

Beyond the Tribunal, de Wit was aware that the reason he had been brought in as MD was "to get MCPS a place on the European map". Board thinking had changed since the overtures from PolyGram to set up a European Central Licensing deal with MCPS had been rejected (*see ECL and Cannes Agreement section in this chapter for details*); a revised priority was re-establishing MCPS influence on the processes and decisions of the Continental European societies, in view of the significance of the Anglo American repertoire which they were now administering through proliferating ECL deals with music multinationals. And that frankly meant that the UK society must have involvement in one or more of those deals. In 1992 de Wit went to talk to GEMA and Germany and SACEM in France in order to set up the joint European Licensing bureau BEL for joint handling of the EMI ECL agreement.

Licensing and distribution

Sandra Cox, who in mid-2002 succeeded long-serving MCPS Executive Director Chris Martin in that demanding role with overall responsibility for the society's income and business, had joined MCPS in the Finance department during the BPI-MCPS royalties Tribunal in 1991, and gained the immediate impression that huge changes were taking place directly because the record industry on one side and the musical works copyright owners

---

5 see Alliance chapter for full account

Sandra Cox, Executive Director MCPS

(writers) and copyright holders (publishers) on the other realised that MCPS was the most convenient way to deal with the post-1988 Act "free market" for mechanical rights. She saw the introduction of the Audio Products (AP) Agreements, and realised that they were an enormously significant development for both sides of the music industry. These agreements remain the bedrock of MCPS activities and processes.

Very briefly and simply, AP1 offers a blanket agreement whereby the licensed record company can use any works in the MCPS members' repertoire, but has a duty to give notice of intention to record a work and to request clearance and provide the necessary information about the planned record release. This is all in what is known as "label copy": the information about titles, authors, publishers, artists, record producer, catalogue numbers, track timings, "P and C" notices (respectively about the rights in the recording or "phonogram" and year of its first publication, and the rights in the artwork). This information will probably be found somewhere on the packaging, but not necessarily on the label on the disc itself. Traditionally the AP1 Agreement was aimed at major record companies, though for various reasons that is not always the case now. Licensees report their sales to MCPS quarterly in arrears. The AP2 Agreement offers product-by-product licensing, more suitable for record companies which issue fewer releases and use fewer works in the MCPS repertoire. In this case a specific quantity of manufactured recordings is licensed after payment of the royalties and a copy of the MCPS clearance goes to the manufacturing facility, which links with monitoring of pressing plants. There is also an AP2A Agreement which is similar but which allows manufacturing to take place before payment is made. This method of licensing and the way that MCPS systems link data on copyright works with data on recordings and data on products, result in a distribution model for mechanical royalties which is completely different, and far less complicated, that the one used by PRS for performing rights. MCPS royalty calculation involves "known quantities" at every stage: numbers of discs to be pressed or sales information; PPD (published price to dealer) on each product and the value of the percentage of that; detailed predetermined apportionment of licence fees; works matched against recordings and products; and precise information about ownership and shares of revenue due to writers and publishers. Distributions can therefore be "line-by-line", linking the payment to the licensed use of a copyright in a straight line.

MCPS has the full picture – the price, quantity and licence rate, the total royalty for each product and the calculation for each copyright owner pro-rated according to the duration of each musical work on the recording. Significantly, for an agency which takes no assignment of rights but operates by specific mandates, this system contains information about all works used, regardless of their ownership or whether MCPS is mandated. This means that errors can easily be checked because there are no unknowns and changes in ownership or mandate do not require new basic data to be sought. The eventual invoice to the licensee is, however, based only on the proportion of the product "owned" by MCPS.

Of course, there are also licensing schemes for audiovisual product such as videos and for DVDs; for CDs which are not sold directly but given away (for example as "cover mounts", attached to the covers of magazines, a major and growing part of MCPS business in late 2003); for non-retail usage such as broadcast, and premium offers or tokens (exchanged for music products by consumers of some non-music product); novelty products using copyright music – such as toys and clothing incorporating sound

MCPS Royalties

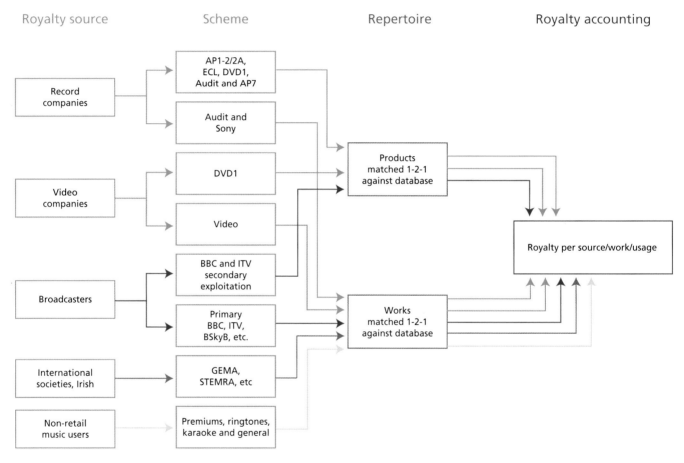

Although there are a number of exceptions dealt with in different, individual ways, the examples chosen for MCPS represent by far the greatest part of all royalties collected and distributed.

Record companies, video companies, broadcasters, etc., submit both royalties, details of the product (e.g. of an album) or tracks and the number of sales, pressings or broadcasts, according to the source.

The royalties are charged in accordance with the scheme and forwarded, via analysis against the specific details for which they were collected, to the members, net of the commission agreed for the scheme.

Members' statements include all the important details for each line, and in every case the royalty paid is linked back to actual sales of the specific product or usage of the work.

Source: The MCPS-PRS Alliance

chips; multimedia products like CD ROMs and the increasingly important online music distribution. And import stamps remain a source of revenue.

The story of a licensing body is obviously primarily a story of licensing work: how it is done, attempts to do it better, the people who do it, the tools and techniques at their disposal and the results achieved. Part of that story has to be the development of the biggest tool in the toolkit, the computer.

Montgomery had set up a dedicated IT department soon after his arrival. Not too long before that and very much within living memory, MCPS staff (as did their counterparts in PRS) worked with systems which were still predominantly paper-based, even though computers had been involved in the process for some time. At its worst the job of checking the identities of interested parties (IPs) in a particular copyright could involve an MCPS staff member in searching through 17 different information sources, some with exotic names like Dead File, Non-Dead File and even Dead-Dead File. Into what must at times have sounded like a data necropolis stepped fresh IT expertise. John Rowe is credited by many of his colleagues (and by MCPS members close enough to the administration to be aware of such things) as the thoughtful and sometimes dogged architect of the society's improved systems, which to a great extent won them heightened support from their members. *See the MCPS IT section*

MCPS licensing activity continued to expand in line with growth in the use of the mechanical right and development of new markets for recorded products. In the early 80s the manufacture and retail sale of music videos was growing, and an appropriate licensing scheme was negotiated with the BPI. The first MCPS-BPI Music Videogram Agreement ran for two years from 1 January1988 but was backdated to October 1986 – indicating that it was probably agreed sometime in 1987, the royalty being 6% of PPD. During these negotiations, MCPS made what some former managers describe as "major concessions" to the record

industry in terms of relating the licence rate for the new music product to that for the established audio recordings. The view is that these continue to echo down the years because they are the historic cause of the problems faced in the late 90s and early 2000s as MCPS struggled to put in place what it believed would be a satisfactory answer to the licensing first of CD (digital Compact Disc) and then of DVD (Digital Versatile Disc).

In March 1983, the digital Compact Disc was launched in the UK after its launch in Japan in October 1982 and slightly ahead of the USA launch in August 1983. Although no one had an optically perfect crystal ball, it was obvious that the digital CD was intended by the record industry to replace vinyl. As things turned out, vinyl sales proved remarkably resistant to these death threats, just as they had previously thwarted predictions that audio cassettes would kill them off, but CD did rapidly become the mass market recorded music format. UK CD trade deliveries grew from 300,000 in 1983 to 29.2 million in 1988 (more than doubling and sometimes tripling each year). In 1989 they reached 41.7 million and overtook LPs; in 1992 sales hit 70.5 million and overtook music cassettes (which were soon after that to start declining dramatically as a music format virtually to the point of extinction today). CD sales comfortably broke the 100 million level in 1994. Then growth slowed dramatically, first as the early and long-lasting boom in replacement of vinyl albums with their CD equivalents ran out of steam and then as online distribution (mostly illegitimate) of music hit retail sales of legitimate product and inflicted continuing damage to that market. The UK CD market held up better than that in the USA and Continental Europe, and in 2002 stood at 221.6m units with a trade price value of £1077.6m.

So in 1984 MCPS needed to license manufacture of this new audio format. This licensing agreement was particularly important because of the potential of the digital CD format to develop as a carrier of any kind of digitised information, not only recorded music – as would indeed happen with sophisticated variations on audio CDs (such as the MiniDisc and several kinds of "super CD" formats) and then with DVD.

A major influence on the UK CD licensing agreement proved to be the German Society GEMA, whose actions were believed by MCPS management at the time to compromise their negotiating position with the BPI from the outset. At that time there were only two CD manufacturing plants in Europe and both were in Germany; the Dutch music multinational PolyGram's factory was in Hanover and US record company RCA manufactured at Gutersloh. These manufacturing operations were licensed by GEMA at what the MCPS managers and directors regarded as too low a royalty rate. Even after 20 years in which reflection would be expected to mellow, Graham Churchill asserts that GEMA effectively "gave away greater concessions than were necessary".

MCPS wanted to negotiate on the basis that the compact disc was like any other recorded product, but the BPI's hand had been strengthened by GEMA's decision on a low rate. They pushed hard for a reduced royalty, in effect asking the writers and publishers to contribute to the cost of developing and launching CD technology by helping the record industry to recoup its investment. Churchill recalls: "We eventually came to an agreement with which neither side was very happy, so it was probably on balance the right one." In 1988 the UK rate for CD was 6.25% of PPD plus 29%. The record companies took the same "recouping investment" approach in their contracts with recording artists, basing royalties on dealer prices, and this course of action led to a number of bitter courtroom disputes between artists and their record labels in the mid and late 90s as the fairness of these reduced royalty rates was disputed, such as the suit brought by George Michael against Sony Music.

Auditing and Field Force

Alongside its efforts to sharpen up its own performance and to offer members and potential members the benefits of such improvements, MCPS was tackling the performance of its licensees.

MCPS had had an audit function for a long time, but it had been largely inactive and correspondingly ineffective. A dedicated Audit Department was set up during the BPI Agreement renegotiations. It began regular audits of reports from record companies, and quite soon exerted a significant impact on licence revenue as widespread errors were uncovered. Many of these were computer and accounting errors, but there were also instances of deliberate misreporting. Most of these were fairly small, but there were a few major, even blatant, transgressions; the largest single settlement paid as a result of an audit was £1m. The MCPS Mounties almost always got their man, and there were very few who got away with it. Churchill still remembers with amused and grudging admiration the ingenuity and flamboyant disregard for copyright law which was occasionally displayed by determined individuals who cannot, for obvious reasons, be named. His colleague, Mark Isherwood, who at one time was responsible for MCPS broadcast licensing, was involved in an issue which, whilst not directly under the "auditing" heading, did have some Mountie determination behind it. In the late 80s MCPS won agreement from the BBC and ITV on a deal whereby programme cue sheets (details of music which had been broadcast, from which MCPS calculated royalties payable) which arrived after a nominated cut-off date before the annual MCPS broadcast royalties distribution, were charged for again at the same rate. As a result, both major broadcasters found themselves paying large additional invoices on a number of occasions. This led directly to two beneficial developments. The broadcasters invested in improved systems so that they could do their cue sheet reporting more quickly and efficiently, and MCPS was able to move to two broadcast royalty distributions a year.

Another important development was the setting-up of a very active field force, similar in some ways to the PRS Licensing Inspectors but with a remit to be the eyes and ears of MCPS away from head office in Streatham. Their role was to get to know the people who owned and ran the then numerous record pressing plants all over the UK, the record importers and distributors, and the regional broadcasters. The information they gleaned helped MCPS to sustain a more accurate picture than before of what was really going on in the market place. The field representatives, who later developed into the society's regional management, also had an anti-piracy role, watching for counterfeit cassettes of commercial recordings on market stalls and investigating as far as possible into the "bedroom recording industry" which supplied those illicit street traders. Lastly they were also out there most definitely to be seen, and to make MCPS' presence felt a long way from Streatham; to "project power" in the popularised military jargon of the early 2000s.

The 90s and 2000s have seen many businesses, including the rights administration organisations, replacing their traditional local presence and personal accessibility of company representative with highly efficient call centres. The question of what will fuel the old incoming information streams, and how useful regional and local networks of formal and informal contacts can be maintained is frequently debated but the trend to centralised customer relations handling continues.

Setting the mechanical royalty rate and negotiating agreements for its application to record producers for the use of copyright musical works was and always will be a core activity for MCPS. But an agreed rate and an associated licensing deal must be enforced for the process to work and be of value to rights owners. It is the nature of individuals and businesses when presented with a deal to look immediately for ways of legitimately making it work to their own advantage or illegitimately subverting or avoiding its requirements. It was music industry lore in the 70s and 80s that many factories were sending at least as many illicit pressings out of the back door as legitimate and licensed pressings were leaving from the front door. Lore also related that the practice was far more common in certain European countries than in staid and generally better-behaved Britain.

The strength of the vastly improved mandates given to MCPS after the abolition of the statutory licence in the 1988 Copyright Act meant that soon afterwards MCPS was able to introduce and win acceptance for a code of practice for record pressing plants, and not too long after that was able to demonstrate that the code had force behind it, when a major raid on an infringing factory was successfully conducted.

In 1989, MCPS decided to strengthen its position in terms of checking and enforcing licence terms by seeking inspection and audit rights at record manufacturers (which at that time were still numerous and spread all over the UK and Northern Ireland, and the Irish Republic), to complement their right to audit record companies. MCPS had been using a variety of detective strategies to monitor the output of record pressing plants, even to the extent of checking the volumes of polycarbonate raw material which was being delivered and utilised against the expected usage based on licensed orders for pressings.

MCPS drew up a new agreement and arranged a meeting which was attended by some 350 representatives from manufacturing companies, whose mood was definitely not as smooth as their surroundings, as they voiced their fury to the MCPS team of Montgomery, Churchill, and legal adviser David Lester. No one who was present claims to have enjoyed the meeting very much, but it led to the formation of a joint committee to discuss the issues, and in 1992 a new agreement did come into force. The Manufacturers Code of Practice did not itself cover audit rights, but it committed manufacturers to delivering manufacturing details and answering specific questions about the pressing activities of record companies with the guarantee of the provision of comfort in the event of litigation.

63

Licensing new forms of entertainment – no longer just "audio products"

Protracted negotiations (some would say battles royal) of licensing terms remained a feature of MCPS life. From 2000 onwards, negotiations between the record and publishing sides of the UK music industry over the licensing of DVD (Digital Versatile Disc) were to make the CD licensing duel seem like a good-humoured difference of opinion. DVD is an audio-visual product which also offers the user control and search facilities for content – almost always including copyright music, and can contain several layers of information. DVD is gradually replacing videotape as a format for releasing feature films for sale to the public but is also an increasingly popular format for audio-visual music releases and (one of MCPS' arguments) even a substitute for the CD. Eventually, in May 2003 MCPS unilaterally issued a DVD licensing scheme based on 10% of PPD after prolonged stalemate and then breakdown of talks with the BPI. It was intended both to get the ball rolling in terms of DVD licensing and revenue streams for publishers but also MCPS took the view it had no alternative since negotiations with the BPI were proving fruitless. The BPI's response was a referral to the Copyright Tribunal. As 2003 came to an end, the Tribunal hearing remained a possibility but not a certainty as negotiation between the two sides continued

For different reasons and in a different style, the two sides of the music industry were simultaneously in a similar long-running, often frustrating set of negotiations on the joint licensing of internet music distribution by record companies. This was a practical illustration of the term "convergence" which had been much-used, sometimes misused and probably over-used in the 90s.

This meant the increasing tendency for different types of entertainment to "converge" in new multimedia formats and to be delivered to the consumer in ways which required the use of several different kinds of copyright at the same time. Legitimate distribution of copyright recorded music via the internet was very slow in arriving, while piracy on a breathtaking global scale had successfully captured the hearts and minds of a generation of music consumers via free sharing of digital music computer files.

In very recent years, the music industry has, through litigation against infringing service (and in 2003 in the USA, even against individuals downloading unlicensed music files in their homes, in an unprecedented and very tough campaign by the record industry association the RIAA) helped the establishment of legitimate copyright music internet distribution. This required for the first time that MCPS and PRS should offer a joint licence for use of both the performing and mechanical rights. *See Alliance chapter*

In order to maintain the thread of the MCPS' UK licensing story, some large strides in timing have been taken here. There are important gaps which now need to be filled in.

A major issue emerged in the late 80s on an international scale. The record industry was by then dominated by multinationals: EMI, PolyGram, RCA/BMG, CBS/Sony and MCA each embracing both record company and publishing operations and some having much wider business interests involving a variety of entertainment-related intellectual property. As global companies they were increasingly impatient with territorially operated mechanical licensing, and they wanted central licensing deals and the financial benefits they believed should arise from these as a result of greater cost efficiency for the music publishers via their collective administration societies.

Montgomery and his management team were very aware of the mood and the trend. They urged that European central licensing (ECL), which any society within the European mechanical rights societies' umbrella organisation BIEM had a right to offer via its reciprocal agreements with other European societies, was inevitable, imminent and irresistible, and that MCPS should seek to set up such deals earlier rather than later. The reaction of their Board and their publisher members in general was negative. The proposal was quite strenuously resisted, mainly because it threatened the publishers' freedom to deal individually by requiring that any ECL had to be an agreement with MCPS as a collective administration organisation.

Bob Montgomery made a presentation to the Music Publishers' Association, and thus by its very nature to the MCPS membership, suggesting that MCPS would license RCA Records throughout Europe in a landmark central licensing agreement. Despite the persuasive nature of the argument in favour of such a deal, the music publishers, led by Peter Smits of EMI Music Publishing, firmly opposed what they perceived as creeping paralysis regarding their position of control and effectively the meeting instructed MCPS to leave well alone. This issue of European central licensing began a chain of events of very great significance to MCPS, with links which connect to key aspects of the way its business is done today.

European Central Licensing and the Cannes Agreements

Until the early 80s, European mechanical collecting societies operated strictly on a territorial basis, representing local members' interests under membership agreements and the international repertoire by reciprocal agreements with other societies. The European Commission had been uneasy about both the exercise of territorial rights and the monopolies enjoyed by collecting societies. It indicated its intention to displace those with the concept of "freedom of movement of goods".

An important development came when the Commission objected to GEMA's attempts to license record manufacture which was taking place in Germany under licence from copyright societies in other European Union territories. There was also a European Court decision that GEMA had no right to impose a top-up royalty on records imported from the UK – this being the difference between the BIEM rate applicable in Germany and the lower statutory rate applicable in the UK. Major record companies had manufacturing, marketing and distribution operations in Europe which reflected their own structure as multinationals, and these decisions strengthened their arm in dealing with societies' irritating (to them) territoriality. A record company operating across borders could now seek the best available European licensing deal centrally, knowing that once a licence had been granted for one territory it was free to distribute the licensed goods to any other territory in Europe without incurring a further royalty. European Central Licensing (ECL) was what they wanted and it was inevitable that some societies would seize the opportunity to give it to them.

In 1986 PolyGram approached several societies, including MCPS, with a proposal that it be granted a pan-EU licence from one single source, and that they should centralise their royalty accounting at the same time. The MPA and MCPS turned down the proposal. In fact, the Dutch Mechanical Society Stemra did

Crispin Evans of Universal Music Group, a member of the Boards of MCPS, PRS and the MPA.

Universal Music Publishing

that ECL deal with PolyGram in 1987, but without the central accounting. Stemra also had an ECL with CBS. GEMA in Germany did deals with BMG in 1990 and Warner Music in 1991. The French society SDRM did an ECL deal with Sony in 1993. EMI's ECL deal led in 1994 to the formation of BEL (European Licence Bureau) as a means for GEMA, MCPS and SDRM to handle the deal together in an attempt to rationalise the "ECL business". Later after PolyGram moved its ECL to MCPS, Stemra joined BEL.

The proliferation of ECL deals threatened the societies' local monopoly and possibly the existence of some. So ECL was initially opposed by those societies without a central licensing deal. It was not a fight that could be won, given the EC's support for the competition principle enshrined in these deals, and given the pressure of demand from record companies as the core and by far the most important mechanical rights licensees. Inevitably downward pressure was put on society commission rates while there were enforced improvements to speed and accuracy of royalty processing. But one outcome was that publishers lost revenue when inter-society competition replaced co-operation, as the record companies shopped for the most attractive deal (which included "rebates" from their licence fees – lowering the overall revenue for licensors).

The early ECLs, as explained by Crispin Evans, Senior Vice President International, Legal and Business Affairs Universal

Music Group (formerly PolyGram Music) and member of all three – PRS, MCPS and MPA – Boards, "were done in the face of opposition from music publishers, who were particularly keen that central accounting should not be developed because rights are owned on a national basis in different countries by sub-publishers who stood to be cut out of the picture altogether – which was not acceptable".

However, the original PolyGram-Stemra ECL became the model for all such agreements. The competition between societies and their offering of financial inducements to record companies to attract their business sharply-focused publishers' attention because, in Evans' words "it was essentially our revenue, not the societies', which was being used for these financial inducements." MCPS members were told the level of such financial inducements being offered by their society, but no other societies made such revelations. An estimate was that about 2.5% of publisher income was being "handed back" to record companies.

The UK publishers took various actions, including forming a new copyright society EMRO (European Music Rights Organisation) in 1992. It was intended as a means for UK publishers to have the option to withdraw their mechanical rights from the Continental European society network and place them with EMRO, which could then be a single mechanical rights society for the whole of the EU, acting as MCPS does under the direction and control of its owner, the MPA. As Evans described it: "EMRO was a flag which flew but never did anything else – it never went into battle". EMRO continues to exist and could, as publishers occasionally point out, be reactivated MCPS' reputation in Europe was at the time damaged by the EMRO affair. Nevertheless, former MCPS MD Frans de Wit regarded it as a significant lever in his talks with GEMA and SACEM on the setting up of BEL, as mentioned above. When EMRO was "mothballed" in June 1993 (EMI and Warner Chappell withdrew support), MCPS said it would seek its own ECL deals, and did. It was later affected again in terms of its relationships with Continental European societies when a "mini central licensing organisation" called Music Rights Society Europe (MRSE) was set up in 1995 by EMI to collect royalties from just one album, Simply Red's Life. This development was not pursued, however.

Fresh steps were taken by MCPS, which offered PolyGram (as its ECL was transferred from Stemra) the inducement of direct distribution. Devised by PolyGram Records, PolyGram Publishing and MCPS this was an ECL scheme under which royalties flowed in foreign countries not to the national collecting society but directly to their members, including the UK publisher's European sub-publishers. In PolyGram's view this would have removed "the middleman", saved administration costs and speeded distributions. It was, predictably, met with even greater horror and louder cries of protest from Continental European societies than the earlier central accounting idea.

As Evans pointed out, direct distribution was briefly implemented, and worked. But in the face of an escalating bitter dispute and retaliatory action, a meeting of the major music publishers and European collecting societies was called at Midem[6] in 1997. Incidentally, this was held in the casino (presumably chosen without any intended ironic reference to gambling or stakes which might be won or lost), and its outcome was originally called the Casino Agreement. Evans is one who rather regrets the later change to the more prosaic title of Cannes Agreement[7].

This was an early, and toweringly large, milestone for John Hutchinson when he had only just been confirmed as Chief Executive of MCPS, prior to the formalisation of the MCPS-PRS Alliance. He was attending Midem for the first time, and found himself involved in a business-changing, potentially debilitating, development which had been in the making before his arrival but which proved to be one of the biggest issues he would have to deal with on his watch as Alliance CEO.

In a speech to the Alliance management in November 2000, Hutchinson was referring to the Cannes Agreement among other thing when he said: "I have often compared my arrival at PRS in 1995 to being parachuted into a battle zone. What I did not expect was to take on another theatre of war at MCPS while continuing to fight PRS battles." As he saw it, MCPS was already under fire – to maintain the metaphor – for its inability to follow through efficiently on the ECL deal it had won with PolyGram, and for offering direct distribution. MCPS was in imminent danger of being hopelessly overstretched. In effect, Hutchinson summed up, they were doing something they had not got the systems or the organisational capacity for, at a price they could not afford, while breaking the "rules" in that they were cutting across all accepted and established procedures and agreements in their business sector.

Although some publishers appeared to want direct distribution, it was clear that most wanted better all-round cost-efficiency and lower administration charges from the European societies, and were prepared to use the former as a bargaining chip to achieve the latter. Also, Hutchinson sensed that commitment to direct distribution at MCPS Board level was not great, while opposition from Continental European Societies was huge. Not only did he see the need for peace to break out for everyone's sake, he was also aware of the acute danger to a UK Chief Executive who got embroiled in this war (to which he was a very late entrant) and ended up on the losing side. So support for the Cannes Agreement was the only sensible course of action.

The Agreement took effect in July 1997 but was only completely signed off in November that year; with an extension it ran to mid 2002 and was succeeded by the Cannes Extension Agreement.

Briefly, the first agreement demanded that societies should reduce their commission rates in a series of steps from wherever each of them was at the beginning of the agreement to a weighted average of 6% for phonomechanical royalty administration on

---

6 Marche International des Editions Musicales, the largest and longest running event for the global music industry, and undeniably the major junket for that industry every year. As well as its importance for business, the importance of the week of French food and wine offered to self-confessedly overworked music industry executives, and the blasé attitude affected by old Midem hands, was once summed up in a headline by the then *Billboard* Editor Mike Henessey as "MIDEM – Must I Damnwell Eat Moules"

7 Although this did result in the now famous statement by the then head of SACEM, Jean-Loup Tournier, when complaining of pressure from the publishers – "I came to Cannes, not to Canossa" a reference to Henry IV's enforced and humiliating walk barefoot in the snow to win the lifting of his excommunication by Pope Gregory VII.

every licence they issued based on shipments of records (not manufacture – so in the UK this essentially means AP1, although AP2A Agreements are also included); and they would do this in line with time segments in the Agreement, which had the significant effect of enabling publishers, at pre-defined intervals, to conduct audits together with the societies' of their compliance. Other elements of the agreement included implementation by all the societies of Common Works Registration; and the publishers' *quid pro quo* prohibition of direct distribution.

Though already a well-controlled, low commission organisation, MCPS had to volunteer then to be tied down as tightly by this first Agreement as the worst-offending, highest cost mechanical rights society. Because the agreement was based on a reduction in the average commission rate, allowing variations within and between societies, it had a far more serious impact on a large society handling a high volume of relevant licences, such as MCPS, than on some smaller societies. Had Hutchinson been able to do so then, he would have negotiated a first Cannes Agreement much more like the second. It exchanged a rigid one-size-fits-all approach to one which offered prescribed, and decreasing, commission levels via a more sensible and flexible arrangement taking into account the circumstances and performance of different societies. Had Hutchinson been able to influence the environment in which the first Cannes Agreement was formulated he would have tried to make it "a co-operative, collaborative environment – a tough one for societies but nevertheless collaborative". This in his view would have prevented society in-fighting over ECL deals and so been a defence against undue pressure for a deal which was harsh as Cannes. In all however, Hutchinson's view was that having the two Cannes Agreements has been better than not having them at all.

Piracy at home – and around the globe

To begin with a question: where might every official Beatles album ever released in the UK, plus several bootleg live concert recordings, plus recorded interviews, plus thousands of photographs of the artists, plus all the printed lyrics of all the songs, have been found together and bought for the grand total of £5? Answer – on a single illegal CD ROM created using MP3 digital data compression technology, and sold over the internet by creative, enterprising, blithe and utterly unscrupulous pirates. This is just one story in the case files of IP anti-piracy operators, of which the MCPS Anti-Piracy Unit (APU) is one very active example.

Music piracy is often thought of as a problem exclusively for the record industry – because it appears to be the work of recording artists and the rights of the companies which produce their recordings which are being pirated. But of course the millions of appallingly-amateur to frighteningly-clever bootlegs, counterfeits and other pirated products over the past 40 years have also infringed the rights of those who wrote and published the songs.

The most active phase of anti-piracy activity on behalf of those rights owners has been recent, within the Alliance, although it began within MCPS. At the head of the APU since its inception, senior Alliance Legal team member Nick Kounoupias has not only pursued but documented the long fight, against illegal recordings initially sold via mail-order and market stalls, and in the new century increasingly via the internet.

He has needed regularly to stress the correct terminology. Bootlegs were unauthorised recordings of live performances, or sometimes stolen "out-takes" from studio recordings: people who bought the poor-quality, badly packaged reproductions (usually tape cassettes, largely made by genuine fans of the artist in question, but also vinyl LPs made by commercially-minded pirates) knew what they were buying and usually did so because the material was not

Online Piracy

Unlicensed Ringtones / clips / downloads / misc

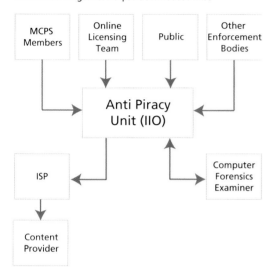

Comparison with other APUs': Budget and Personnel

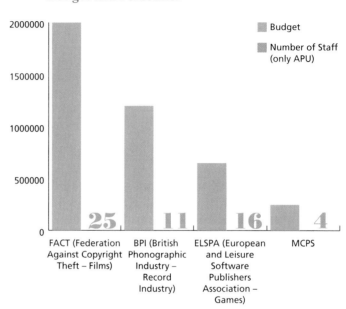

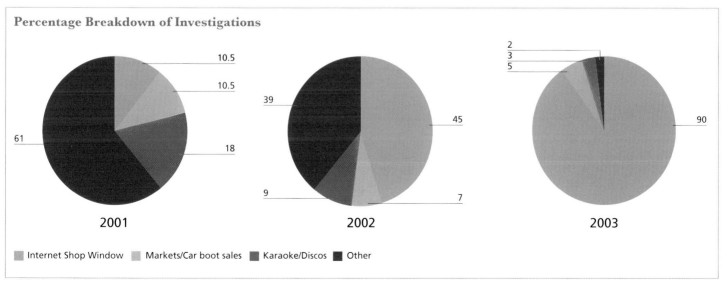

Percentage Breakdown of Investigations

2001

2002

2003

Internet Shop Window   Markets/Car boot sales   Karaoke/Discos   Other

Source: The MCPS-PRS Alliance

legitimately available. Counterfeits (LPs at first but later almost exclusively tape cassettes) attempted to fool the public by looking like the original, even if the majority had such poor imitation packaging that the buyer's appallingly poor eyesight, or more likely willing complicity in the crime, was a safe assumption. Kounoupias draws a third, less well-understood distinction, which is that "a pirate recording is one where there is an authorised duplicate of a sound recording embodying copyright musical works which is then released under another description and with different packaging and graphics".

Record piracy dates back to the early 60s, but expanded hugely in the 70s with the arrival of the cassette tape, far easier and cheaper to manufacture illicitly than vinyl records. In the mid-90s came the recordable optical disc, and pirated CDs took over the illegal market. Kounoupias pointed out that this was a critical development for several reasons. Digital format improved sound quality and speeded up the process of copying commercial recordings. Most importantly, the quality did not degrade with successive copies as it did with analogue tape. Then "the temptation to copy music has worsened during the last 10 years because of the ease with which music can now be uploaded and downloaded via the internet: illegal files containing official recordings as well as live performances are being exchanged and downloaded on a massive scale". Two forms of internet piracy have developed. These are "online piracy" – the trade in illegal

Nick Kounoupias, Senior Alliance lawyer and Head of the MCPS Anti-Piracy Unit

music files without any physical product involved; and "shop window piracy" which can be defined as the trade via the internet of illegally manufactured CDs and CD ROMs and latterly DVDs.

Another related topic with another truly sinister story of its own has been the increasing evidence of links between the lucrative trade in copyright piracy and major criminals in search of funding or additional profit, terrorism of all nationalities, and organised crime syndicates.

The average capacity of computer hard drives has rocketed from four gigabytes in 1999 to almost 60 gigabytes in 2003, with all the potentially grim implications that has for copyright owners (and this process will continue). Kounoupias explained that technological change had "given rise to a new breed of criminal", one who does not wish or need to take the risk of selling illegal goods openly in a street market. Internet shop window piracy, which is now probably the most significant problem and an estimated 92% of the MCPS APU's day-to-day work (up from 10% in two years), allows the trade to be carried out from the safety and comfort of the pirate's home. The safety is not actually as great as assumed by the pirate, since anti-piracy efforts can trace his physical address through his electronic "tyre tracks".

Apart from the APU ingenuity which is used to counter the pirates' ingenuity, all possible legal remedies and aids are called into service. "MCPS" is a registered service mark (registered in February 2002 as a certification mark). All record companies are required to use this mark if their product is licensed by MCPS, which brings advantages when it is necessary to sue or to prosecute for trademark infringement.

In the past 20 years, the entertainment industries have acknowledged the fact that, in order fully to combat piracy, they needed to create their own APUs, as well as (and with increasing effectiveness and intelligence) working through the police and local Trading Standards Officers. The MCPS APU was set up in 1994 in response to MCPS members' demands, and grew to a full-time staff of seven investigators. Some years earlier the record industry set up the BPI APU. The UK film industry has FACT (Federation Against Copyright Theft) and ELSPA (Entertainment Leisure Software Publishers Association) works on behalf of the computer games industry. In 2003 these organisations had a combined budget in excess of £6m a year. Technological developments have led to a convergence of copyright piracy across different industries. It is now common for anti-piracy investigators of the music, film and computer games industries jointly to raid the same pirate who is infringing everyone's rights equally and without favouritism.

Kounoupias has long favoured even closer APU co-operation, pointing to an estimate that a combined APU could operate for lower cost, with no diminution in the available investigative and forensic examination capabilities; such a move has already been successful in the Netherlands in the shape of the BREIN organisation.

Conjoined twins – MCPS and IT

The development of information technology at MCPS is more closely intertwined with the development of the organisation itself than is the case with PRS. Those who have, or at various times had, the job of managing the work of the mechanical rights society generally agree that the history of one is essentially the history of the other. This reflects the nature of the company first as a company owned by shareholders who expected dividends, and then as an agency which was wholly owned by the trade association whose members were its clients, MCPS always regarded itself simply as a business serving other businesses. So its business systems – from paper to electronic – carried it forward, served it on a daily basis, and in a tough kind of virtuous circle defined its character while the systems themselves were being defined by client demand and the market. MCPS managers past

and present share some pride in describing the organisation in terms which emphasise the consistency of its role, and of the way that role was delivered: always a member service, always cost-conscious, always cost effective, always business-led. The "member service" item in that list does not to any significant extent include the extensive and expansive "member relations" and what can broadly be termed cultural, activities which are so important in the traditional authors' membership societies, including PRS. So MCPS activity has always been tightly focused on delivering a relatively straightforward business service in return for pre-set commission rates. And that service has always been licensing the mechanical rights where it had its customers' mandates to do so, collection of certain data and related distribution of money.

Before the purchase of MCPS by the MPA in 1976 information technology was not a visible feature in the landscape. MCPS did none of its own data processing. As mentioned before, this was supplied externally, was limited in scope and in the mid 70s was facing the end of the road where support from the supplier was concerned. This situation meant that the salvation and rapid improvement of IT had to be a priority for several years.

There were no databases as such. The MCPS Tune File offered 15-character identification of works titles, with 10-character ID for the writer(s). This was used when compiling printed royalty statements for members, but the key to doing the organisation's work was a huge card index which was used in an entirely manual process of royalty distribution calculations. These were based on statements of record manufacture and sales which were at that time compiled by the licensees themselves – the record companies – and arrived at MCPS as paper documents which needed matching to copyright owner information, and "tune coding" to produce the royalty distribution paperwork for the publishers.

Database management systems were created in Adabas (which proved to be a very good, robust, long-lived platform), and MCPS was able to develop its own in-house distribution system. In the

Former MCPS Director of Systems and current Alliance Director of Planning and Corporate Service John Rowe (left) with Jonathan Hodgetts, Information Security Manager whose responsibilities include the PRS Archive which was a valuable resource in the research for this history.

late 70s the enticing promise MCPS made to publishers, linked to the new Membership Agreement of that time, was monthly distributions, which led soon to weekly payments of some royalties as money was passed rapidly and continuously through the system to members alongside monthly statements. Behind the delivery of that promise lay the phenomenally hard work of achieving it on inadequate systems and hardware. The memory of the long hours and sweated labour remains fresh for those who were involved.

Keith Lowde, Finance Director from the early 80s, recalls that in the 70s the IT senior management had "done an excellent job of defining the data relationships and programmes necessary to develop a database which could be used by various applications" but poor management in some areas worked against efficiency in an increasingly computerised environment. A good IT team had been recruited but was seemingly not properly directed, and the views of those who had to operate the systems to do the work of

MCPS had often been subordinate to the need to present the operational situation in a better light than it deserved to the Board of the time. By the mid-80s, Lowde recalls, systems development became a user-led activity, which brought significant change.

John Rowe was one of the team putting in the sweated effort in the 80s. He went on to be MCPS Director of Systems and Distribution and is currently Director of Planning and Corporate Services for the Alliance. "We were a distribution company – that was our purpose and our mantra. No matter what, we had to make those monthly distributions, and we never failed in that. This broke the mould." But however much the publishers might have appreciated the mould-breaking MCPS offering, it was not enough to entice the majors to give the society the mandate to license their lucrative core business on their behalf. MCPS was still only handling a fraction of the licensing for recordings and record manufacturing in the UK, with the big publishers preferring to license their copyrights directly.

Meanwhile, the MCPS IT team was putting in systems which could auto-match copyright ownership data to radio log information under the MCPS blanket agreements with broadcasters. The algorithms were essentially those used for putting new works into the database on a daily basis, which is also a "matching" process. In one version of history, this and other developments in systems and processes were achieved faster at MCPS that at PRS; another version counters by stating that PRS was always able to automatch even when it was using ICL. The two statements can almost certainly be reconciled at the appropriate level of detail. However, it is inarguably true that MCPS was perceived to be moving faster and more efficiently where IT was concerned, although the two organisations' needs were similar at a technical level (but different in volume in some areas). The reason, expressed in various ways by various people who were involved but possibly best summed up by Rowe, was that "at MCPS we had the devil driving us: we had no money and we were very close to the business we served, which demanded that we found a way to do this work – so we did". MCPS systems also had an undeniably much less complex job to do than PRS systems; processing data relating to audio products involves relatively simple calculations involving factual numerical data on audio products made or sold, the tracks on those products, and the price on which royalties are to be calculated.

The milestones and historic turning points – triumphant or disastrous – in MCPS' life are few, again underlining consistency: as mentioned previously, the first was the amalgamation of mechanical rights organisations into MCPS in 1924, and the second was the purchase by the MPA and the business modernisation which that drove forward. As the works database was created the third, enormously important, new chapter was about to begin.

The full mandate for licensing audio products was finally given by publishers to MCPS in response to the 1988 Copyright Act. This was the impetus for the creation of the AP (audio products) Licensing schemes which became, and still are, the core and majority of MCPS business. Created in order to serve the publishers' post-1988 need for collective negotiation of rates and management of licensing and distribution, the AP schemes also had a considerable impact on the licensees. Record companies had for decades maintained their own royalty departments and separate databases (one of the longest-established and most comprehensive being that of EMI, of course, as befitted its position as the original British record company). These departments were no longer needed, because the AP schemes organised all kinds of audio product licensing, and MCPS systems were at last able to handle the process from licensing, through generating invoices based on pressings and sales of recorded product, to integrating with royalty distribution systems. It is not an exaggeration to say that the AP Schemes changed the way the publishing and record businesses worked in at least one major area of administration.

A crucial IT development was the creation of an Agreements database which stored details of agreements between the copyright holders, the writers and the publishers to whom they assigned their rights. So it contained information about the allocation of their respective interests in individual works and entire catalogues of music. The size of the task of creating this database is illustrated by the fact that it took the head of the copyright department and his team a full year to put 10,000 individual works into the system with all their associated agreement information. It was a very big piece of IT design and development work to achieve consistency and reliability in operation, Refinements are still being added by at least one software developer who worked on it originally and is still with the company.

The MCPS' crowning achievement in the way they stored this information electronically was that they constructed the system to automate the whole chain of change in various databases if musical works ownership (therefore agreements) changed. The PRS systems could not do this; the change of ownership of a catalogue of thousands of works meant that all their data had to be updated manually. The kind of automated system developed by MCPS was one of the planned vital components of the PRS PROMS system which was in development close on MCPS' heels at the end of the 80s. The collapse of the PROMS project in 1993 might possibly have caused some quiet glee in the MCPS ranks, but there was far less satisfaction taken in the PRS failure than there was pride taken in MCPS success and time leadership in this area. This understandably contributed to the conviction within the mechanical rights organisation that it had unassailable superiority in efficient IT systems. This assumption underpinned both the unsuccessful and later successful attempts to bring MCPS and PRS together operationally.

The MCPS Agreements database was, of course, part of a bigger IT and business systems picture. In the mid-80s MCPS had been brought an idea which filled in another important area in that picture.

The route this idea took began at the north London office of the poll and market survey company Gallup, which was responsible then for compiling the UK record sales charts every week. Gallup was approached in 1985 by the National Sound Archive (part of the British Library): it was, and remains, the main British repository for sound recordings, including copies of commercial recordings issued by UK record companies, which are required to deposit copies of all new releases with the Archive. It had amassed over a million recordings, and needed to create a comprehensive catalogue of these, as a resource for research and in order to control and keep track of the constantly growing collection. It wanted Gallup to provide the technical expertise for creating this catalogue, to the proposed mutual benefit of the two organisations. In charge of the Charts operation at Gallup was Godfrey Rust, who saw potential for the idea but not in terms of Gallup's needs (the chart compilation only required part of the information which the NSA wanted in the proposed in-depth catalogue). Believing that a valuable central database could be created for the whole music industry, Rust took the idea to PRS, BPI, PPL, MCPS and the eminent music magazine *Gramophone*. Of these, MCPS showed the greatest interest: it already obviously had a recordings database, and needed to expand and improve it. In Rust's view, there was "a 75% overlap" in the interests of NSA and MCPS in such a catalogue project. With the encouragement of MCPS top management, particularly Bob Montgomery and Keith Lowde, the NSA and MCPS agreed to set up the project, named National Discography, in 1987. "Happily, I completely underestimated the resources which would be needed," recalls Rust, "or they would never have started work on it."

The project took time, but gradually the MCPS team built a Licensing database linked in logical sequence to a Products database (listing all the different recorded products on which a particular recording has been included), linked to a recordings database (listing all the various recordings of a particular musical work) linked to a Works database (which identified the individual copyright works owned by publishers). At the Product database level the National Sound Archive could add the information it held, completing a data entry which was then of use to both MCPS and the NSA, and which could be checked by MCPS for accuracy against label information on recordings stored by the Archive.

At the Works database level, there was a link to the Agreements database, completing the entire suite of information which was needed by MCPS to licence and distribute. This system and the constantly growing data it held, and the facility for updating it rapidly so that accuracy of the data at any time was reasonably good, attracted interest and came to be regarded as significant. Over following years through the early 90s National Discography appeared to have potential for commercial exploitation, but for various reasons this was not successful. It was not something MCPS really knew how to do; copyright owners were nervous about losing control of access to essential and valuable business data. This line of exploitation was not part of publishers' core business and they were unwilling to spend money on marketing it.

In 1988 the sudden huge growth in the amount of business going through MCPS had demanded that the databases be as comprehensive and as accurate as possible (and the possession of databases of a provable level of quality would be a factor in MCPS' favour in the 1991 Copyright Tribunal when the organisation's administrative abilities were challenged by the BPI as part of its case). MCPS applied a policy of employing people who were experts in particular musical fields, and could use their expertise to identify exactly which works were involved in which recordings and products. The aim was high quality data through high quality repertoire identification, which is particularly important for MCPS which is expected to deliver "line-by-line" distribution.

The repertoire expert approach also won credibility with specialist music publishers, who would then give their licensing mandates to MCPS on the strength of a confidence that their repertoire could be identified and their royalties paid to them. One example was the dance music market which enjoyed huge growth in the 90s, but which operated very differently to the traditional major and established independent record company sector of the business.

It rapidly created many different types of dance music, often linked to the creativity of club DJs, and notable for its wholesale use of samples – extracts from existing commercial recordings (copyright recordings of copyright works) which were then worked into new live DJ performances and into new recordings. It was an intellectual property nightmare which gradually improved when litigation forced dance labels to take a legitimate path to sampling by doing deals with the copyright owners, and when the dance music sector came to realise that their own copyrights could be infringed. Their confidence in the dance repertoire specialists at MCPS led many to join the society to earn royalties from the licensing of their rights. The story was similar with specialist classical and blues publishers. In the late 90s, after the setting up of the Alliance and as part of the change process which combined the two societies' staffs and different ways of working to lower cost, the specialist repertoire expert gradually ceased to be part of the MCPS business strategy. The cost efficiencies are welcomed and applauded by MCPS members, but there remains some regret at the loss of the music specialists.

The next great challenge to IT was also the next milestone in MCPS business development, underlining the assertion that "business" and "IT" are pretty much the same thing for the organisation. This was the winning of an ECL deal in 1996.

It meant MCPS must handle huge volumes of licensing data, including different currencies, different rates – not only the BIEM mechanical rate (as opposed to the UK rate struck with the BPI and its members) but local variations of BIEM – and different types of products.

The size of this challenge prompted acknowledgement that it would make great sense to share the operational burden – reviving and strengthening the long-held positive views of collaboration with a "natural partner" such as PRS. It was not mere coincidence that the drive towards alliance between the two was successfully resurrected and taken forward in that year.

Shortly before work began to put the MCPS-PRS Alliance together, an amendment to the 1988 Copyright Act gave performers on recordings a right to remuneration for their contribution. The recordings performance administration organisation PPL had the task of distributing these payments, and found it had problems of lack of data, similar to those which MCPS had quickly to overcome after the Act first came into force in 1988. PPL had the choice of building a new database and systems itself at breakneck speed, or going to MCPS. They decided sensibly to do the latter. PPL needed electronic data comprising the individual recordings with their respective sound recording owners, and relevant contributor data (meaning in this context all interested parties to a sound recording such as performers –from individuals to orchestras, producers and so on, who would be entitled to claim royalties). As MCPS had already developed a database on the principle of needing to identify each different recording and had, or could easily develop, the ability to capture sound recording information on sound recording owners and other contributor data, there was an option for PPL to receive from MCPS electronic data to drive their distribution efforts. This was an option PPL took up. Although arguably self-extinguishing over time, because it inevitably created new data owned by PPL which could – and PPL decided it would – allow that organisation to do the job alone after a time, the deal was a useful revenue earner for MCPS. The Service Level Agreement ran for five years until PPL and the major record companies set up their own database, CatCo, as a result of their need to develop data formats which could deliver information from each PPL member to the society directly. However, technical and PPL/MCPS collaborational developments continued, and because a goal is to facilitate PPL members' wish to send their data just once to one point, MCPS continues to have a vested interest in a successful CatCo in order to meet its own future plans for automation of processing.

The PPL deal had originally been seen by some of the MCPS executive team to support an idea which had been simmering in that camp for several years. This was that their databases and systems had the potential to offer a "content management" service for the whole music industry, and even beyond that to all administrators of all kinds of intellectual property rights. However, MCPS was never in a position to take this idea forward.

Yet that train of thought was boarded by other hopeful passengers, and so this story is taken up in the Alliance chapter, which also deals with the international context.

The MCPS website is a www.mcps.co.uk

Recent MCPS Chairmen[8]

1972	Leslie J Abbott	Keith Prowse Music Publishing Ltd
1976	Robert Kingston	Peer Music (UK) Ltd
1985	Derek Knibb	Carlin Music Corporation
1992	Terry Foster-Key	EMI Music Publishing Ltd
1995	Jonathan Simon	Moncur Street Music Ltd

8 It proved impossible to compile a complete chronological list of MCPS Chairmen and in preference to presenting a list with large gaps in places, only the chairmen who served in the past 30 years have been named.

MCPS Revenue 1988–2002

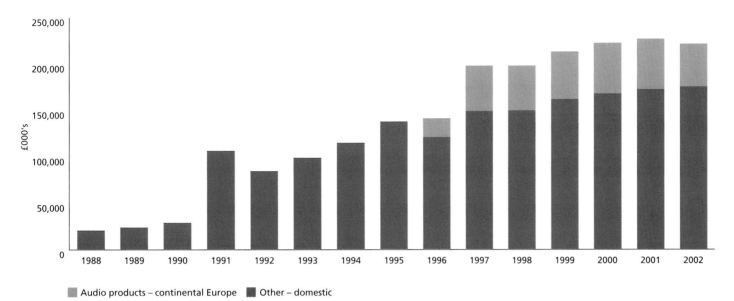

The impact on revenue of the 1988 Copyright Act and the 1991 MCPS-BPI Tribunal decision can clearly been seen reflected in the figures from 1992 onwards..
The contribution to revenue of the PolyGram ECL deal starts to be seen from 1997.

MCPS Commission 1988–2002

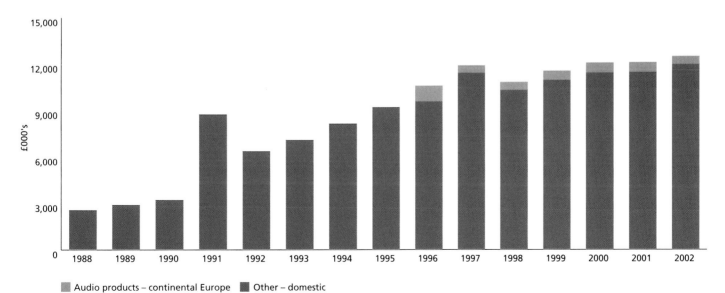

This is the MCPS operating revenue (corresponding to the PRS administrative costs deducted before royalty distributions, but in the case of the mechanical rights organisation based on pre-stated commission rates charged to members for various types of mechanical licences administered). After 1997 commission rates were limited by the Cannes Agreement, and from 2003 onwards the amended terms of the Cannes

Agreement Extension should have a positive effect.

Source: The MCPS-PRS Alliance

77

MCPS Revenue 1998–2002

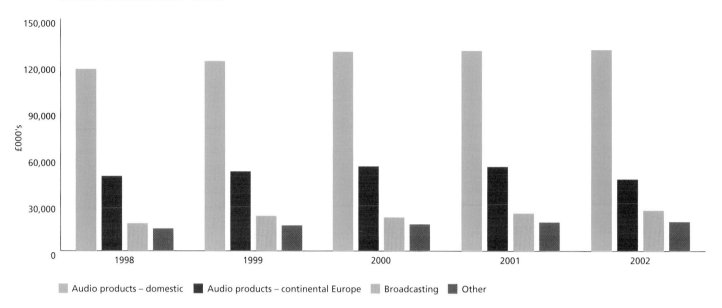

Legend: Audio products – domestic | Audio products – continental Europe | Broadcasting | Other

The question highlighted by this chart is whether the rising new revenue sources can or will substitute for the declining traditionally dominant sources. Domestic income from Audio products has effectively been flat for three years and can be expected to fall; as the AP market continues to decline worldwide the continental European figure can also be expected to fall. Broadcast income is expected to rise and to embrace a wider variety of music usage; other income includes multimedia, online and mobile phone ringtones licensing – all of which have good potential for growth.

MCPS Commission 1998–2002

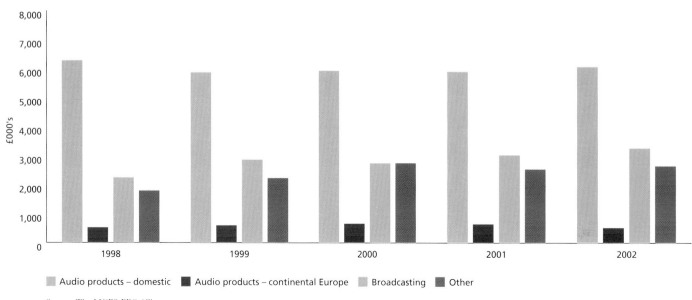

Legend: Audio products – domestic | Audio products – continental Europe | Broadcasting | Other

Source: The MCPS-PRS Alliance

Introduction – modesty, vigilance and encouragement of British composers and authors.

An epilogue at the beginning of a chapter is a rather non-standard approach, but words written to end the first history of PRS by company Secretary Charles James make a good introduction to the society's updated story.

In 1952 he summed up: "The achievements of PRS were not easily gained. It has engaged in a constant struggle for recognition of the right of the composer, the lyric writer, and the music publisher to a proper reward for the public performance of their works both at home and abroad. In effect, it has become an international clearing house for the performing right and its product, and in an age of mechanical music it can modestly claim that by its vigilance it has in some degree encouraged the creative talent of British composers and authors."

The cautiously modest tone may be dated, but the statement stands just as well now as then. In fact its relevance is heightened by the recent development of technology which puts electronic distribution of copyright music within the power of anyone with a link to e-mail and the internet. The need to maintain this vigilance and act effectively has meant that the pace of change inside PRS has in recent years been as great or greater than that outside it, as this history shows.

What is PRS? It is a membership society for creators of music and lyrics, which on their behalf collectively administers the part of their copyright known as the performing right. The 1988 Act defined a bundle of rights embracing the right to perform a work in public (by live or recorded or broadcast means), the right to broadcast (by whatever means that broadcast is then transmitted); and the right to include the work in a programme transmitted by cable (which includes the internet). To do this, PRS takes an assignment of its members' performing right. One of the best descriptions of PRS is the one which was regularly used in PRS' Yearbooks: that it exists to do collectively for music creators that which they would find impossible or too costly to do individually, the licensing of every usage of each of their works, the tracking

of licensed performances and the collection of royalties. In recent years, the possibility has been raised that technology and new service providers will enable copyright owners to do all this for themselves. If that happened, collecting societies including PRS would, logically, not be needed and would cease to exist. However, there is a strong argument that the collective strength and efficiency which writers gain from their societies is actually more

' cartoon from the Daily Mirror, *22 April 1965*

Although busking is one kind of "public performance" of copyright music, PRS has for practical reasons seldom been able to license it, but the 2003 scheme for allowing buskers to play on designated pitches in London tube stations was an opportunity for the society to issue a licence to London Underground. This cartoon was first reproduced in the 1988 history of PRS, *Harmonious Alliance*

needed now than ever. The purpose and objectives of the society have been carefully and at varying length described many times for many different audiences: members, licensees, the press, Parliament and Government departments, the Monopolies and Mergers Commission, The Copyright Tribunal, consultants and suppliers, the rest of the music industry, the international community including the Directorates of the European Commission, students and charities. Back in 1955 in the first issue of *Performing Right*, an early incarnation of the society's membership magazine, Licensing Manager Ernest Ford wrote: "The Society's rights extend to every public performance of the music in its repertoire, from that at a symphony concert in the Royal Albert Hall to that by a street mendicant". The statement is true today, although any self-respecting busker would now object to the implication that he was a beggar. An interesting fact is that until mid-2003 such street performance remained impossible to license. However, when buskers on the London Underground were given legitimate "pitches" in stations and allowed to busk on a rota system, PRS promptly licensed the operators London Transport, in line with standard practice of licensing the "venue" and not the performer.

PRS has never really been helped by its name. It is perfectly accurate, and the term "performing right society" is currently used around the world to define all collective administration organisations for this bundle of music rights. But as a name for the UK organisation, it has done little to make recognition of its role easy. And generations of PRS employees who have answered the conversational question, "Who do you work for?" have resigned themselves to seeing the questioner's eyes glaze over with incomprehension when hearing the answer.

Fifty years ago PRS Chairman Leslie Boosey explained his frustration with the name at the 1953 AGM. Tired of jokey questions about "performing elephants", and of even less amusing evidence that many people thought The Performing Right Society was "an organisation buying up copyrights for the benefit of

shareholders", PRS had applied to the Board of Trade for permission to change the name to The Society of Composers, Authors and Publishers of Music Ltd. This style of name would, it was thought, explain what the organisation was, and would be similar to that of the American Society of Composers, Authors and Publishers (ASCAP), or the French Société des Auteurs Compositeurs et Editeurs de Musique (SACEM). In fact it would have been more similar to the latter because the UK society has never seen any need to include its nationality in its title and neither has the French society, but the latter had the reasonable excuse that it was the first music rights society which ever existed. The Board of Trade rejected PRS' application because of the potential confusion with the name of The Incorporated Society of Authors, Playwrights and Composers (possibility of any confusion is difficult to believe, but the BoT thought it a real danger at the time).

The longer a name is in use, the more difficult it becomes to change it, and there appear to have been no further efforts in that direction. However, when (in preparation for the 75th anniversary) the PRS logo was redesigned in 1988 by The Jenkins Group, the Chief Executive stressed that the new logo put the emphasis on the initials rather than the full name "which is ambiguous and misleading". The redesign also added to the logo the excellent line *Giving Music Its Due*. The fact that they resisted the obvious temptation to put an s on due made this an elegant pun which certainly helped to brand PRS as an organisation associated with music as well as hinting at both moral and financial justice.[1]

The importance of the law was well understood. When the UK performing right society was set up in 1914, it needed every sign of authority it could muster as it almost fearfully started its job of licensing music users who had always enjoyed freedom from such licence fees. Knowing that it would be greeted with much the same general enthusiasm as a flu epidemic, PRS quite rightly carried the shield of copyright legislation as obviously as it could. For most of the society's existence, the law featured heavily in

---

1 That line has, of course, provided the title of this history. It was dropped from the PRS logo, with regret on the part of many including staff, when PRS and MCPS set up their alliance in 1997 and their two logos were joined above the new explanatory wording *The Music Alliance*. That "line" in turn proved so successful a tag for the new organisation that it caused a new and different set of problems – *see Alliance Chapter*.

PRS agendas, and in communications to members, music users and the public (the significant change in emphasis to "marketing the value of music" is very recent). So it is not surprising that James' epilogue brackets PRS history to that date by stating: "It commenced its operations under a copyright law based on the principles laid down in the Berlin International Copyright Convention of 1908, and in 1948 those principles were strengthened in the Convention as revised at Brussels. Alterations in the present Copyright Act of 1911 will be necessary to conform to some of the revisions. This book goes to press before the result of the deliberations of the [Board of Trade Copyright] Committee can be known, but it is reasonably certain that in due time the Act of 1911 will be replaced by one which meets the changes which have taken place during the past forty years."

That new Copyright Act was signed into law in 1956. There would be another in 1988, and further Copyright Regulations which came into force in October 2003. The business and technological environment which would be in place by that time could only have been guessed at by a few very prescient individuals in 1951.

The job of licensing and distributing was and remains complicated. *Performing Right* magazine described the licensing process in the 50s with its many snags and voluminous correspondence. Today well–designed computer systems and modern call centre ways-of-working make that process far faster and more efficient, and keep protracted exchanges of letters to a minimum. But for all the hugely welcome gain in business processes, there has been some loss in entertainment such as an Irish pub landlord whose licence fee cheque arrived with a covering letter in rhyming couplets. Time-worn music users' excuses and arguments still reappear, even if not in copperplate longhand on Basildon Bond notepaper. Reporting requests that "Church Fund dances" should be exempt from PRS fees, the society invokes the Biblical quote that "the labourer is worthy of his hire"; and on another occasion it is clearly thunderstruck by the irony (and the cheek) of trades unions which argued that their music use should be exempted because PRS was also "a kind of trade union". The point is made that these and similar attitudes arise from the users' and public's "failure to realise that property can be abstract as well as material". The same point still has to be made from time to time, although lately the owners and administrators of copyrights have had to face the fact that even when there is a clear realisation that "property can be abstract" there is often no respect for the owner and no qualms about acquiring and using it illicitly.

The complexity of what PRS does has always been an issue. Fifty years ago, Licensing Manager Ernest Ford wrote of the "vast and varied duties of licensing and collecting" (failing even to mention the vast and varied problems of distributing royalties once the licence revenue is collected). Former President Sir Arthur Bliss once congratulated a politician on visiting PRS where he "earnestly studied the subject of copyright which is as technical and complex as, say, atonality or thermodymanics". Advisedly skirting the thermodynamics side of the question, the MMC Report in 1996 acknowledged: "It would be far beyond the majority of copyright owners to negotiate and collect their own royalties for performing rights including both public performance and broadcasting". The Society's own far-reaching review in the mid-90s of PRS royalty distributions, and the data on which they are based, led consultant statistician Professor Frank Kelly and major market research company Millward Brown to go on record as to the complicated (and to them fascinating) demands of PRS' work. And quite recently one of the UK's leading IT consultants acknowledged that the PRS requirements for computer systems were among the most complex – for the size of the organisation – that he had ever encountered.

The complexity arises from the variety of PRS members and their musics; from the variety of music users and the many ways that licensable usage arises; from a very wide range of national and international practices, expectations and demands in this specialist field of activity; and from changes in and interpretations of the law. The PRS story which follows is not intended to deal with all the possible fascinating levels of detail. It aims to give a fair and interesting, but fairly short, account of 90 years.

The PRS General Peformance Licensing Department in the early 30s.

Trying to give music its due – whether it wants it or not

PRS was founded well after the societies set up in major European territories, such as SACD (France, 1791), and the composers' and authors' societies in France (SACEM 1851), Italy (SIAE 1882), Austria (AKM 1897), Spain (SGAE 1901), and Germany (GEMA 1903). This was not because British composers and publishers were unaware of the potential source of income, or of the success of those European societies which were well-established and continually increasing in number. It was partly because UK music users had a very powerful voice in a highly profitable British entertainment industry in the late 19th and early 20th centuries and they certainly did not want to pay performing right licence fees. But predominantly it was because the music publishers did not want such a society, for reasons explained further on.

Referring to the founding of PRS in 1914, Professor Cyril Ehrlich wrote in *Harmonious Alliance:*[2] "The pioneers' task was daunting. First they had to recognise and come to terms with a fundamental technological, economic and cultural revolution which was beginning to transform society's use of music, and therefore the opportunities and risks for everyone in the industry. The shape of things to come could be discerned …only by men of unusual vision. To assimilate this knowledge and adapt to the new conditions required unusual flexibility and adroitness… reappraising, perhaps reversing, long-established procedures… [attacking] deeply ingrained attitudes, preconceptions and behaviour, not only among the general public who had to be persuaded to pay for new forms of [music] consumption, but even within the industry itself".

The description of the pioneering days remains strikingly apt in today's circumstances; only the detail is different. Music creators and copyright owners see the first few years of the 21st century dominated by the continuing battle to realise the value of their rights in the "everything's free" environment of digital file

2 This history, which took the story up to 1988, was commissioned by PRS as part of its 75th Anniversary celebrations in 1989. It was published by Oxford University Press, but is now out of print.

exchange on the internet. The music industry worldwide struggles to adapt to survive and possibly even prosper through the challenges of such change. It is aware that its business model must change but, probably inevitably and excusably, it is currently fighting tooth and nail with technology, legislation and litigation to take most of its traditional business model into the future. In this the industry is often accused of working against its own best long-term interests, although the traditionally "rights-based" thinking of the writers and publishers is favourably contrasted with the "product-based" thinking of the record business.

Back to around 1914, however. The infant PRS, when it timidly started taking its first steps, also met hostility for an historical reason. Exploiting the performing right provisions in the Copyright Act of 1843, a certain Harry Wall had in 1875 set up the "Copyright and Performing Right Protection Office". Having managed to buy up many old music copyrights he used the Act to demand the £2 (about £75 at 2003 value) damages-plus-costs from many unwitting copyright infringers – usually for small local performances where the organisers and performers could easily be intimidated into paying under threat of legal action. Wall would offer to scrutinise programmes for "infringing" material, for a hefty fee of 2s 6d (now about £5). He was probably not the only such dubious entrepreneur in the absence of an official *bona fide* performing right society, but he became notorious when he was exposed in evidence before an 1882 commission of enquiry. This led to prompt legislation to protect the public from "vexatious proceedings" to extract performing right penalties, but Wall continued as vexatiously as before (no country-wide instantaneous exposure in the mass media in those days). In 1888 the £2 minimum penalty was dropped and such matters had to go to court for an assessment of damages.

Public recollection of Wall's behaviour was the albatross around PRS's neck in its early days, but Wall had been indirectly responsible for PRS being formed. So appalling was this man's reputation that in 1903 Alfred Moul, SACEM's representative in the UK, sued over a comparison by William Boosey between his activities and those of Wall (*see below*) , and left SACEM to devote himself to the formation of a British performing right society. Although Moul eventually gave up this crusade in despair, Pierre Sarpy took up the cause and helped publishers eventually to set up PRS when they finally overcame their prejudice to the performing right as being detrimental to their traditional printed music business.

The opposition they faced is illustrated by some quotes from William Boosey[3]. These anything but diplomatic and balanced views are all the more interesting because they came from the music publisher who was later to change his mind so completely that he became the first President of PRS when it was eventually established. With Moul very much in mind Boosey condemned "foreign composers and publishers [who] insist upon vexatious rights of performance that never have been, and never will be, understood here [in the UK]". Boosey cited several reasons, including the "notorious circumstances" of the activity of Mr. Wall, and the huge business of selling printed music of popular songs and tunes (small works) under a royalty system which meant he would want no hindrance to his works being performed. In this Boosey assumed that active licensing of the performing right would hinder public performance.

There was quite lot of truth in that assumption, even though Boosey overcame his own arguments at some point (his autobiography, written many years later, cited the 1911 Act's treatment of "mechanical music" and also claims that he foresaw the way the music market would change, although hindsight possibly played a greater part than foresight). PRS would meet much resentment from music users, and many would claim that it curtailed or prevented their music use, although there were relatively few high-profile cases of that actually happening. Over 80 years after PRS was founded this perpetual source of potential friction between PRS and its "market" was tackled through a process of downplaying the (still paramount) legal requirement for a licence while promoting the concept of "selling" the advantages

---

3 Although of the powerful and greatly respected music publishing family of Boosey, and having begun his career in the family firm, William went to work for Chappell in 1894.

of a PRS licence, as access to a world repertoire of copyright music which could be shown to be a valuable aid to increasing trade in all kinds of businesses.

The sheer persistence of SACEM in protecting the performing right of its own writers in the UK was certainly one factor in the change of attitude towards setting up a UK society. SACEM litigated frequently, and won. A Manchester concert agent, taken to court for refusing to pay SACEM's £5 fee in relation to use of a military march in the French society's repertoire, wrote to the *Manchester Guardian* to attack not only SACEM but the performing right generally. He described attempts to protect and license the right as "a terror"."

Then, with the kind of piously-expressed self-interest which today is echoed in many "justifications" of private piracy of copyright music through the internet, he wrote that public interest called for "such a delightful thing" as music to be free to all who wanted to perform it while "composers should be remunerated by the sale of copies and not by vexatious restrictions".

Surely even among those writers and publishers who would at the time have agreed with him, a premonition that such an approach *might just* not be sustainable in the long term must have led to a thought that protection and administration of a right which earned little today was the only sure way to ensure that it continued to exist into a future, when it might well earn much more. Had the views of that Manchester concert agent and many music publishers and writers themselves prevailed, the establishment of intellectual property (IP) as the bedrock of the creators' side of the music business would not have happened, and composers' and songwriters' income could have disappeared as the sales of sheet music dwindled from their peak of 20m pieces in 1898 to a small fraction of that in the early 2000s[4]. Happily the recognition of the supremacy of IP, however grudging at first, would also offer recorded music a viable commercial future which it might have been denied.

Getting started

It was certainly not any real change in the market which led to the formation of PRS. The publishing business then comprised mainly small family firms which inevitably had little fondness, or resource, for major investment and which naturally resisted innovation. It remained more concerned with piracy of sheet music than with the implications of the supremacy of the recorded music industry and the impact of broadcasting, and it is fair to point out that in 1914 the enormous changes to the entertainment industry which both would cause required great foresight to evaluate.

The first PRS AGM was in the society's new two-room office at 32 Shaftesbury Avenue in the heart of London's theatreland, on 1 April 1914. Clearly there was no timid superstition about such a seminal event being held on April Fools' Day. Leaving aside the pragmatic coincidence with the start of the financial year, it would be nice to think that it was even a gesture of defiance to all those who were to try, unsuccessfully in the end, to make a fool out of PRS as its history unfolded.

The first name written into the PRS membership list was that of Liza Lehmann, most famously composer of *In a Persian Garden*. Her grandson, the composer David Bedford, is the Chairman of PRS as this history is written and sent to print, as he mentions in the Preface.

William Boosey and his supporters had carved PRS out of some pretty unpromising material as far as any real sense of writer and publisher unity was concerned. The founders and first signed-up members still disagreed on many issues, and of course PRS could not license the music of those who declined to be members – which inevitably led to impossible-to-satisfy demands for a full list of every title controlled by PRS to be provided to every licensee (and updated and resupplied at frequent intervals, presumably).[5]

---

4 Direct comparison is difficult because sheet music sales ceased to be stated in units and today are reported by the MPA in value terms. The term "sheet music" always embraced albums of songs; the trend over the past couple of decades has been much more towards collections of printed music in books (folios) particularly collections of popular music.

5 Such demands for lists continued to be part of the militant music users' armoury, brought into service now and then. Fortunately UK Courts are sympathetic to PRS' argument that it would be excessively onerous for the society to supply a list showing all the approximately 16m titles in its repertoire, and so have not compelled production of such a dosument. The courts are generally satisfied that PRS is willing to invite any music user to inspect its database of works.

Coming out fighting

All of this gave the still-trenchantly opposed music users plenty of opportunity on the one-hand to ignore PRS and on the other to attack it. However, with some publishers still loudly criticising PRS as "un-English and inquisitorial" (as in the pages of the *Daily Telegraph* in July 1914), the music users hardly needed to expend too much of their own energy in their cause. While some publishers tried to strangle the infant society by simply refusing to join – unanimity and control of the whole UK repertoire being essential to PRS' long-term survival and success – others put prominent notices on their sheet music that it could be performed without a licence. Meanwhile, offering an argument which would later be persistently pursued by both broadcasters and the record industry, the Moss Empires theatre group insisted that performances of songs in their shows helped to sell copyright music and so enriched writers and publishers without need for licence revenue. The opposition did meet some brave resistance led by the eminent writers of the day, including Lehmann and Monckton on the PRS Committee. They campaigned in terms of justice, application of an existing law, and pragmatic appreciation of how the market for music performance was changing and developing. In support, Boosey dismissed "timid composers and timid publishers" and insisted that PRS should get down to some kind of work.

That line of work had two obvious and essential strands: setting up contracts with the overseas performing right societies already in existence, and finding a way to license music users in the UK. The first task was relatively easy, and a reciprocal agreement with SACEM was, predictably, soon established, with others following rapidly in pursuit of mutual benefit. The second was fairly easy to start (building on the spadework already done in the UK by SACEM by initially adding the PRS repertoire to the French society's existing licences, raising the licence fee accordingly and sharing the revenue) but would have to be accomplished in the teeth of angry, determined and at times highly organised and well-

Pictured at a PRS event in 1947 are (*left to right*) PRS Chairman Leslie Boosey with composers Zoltan Kodaly and Eric Coates . The latter was one of the society's first members in 1914; although he briefly resigned soon afterwards under pressure from those who believed that the enforcement of the performing right would discourage performers from using copyright music, he was persuaded to rejoin by the General Manager Pierre Sarpy.

resourced opposition. Still there were early successes. Moss Empires had come in like a lion but went out like a lamb; as did several major hotels and restaurant chains; and two guineas (£2.10) a year was won from the London County Council for civic band concerts.

Sarpy, with his rare accumulation of knowledge and experience in a highly specialist business, was the best person to do the job, and he was given the maximum power to act by the PRS Committee who assigned their rights personally to him and funded his team of licensing agents. As remains the case today, PRS set out to increase its licensee coverage by approaching trade associations which could reach agreements on behalf of (or recommend agreements to, or at least give access to lists of) operators in a variety of business sectors using music.

Even where there was no open warfare, the process was difficult for other reasons. Many companies had feet in both camps; for example, music publishers with interests in theatre ownership or concert promotion. Composers came under varying degrees of pressure; the rich and well-organised PRS Archives include a copy of a handwritten letter from young composer Eric Coates resigning his membership only a few months after he joined in August 1914 because he had been told his music would be boycotted by performers if a licence fee was demanded (a slightly odd threat since performers did not pay the licence fee; the venue did and does). As he had to do with others, Sarpy found a way to win Coates back, and he went on to be a PRS Committee member. Gradually more writers joined, and the membership of the commercially very successful of their day gave PRS a much needed boost. Then, as now, publishers encouraged their contracted writers to join the society.

Sadly, the year of PRS' birth also saw the start of World War I. That affected European reciprocal agreements and the PRS membership of composers whose countries of origin were now

"the enemy". On the other hand, in the UK there was full employment, however grim the reason for that; people had money to spend on entertainment and a spirit which demanded music as an antidote to fear and tragedy. The patriotic songs written in those years illustrate the point, quite apart from the insatiable appetite for entertainment in music halls, cinemas, dances, tea rooms and just about everywhere else the public might congregate to forget the war for a short while.

The war ended, finding PRS stronger, more experienced and better prepared for its job. It needed its strength, because the death of General Manager Sarpy in 1915 was a great loss of a wise man and a serious setback to practical progress. His replacement was a man described by Prof Ehrlich in *Harmonious Alliance* as "a solicitor by training, an office tyrant by vocation and a litigant by temperament". Although H S J Booth was a disaster in terms of staff, membership and public relations, he did do a lot to demonstrate that PRS was "not to be trifled with" even if at very high cost in legal fees. He knew, however, that to succeed with a licence infringement case in court PRS needed accurate evidence. He set up "a corps of agents, reporters or inspectors" who had musical knowledge and could check unlicensed premises and identify whether copyright music was being played there. Agents were paid admission costs (if they had to pay to get into premises using music – and the expense claims for visits to the more raffish areas of cities must have been interesting), their travel, and 7s 6d (37.5p) per visit. This was the beginning of the PRS field force – and the work of PRS inspectors would not significantly change until the mid-to-late 90s, when the licensing emphasis changed from law enforcement to marketing, and systematic checking of what was being played in premises became part of an ongoing professional, statistically-based market research exercise. The need for evidence of copyright music being played in unlicensed premises remains today of course, and many solicitor's letters and writs are sent to infringers every year, although the amount of litigation which needs to have its day in court is not as great as in early times.

Post-war peace did not break out for PRS. A boycott of certain PRS publisher members' music led by the Musicians Union (protesting at PRS charges) was followed by attack from another union – the British Music Union, representing music users (founded by dancing teachers). Its aim was to destroy PRS. They used the society's own weakness against it. PRS did not have the solid support of all UK music publishers, and the BMU was able to offer its members a list of "free music", which was out of copyright, or was copyright music where a non-PRS publisher was waiving the performing right. The BMU also tried several times, unsuccessfully, to get a Private Members' Bill passed which would have restored copyright law to its pre-1911 weak state.

Increasing financial strength was one reason PRS survived and eventually prospered: it did its job, it brought money in and distributed it (at high administration cost, about which there is little evidence that members complained) and its efforts meant that it benefited from increased use of copyright music in the businesses it licensed. For example, the film industry boomed in the 20s, with huge and varied repertoires, concentrating on the "light" music which happily was mostly controlled by PRS, being used by the pianists and pit orchestras who accompanied the silent films. Printed music offered collections of mood music: early examples of selections "without which musical directors of all cinemas should not rest content" include *the empty cradle* and *funeral – the last journey* at the tear-jerking end; through such dramatic offerings as *tumult, riots, confusion, horses stolen* and *burglars in the house*; to the peace of *salvation, safety at last*, and even *unbounded joy*. A far greater range of such music, with less melodramatic titles, is today offered by library music publishers in categories to suit the content of radio and TV programmes, films and ads. Today, however, the music is recorded, digitised, and available from production libraries as CDs or via the internet.

The problem of success

Licensing and collecting fees were two huge tasks, and battles, for the developing PRS. But by the 30s, the situation was beginning to illustrate the yet-to-be-coined warning: "be careful what you want – you might get it". Once a society succeeds in collecting money in reasonable amounts, distributing it is the next big problem.

Harmonious Alliance neatly states:" The society's first exercises in distribution were based upon procedures which were too rudimentary to satisfy members and too ambitious to be practical." After troublesome early attempts to insist that licensees provided detailed lists of music they used (a requirement which survives as a largely uninvoked precaution in PRS Public Performance Licence Agreements even now) an "unacceptably clumsy and divisive distribution classification system" was introduced. This was based on the classification of members "according to their status and the character of their works" aligned with whatever data could be acquired about actual performances of their works. After recent decades of hard-won battles to obtain playlists and cue sheets for broadcast, film and advertising; an MMC Report demanding greater fairness, accuracy and transparency from PRS; a long and careful process of simplifying distribution rules; a huge research exercise into whose music is being performed, where and how much; and years of improving the quality of data held on members and their works, MCPS-PRS Alliance managers and staff in 2003, reminded of those original distribution methods, would have difficulty deciding whether to laugh, cry or faint.

The first PRS Distribution (recorded in a Statement of Apportionments) was for the three years from 1914 to 1917. A total of 270 composers, authors and arrangers, in eight "classes", received a total of £5343 5s. 0d, and five classes of publishers totalling 16 companies received in all £2662 10s.0d, while two affiliated societies (French and Italian) received about £3000 between them. The details of the individual apportionments were published in the *PR Gazette*, though such publication of members' financial information was subsequently utterly forbidden, and remains so. Top earner was Lionel Monckton with £150, and Nathaniel D. Ayer earned £100. The next "class" received £75 each and included Edward German and Haydn Wood. In the £50-each class were Percy Grainger, Eric Coates and Liza Lehmann. Of the publishers Chappell received £350 as the largest earner.

However, even today few would argue with Professor Ehrlich's comment that "nothing connected with the process of [PRS] distribution turned out to be simple". And John Axon, PRS Executive Director, would agree that through its lifetime PRS has built mazes for itself to negotiate mostly out of a desire to do the best for everyone in an imperfect world. As Ehrlich elegantly put it: "Complexities which might …appear unnecessary arose from rational attempts to appease conflicting interests and grapple with problems which were intrinsic to the society's functioning".

Changes in the market, the growth of the BBC and public popularity of radio, the noticeable beginnings of the decline in printed music sales, and the rise of farsighted, more broadly business-minded publishers (with Fred Day of Francis, Day and Hunter on the white charger way out in front), all contributed to the long-delayed truce and then alliance in 1926 between PRS and virtually the whole publishing sector. This gave PRS, its writer members who by then included all the most successful and best-known, and the publishers who already supported it, the strength

of repertoire control on which depended its assurance of survival and ability to be truly effective.

One thing remained unchanged: the endless succession of problems, battles and threats which PRS had to deal with put its increasing strength regularly to the test. In an effort to avoid live broadcasts of bands turning into "plugging" sessions for particular tunes (band leaders being paid by popular publishers to play and announce them), the BBC decided to ban the announcement of titles. Publishers were infuriated and PRS found itself in dispute on their behalf, demanding that the BBC honour its contractual obligation to "duly and adequately announce" the music it played. The PRS-BBC licence contract slid into serious dispute and relations soured. Eventually the BBC gave way on announcements, the licence was renewed and goodwill restored.

No pause for breath, however. The International Council of Music Users Ltd succeeded the British Music Union as PRS Enemy No1, uniting a variety of music users in another lobby to influence Parliament and public with the goal of changing copyright law to "remove the necessity for the existence of PRS". When the notorious Tuppenny Bill easily got its Second Reading in November 1929, PRS faced what was probably the single greatest crisis in its life.

The Bill proposed two potentially devastating amendments to the 1911 Copyright Act. Firstly, publishers would have to print a statement asserting their rights on every piece of sheet music (negating all the efforts to have the performing right assumed *as a right* and thus avoid national chaos and complementary problems with international agreements). Secondly, and more perniciously, the amended Act would provide a compulsory performance licence "insofar as [the right has] been retained by printing the required notice" with a fixed maximum fee. The fee proposed was two old pennies. Significantly, the BBC was PRS' ally in opposing the Bill.

Enter barrister, author, librettist and later MP, A P Herbert. Not for the last time he put his formidable talent with words into the

Composer Ralph Vaughan Williams, an eminent member of PRS but an opponent
of the society's cause in the battle over the contentious Tuppenny Bill.

service of PRS, and tore the Bill to pieces with a combination of
forensic analysis of its practical stupidity and anger at its
unfairness. Calling it a "fantastic measure" which was intended to
destroy composers' earnings, he asked how two pence could be
shared between writer and publisher; whether it was supposed to
pay for the use of foreign works as well as British, and for "the
manufacture of 100,000 gramophone records"; and whether this
approach should be extended to other creative works – a tuppenny
Forsyte Saga, or Chaplin film. Humorous even when furious, he
remarked that if one stage musical work could be performed for
tuppence, "for a bob (a shilling – now 5p) you could run a
repertory season".

Herbert denounced the Bill as rotten at its heart, and told MPs
they had disgraced themselves by allowing it to slip through to a
crucial legislative stage unopposed. He thundered in a style which
today's polite professional lobbying organisations would, sadly,
never dare to dream of using: "No man should waste a minute in
attempting to amend it: it must be killed dead as an insult to the
craft of music."

There were many other PRS supporters. Signatories to a
Confederation of Arts denunciation included Arnold Bennett,
George Bernard Shaw, Virginia Woolf and the heads of
RADA and the National Gallery[6] The press weighed in on the
side of the creators, demanding to know why anyone should
expect to use another's property without paying fairly for it.
The *Morning Post* and the *Daily Mail* specifically defended PRS
(in a way which brings tears to the eyes of the author of this
book, herself for some years in charge of the society's public
and press relations). PRS was not "a tyrannous body" or a
"vampire" but a protector of composers. Its fees were not
"arbitrary, excessive and ill-defined" but were to a scale of
charges which were made public. The *Evening Standard* went
so far as to describe the Bill as insane.

More moderately, led by Leslie Boosey, PRS addressed a careful
portfolio of facts to Parliament. The Tuppenny Bill was killed.
PRS' value as a source of collective administration of rights for
composers and publishers was fully supported in a Select
Committee report. In wording similar to that which would be used
by the Monopolies and Mergers Commission over 60 years later,
the Committee judged that PRS was "undoubtedly a convenience
and almost a necessity" for creators and copyright owners and for
music users. It was probably "the only practicable way in which
the composer can collect his fees for performing rights in any
adequate manner". But there was a grave warning: PRS was a
monopoly and so *could* abuse its powers (for example by refusing
to grant licences) and so there should be some arbitration for the
music user to appeal to, such as a tribunal.

6 But one eminent composer, Ralph Vaughan Williams, who had little interest in performing
   right fees and objected loftily to the licensing of "musical entertainments in country villages"
   supported what he viewed as the "real grievance "of the Bill's promoters and warned against
   PRS "intimidation".

PRS had won this battle, but it had to be aware that there were complaints from users about the rough justice of blanket licensing, which it was claimed forced users in effect to pay for the use of that whole (world) repertoire – a bargain if you were using that whole repertoire – when they might actually only be using a very small part of it. This argument has recurred many times. It seems logical from some users' point of view, but has always been robustly defended by PRS. The society maintains that the music users are paying for a licence: this entitles them to use whatever music they wish to use from the entire repertoire, and it frees users from the obligation and administrative cost (potentially huge, in some cases) of contacting every copyright owner individually for permission to use that chosen music. To that long-standing and consistent response PRS would today add that the music user is getting access to an enhancement to business; use of the right music in the right way for any business can and does contribute to success and profit.

However, it is fair to say that the apparent complexity of PRS Licence Tariffs stems to some extent from efforts to make the justice a little less rough by considering specific kinds of usage and their relative likely value to the user, and negotiating or defining detailed variations on licence fees accordingly. But segmenting the repertoire and licensing it in parts has never been conceded by PRS, nor demanded by the Copyright Tribunal in any specific case or by the Copyright Act generally.

The depression of the 30s sent sheet music sales into a headlong dive, made worse by the fact that record sales also plummeted; films coincidentally acquired soundtracks and radio blossomed as home entertainment much cheaper to acquire (and play) than a piano.

In these times it was probably sensible for PRS to act cautiously in its licence fee demands, to consolidate the goodwill it had won in the Tuppenny Bill battle and to avoid seeming greedy when businesses everywhere were in trouble. But its members, particularly the naturally more aggressive pop publishers, wanted PRS income to rise rapidly to make up for what they were losing

elsewhere. Adverse external circumstances triggered, not for the first or last time, expression of many members' vague underlying discontent, not just about low licence fees but also about slow and inaccurate distributions.

Those were long-term problems which PRS could not tackle quickly. Meanwhile, it had to adapt to a changing market for the public performance of music, which increasingly involved recorded and broadcast ("public rediffusion of music") formats as well as live. Inevitably, litigation had to settle arguments, deciding that there was no difference in substance between a hotel engaging a band to play for diners and dancers and the same hotel piping a radio broadcast through loudspeakers.

This sensible judgement did spark some mild hysteria about the prospect of PRS wanting to license people listening to radios in their home, the loudspeaker in the radio set having replaced the headphones of the earlier cat's whisker and crystal contraptions. Of course, PRS had no such intentions, and the law did not allow it to do so, but such public overreaction is something the society has had to cope with at times. Another example was the early 90s attempt to start licensing the use of music at private wedding receptions: this was abandoned after a stream of (often good humoured, but insistent) adverse public and media reaction.

World War II

As PRS celebrated its 25th birthday, war with Germany was declared. Initial swinging regulations which shut down all forms of entertainment (a 6pm curfew on all venues to prevent loss of life in the expected massive bombing and the BBC reduced to public announcements with a few gramophone records to lighten marginally the leaden atmosphere) were soon relaxed. In fact, in Britain World War II sparked a boom in public entertainment, the psychology of which needs no explanation. The exception was television, where service was suspended for the entire war.

Although PRS income was sustained, its administrative work became a nightmare with skeleton staff, office evacuation, communications clamp-downs, agencies overseas closed down (eg Hong Kong when Japan entered the war) and power supply problems hitting the innovative, in collecting society terms, electric calculating machines of which everyone was so proud. But ingenuity and determination took over, and distributions were not only made but mostly made on time. The story was happily similar in the other European societies, even though no revenues were allowed out of occupied countries. Legislation was needed to allow PRS to go on licensing and collecting for rights owners in enemy territories, but the revenue was passed to the Custodian for Enemy Property while hostilities persisted. On the humanitarian front PRS allowed dislocated composers, writers and publishers (mostly Jewish) to join PRS regardless of Nazi authorities' objections.

The war brought great change to the way people lived their lives, and even though most of the public had never heard of the society, PRS was tangentially but unshakeably attached to public lifestyle. The huge influx of workers into factories needed distraction from fear, fatigue and the monotonous stress of munitions assembly lines. Entertaining background music was one pretty good answer to that need, enormously stepping up the "rediffusion" of broadcast music through loudspeakers. The BBC's programme *Music While You Work* was born, and became a daily outlet for modern popular music which had previously been so under-represented on radio. A stopgap licence fee (one guinea – £1.05) for factories was set up by PRS, with such totally uncharacteristic lightning speed that it probably suffered from a bout of corporate dizziness. Inevitably when tariffs *were* worked out (based on factory size, number of workers and areas where music could be heard) there were the usual objections, press debate, questions and speeches in Parliament and High Court test cases which supported the PRS position.

One of the most-performed songs associated with World War II: the English lyrics sung to the original marching tune became hugely popular with British troops and public, who thereby "captured" an enemy song and made it their own.

PRS has had to deal with one particular argument countless times over the decades, and the gist of it always remains the same. The user starts from a position that somehow, for any of a variety of reasons depending on specific circumstance, there is a good case for the music used in a particular business to be very cheap or free. This stance only ever applies to music use, not any other goods and services the business might use.

Essentially, the script hardly varies, and is typified by this "conversation piece" written in 1943 by eminent PRS member A.P.Herbert (the specific suggestion here is that munitions factories should be exempt)

In this particular case – after all, there's a war on – there are all these people making munitions, and *Music While You Work* is intended to help them along. I should have thought [PRS] might stretch a point.
And let their work be performed for nothing?
Well, in the circumstances, yes
Has there been any proposal to waive fees due to holders of patents...?
Not that I know of.
Are newspapers and cigarettes distributed gratis in the munitions factories?
Probably not
Very well then.

Over the years one side of such conversations has taken various forms – "After all it's part of education"; or "It is a start-up industry and hasn't any money"; or "It's a charity"; or – oddest of all, but apparently entirely logical to the licence fee objector – " They [name any major pop writer/performer] earn enough already". The "music should be free because it's digital and I can file share for nothing and anyway CDs are too expensive" argument of the internet boom is, however, in a class of its own for aggressive illogic.

The regularity of these public clashes finally led PRS to think more constructively about its public relations, and in fits and starts it began to improve its written communications, its press contacts and its relations with MPs and public bodies.

After the war came reconstruction. Alongside rebuilding its own administrative structure, PRS needed to take the lead in getting the international network of performing right societies working again. Its expertise and experience, enhanced by the fact that its work had not been interrupted during the war, were called on to help continental Europe. For example, with their unerring talent for creating sinister acronyms, the Nazis had replaced GEMA in Germany with an organisation called STAGMA, and PRS was invited to help reinstate the legitimate society, which it did. Meanwhile Leslie Boosey worked very hard to bring the international authors' societies' confederation CISAC back to life again. At home, the job of reviewing and updating obsolescent licence tariffs and creating new ones in response to new usage was a major post-war task, not to mention the endless round of renegotiations of broadcast licence contracts.

While the society was picking up its old threads and spinning a few new ones, its members were also getting more organised. The Composers Guild had begun in 1944 and soon after the end of the war its near-200 members included most of the well-known British classical and light classical composers; it also had a sub-group of composers for film.

Reflecting a broad division of membership which was maintained until unification of music writers' organisations in 1999, the British Songwriters Protection Society was founded in 1947, later becoming the Songwriters Guild of Great Britain, then BASCA, the British Association of Songwriters, Composers and Authors. It was a foil to the Composers' Guild for popular songwriters (though membership overlapped, Noel Coward being one eminent member of both organisations). Characteristic of BASCA was its accessibility to a very wide membership, from new, amateur, would-be popular songwriters to those who could be said to have "made it" in every possible way.

A complete contrast was very deliberately created much later, and marked the increasing political awareness among some writers. Current PRS Chairman David Bedford was one of a group of composers (including Howard Blake and Nicholas Maw) who reached the view that the Composers' Guild, of which they were members, was not doing anything at all for media composers, and very little for its classical membership. They founded the Association of Professional Composers (APC) which took a very active role in pursuing its members' interests. Its membership was exclusively for fully professional composers (not songwriters, who properly belonged in BASCA). There were never more than about 250 APC members, invited or selected to join with a requirement that they had to be earning enough to be PRS Associate members. Big APC issues included fighting for the PRS classical subsidy to be kept when in 1989 pop songwriter Mike Batt on the PRS Council first suggested its abolition; and the insistence by broadcasters who commissioned music for programmes that they should be given publishing rights.

These battles made Bedford, who became Chairman of the APC in 1989, a much more politically aware writer who wanted active involvement in writers' organisations. The same was true in varying degrees for other leading members of writers' organisations who went on to contribute as writer Board members for PRS and MCPS, including the long-serving BASCA Chairman Guy Fletcher.

One early crusade for the writers' guilds was against the increasing "Americanisation" of the output of broadcasters and cinemas. The campaign was not a success, mostly because it was attempting to resist a shift in public taste. Years later, with Americanisation

jargonised into "US cultural imperialism", other nations, particularly France, would take a firmer, Government-backed stand which saw the introduction of quotas for the use of "national" music in broadcasting, but which had similarly small impact on mass public preferences. In fact, such quotas in the UK were called for by some members at the PRS 1961 AGM, but this was not pursued.

Besides all this, the 50s and 60s and were just over the horizon, and about to transform the UK entertainment industry with rock 'n' roll, the cult of youth, booming disposable income for post-war baby boomers, pirate pop radio and then BBC capitulation to the demands of that audience, enormous increase in TV music use and a record industry which found it had a licence to print money.

The boring but essential counterparts to the frantic hedonism of those times included the approach of a new Copyright Act. This was a revision of the 1911 Act in the light of technological developments and updates to the Berne Convention, which granted an exclusive right to writers in respect of public performance of their works but left the details to national legislation. Interestingly, PRS was in 1951, five years before the 1956 Act, reassured by Harold Wilson, then President of the Board of Trade, that he believed the society was functioning well and saw no reason for any referral to the Monopoly Commission (as it then was). Nevertheless, PRS wisely decided to monitor and lobby the Committee set up to review the 1911 Act. It was right to be vigilant, since the Committee was soon faced with evidence of all the old antagonisms against PRS from groups of music users (but again excepting the BBC). While the Committee largely took a positive view of PRS, it had some harsh criticism of the "arbitrary and autocratic" behaviour of PPL in its licensing of public performance of commercial recordings.

It is worth noting that this was one of many occasions when PRS discussed changing its name (often described as unhelpful and confusing in terms of expressing what the society did). The added edge this time was PRS was keen not to be confused with the much criticised PPL.

Market change

The PRS name did not change, but the organisation did in response to revolutionary change in music, the market for music and the accessibility of music – increasingly in recorded and broadcast form and increasingly mobile via portable radios and then tape cassettes. The number and variety of premises using music in their businesses also mushroomed, helped by facts such as changes in the drink laws (which encouraged pubs to use music); the rise of companies which provided ready-made selections of pop music on cassettes and sold these into premises as background music; and the then novel, now essential, accompaniment of music to sports events and exhibitions and on coaches and aircraft and in shops.

There were other far-reaching changes around that time. Fuelled by youth culture and disposable wealth came the rise of the rock and pop singer-songwriters, with The Beatles out in front creating their own myth, madness and multinational empire. This made music the sort of big business that the financial press wrote about and heavyweight accountants worked in. The performer was now frequently also the writer and soon was also the music publisher. A surprisingly large number of them made, held on to, and increased fortunes which much less than a decade before would have been impossible to imagine or predict. The writing talent and success of the 60s wave of British music makers who conquered the world's markets contributed to the trebling of PRS income between 1965 and 1975 because they were all PRS members.

Success of British composers around the world, and particularly in the US, in the 60s led to the trebling of PRS income between 1965 and 1975. Leading the period of British dominance of the global music market were PRS members John Lennon and Paul McCartney

Four eminent PRS composer members at the 1975 AGM (*left to right*) Malcolm Arnold, William Walton, Vivian Ellis and Lennox Berkeley

Tariffs which really kept pace with inflation were also important, and the surge in global commercial success for British music also propelled success for the works of 20th century classical composers including Benjamin Britten, Sir Edward Elgar and Sir Malcolm Arnold.

PRS had to seize these opportunities and deal with the changes in the music business on behalf of its members, inventing or reinventing the wheels to keep things rolling forward. Its new spirit of opportunism also led it to apply for a Queen's Award for Export Achievement, which was granted in 1971. Understandably, no one remarked on the slightly ironic coincidence that this was the year in which The Beatles, who had largely driven that export achievement, officially split up.

In its first 50 years, PRS spent much of its time and energy fighting for survival and recognition within whatever level of protection the copyright law provided at any time. This made for a story full of big events dealt with on a grand scale by notable personalities among its officers, administrators and members. There was a parallel equally interesting but not so grand and personality-filled story. The history of a collecting society is primarily a story about licensing and distribution, and that deserves to be told in its own right, as it is later in this chapter.

Business change –management, philosophy, information technology, legislation and PR

Picking up the broader story of the society from the 60s calls for some focus on the management of PRS. The pattern of change included some significant changes in senior personnel, and in their style. Following Head of Legal Affairs Denis de Freitas into the top echelons of PRS came Michael Freegard in 1964 and in 1966, the year that Leslie Boosey resigned as Chairman to become President of Honour and was succeeded by the songwriter Paddy

Roberts, Freegard became Company Secretary, and only three years later he was made the society's youngest ever General Manager.

During three decades at PRS Freegard worked on making the management of the Society more professional. In retirement in 2003, he observed that the process was still going on, although some of the concepts of "good management" had changed over time (very broadly) from inwardly paternal and outwardly culture – and revenue – oriented, to inwardly and outwardly commercially minded and structured.

As CEO, Freegard saw his primary objective as increasing PRS income and paying the cost of doing that. His business philosophy in pursuing such goals chimed with that of his predecessor Royce Whale but reversed the attitude of Whale's predecessor Leonard Walter. It was to be partly reversed again by John Hutchinson, who would tackle cost-cutting and income growth with equal aggression. Walter had been determined to "reduce cost at all costs". This was partly in reaction to the limitations on PRS income which were continually threatened and occasionally enforced by the Performing Right Tribunal, and partly because the society's efforts to license certain types of users, particularly smaller business premises, were hesitant and ineffective bringing in small amounts of revenue.

Freegard believed then, and believes now, that it was better to spend more on enforcement to generate more licence income. Looking back, he states firmly: "I'm completely unrepentant. It was essential to ensure that the performing right was respected and valued by going after all possible revenue. We had to improve our licensing efforts, which in some areas were feeble." He remembers an annual meeting of Licensing Inspectors in the mid Sixties: it was held in the smallest office on the top floor of Copyright House because there were then only six Inspectors to cover the whole of the UK. Whale quadrupled the number of Licensing Inspectors, and Freegard determinedly furthered the process, in the clear knowledge that costs would rise. His plan was helped by The Beatles phenomenon and the allied big rise in PRS international income. This allowed him to take domestic costs up while maintaining the overall expense ratio.

It was also a time when the use of music in business – retailers, cafés, bars, restaurants, factories and offices and more – was beginning its growth towards what some members of the public decried as saturation of the environment. Those who used that description did so with either pain or approval, depending on their attitude to music being unavoidable in so many circumstances. A movement called Pipedown made some impact in the press, demanding freedom from "piped" recorded music in public. Despite the fact that at least one PRS Board Director (a very successful classical, TV and film composer) cheerfully announced that he himself was a member of Pipedown, from the mid 90s onward PRS increasingly encouraged businesses to use copyright music to "add value" to their offering (*see Licensing and Distribution section*).

Even by the mid-80s PRS licences were becoming better understood (if not better liked) by small music users, and the economics of collecting such licence fees became more realistic as revenue growth in that particular area grew considerably in relation to the collection costs.

The PRS Board tended to agree with management, and composers and publishers were generally supportive at the time. But Freegard's period at head of the company was marked by the growth of a conflict of legitimate demands (more activity, more efficiency, and more communication v. lower administrative cost) which has become a way of life for PRS and many other societies. This conflict has been addressed in many ways and through various initiatives, some successful some not, but all generally focused on better ways of handling data and processes via computers (*see IT section*).

Throughout Freegard's time as Chief Executive a continual increase in data (more members, more licences, more works, more agreements, and more performance information) and demands for more accuracy pushed up spending on administration. This happened as the pendulum started to swing again on the issue of costs, because of changes on the PRS Council, particularly as new business-focused executives at management level in big publishing companies replaced individual and family firm entrepreneurs who were "music men".

Freegard's tenure at the head of PRS included the very long period of preparation for new and updated UK copyright legislation to replace the 1956 Act. The highest public profile and the most intense, at times vitriolic, lobbying related to the music industry's calls for a statutory levy on domestic recording equipment and tape. This was to compensate music copyright owners for the use of their works in unlicensed recording of broadcast and commercially recorded music by people at home. This rather long-winded concept was rapidly encapsulated in the phrases "home taping" and "blank tape levy". The rights in recordings were the issue here, and as the BPI battled on behalf of the record companies, it was supported by the Music Copyright Reform Group (MCRG), through which writers and publishers' interests were jointly lobbied for by PRS, MCPS and the MPA.

Issues relating specifically to the performing right were to some extent and perhaps conveniently eclipsed in public controversy during the prolonged furore over the blank tape levy as the BPI and opposing organisations such as the Consumers' Association and the European Tape Manufacturers squared up to each other, their respective PR and government relations machines at full throttle.

The Government's attitude to the "performing right" indicated that this was not the focus of change in the law nor, at that point, was there any active Government interest in PRS administration. While the DTI received many complaints from music users about performing right licensing, the level of tariffs and PRS licensing activity, the Government generally fell back on the existence of the Tribunal as a response, rather than taking a fresh legislative or regulatory approach.

As well as increased Government relations, public relations in all senses were a focus. PRS was an unheard-of and seldom heard-from organisation. Freegard worked on establishing identity and communications. In asking his Board to commission Professor Ehrlich to write *Harmonious Alliance* Freegard wanted not only a history of PRS but a means of making the society and its work better known. It was published in 1989 when the 75th anniversary celebrations brought PRS more positive publicity than it had won in the past, so crowning years of steady PR effort.

As an advocate of improved PR, Board member and future Chairman Wayne Bickerton had become Chairman of the society's PR Committee. In 1988 it commissioned a new PRS logo and corporate image to be designed by The Jenkins Group to coincide with the 75th anniversary in 1989. Michael Freegard stressed that the new logo put emphasis on the acronym PRS and the line Giving Music Its Due to describe what PRS does, rather than on the society's full name which was considered "ambiguous and misleading". The celebrations included an anniversary launch at the Theatre Royal in Drury Lane, a gala dinner at London's Guildhall, an anniversary regional meeting for members at the Queen Elizabeth II Conference Centre in Westminster, and the launch (originally for only two years but eventually long-lived) of the Composers in Education scheme proposed by the Deputy Chairman Publisher Andrew Potter. There was also the creation of a new corporate video by the inventive and successful Video Arts company: it featured a tune written by three PRS composers and performed in many different musical styles – with the effect that every member of PRS staff could not only remember the tune but exasperatedly admitted they could never forget it. Sadly, the Post Office refused to issue a commemorative stamp because it only considered centenaries for such an honour. PR, in the sense both

The PRS 75th Anniversary dinner at The Guildhall in London in 1989 was attended by HRH Prince Edward (second left), who is pictured here with (*left to right*) lyricist and PRS member, and currently President of the British Academy of Composers and Songwriters, Tim Rice, PRS CEO Michael Freegard and President Vivian Ellis.

of press and public relations, had previously never really figured much in PRS priorities, though the need for clearer and more sympathy-inducing communications had been sporadically acknowledged. The attitude characterises the society as it was in its first half century – rather self-absorbed, standing aside from the flamboyance of the music business, lofty in its stance and language, addressing its members with the distant politeness of nobility, and as far as possible not addressing anyone else very much at all.

The idea of indulging in PR was long frowned on by the Board as undignified publicity-seeking of an undesirable kind. Freegard remembers introducing it by stealth, in the guise of a department with a suitable Civil Service title of Information and Publications, serving the needs of public/press, membership and licensing communications. This function later became Public Affairs, still avoiding the unwelcome initials PR (but incidentally creating potential confusion with the broadly adopted meaning of Public Affairs in the commercial world as embracing Government and investor relations). Reflecting the changing style and approachability and branding of PRS, this function later became Corporate Communications. As such, it was greatly and actively supported by the profile - and marketing-minded Chief Executive from 1995, John Hutchinson, as he very publicly wrought major continuous change over a decade.

Further change in attitude and structure was reflected in the 2002 decision to drop the "corporate" aspect of the work and the title and bring greatly expanded communication with members (of PRS and MCPS collectively) to the fore in the MCPS-PRS Alliance (*See Alliance chapter*).

A communication issue was in a way one of the triggers for a notable clash between the PRS Board and one of the society's members. Although the details are not relevant here, the episode illustrated attitudes which were to alter rapidly thereafter and speeded constitutional change which was already in train, as well as providing an interesting footnote to history of company law. Writer and publisher PRS member Trevor Lyttleton demanded a list of PS members eligible to vote together with their voting status. He was denied access on the ground that provision of such information would be tantamount to disclosing the earnings of the members concerned – information which is confidential (the entire Membership list *without voting* status being readily available in accordance with company law at that time.). Legal action followed. A High Court decision in the society's favour was reversed by the Court of Appeal. Legislation followed in the form of a Companies Act amendment which dealt with classes of membership of companies limited by guarantee: this effectively required companies limited by guarantee, such as the society, to disclose in any statutory register of members the class (and hence voting status) of membership held by each member. But PRS had already accepted the need for a change to its Constitution,

extending voting rights and amending membership criteria. In the 80s, the Society set out on a road to greater openness and approachability, although progress was seen by many as neither rapid nor broad enough.

Growth and change of attitude in membership

During the anniversary year a special presentation was made to PRS member Paul McCartney by the society's Life President, composer Vivian Ellis.

Membership had been growing rapidly. For a long time, writers tended to come to PRS via recommendation or insistence from their publishers (both benefited); for example, The Beatles joined because DJM founder and owner Dick James told them to. Later PRS also went out to find members, and the issue would arise of keeping them in the face of unacknowledged competition from other societies particularly, it was thought, from the American societies which were in competition with each other.

Growth in numbers was allied to changes in attitude. Looking back, Freegard saw this as a change from gratitude for whatever PRS could do for them and appreciation of whatever royalties flowed to them, to a view of themselves as both owners and clients of their society, demanding what they saw as their due.

Andrew Potter, an elected publisher Director of PRS since 1986 and Chairman from 1996 to 2002, noted the unusual turnover among publisher Directors in the late 80s. This would prove to be significant in sparking change, although it was less organised revolution than very rapid evolution and its forward role was a lot less obvious at the time than with hindsight now. He was one of a number of young contemporaries who brought new ideas and attitudes from all music publishing sectors, classical (Potter from OUP), film and TV music (Maggie Rodford from Air Edel), pop (Steve Lewis from Virgin). Each of the new arrivals wanted to see more rapid change and development of PRS, although their approaches varied from patient persistence to open irritation with management ethos and procedures. Equally important was the progressive change in the representation on the Council of the major multinational music conglomerates, into whose hands the real power in music publishing was rapidly shifting. They brought a harder-nosed attitude towards what the society was doing and how it was doing it. Potter sums it up: "PRS stopped being a gentlemen's club and became a business."

The writers on the Council not only revised their representation much more slowly at that time, but also viewed the changing style and agenda of the publisher Directors with wariness often amounting to suspicion. Pop songwriters Mick Leeson and Pete Waterman (who chose to join as a writer though he was also a publisher) brought a more robust and questioning attitude with them in the early 90s. The traditional PRS philosophy of the cultured collective, believed in and applied firmly by Michael Freegard in over 20 years as Chief Executive, needed to find a way to work with the new business philosophy. It was never going to be easy. The increase in tensions and a generally more

The headquarters of PRS since the early 60s and home of the MCPS-PRS Alliance, Copyright House in Berners Street, London W1

demanding and attentive attitude from increasingly knowledgeable, focused and progressive Directors might not have been comfortable for some on the Board, and even less so for top and senior management, but they built up impetus for useful re-examination of long established attitudes and practices. And they were inevitable. It was equally inevitable that some babies would exit with the bathwater in the rolling process of change.

A response to a more demanding membership, looking for greater efficiency and cost effectiveness, necessarily included improvement in automation of essential processes, storage and use of data and calculations. In the late 80s, it was decided that rather than tinkering further with systems piecemeal, a far bigger and more comprehensive plan would be put in place. This project bore the acronym PROMS[7] for Performing Right Online Membership System. At the time it seemed to hold out the prospect of automating much manual work. Freegard recalls being sceptical, but early demonstrations were very impressive and fears

7 see IT section

A PRS member as well as one the world's most famous conductors of all time, Sir Malcolm Sargent is pictured here in the Albert Hall during the traditionally riotous last night of the Proms (the annual Promenade Concerts).

diminished. But PROMS was to fail in its objectives, leading to considerable pain, upheaval and management change, and to Freegard's own departure. This catapulted change to the top of the agenda. In Potter's words: "Things had been building up to something in the 80s, and it turned out to be PROMS, which was symptomatic of a system which could not cope with change."

In 1994 an independent examination of its own corporate governance – how the society governed itself – was a significant step for PRS. This also anticipated the 1995 Monopolies and Mergers Commission enquiry, itself another major milestone for the society, and some would say the most important milestone of all. To quote Potter again, stating a view held by many contemporary and subsequent Board Directors: "The MMC report was the best thing which could have happened to us". The

senior management view would be one of agreement, but those who were involved at the time point out that the MMC Report really formalised a stream of analyses and recommendations which were put to the MMC Panel by PRS managers themselves.

The PRS Corporate Governance Review

Playing in Tune was the title chosen by Professor Tom Clarke, the DBM Professor of Corporate Governance at Leeds Business School, for his 1994 report on how PRS was, and should be, run; and its communications with its membership. Chairman Wayne Bickerton, who had pushed hard for this review to be commissioned and later strongly supported the implementation of its recommendations, commented at the time of Clarke's appointment: "Having consistently supported the proposal that [the PRS Board] should undertake a corporate governance review, I welcome the appointment…the company as a whole is also conducting a business processes review as part of a total continuous improvement initiative". The scale of self-examination and reorganisation which Board and management embarked on after the failure of a major computer system project, departure of the CEO and most of the top team, and evidence of great discontent in some sectors of the membership is reflected in that comment.

The executive summary of Clarke's report noted the recent exposure of weakness in the PRS information systems and the deterioration in the relationship between management and Board. It stated: "However, if PRS is to engage as a productive partner in the joint venture with MCPS (*referring to the ServiceCo project of that time – see Alliance chapter*); to capitalise on the considerable opportunities emerging for developing PRS business; to respond effectively to the series of challenges ahead presented by multimedia technology and international relations; then it must establish a more professional, focused and proactive mode of governance".

Anticipating resistance to proposals for altering the "long-established representational structures" for sectors of the membership on the Board, Clarke urged that "what the membership of PRS requires above all else is a highly efficient Society, which is an effective custodian of copyright data, and very cost effective in its handling of the financial transactions which form the basis of the Society's work".

His recommendations included:

The then 24-strong Board to be halved to six writers and six publishers (as illustration it was mentioned that the Main Boards of BT, Shell and BP then numbered 13, 10 and 16 respectively). Also a retirement age of 65 to be set for all officers of PRS (Board and executives)

Small Board committees focusing on different revenue streams and functional areas of PRS to be set up, involving previous Board members initially

Two external directors to be appointed, drawn from relevant backgrounds (IT, finance, high tech industry etc). Also two Executive Directors to be appointed from the senior management of the company

Creation of programme of directoral development for Board members and clear written definitions of their roles, duties and responsibilities

A full-time salaried Chairman and a Chief Executive given full responsibility for running the business, concentrating on strategic development, supported by a senior management team to coordinate the operational control of the company

The practice of meeting, on a regular basis, representatives of the membership – major publishers and writers, the writers' guilds etc.

After much deliberation, the Board decided to reduce its elected membership by only two seats on the Board, believing a wide range of musical and membership opinion at Board level was essential. Most other recommendations were carried through either to the letter or in the spirit of Clarke's report.

If the elected Directors had any lingering subconscious wish to slow or even reverse that process of change, it was not evident in their choice of a new Chief Executive in 1995. John Hutchinson would energetically, enthusiastically, strategically and ruthlessly accelerate, broaden and vigorously proclaim change and a business ethos almost from the moment of his appointment.

The Corporate Governance Report thinking was supported, amplified and acted upon by Hutchinson to an extent only hinted at by Clarke.

Hutchinson's personal and professional impact was felt, greatly admired and sometimes equally greatly resented, at every structural level and in every sphere of PRS activity. One key area in which his approach differed significantly from the traditional PRS approach, represented notably by Michael Freegard, was international relations with its affiliated societies within CISAC. The best perspective can be offered by looking at the broad history of PRS international relations here.

PRS in the global society network

PRS has played an important role in CISAC's history, not least through Leslie Boosey who in 1946 became the first publisher to be elected president of CISAC. During World War II and its aftermath, Boosey was extremely active in helping to preserve CISAC. He organised the evacuation of its office from Paris to neutral Switzerland and participated in the reorganisation of societies in several European countries including Germany. In 1976, CISAC's 50th anniversary, Boosey was awarded a CISAC gold medal. He ensured that PRS was influential and at the heart of the always growing international network of music copyright societies. The CISAC Congress of 1947 was organised by PRS in London and the society was to host the Congress again in 1964 and 2002.

So there developed a strong PRS tradition of solidarity with CISAC, and this was willingly inherited by Freegard when he came to run the society. His view and that of his peers and contemporaries was typified by the language of the time: reference to sister societies whose executives were colleagues; sister societies which were partners in lobbying Governments and intergovernmental organisations such as WIPO and UNESCO[8]. Taking a very active role in furthering the international aims of CISAC in terms of copyright protection was an important part of the work of member society heads, as was serving on the CISAC Executive Bureau as Freegard did (for a period as its Chairman). With both PRS and MCPS as members, GESAC[9] was founded in 1991 to represent the interests of authors and publishers in the European Union, particularly in their relations with the European Commission in Brussels.

This solidarity proved important in the early 60s, when concerted effort from developing countries to obtain exemptions from international conventions on copyright and intellectual property licensing, in order effectively to obtain free access to literature and music, needed to be resisted.

Freegard reflects that the need for CISAC to be a forum for co-operation came to mean that issues between member societies were not allowed to become prominent, and the CISAC model reciprocal contract remained accepted and essentially unchanged

for many years. Some societies and individuals were troubled by some of the distribution practices of certain other societies[10], but this was superseded by the principle of co-operation and common cause. By way of polite "policing", some societies appointed their own representatives based in key countries, to visit the affiliated society there regularly and use their knowledge to check what was being done. PRS had such representatives in France, Spain, Italy and Germany, and the societies in those countries had similar representatives in London. This system was useful in terms of gaining regularly updated general information but was of questionable value in terms of any "auditing" of distributions.

Although in 1980 a PRS delegation visited JASRAC in Japan for an exchange of information, later in the 80s a more formal system of executive teams making investigative "technical visits" was introduced. PRS, BMI and ASCAP decided to set a good example, and started by making such visits to each other. But the main concern was with some of the practices of continental European societies (income due to the UK and USA from Europe was greater by far than that from the rest of the world).

The PRS Board had pursued a policy of supporting Freegard's view that major societies should take a long-term view of assisting the work of CISAC, "investing in the future", and in the 80s and 90s this appeared to bear fruit. Useful regional committees were formed and started to tackle real issues, and new societies were encouraged and helped to establish themselves. PRS was "parent" to a number of these in territories which had been under British rule or protection such as Hong Kong, Singapore, Zambia and parts of the West Indies.

In the early 90s, there were two issues which stood out from the many. One was the increasing complexity of the society's activity, and the impact of that on costs. The other was what Freegard describes as "a growing xenophobia on the part of the publishers towards foreign societies and particularly the continental European societies". Some would question the term

8 World Intellectual Property Organisation. United Nations Organisation for Education, Science, Culture and Communications.

9 Groupement Européen de Sociétés des Auteurs et Compositeurs

10 The term "black box" was used to mean money which any society had not distributed – to its own members or to an affiliated society – because of its inability to identify any real or alleged Interested Parties in the copyright. After a period of time most societies would put this black box money to use within their own organisation. However, the PRS approach was always to distribute all distributable income in any given year, and not to hold any black box funds. It makes available information on Unidentified Performances and when IPs came forward to make a legitimate claim, the due royalties were paid from current income . It is easy to understand why the idea of "black boxes" annoyed UK society members particularly.

The presentation of the first PRS John Lennon Award in 1988 by his widow
Yoko Ono and former Beatles record producer George Martin

"xenophobia", but there is no doubt that in what were to be the
last years of Freegard's long career with PRS the publishers on the
Board increasingly voiced doubts and dislike for many of the
practices of most of their affiliates in Europe, and this discontent
was progressively evinced by the writer Directors too.

The highly visible and audible splash which first disturbed the
surface, and started the eventually far-reaching ripples and waves
in international relations, was delivered by one of PRS's best
known groups of members, the rock band U2. They decided to
challenge first their own society and, through it, the European
societies on a range of administrative and accounting issues
affecting both the amount of royalties they received for popular
concerts of their works and what they regarded as the
unreasonable length of time they had to wait for payment of
royalties attributable to live concerts at which they were
performing their own compositions.

This challenge in its early stages threatened to become very
acrimonious. It could have destroyed the relationship between
the society and a group which was among the most famous and
respected of its members and, in turn, could have led to a series
of similar conflicts with other major singer-songwriter members.

Dealing with that situation involved almost three years of
discussions and diplomacy. This process involved the legal teams,
senior management, the Chairman Wayne Bickerton and later
John Hutchinson after he took on the Chief Executive role in
1995, as well as the band's management, legal representatives
and publishers, and the heads of European societies which were
drawn into the issue and which in time moved to accepting the
key principles that administration charges for international concert
tours should be reduced and the payment of royalties could and
should be speeded up.

Litigation against PRS for breach of European competition rules
was begun by U2 in 1994, not long after which PRS joined the
European collecting societies as third party proceedings; but
eventually negotiation and joint review of the real issues led to
three beneficial results. The first was that U2 and PRS settled the
financial issues out of court. The second was that the incremental
deductions made by various societies which licensed parts of
major international concert tours were challenged and reviewed.
The third was accelerated improvement of practices within
PRS for which, it must be said, the MMC's investigation and
publication of its Report at the beginning of 1996 were also
significant catalysts (*see Appendix on MMC*). The MMC took into
consideration a number of issues raised by members, including
those at the heart of the dispute with U2. Its recommendations –
which PRS was obliged to follow – included allowing members to
require re-assignment of live public performance rights in works of
which they were composers. Once the society had set in train
implementation of this, it willingly accepted that it had little
option but to concentrate efforts on giving members reason to stay
in the collective fold, and so it offered greatly improved service
in respect of administration of concert tours while significantly
reducing the costs deducted from that royalty stream.

PRS Chairman from 1996 to 2002 Andrew Potter's view was
that U2 and their publisher (PolyGram Music – now part of the
Universal Music Group) deserved credit for being "change

makers", attacking arbitrarily set "administrative" deductions by collecting societies and forcing more businesslike behaviour. He and others believe that continuing rolling improvement in society practices and in their attitude to fairer treatment of copyright owners can still be traced directly to the U2 case. In fact, inter-society relationships were never to resume their appearance of glasslike stillness again, and over a decade later many of the developed world's current generation of collecting society executives, and possibly also most Board members, would probably agree that this is no bad thing.

Executive Director, Membership John Sweeney, with full support and active input from Hutchinson, overhauled PRS attitudes, communications and rules on cost deductions: these started to reflect the actual cost of particular kinds of licensing and distribution (broadcasting costing by far the least and general public performance the most). PRS specialist managers worked increasingly closely with bands and their management to speed up and maximise their tour income. In a bold but successful move, PRS capped its administration charges for live tours and allowed bands to opt to administer their own tours while offering a PRS service in that area which deliberately competed on cost and efficiency with any arrangements the band might make for itself. As a result, the opt-out was very rarely pursued.

Change, greater transparency, greater efficiency and business pragmatism in collecting societies had all been inevitable, but the growing need for them had been largely ignored. In recognising such hitherto alien concepts as market forces, customer power and the fact that they were actually part of a global network of financial services organisations, societies have undoubtedly moved forward, as most would agree. More detailed debates about how much, how far and in what direction change should continue, about who should lead and who should follow, what the advantages and costs might be, and about how much of the baby has been thrown out with the opaque bathwater, can and will legitimately continue, of course.

Freegard frankly assessed his position at the time as being "insufficiently aware of the need to tackle reform in the European societies". In another example of the way that change – though linear in the long term – tends to go through generation cycles, John Hutchinson would early in his tenure demonstrate a totally contrasting attitude. European societies were an early target for him, and with no personal history of involvement in this business he was free to take a comparatively aggressive and uncompromising stance on PRS' behalf. The issue which crystallised the feelings of frustration and demand for change among PRS members, led by their elected representatives on the Council, was that of "social and cultural deductions". Briefly, this was a well-established practice, written into the CISAC standard reciprocal agreement between societies, whereby societies were permitted to hold back a certain percentage of the royalties they were due to pay to a sister society and apply the funds to social and cultural activities largely assisting their own national membership. The basis of the deduction being a percentage, this inevitably meant that the societies whose members' works earned the most internationally suffered far greater deductions in money terms than the societies whose members' works received few if any performances outside their own country. And the long-term global commercial supremacy of UK (and US) popular repertoire inevitably meant that far more was deducted from royalties due to PRS from its sister societies than PRS could possibly reciprocally deduct from outgoing royalties.

Freegard's firm view on the issue of social and cultural deductions by CISAC societies as changed little. "I thought they were rather a good idea, and believe that opposition to them stems from lack of understanding that licence tariffs in Europe were, because of their societies' cultural stance, established at much higher rates than in Britain. Affiliated societies in Europe resented sending so much money to the UK, which had the dominant repertoire in the growing pop music market, while getting so little back". During a Tribunal on dance hall tariffs in the 50s, an executive of the Italian society (called as a PRS witness) was told the UK tariff for a particular type of music usage and assumed it was a weekly charge; it was in fact the *annual* fee.

The social and cultural deductions smoothed out some of this difference and, Freegard is convinced, avoided a sustained attack on the level of PRS tariffs from European societies. While the reciprocal deductions which PRS could and did make were not full compensation for money withheld by affiliated societies they were not insignificant (a fact which Freegard thinks became lost to view among UK members as the argument gained pace and heat during the 90s). The way reciprocal deductions worked was also important and also little understood. For one thing, they had been initiated between ASCAP and PRS in order to balance the discrepancy between the huge overseas performing right earnings of American writers and the much smaller earning from UK copyrights. As such they had worked in PRS' favour.

A complementary example might have been a 9.5% deduction by SACEM from what it was due to remit to PRS in a year. PRS would make a 9.5% deduction on what it was due to remit to SACEM. In recognition of the fact that about 1% of PRS revenue was being devoted to Donations and Awards and the PRS Members Fund ("social and cultural" activity, it was thought),1% of the deduction would be retained and 8.5% added to the amount of incoming SACEM payments, which were then distributed to members. In terms of monetary value this, of course, worked in favour of the French society because PRS copyrights earned far more in France that SACEM copyrights earned in the UK.

Former PRS Chairman Wayne Bickerton, who for two periods between January 1994 and November 1995 acted as Chief Executive after Freegard's departure, strongly takes issue on these points. He asserts that as a Director he had consistently disagreed with the CEO's view that social and cultural deductions by overseas societies had some balanced and potentially beneficial place in the overall working of the essential international society network. He shared the objections of many of his peers that the dominance of Anglo-American repertoire in music performance globally meant that the deductions from PRS overseas revenue were disproportionately and unjustifiably high, and that the provisions of the standard CISAC reciprocal agreement of the time, which enabled these deductions to be made, needed to be addressed and changed. Additionally his view was that dissatisfaction with these deductions had been amply signalled by Board members, including himself. After taking the Chair this issue was one of his priorities. One initiative he led was to set up a grouping of societies administering the market-dominant repertoire (PRS in the UK, ASCAP, BMI, SESAC and SOCAN in North America, and APRA in Australia).He explained: "To further pressurise the overseas societies, I instigated the formation of AARS [Anglo-American Repertoire Societies]. For the first time CISAC societies had to deal with a body representing the combined interests of Anglo-American writers and publishers. This clearly put the issue on the agenda for CISAC and much heated debate took place during my term of office." The AARS grouping was relatively short-lived, having as Bickerton asserts, firmly and formally put the issue on the European societies' agenda.

CISAC social and cultural deductions were in the forefront for some time, but the change in attitudes, expectation and demands from sections and vocal individuals among PRS members developed across a broad front over several years and touched on costs as well as income, on distributions, information and other aspects of administration. Recalling the growing voice of discontent from members at that time, Freegard lists their main points and adds his own thoughts. UK writers and publishers saw deductions of all kinds as "members' money being taken": Freegard's standpoint was and is that the revenue collected by PRS "was not anyone's money until it was distributed".

Publishers initially and the "more worldly and politicised composers" saw PRS as an agency collecting money on behalf of its members: Freegard felt and still feels strongly that PRS' work was "a collective effort to create a pool of income to distribute to members".

A measure of the change in attitudes over the past 15 years is the fact that such statements today would be the basis for heated debate in many European and North American societies and would be subject to outright rejection by some. Yet Freegard's position (it could be termed a philosophy) was a very widely held and traditional collecting society view of the purpose and nature of their organisations and activities, and it was seemingly

accepted by most members of most societies up to the mid and late 90s.

"The ideal is for the individual creator to license his copyrights directly," Freegard asserts, "where that is possible and where the creator is not subject to monopolistic users. But where collective management is best, it should be collective. Distributions should be made to individuals in relation to good and sensible rules, but I believe it is a mistake to trace every payment directly to an income source." In line with this philosophy, Freegard continues today to favour practices such as weighting the value of classical performances, and smoothing out the drop in writers' earnings as their music goes out of usage (and they grow older) through

Pictured at the Guildhall School of Music and Drama for the presentation of the 1989 Vivian Ellis Awards are (*front row, fourth left to right*) current MCPS Chairman Jonathan Simon, Vivian Ellis, lyricist Don Black, singer Petula Clark, lyricist Tim Rice and theatre critic Sheridan Morley

the old PRS earnings equalisation scheme and the unlogged performance allocation.

Since leaving PRS Freegard has seen this philosophy publicly re-examined and debated, both in the MMC Report published in1996 and in PRS AGMs and membership publications, and replaced by a business-orientated approach.

Without suggesting that these two approaches are anything other than equal while different, he holds that the "rough justice" of the collective/cultural philosophy worked in the particular context of rights societies, concluding: "I remain entirely in favour of the cultural approach". He reminds himself that towards the end of his tenure he did, however, see the cultural change which was coming, but did not appreciate its extent, nor the speed with which it would arrive, admitting "it rather crept up on me".

His model as Chief Executive was Leslie Boosey, whose leadership of PRS had been characterised by moderation (some would say reticence) towards music users, and great concern for culture, but that leadership had avoided many unnecessary battles and helped to win some significantly necessary ones.

Culture change within PRS

Apart from cultural issues at CISAC and society level, it is worth touching on the culture within PRS; this changed significantly in the decade since Freegard left the society (some would say changed beyond all recognition and, depending on who was speaking, that would be a cause for regret or for self-congratulation). Prior to the change, in the view of the man who led the society then and for so many years before, the PRS management was probably seen as "a bit stuck up, a bit apart" by the members and by other organisations such as the guilds (BASCA, the APC, and the CGGB)[11], MPA, MCPS and, to an even greater extent, the record industry bodies such as BPI and PPL. "That was probably my fault,"admits Freegard. "I don't naturally gravitate towards the pop world ethos, so I did not socialise much in a predominantly pop-oriented music industry, which meant that PRS was somehow felt not to be joining in. I saw PRS as an essential tool for the music business but, yes, a bit apart."

During Freegard's tenure another change which had cultural and management elements took place, as recalled by the man responsible for it. The role of the PRS Chairman underwent significant development in the early 80s. This can be attributed to the efforts of songwriter Roger Greenaway. In the second half of 1981 he was approached by Richard Toeman (the then Chairman) to follow him as the next Chairman of PRS. Greenaway was flattered but hesitant. "I felt I was not up to the job and since I was still at that time, a very busy writer and producer I really didn't have the time". Greenaway's supporters on the Board persisted and promised to help him. After much thought he offered to stand for the Chairmanship from January. Toeman accepted and chaired for a fourth year until Greenaway succeeded him.

Before starting he had a couple of significant visits. One was from well-known composer and Board member Steve Race; the other was from Greenaway's own publisher and old friend Dick James.

---

11 British Academy of Songwriters, Composers and Authors, the Association of Professional Composers and the Composers' Guild of Great Britain. The membership of these organisations inevitably greatly overlapped with that of PRS, but collectively was much smaller while including (particularly in the case of BASCA) many aspiring or barely-active writers who were not eligible for PRS membership. All three had close connections with PRS, including funding assistance. In 1999 they merged and relaunched as the British Academy of Composers and Songwriters (BACS) which is generally abbreviated to "the Academy", and became fully financially independent while maintaining very strong links with PRS and indeed having its headquarters within the Berners Street offices of the MCPS-PRS Alliance.

Both offered good advice and asked the new Chairman to consider looking at certain aspects of PRS business that bothered them. "At that time there was no Chairman's office at PRS and apart from Board or Committee meeting days (meetings would go all day then) the Chairman seldom visited PRS, mainly because with the exception of Paddy Roberts, a composer who took the chair back in the 50s and who lasted only a year, all Chairmen had been publishers. There was a strong resentment among the publishers and one or two writers on the Board because they felt that, although they seemed to discuss and debate matters interminably, at the end of the day they were there to rubber stamp what the top managers wanted."

To break down that perception, or reality, Greenaway set up a Chairman's office; he ensured that he was at PRS throughout every Monday, all day on meeting and committee days and randomly as and when he felt it necessary. He also pushed for changes in management practices and flow of information to the Board. The CEO of Boosey & Hawkes at the time, Tony Fell, asked the new Chairman to see to it that in future the Board could see the annual budgets and projections before they were finalised. Greenaway persuaded Michael Freegard to change the long-held view that budgets were not necessary as the business costs were 80% labour-related. A financial controller was recruited (and PRS also took on one of the much-liked but initially unsuccessful candidates for the role, John Axon – who over 20 years later is Executive Director for PRS within the Alliance). From then on the Board took part in the budgetary process.

Greenaway recalled: "In order to try to improve relations between the Board and managers I set about learning the business. I decided the best way would be to 'walk the floors' and to interview in camera as many of the workers and middle managers that I could. Without losing or compromising any trust put in me by the staff I managed to get a handle on the general way PRS ticked. Slowly but surely I was able to convince senior managers that I had no intention of micro-managing business and that I really was

genuine about trying to improve the relationships they had with the Board. I believe I succeeded up to a certain extent. Tensions between Board and management seemed a lot less frequent as time went by. Because of this there was certainly a more friendly, almost convivial, atmosphere between writer and publisher Board members. The one seemed to improve with the other".

Greenaway also had to play a diplomatic part in fulfilling the Board's wish to replace Denis de Freitas, and then dealing with adverse Board reaction to de Freitas' appointment to run Music Copyright Overseas Services (MCOS) which Freegard set up to deal with PRS royalty agencies abroad; and eventually bringing Robert Abrahams into PRS as Director of External Affairs, with a legal and international relations role.

During the third year of Greenaway's tenure it was decided that Ron White, CEO of EMI Music Publishing Ltd would succeed him. Sadly in 1985 White fell victim to cancer. Greenaway agreed to be Chairman for an additional year pending White's recovery, but although the latter took over in 1987 he died halfway through his chairmanship, a real loss to the industry and to PRS.

Greenaway reflected: "If I had to stake a claim to any achievement during my Chairmanship it would have to be the setting up of the Chairman's office and convincing the Board to treat the office of Chairman as equally important to that of the Chief Executive, and properly to compensate the position financially".

Greenaway's efforts can be described as having brought about one change in the society's culture. Later, alongside his extensive restructuring of management and business practice, John Hutchinson's most pervasive change at PRS would also be to its culture. As an earlier CEO who had sustained a very different corporate style and thinking, Freegard's view is that this subsequent culture change has been largely to the good, including the distinctly more commercial and business-minded approach of

Roger Greenaway

PRS as a society, and certainly the MCPS-PRS Alliance as an operating company. One result has certainly been that things have greatly improved for successful writers and publishers, though Freegard feels that they have become worse for the relatively unsuccessful. Objectively evaluating change since his departure, and seeing it as broadly positive as well as inevitable, presented Freegard with no difficulty; dealing with, even having to initiate, such far reaching change himself would, he frankly admitted, have been asking too much at the time. Indeed the PROMS[12] failure which led to his resignation "was in a way something of a relief".

So a relatively short time after taking the PRS Chair at the beginning of 1993, Wayne Bickerton was placed by his Board in the position of acting Chief Executive. It was to prove a tremendously demanding period for him, for the Board and for the Society's management. Bickerton comments: "I was told on more than one occasion that I had been handed a poisoned chalice. Having just been subjected to a major robbery at home I did not think anything could produce more stress – I was wrong." Bickerton's absolute priorities, recognised then and recalled now, were "to deal with the loss of confidence both internally and externally, and to restore an effective working relationship between the PRS Board and the management – and to allow the management to manage on a daily basis". His stress on the last issue reflected the already-mentioned very serious disturbance in trust between elected Directors and managers; this had led to a determination in the minds of some Board members to "run" the company at a level which was not really possible, desirable or

proper in governance terms for a Board to attempt. Addressing that conflict was a prime task for the Chairman/Acting CEO. "PROMS took the lid off PRS and everything was then open to question," Bickerton explained. "I wanted a new PRS, one that could deal with the requirements of the membership in a proactive way. This was why I called for a corporate governance review, and with Professor Tom Clarke's help we eventually accomplished that big, positive change and succeeded in modernising the Board structure. I also felt that the pop industry's view of PRS being an ivory tower with little or no communication with membership was a matter of concern. That view was endorsed when I invited major publishers to lunch to discover it was their first visit. With the help of Terri Anderson [Communications Director] I arranged regular industry lunches, and created a more effective dialogue with the BPI, PPL and the broadcasters."

Another task arising directly from the PROMS cancellation was recovering some of its cost. Led by Bickerton and the legal team the society drove determinedly towards action against the project consultants LBMS, and successfully reached an agreement which saw a substantial proportion of the consultancy fees repaid to PRS over an agreed three-year period. A concurrent task for Bickerton and the IS division was to replan the future of the society's IT while keeping the existing computer hardware and software working as efficiently as possible.

Both writers and publishers on the Board had, as mentioned above, already been expressing increasing dissatisfaction with income flow and deductions by affiliated societies. This issue was another which Bickerton believed had to be tackled firmly, even aggressively. "Modernising and improving PRS reciprocal agreements, including tackling the issue of social and cultural deductions was essential", he recalled. "The problems with U2 also served to highlight the old-fashioned and unfair manner in which collecting societies dealt with the administration of live performances. Much did change. For example, I was delighted

---

12 Performing Right Online Management System – the bold "quantum leap" in IT to computerise and integrate many aspects of PRS operations. System design and quality of data proved too poor for the project to succeed and it was abandoned. See PROMS account in this chapter

that I eventually succeeded in getting JASRAC to pay royalties for the performance of foreign repertoire in Japan at the same rate as that for performance of Japanese repertoire". This was one example of a beneficial result from the increased level of "technical visits" to affiliated societies to review and discuss issues affecting UK income and how this was affected by local distribution rules and other factors. A broad review of international relations and reciprocal agreements was also set up, in the reasonable belief that PRS members' income could only benefit from these issues being widely examined and acted upon.

Domestically he became an early Board-level champion of change in the way PRS approached public performance licensing, strongly supporting the proposals of Clive Thomas (*see Licensing and Distribution section*) to move towards a marketing and selling approach as opposed to the traditional approach of copyright law enforcement – summed up by Bickerton as "the approach of a business trying to maximise its revenue rather than a collecting society going through the motions of licensing".

Reflecting on his schedule of competing priorities at the time Bickerton admitted: "The list at times seemed endless – PROMS, corporate governance, U2, the issue of IMRO[13], the MMC Enquiry, distribution systems, then ServiceCo[14] and more. I reached a point where I was filled with dread whenever I got a call from Brian Wilkinson [Company Secretary] or Nick Lowe [Director of Legal Affairs] to say he wanted to see me about something important which had just come up."

To this (incomplete, it needs to be noted) list, he added: "I was disappointed by the attitude of many figures in our own industry at the time – an attitude actually stated by one publisher who was prominent in the industry organisations as 'let's kick PRS while it's down' – a big disappointment, from people who really should have known better.".

Bickerton's term as Chairman in fact included two periods as Acting Chief Executive. Edward McLean joined PRS as Chief Executive for five months in 1994, and on his departure the Chairman again took on the CEO role.

On a deservedly much more positive note, almost a decade later when asked to state his achievements in that difficult time, Bickerton mused: "Perhaps other people are better judges, but I believe corporate governance, international improvements and, perhaps above all, helping to facilitate a better working relationship between the Board and management were my achievements. It should not be forgotten that despite all the issues that were dealt with at this time PRS managed to reduce its administration costs to 15% and increase its revenue by 20% – that is, £30m. Under the circumstances that was a significant achievement by my team. I think I helped to create a more open PRS in its own eyes and that of others. And we had dealt with almost all the important issues raised in the MMC Enquiry before I completed my term."

Inevitably, several of the crucial issues, problems and initiatives which were at the head of Freegard's agenda when he left, or were added in the interregnum of Chairman Wayne Bickerton, were still at the head of the business agenda taken up by John Hutchinson was he took up the Chief Executive role.

A new Chief Executive, and even bigger change

PRS announced the appointment of John Hutchinson as its new Chief Executive on 19 September 1995. A Fellow of the Chartered Institute of Bankers and a Companion of the Institute of Management, at 51 he brought the experience of a career in banking and financial services. That career had begun with a long initial association with Lloyds Bank in various senior management

---

13 The PRS licensing arm in the Republic of Ireland had gained an identity as the Irish Music Rights Organisation, in 1988. In the early 90s the major issue of its becoming a separate and independent society was under protracted and at times difficult discussion – although this eventually led to a successful conclusion in terms of ordered separation of the new national society from its UK parent.

14 The proposed jointly-owned service company for PRS and MCPS business. *See Alliance chapter*

posts, progressed through positions on the Main Board of the Nationwide Building Society, and taken him to the role of MD of VISA UK with responsibility for card and retail payments systems and public relations.

While a collecting society can be described essentially as a financial service, the move for Hutchinson was into a business he knew nothing about and, as he was to discover, into a company which tended to think of itself as a society first and a business second.

With a thoroughness which was soon widely recognised as a Hutchinson characteristic whenever he needed to accumulate knowledge in order to formulate for himself a strategic move, he used his experience in merger and takeover business to assess and assimilate the company he was considering heading. He remembers: "The 1994-95 *PRS Yearbook* told me a lot. On the cover I saw my favourite album artist, Annie Lennox, and my favourite pop composer of the time, Freddie Mercury, which was exciting. That was backed up by a lot of information inside which told me the organisation was one which was financially viable and strong, but had a lot of old ideas and practices hanging around its neck." The 1995-96 *Yearbook* came out just before he arrived at PRS, and confirmed both opinions. It strengthened his view that the cost to income ratio was high, and other ratios were poor and needed tackling (eight years later he was willing to make the point that one of them, the level of debt in Public Performance licensing, has had to work through to the front of many pressing priorities, and was only in 2003 being tackled aggressively and sustainably, after years of merely being controlled).

When he started work at PRS Hutchinson was pleased to find that his first impressions about the likely "stuffiness" of management (largely from the then still persisting practice of printing a page full of stiffly formal photographs of managers in each Yearbook) were largely dispelled on meeting the small senior management team which had been working tirelessly to achieve forward motion

The first *PRS Yearbook* to feature pictures of artists who are also writer members of the society on its cover was also the first PRS Yearbook seen by John Hutchinson when he was preparing to join the company as Chief Executive in 1995.

in the difficult period since the resignation of Michael Freegard. "I was pleased and surprised to find that these few people really were a team, trusting each other and working together – even though it was obvious that they were rather tired and stressed."

A lot of loose ends dangled outside the attractively presented but firmly controlled coverage of events in the *Yearbooks* he had seen. He had noted that a previous computer "disaster" of some kind had clearly happened, but no one was dwelling on it in those particular annual reports; some sort of joint operation called ServiceCo had moved off the buffers but apparently run out of steam; the PRS operation in the Irish Republic was separating itself, with hints of some difficulties and discord which were again not expanded on; changes in management had made the page of "mugshots" he had first seen outdated by the time he arrived at PRS; a CEO whose tenure had been very short was given no more than a passing reference; membership dissatisfaction and the pending outcome of that via an MMC enquiry remained unresolved. His researches intrigued, informed and encouraged him: "PRS was a service company in which I believed I could use my core competencies to good effect, but I asked a lot of questions in interviews for the job". He still has the Visitor lapel tag from his attendance at Berners Street for his final successful interview on 8 August 1995 (a significant date for the additional reason that it was his birthday). He took up his new role on 6 November.

The issue of possible closer co-operation between MCPS and PRS was already in his mind. He had for unconnected reasons recently been talking to broadcasters, and had heard some well-rounded opinions about collecting societies – PRS, MCPS and PPL. His self-questioning then about the multiplicity of organisations doing seemingly similar, even overlapping, jobs, and his access on arrival at PRS to reports about the ServiceCo initiative strengthened quite early into a belief that these organisations ought to work together. Exploratory talks with PPL about possible co-working had already taken place (and almost a decade later in 2003 were taking place again). "It seemed to me absolutely barking mad that this collaboration should not happen," was the characteristically rapid and trenchant Hutchinson verdict.

From the outset, Hutchinson applied a policy of working with the experienced and knowledgeable senior management he had inherited, rather than parachuting in new troops. Evidence of this is the fact that he only ever brought two new people into the company at director level: Pablo Lloyd as Finance Director in 1996 and (after Lloyd moved on to the University for Industry) his successor Steve Porter in 1998, who in later restructure and consolidation of the MCPS-PRS Alliance top management became Chief Operating Officer.

John Hutchinson's first Chief Executive's Committee in 1996. Pictured (*standing left to right*) are Secretary and legal Counsel David Uwemedimo (now the CISAC Regional Director for Africa); Internal Auditor John Standish; IS Director and now Chief Information Officer for the Alliance, John Rathbone; Director of General Performance Licensing and now Executive Director PRS, John Axon; Financial Controller Tony Ghilchick; Director of Membership John Sweeney; Director of Broadcast Licensing Nicholas Lowe; with (*seated left to right*) International Councel and later Director General of British Music Rights, Frances Lowe; Director of Planning and Corporate Communications Terri Anderson; John Hutchinson; Director of International and now consultant on agency territories, Diana Derrick; Director of Human Resources, Karen Robertson.

Hutchinson's high priorities on arrival in late 1995 were putting a strategic business planning process in place, revitalising IT progress, keeping the momentum in income growth, improving member relations, and internally raising morale and improving communications. Within the "rather tired and stressed" senior team he found in place, all those priorities had an existing manager except for business planning. Following his use-what's-available policy, he added to corporate communications Terri Anderson's role the responsibility for getting a strategic planning process under way. Through the first draft three-year plan Hutchinson and his team were able to bring an objective of creating business sector and international alliances to the attention of the PRS General Council as it was then called. The soon-agreed change of the General Council's title to that of Board (and the refocusing on Companies Act requirements which went with that) was another very early indication of how Hutchinson saw his role and that of the organisation he was now running. These changes acknowledged the primacy of the fact that PRS was a business, and a sizeable business at that.

It is interesting to note when looking at the business plans produced for PRS in 1996 and 1997, and for the Alliance since then, that the themes, priorities, broad strategies and tactics which were thought through and recorded in the first formal PRS three-year business plan are there in the five-year Alliance Plan set out in 2002.

"So from the beginning we knew what we had to do, but we had a few alligators to clear out of the swamp," Hutchinson summed up. The alligators included two Copyright Tribunal referrals from BSkyB and British Airways; the dispute with the extremely prominent PRS members and international music supergroup U2; the MMC Report, which was confidently expected to recommend major operational and governance change and improvement; getting compensation for the PROMS problems; and improving member communication (which John Sweeney as the relevant senior manager had already started to implement). Hutchinson listed these and other issues with easy recall eight years later by way of illustrating the "interesting times" at PRS into which he had found himself pitchforked.

He was acutely aware that he was "very much alone". Every previous new role in his career had been eased by his familiarity with the business he was in and the people in it, giving him some kind of continuity underlying the newness. This was not the case with PRS. In 1995, from President, Chairman and Board directors, through layers of complex workaday detail and the many variously located managers and staff who dealt with them, to a membership with two very different (writer and publisher)

faces, Hutchinson had to start at a run down an unmapped new career path. One tactic he used for dealing with that was to "be my own team till I got my own team around me". Part of that was to do nothing to soften the impact of his management style, which was unfamiliar to the organisation. He reasoned that various aspects of his professional skills would be duplicated in those who would be his direct senior reports, and therefore the unique aspect of his role must be to deliver "galvanising" leadership. "So I decided I was going to lead. I had wanted to be a CEO for some time and I had the opportunity to be that in the fullest sense. My diagnosis was that PRS did not need micromanaging by me, but it needed vision, some icons, and impetus. Of course there is a lot of luck in business management, and I had some".

Part of that luck, after an arduous first three months in the job in which he "had so many streams of activity going that I hardly could be aware of them all in detail", was the publication of the MMC Report in February 1996. It not only pointed in the direction Hutchinson wanted PRS to go, it validated the work which had already begun. The MMC Report undoubtedly helped the Chief Executive to insist on tough decisions being made by the Board. In all this, Hutchinson was strongly supported by his new Chairman. Andrew Potter succeeded Wayne Bickerton as Chairman in January 1996 and the warm, constructive and mutually respectful working partnership which the two, Chief Executive and Chairman, established contributed enormously to the steady advance of change in PRS and very soon to the establishment of the MCPS-PRS Alliance. Hutchinson greatly appreciated the value of that relationship during Potter's two consecutive terms in the Chair through six enormously eventful years. In 2003, with corporate life no less lively and demanding than it had always been, he also paid great tribute to the contribution of the other two Chairmen who have worked with him. Jonathan Simon as MCPS Chairman and as a PRS Board Director, and composer David Bedford who succeeded Potter as PRS Chairman from January 2002 after serving as his deputy; both continued the good working relationship needed to make progress.

Personalities at all levels inevitably made an impression on the new, but fast taking command, Chief Executive. One was the then President of PRS, the composer Vivian Ellis. A celebrated writer and musician, he was also a vital but very elderly man of strong character and waspish sense of humour. He had a sense of the ridiculous and the banal: he was famous, or possibly notorious, by then for a habit of delivering during proceedings frequent cuttingly witty asides, uttered in a deceptively soft tone which could actually be heard at whatever distance he chose. It was not long after becoming PRS Chief Executive that Hutchinson was able to demonstrate his soon-acquired affection for Vivian Ellis (occasionally tinged with exasperation, as was everyone's) by organising a 91st birthday party for the President in the PRS Boardroom. To the surprise and pleasure of all present Ellis went to the piano, announcing that it would probably be the last time he would perform, and sang several of his own songs. He finished with *This Is My Lovely Day* and it is quite possible that he was aware of the hint of prophecy in the lyrics of that song since shortly afterwards Vivian Ellis died peacefully. He was the last President of the society. No one has been appointed to that position since.

For all Hutchinson's ability to be ruthless in driving through major change in ideas, plans, Board and management structures, international relationships and ways of working, he asserts his belief that every organisation should have a solid sense of its own history. He has acknowledged and appreciated Michael Freegard's important role in shaping the history of PRS for over 30 years and managing it through to hugely improved income levels in that time. That the new Chief Executive invited and warmly welcomed his long-serving predecessor to social events involving PRS management was reassuring to people who were very aware

of the antagonisms which the PROMS failure had aroused at Board level.

Hutchinson's arrival at PRS launched, or coincided with (as always, both are probably partly true) a shift in gear and increase in speed which meant that milestones were passed at a much greater rate than ever before. His own list of these milestones starts with the MMC Report. This he immediately recognised as a gift, the first pages of the map book he had arrived without. He was able to begin using that map, taking the Board and management with him. The MMC Report was, as attested by many, a valuable turning point for PRS. Hutchinson's close ally in using the recommendations as a basis for positive change at Board level was Chairman Andrew Potter. Woven through the Report's recommendations were as many implicit invitations to the Board Directors to take a more active, but properly defined, role as there were proposals for action from management. The PRS Board, as it digested the content of the report with the encouragement of their Chairman and Chief Executive rose to the challenge of being a more engaged, strategic-thinking body, and in turn were served by a new-style management which offered a framework for Board and managers to work together on strategic planning. Better regular reporting on company and management performance was instigated, replacing what many directors felt was a stream of poorly connected "over-information" with shorter, clearer and more targeted information which could be – and was – frequently adjusted to suit the real needs of a Board charged with controlling and as appropriate directing the company rather than attempting to run parts of it on a day-to-day basis. An increasingly confident PRS Board was also able to turn its attention more constructively to a generally-agreed new priority – communication with the membership. The Chairman and Deputies became unfailing attendees at a series of regular regional members meetings, always supported by several other Directors, predominantly writers but also publishers. In Potter's recollection (and that of everyone involved) the Board began to enjoy a far better sense of co-operation and equal working, tackling real issues more effectively than ever before and making increasingly effective use of the variety of knowledge, talent and experience among its elected directors. That variety was maintained through numbers: after careful consideration of the MMC Recommendations on Board size (*see MMC Enquiry Appendix*) the Board decided not to decrease the number of directors.

Next came a milestone acknowledged by Hutchinson as the biggest on the route: the opportunity to create an alliance with MCPS. Different views persist on whether its arrival only months into the reshaping and replanning of PRS was good timing, but the chance arrived when it did and had to be seized then.

At a joint planning meeting for Board Directors and managers in May 1996, the possibility of trying again to collaborate closely with MCPS was raised openly (by PRS Board Director and MCPS Chairman Jonathan Simon) for the first time since the demise of the ServiceCo idea. The following month the MCPS CEO Frans de Wit left the company. Hutchinson and his PRS senior management team decided quickly that they should push a door which was suddenly ajar. What they did not realise was that the door was wide open, and MCPS Board and managers were broadly as keen to walk through it as the PRS side was.

The account of what then ensued is given later in the Alliance chapter, but asked for his personal speculation on the timing of the alliance opportunity, and whether there had really been any real danger that it might again fail to proceed, Hutchinson recalled: "Already by June or July 1996 there were [MCPS] people who were saying 'but he's PRS…PRS is different…can a PRS person manage two very different businesses?' So it is possible that had this opportunity come after I had been with PRS for longer, things would not have gone ahead in the way they did."

1996 ran past a number of other milestones for PRS. One was the resolution of the dispute with supergroup U2 (the early stages of which had been during Wayne Bickerton's term as Acting CEO)

without the long-threatened High Court battle. Better still, close co-operation was established with the group over the way the licensing of their then forthcoming European concerts would be handled at the PRS end. The conflict with U2, in some ways, became a signpost to one of the major parallel paths of policy which Hutchinson would follow. It possibly prompted Hutchinson's thinking on some key matters from the outset, as he absorbed information at an astonishing rate about a business sector of which he had no previous practical experience, but in which he was soon to be acknowledged as an innovative (if occasionally wayward) thinker and change maker. For him U2 were important people who needed to be negotiated with; on another level they were a lighthouse beam illuminating business practices in the collecting society world which were a puzzling affront to his trained commercial financial services mind. As mentioned earlier, like other top pop groups U2 undertook regular international tours, performing to many thousands of fans in large stadia all over Europe and other parts of the world. The performing right payments for each tour could total hundreds of thousands of pounds but in some cases the group had to wait up to two years to receive their foreign royalties and the administration costs were often exceptionally high.

The U2 case was highlighted in the MMC investigation, which had yet to report when Hutchinson took office. As a result of that report, Hutchinson and the PRS Board committed themselves to what can, without exaggeration, be called an internal revolution. Hutchinson had persuaded elected directors to alter the name of the PRS General Council to that of Board and this was one of the series of steps which changed the structure, ideas, ethos, terminology and behaviour. These internal changes very soon fed into international relations. And it all proved to be the beginning of a continual rolling process of change and development led by the current Chief Executive.

Driven by the U2 case PRS pledged itself to persuade its European colleagues to reduce their administration fee for large-scale pop concerts to a maximum of 15%. At this time the most influential figure in the world of European authors' societies was Jean Loup Tournier, head of the French society SACEM and later President of CISAC. PRS decided that if Tournier and SACEM agreed to the 15%, it would be easier to get other European

societies to follow suit. Accordingly Hutchinson and International Director Diana Derrick negotiated with him first. When Tournier agreed, a whirlwind series of visits to other European capitals followed. Many, but not all, societies were persuaded to modify their rules.

Another immediate and inherited problem for Hutchinson when he first arrived had been dealing with the proceedings and then the decisions of what he has described as "a runaway Copyright Tribunal" – the BSkyB tribunal in which the proposed new PRS licensing deal was in all key aspects rejected.[15]

The other PRS milestones in that year related directly or indirectly to the MMC Report, and comprised a series of changes and developments which affected every level of the society's activity from Board to departmental. Of those which affected the membership most directly and obviously one which caused controversy was the ending of all awards and distributions of revenue which could be described as "subsidies" of one part of the membership by the others. And of those, the greatest pain and dispute was caused by the termination of the classical music subsidy. Even after prolonged explanation and consultation the strength of feeling about this move was such that prominent members of the classical music fraternity sought and achieved a Parliamentary scrutiny of the PRS action. Hutchinson believes that the House of Commons Select Committee hearings, which vindicated the PRS position, were a notable turning point in confidence at PRS Board level. The Board, he believed, had been genuinely nervous about following through their justified but unpopular decision, even though it had been communicated and implemented in every way in accordance with the spirit of the MMC Report. A very public examination of what had been done and why had given full support to the CEO and Board, and this had a noticeably positive effect on PRS confidence in policy-making and firm action from then on.

PRS member, Ray Davies

15 see PRS Licensing and Distribution section

The Select Committee decision also indirectly drove forward the setting-up of The Performing Right Society Foundation because although it was and is a source of funding and encouragement for all genres of music, it was in some part intended to give financial encouragement to classical composition and performance in general by some means other than subsidising the royalties of individuals. The creation of, and almost immediate recognition and approval of, the Foundation represent for Hutchinson an important, entirely beneficial development. Not only did it see PRS "grow up" in the way it handled its voluntary obligation to promoting musical creativity and diversity in Britain, it also dealt in a fair and statesmanlike way with the issue of "supporting culture". Although, supported by his Board, Hutchinson had roundly criticised the way that affiliated societies in Continental Europe operated social and cultural deductions, he had some respect for what many of them were trying to do in terms of encouraging cultural activity. The Foundation, incidentally (but from Hutchinson's point of view not accidentally), allowed PRS to step onto even higher moral ground. By taking a superbly well-organised and imaginative approach to cultural subsidy, using funds allocated from UK distributable revenue only and not deducted from what was due to other societies, PRS stood by its principles and strengthened its position on this issue.

Internally, in the first year of Hutchinson's tenure, an important requirement for management was something which he has referred to as a vision, or icon: a means of inspiration and empowerment rather than a marker of a specific time or event. His senior management knew they needed to achieve a great deal, but felt hamstrung by apparently conflicting objectives. They were to do spectacularly more and better but they were also to deliver significant cost savings, and their perception was that they had to do both at the same time.

Hutchinson set up a "tablet of stone". He told his top team that he knew that in the short term costs had to rise, but the medium and long-term objectives could not be compromised. So the tablet read "Thou shalt make all the graphs go in the right direction". The cost to income ratio was the key; income had to rise in order for costs to rise, and if that was achieved management could rightly claim successes which would lead to greater trust and freedom to act coming from the Board. The PRS approach of aligning cost/income ratio to "member value" (income and all other benefits), in a matrix for optimum performance as a service organisation, may in 2003 seem the obvious and only one for any collecting society. Before the mid-90s there seemed nothing obvious about it to many societies, and the change in thinking and expression appeared to remain peculiar to the UK for some time. So, when in September 1998, Hutchinson attended a General Assembly of the French society SACEM, he enjoyed some private pride in seeing its mission stated as being "to get the maximum collections at the lowest cost and to distribute them as speedily and accurately as possible with the lowest possible deductions", wording very close to that he had used to PRS Board and management in early 1997 and to many different audiences.

Unequivocally another milestone for Hutchinson as PRS Chief Executive was achieving a 13.9% administration cost to income ratio in the years 1997 and 1998. It was the lowest achieved for many years before and all years since. Hutchinson and his team knew they had over-achieved, and that substantial necessary investment was in the wings. In fact it was the Alliance which made this PRS extra low cost year possible, because without the Alliance it would have been necessary to invest heavily in new systems earlier.

Under Hutchinson the international strategy of PRS was certainly to be more robust and at times confrontational if that was thought necessary. By late 1995 it was already focused on two priorities: a replacement bilateral contract (CISAC reciprocal ageement) to be offered by the society to its foreign partners, and regular and rigorous technical visits to foreign societies.

The existing bilateral contracts were based on a CISAC-approved model that detailed minimum conditions for the transfer of monies between national societies. The new PRS contract included a clause that payments to PRS members would be exempt from the 10% deduction, that administration costs would be capped and that PRS would have a right to audit the accounts of other societies. The attempt to replace the old CISAC-style contract had mixed results in the 1990s. Generally, the new societies emerging in eastern Europe and in the Far East, eager to represent the PRS repertoire, were willing to sign. Often, the initial contacts were made at CISAC Congresses. At Washington in 1994, the PRS International Director was approached by officials from the newly- formed Chinese authors' society. This was followed by a visit to China by PRS Chairman Wayne Bickerton, where he signed one of the first bilateral agreements between the Music Copyright Society of China (MCSC) and a western society. A similar process took place with the Cuban society (ACDAM). In contrast, in western Europe but also in Africa, there was considerable resistance to the new PRS contract. The main sticking-point was the reluctance to give up the 10% social and cultural deduction from royalties due to PRS members (*dealt with in more detail earlier in this PRS chapter*). Nevertheless, the more aggressive attitude of PRS, led by an assertive Chief Executive who had never been part of the old CISAC ethos described by Michael Freegard, brought improvements even in Europe, such as increases in advance payments and greater transparency of practices.

However, one very big change which Freegard had wanted to bring about was the union of PRS and MCPS. He saw the joining of the two UK music rights licensing and collecting organisations as simple common sense. His intention then was to merge the two organisations completely, following the models of GEMA in Germany (where the performing and mechanical rights have always been administered by a single society) or SACEM/SDRM in France (where there are two different identities for the performing and mechanical rights societies, but there had always

been a single organisation). He accepts that might have proved impossible to achieve entirely, but that would have been the aim. That initiative was pre-empted (some would use the stronger term "thwarted") by the MPA's purchase of MCPS in 1976 which is dealt with in more detail in the main MCPS chapter, as is the unsuccessful move towards a joint venture in 1993.

When the opportunity for MCPS-PRS joint working arose again in 1996 it was seized by Hutchinson and his senior managers, and by many Board Directors and taken forward with speed and determination which was intended to ensure that it happened.

Licensing and Distribution

The PRS approach to exerting its powers to license was originally and for a long time tentative and amateurish. When it was formed, PRS expected a fight from users over the rates it wanted to charge, so it aimed for low "acceptable" rates and then naively believed that once a rate was set the users would willingly pay. This proved to be untrue. Outright hostility, refusal, tirades in the press, Questions in the House and litigation were all liberally used by music users in early attempts to curb the society's licensing attempts, or even force it to abandon its operations altogether.

Even today licensees' willingness to pay cannot be said to match the public enthusiasm for buying Lottery tickets, but years of dogged persistence (politely at the door or more robustly in the courts) and improving communication have brought change. First came acceptance, then better understanding that there is a good case for paying creators for the use of their work and the most convenient way was via a single licence from their collecting society. And in recent years another very significant change, initiated by PRS and winning positive response from music users, has been the shift from emphasis on law enforcement to marketing the PRS licence as a valuable business enhancement.

Once it had got its licensing schemes underway, there were many years in which PRS wrapped itself in the comfortable but unrealistic view that those who sought licences voluntarily, or were easily identified and approached by the society to take out licences, were the entire potentially licensable spread of users. Ernest Ford, Licensing Manager in the 50s, actually spoke of licensing "saturation", which was nonsense.

Attitudes to licensing and licensing activity were tackled determinedly in the 60s. At the same time, use of music was increasing. The increased revenue funded more professional activity and a bigger field force to look for unlicensed use. But it was not until the mid-90s that marketing methodology was used to research the likely total size of the music performance market: this indicated significant potential for public performance revenue growth.

Apart from the increase in obvious forms of "public performance", just two examples illustrate new usages which were unthought of until the last couple of decades. Firstly the mesmerisingly monotonous, monochrome ping-pong video games were to give way to polychromic action-packed computer games with sound attached: their erratic electronic bleeps, which intensely irritated one generation as much as they delighted another, were replaced by specially-created background music. Then the explosion in sophistication and youth ownership of cell phones led to demand for music as ring tones, a demand promptly satisfied by PC and telephone access to digitised sound files; these developed from tinny electronic monophonic renditions of barely recognisable tunes to music recordings delivered with reasonable sound quality, and then extracts from original commercial recordings.

Both these market phenomena depended on advancing technology and the apparently insatiable demand for some form of musical accompaniment for almost every human activity. Both

also presented interesting copyright issues and licensing headaches for the music rights societies, but had quite different outcomes.

Computer game producers at an early stage involved composers and were prepared to pay appropriate copyright fees. But the huge growth in the market made the cost of such an approach too high, and a preference for complete buy-out of commissioned compositions followed, putting much of this music beyond the reach of licensing organisations.[16]

Mobile phone ring tones were an entirely different story. What seemed for a while like a passing fad in the very late 90s persisted and grew rapidly into a new business opportunity for ring tone suppliers. Ring tone suppliers need two licences, from MCPS and PRS, but can apply for these at one time via the Alliance.

PRS Revenue streams

There were always three potential revenue streams for PRS to collect. Their size and importance relative to each other has changed at various times, but over the years each has grown to an extent which would astound the society's founding members. They comprise public performance, which is live, recorded or the relay of broadcast copyright music heard in public places; "electronic transmission to the public", which is the transmission of copyright music, live or recorded, by radio and by terrestrial, satellite and cable television and the internet; and international, which is the remittance to PRS of revenue earned by any type of performance of PRS members' works overseas (by way of reciprocal agreements)[17]

Note that broadcast/broadcasting is mentioned twice. This is perfectly correct under the terms of the Act: firstly because any UK-based broadcasting company (from amateur community

16 "Buy out" of creators' rights is a regularly recurring issue in various kinds of music use. Strictly, such buy out of the performing right is possible only if a writer has not assigned that right to a collecting society; however, writers have been known to maximise their income by writing commissioned (computer game, or other) music under a pseudonym which is not registered with their society, and doing a buy out deal for it. PRS has a rate for licensing computer game music, but it is seldom if ever invoked. This may change. The

mechanical right for music on computer games falls into the MCPS multimedia licensing area, with a negotiable rate. Publishers tend to licence this usage directly, however, and because they see it as having strong potential they are tending now actively to seek deals with computer games producers, looking to get copyright music which they control licensed for this use, at a rate which is more attractive to the producers. In 2003, there were indications of a trend towards using specially composed and sometimes quite lavishly

radio/TV and college stations, to the BBC and Independent radio and TV empires) must have a PRS licence to use copyright music in their transmissions; secondly because the use of a radio or TV as a source of entertainment in a public place (any place where the music can be heard by even a handful of members of the public outside the domestic environment) needs to be licensed separately. However, this fact has been and still is regularly seized on with indignation by music users as an objectionable example of PRS and its members "charging twice for the same thing".

The distinction justifying the two different licences is as unpopular as it is clear-cut. The broadcaster pays a licence fee in order to broadcast copyright music, while the pub, restaurant, hairdresser, airline or any other user pays a licence fee in order to use broadcast output as public performances on premises frequented by the public. They are entirely separate activities by separate licensees, not linked in any way under the law. Interestingly, the objectors occasionally include MPs espousing a constituent's complaint, and PRS staff would not be human if they did not feel a little like declaring "checkmate", pointing out that the explanation and justification are enshrined in the Berne Convention – to which the UK subscribes and which therefore the UK Government had taken forward into an Act of Parliament.

It is also important to note that the right to license the inclusion of copyright music in a programme transmitted by cable is what empowered PRS with respect to the internet, although the original explicit distinction between wired and wireless communication has been eliminated by the amendments to the 1988 Act as result of the implementation of the European Copyright Directive. This was never in doubt to the society, but needed arguing firmly and often when music-using websites began to proliferate in the mid-90s, just as the "internet is gloriously anarchic and regulation-free" attitude was in its first flush of joyful naivety. The website creators' inability to place internet usage in the context of "public performance" was an issue, lending weight to the view PRS' name is not particularly helpful to its work.[18] The necessity for an

MCPS licence was probably always easier for users to understand since the creation of digitised music files on computers is not too huge a mental leap from the idea of making a record.[19] As time went on and internet services grew at a phenomenal rate, the blending of previously quite separate kinds of usage in the online environment led to the historic and unprecedented decision for MCPS and PRS to issue a joint online licence (*see Alliance chapter*)

These are all matters which are often misunderstood, and the administration of music rights – particularly the performing right – is undeniably complicated. This illustrates why so much effort has always been needed to explain to licensees, the public and many other audiences what PRS does and why, how and with what authority it does it.

Growth in PRS income is justifiably a matter of pride for generations of management and staff, and should be a source of collective satisfaction to generations of members (even if individuals feel differently at times, with or without justification). This continual and in some periods spectacular growth has two drivers. One is that Tariffs and licence fee negotiations take account of inflation – normally the median between the UK average earnings index and retail price index. The other can be described as "true" growth. This is a combination of growth in the music usage market; better, faster licensing coverage of incremental users, and more accurate tracking of when licences need to be renewed to ensure that these always reflect the updated reality rather than historical information and assumptions.

Where inflation is concerned, it is broadly true to say that through the 20s, 30s, 40s, and 50s it was not a significant factor in overall income growth. During the 60s and 70s that changed significantly, and inflation remained important until the 90s when its contribution decreased, progressively so in the late 90s and into the 2000s when UK fiscal policy has been firmly tied to keeping inflation very low. There are two sides to every coin, and the steadily falling interest rate has recently, but inevitably, had a

---

recorded music for computer games once again, possibly prompted by the enormous improvements in the graphics. Quality computer games were reaching a point where they had the audio visual quality of mini films on a tiny screen

17 These agreements effectively make the members of one society members of every other for the purposes of licensing, royalty collection and distribution, supposedly and ideally enjoying the same royalty calculation regime as national members. Reciprocal agreements

create a "worldwide web" of rights administration. Although agreements are negotiated as between one national society and another, the CISAC standard agreement remains a reference point. The strength of this web has been tested, notably where European Central Licensing of the mechanical right is concerned (*see MCPS chapter*) and there is no doubt that the progressive erosion of national boundaries in a satellite and internet-connected globe well test it further and possibly at some point demand a new approach.

121

major impact on non-licence income; that is, the interest earned by PRS licence income deposited in the bank awaiting distribution to members as royalties.

The true growth, linked both to increased size of the music usage market and PRS' improving effectiveness in licensing that usage, came from several directions.

Public Performance Licensing

PRS firstly achieved a great deal by determinedly pushing to raise tariffs (repeatedly defending its cause and its case in court and Tribunal hearings) while focusing licensing attention on specific sectors of users in a series of combined licensing and trade PR campaigns.

One important issue tested in court was particularly interesting. A prolonged dispute between PRS and the record retail trade culminated in writs being issued by the society in February 1977 against three major retail operations: the London-based shops of Harlequin and Virgin, and Rushworth and Dreaper of Liverpool. The disagreement centred on the playing of records in stores. PRS deemed this to be public performance needing a licence (except where it took place in a soundproof booth). In 1976 PRS set a fee of 13p per square metre of shop floor area, linked to the retail price index that had risen by 15% in 1977. The record retailers rejected this argument and claimed that instore play was ultimately in the interests of PRS members and frequently led to a record sale. The first *PRS Yearbook*, published in September 1977, recorded "an unprecedented large increase" of £4.4 million to £21.6 million in gross revenue in 1976. However, the sum collected from record shop licence fees amounted to £95,447, just 2% of the public performance royalty income of £4.7 million.

PRS had already reached agreement with the major multiple stores, Boots, W H Smith and Woolworths, but the independent record shops mostly refused to fall in line. They decided to defend their position under the auspices of the Music Trades Association (MTA) which established a mutual fund to cover the cost of legal representation. Its own legal advice was that PRS was not entitled to claim a licence fee when music was being played "for demonstration with view to sale, for education of staff and for the detection of faults".

The matter became confused in April that year when PRS lawyers despatched reminders to record dealers who had acquired PRS licences in January 1976 but had not responded to notices that payment for 1977 was due. The dealers in question were aware of the MTA resistance to the writs and were withholding their renewal fees until the outcome of the PRS action was known. Asked by *Music Week* to comment on the general situation and the position of a certain Lois Pink, owner of Sounds Ideal in Wallington, Surrey, who was under threat of court proceedings for withholding her 1977 £12.40 licence renewal fee, PRS declared that her case would be a straightforward claim for non-payment of debt. The writs issued against the major chains were for infringement, but there was "no question of a test case because there is no uncertainty about the law". But a trial in court became inevitable, and the MTA indicated that the Harlequin chain of shops would be the test case.

The issue finally came to the High Court in January 1979, and all parties knew that the outcome would decide the entire issue of whether record shops had to have PRS public performance licences or not. A potential major new revenue stream for PRS members was at stake. Before Mr Justice Browne-Wilkinson, PRS stated that on specific occasions certain Harlequin shops had infringed the performing right by playing music over loudspeakers without possessing a PRS licence. Records and tapes were being played at Harlequin shops "not just at the request of the purchasers but incessantly to promote the sale of the goods". Harlequin claimed that playing music in the shops was a necessity for the record retail business and so could not be regarded as a

---

18 As mentioned elsewhere, when the PRS brand was given a facelift to coincide with its 75th anniversary, the then CEO Michael Freegard stressed that the new logo put emphasis on the initials PRS rather than Society's full name, which was considered "ambiguous and misleading" – partly because it causes many to think that the Society is for performers rather than composers and songwriters, and partly because it obscures elements which have little to do with the popular image of *performance* in the bundle of rights collectively referred to as "the performing right".

19 Nevertheless, it is argued that the term mechanical right is also now misleading, given the changes in technology since music was "mechanically fixed" in a physical recording medium, and that therefore mechanical rights societies would probably also benefit from rebranding

The "beat" for PRS Licensing Inspectors, as the PRS field representatives were known until the change in public performance licensing to a marketing and sales approach in the mid-to-late 90s, included checking all kinds of retail premises for their use of copyright music. Former Inspector in the Dyfed, mid-south and west Glamorgan region of Wales, Jack Harris checks out a local hairdresser in the late 80s.

public performance in the particular sense; PRS agreed it was a necessity but insisted that it was still a public performance and subject to the payment of a performing right licence fee. Harlequin further claimed that, even if it was public performance, record retailers should be treated as a special case; to this the

PRS response was that composers and authors would be able individually to ask the shops for a fee.

Browne-Wilkinson found for PRS, granting an injunction and ordering an enquiry into damages concerning past infringement. He declared he was satisfied that playing records and tapes in record shops rated as a public performance. The MTA decided not to appeal nor proceed with the defence of the other test cases. It announced that "agreement has been reached on a programme of co-operation between the two bodies [MTA and PRS] for the mutual benefit of composers, songwriters, publishers and record dealers". The MTA advised dealers to take out the PRS licence for playing music over loudspeakers in their shops. In cases where shops had been unlicensed since January 1976 when the PRS first sought to impose a fee, the licences were appropriately backdated. The MTA undertook not to appeal against the High Court ruling or refer the PRS performing tariff to the Performing Right Tribunal. PRS responded by making an annual grant of £3,000 over a five-year period in aid of the MTA retail staff training scheme and agreed the payment of costs of approximately £10,000 awarded to the Society by the High Court to be spread across the same five-year period.

MTA General Secretary Arthur Spencer-Bolland said he believed the agreement was a fair and equitable one. The MTA had not considered a negotiated agreement before the court case because "We felt we had a very good case, but unfortunately the moral aspects were overruled by legal argument; the judge merely interpreted the law and decided that, no matter how good the reasons for playing music in shops are, to do so is always a public performance." Laurie Krieger, founder and MD of Harlequin, maintained the stance he had adopted at the outset of the dispute: the PRS demand for a licence fee from record shops amounted to "biting the hand that feeds them".

The Harlequin case underlined the fact that determination to license wherever its members' copyrights were used was one strong and consistent part of the PRS plan for income growth. In addition, the society made two major strategic decisions which were to have a far-reaching and beneficial effect on the way it did its licensing work and on the thinking behind that. Taken together, all these factors were instrumental in delivering to members a more than five-fold increase in total income in the 20 years between 1982 and 2002.

Through the 80s, the PRS licensing function (the combination of the field force of Inspectors and the office based staff) achieved good annual increases in public performance income. Much credit goes to the then Licensing Controller Mike Hudson, whose tactical thinking and negotiating stamina resulted in raised tariffs for retail shops, pubs, hotels and restaurants and proprietary clubs.

In 1988 PRS made a bold attempt to push the tariff for pop music events and concerts licensed under the *Live Popular* Tariff LP from 2% of box office, to 6%. This resulted in a fiercely contested Copyright Tribunal hearing. The 6% tariff was rejected but a rise to 3% was achieved. Other changes which were made around then – and sometimes had to be rigorously defended – included the May 1989 revision of Tariff SS for ships; and in 1990 a proposed substantial increase to the Live Classical Concert Tariff LC began gruelling negotiations which resulted in a 3.3% rate phased in over the following two years. Just over a decade later a further move to increase in this Tariff was cause for considerable friction between the Association of British Concert Promoters (ABCP) and PRS, leading to a Copyright Tribunal reference by the former. As mentioned in this chapter, after the Monopolies and Mergers Commission report in 1996 a series of changes to long-established PRS practices affected, among other issues, the subsidy applied to increase the overall amount available for distribution as royalties on live classical performances. The

abolition of this subsidy, and further changes in terms of the analogous broadcast information used in royalty distributions – after a very wide ranging review in the mid-90s – inevitably adversely affected revenues to classical composers and their publishers. A decision was made to seek better recognition of the value of classical music through a higher Tariff LC.

After many months of negotiation, with a Copyright Tribunal hearing scheduled for January 2004, PRS and the ABCP were able to announce in December 2003 that agreement had been reached on a new level for Tariff LC. Both sides "had wished to avoid a protracted and expensive hearing to the detriment of the classical music community" (the threat of expense and potentially unsatisfactory and disruptive outcomes has on a number of occasions "encouraged" settlement before proposed Tribunal hearings – *see Tribunals Appendix*) Backdated to 1 July 2003 Tariff LC was settled at 4.8% of net box office receipts from concerts licensed under that tariff, with a discount to 4.5% for the provision of all required information and payments to PRS within 28 days.

The significant revival in UK cinema business around 1991 led to action on raising Tariff C. This music-in-cinemas tariff had been previously renegotiated in the 60s. At a fixed 0.575% of (ex VAT) box office it was by the 90s the lowest in Europe. Conflict with the users was avoided by achieving the increase in a series of steps. The tariff was raised to a full 1%, without the Tribunal reference which was more than half expected at the outset.

At various times PRS has been asked to look at working for other rights owners. In the late 80s the literary authors' society ALCS[20] approached PRS to consider extending its licensing of public reception of broadcasts to include literary and dramatic works controlled by ALCS. There was no great enthusiasm among Board Directors; an agency agreement was discussed but not acted on. And in the early 90s there was talk of PRS taking on some

---

20 The Authors Licensing and Collecting Society

level of responsibility for choreographers' copyright licensing/collecting; that also failed to evoke enough interest at top management and Board level.

The 90s saw a period of consolidation under John Crisp, who succeeded Mike Hudson as Licensing Controller in 1991 when sadly the latter was unable to continue his work at PRS due to ill-health. The Licensing function concentrated on improving effectiveness of its own activities, through business targets for managers and inspectors, better incentive schemes, and some concentrated thinking about the systems and procedures which supported the team's work.

The major strategic decisions referred to above related firstly, in the 80s, to the setting-up of regional centres for licensing activity, and secondly, beginning in the mid-90s, to a complete change in the way PRS licensing was thought about, approached, presented to music users, and organised internally; a change from enforcing copyright law to marketing and selling the value of music and the benefits of using music as an aid to good business. This change was then linked strongly to, and facilitated, business planning in which entirely new possibilities for licensing work extending beyond PRS into co-operation and co-working with other associated organisations or companies.

Regionalisation

In the 80s PRS came to realise that to be significantly more effective in something as complicated as licensing the public performance of music, the society had literally to be closer to its business. In this it was moving towards the regionally-based licensing structure of most other European collecting societies. John Axon, then Head of Licensing and now PRS Executive Director and so responsible for licensing revenues for most of his PRS career, describes the impetus at the time as "a need to reinvigorate licensing and get closer to the people who pay us".

The first regional office was set up in 1984 in Edinburgh; the logic was that Scotland was the region most remote from PRS HQ and so most likely to benefit from the reinvigoration and closeness described by Axon. Another underlying reason was that Scotland was in its own estimation and demonstrably "different", having an independent stance and character and increasingly demanding its own identity. Much later, at a time when the Government was promising and delivering Scottish devolution, PRS was to give even greater recognition to this set of characteristics by giving PRS Scotland an identity of its own from a membership point of view, alongside the regional licensing office. However, the process of change within public performance licensing led in 2003 to a major reduction in the manning of this office and a move to smaller premises; all the licensing back office work was withdrawn, but the membership focus remains.

Regional offices were set up during a seven-year period in Sutton Coldfield, Warrington, Peterborough, York and Bristol and within the London head office (for the South-East) with the inspectors covering the region reporting into their own office and the staff in each taking care of customer queries and all the licensing case load, thus fulfilling the objective of getting closer to the people they needed to do business with.

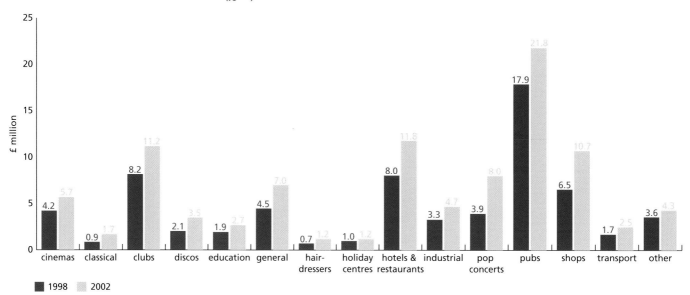

PRS Public Performance Sales (£M)

£ million (y-axis: 0, 5, 10, 15, 20, 25)

Category	1998	2002
cinemas	4.2	5.7
classical	0.9	1.7
clubs	8.2	11.2
discos	2.1	3.5
education	1.9	2.7
general	4.5	7.0
hair-dressers	0.7	1.2
holiday centres	1.0	1.2
hotels & restaurants	8.0	11.8
industrial	3.3	4.7
pop concerts	3.9	8.0
pubs	17.9	21.8
shops	6.5	10.7
transport	1.7	2.5
other	3.6	4.3

■ 1998 ☐ 2002

Source: The MCPS-PRS Alliance

In the mid-90s, alongside the development of the regional offices' activities, a further change in thinking about the whole approach to PRS licensing began to evolve. It would result in no less than a completely new philosophy and business plan, supported by one of the most successful PRS IT projects; and it would require all the regional offices in their original form to close. Two remained, with the revised purpose of concentrating on specific business streams.

In a nutshell, the public performance licensing function would move from a law-enforcement attitude to a selling and marketing and revenue-orientated approach. It reorganised its structure to mirror customer call centre practice which was being adopted in almost every kind of business. And all that was supported by an efficient, tailored IT system which was quite unlike anything the licensing teams had ever had before to assist their work.

With the change of the Licensing Inspectorate into a sales and advisory force (*see below*), it was realised that a functional split was better than a regional one. The offices in Sutton Coldfield, York and Bristol were closed. While the Edinburgh office remained a special case until 2003, 1999 saw a rearrangement which, with occasional adjustment and refinement, remains in place. Corporate and national licence accounts are dealt with by the Warrington office, with the Peterborough office a national call centre for the many small accounts, and live performance and major concerts being dealt with in the London office.

Law enforcement becomes marketing
The beginnings of the new ideas were launched at the 1995 PRS Licensing Conference in Chepstow by Clive Thomas, who had taken over responsibility for public performance licensing. The licensing change of philosophy and practice was encouraged and awarded resources during the Chairmanship of Wayne Bickerton (particularly during the two periods in which he was acting CEO) supported by the members of the Council at that time.

Strong support for the new line of thinking came also from John Hutchinson as Chief Executive from late 1995 onward, and Thomas went on to develop these ideas through numerous generations of plans and changes, including the setting-up of a sales development team. Appointment of an experienced marketing professional was a parallel development. Again, this had no precedent at PRS, although a few other societies such as IMRO in Ireland and BUMA:STEMRA in the Netherlands had similar ideas and were taking them forward in their own ways.

In an energetic atmosphere of investigation and experiment, supported by PRS Board Directors, the soon-to-be marketing and sales arm of the society conducted market research. This showed which standard practices would, and sometimes would not, prove effective in the specialist market of music performance licensing.

Early in-house market research indicated the possibility of big income growth in some sectors, and confirmed the likelihood of high usage of music in less than obvious, and very hard to access, places such as industrial premises[21]. This was linked to some very interesting external academic research[22] on the impact which different kinds of music could have on the buying activity of

consumers in shops and restaurants, commissioned jointly by PRS and PPL[23] (another straw in the wind of change).

The market research led to increased promotional activity, aimed at finding the best approaches to various types of music user, not only to facilitate the licensing of those who were already using music in their businesses but also to "sell" the value of well-chosen copyright music as an aid to doing business, whether that was selling groceries, clothes or computers, or calming a dentist's patients, or subtly persuading drinkers in a bar to buy more expensive wine, or wine from a particular country, or even helping to empty a pub at closing time (by turning the music off!)[24]

But "marketing" *per se* proved not to be the golden key to income growth in this very special kind of business. It was learnt that, contrary to the case in most other businesses, PRS licensing work cannot be done via standard telemarketing and direct marketing. Specialist units came and went, and various methods were experimented with, resulting in the development of a tailored PRS approach which recognises that selling this kind of licence via the idea of selling the commercial value of using copyright music in business environments can only be achieved through use of a variety of personal and technology-based skills.

A new system to serve new ways of working
Ideas about how better to use IT led in the mid-90s to the introduction of one of the organisation's most successful systems projects, the first step in a pattern of change which has been justifiably termed revolutionary. The market research work helped towards making the business case for a major investment in the Public Performance Sales System (PuPSS) which supported the new work methods in licensing.

21 The market research tested the relationship between the number of businesses in various test regions (in each of a range of businesses which as closely as possible matched existing PRS licensing tariffs) and the licensing coverage PRS had at that point achieved. The indications and calculations which arose were used not only to launch schemes aimed at improving licensing levels in certain business sectors, but also to identify better ways of planning licensing activity in future from a marketing and sales viewpoint.

22 Dr Adrian North of Leicester University was already researching and demonstrating the psychology of music as an influencer of consumer behaviour, refining an already widespread understanding in supermarkets, for example that people would move more quickly or slowly around a store, spend more or buy different kinds of goods as a result of hearing different types of background music, often without consciously noticing what they were listening to. He conducted specific further research for PRS and PPL, and assisted in

Just as the concept of market research based "selling" was the application of business thinking which had a long history across all commercial sectors but was new to PRS, PuPSS was based on well-understood and elsewhere widely-used customer relations and customer account management. Essentially the concept is that of the call centre, equipped with systems which enable the staff to view all the information necessary to deal with a customer in terms of running the account and maintaining necessary contact with the account holder.

The significance of importing these ideas and methods into PRS was that the PuPSS database recognised that PRS had customers, who might have multiple accounts with PRS, who should be prompted to report relevant information and renew existing licences or take out new ones, and whose account details often changed and needed to have a traceable history. The old LiVT system recognised licensee accounts but could not link information in any kind of customer management. So the basic (but huge) practical benefit of PuPSS was to automate licensing processes which had formerly required repeated intervention and cross-referencing by licensing office staff. It also allows PRS to talk to the customer and build up a profile of information about his business, then to offer suggestions for using music in that business.

The PuPSS business case, which went before the Board in May 1998 was in the context that "public performance licensing offers the main area of real growth left to PRS", a fact which had been recognised by John Axon and was the springboard for his original regionalisation, and the way that began a steeper public performance revenue growth.

PuPSS is not essentially an IT project although it uses computers (and the same was true of the earlier milestone of the Distribution and Data Review[25] and its subsequent embedding into the way PRS distributes royalties). The business case set out the need for organisation change and improved systems support in the area of public performance licensing. It stressed that there was no

PRS public performance tariffs as at January 2003 (an example)

AC	Aircraft
AS	County, agricultural, horse shows, regattas & open-air events
B	Service & other bands
BO	Bingo (commercial)
C	Cinema performances
CB	Community buildings (run by voluntary organisations)
D	Commercial discotheques & commercial dance halls
DJ	Mobile disc jockeys & karaoke operators
DS	Dance tuition schools
EE	Educational establishments (Government-funded & independent)
FE	Further education colleges
GP	General purposes
HC	Holiday centres
HDB	Hairdressers & Beauty Salons
HR	Hotels, restaurants & cafés; boarding & guest houses
I	Industrial premises, offices & canteens
J	Clubs (proprietary)
JMC	Clubs (members')
K	Circuses
LC	Classical music concerts & recitals
LP	Light or popular music concerts
MC	Motor coaches, buses & mini-buses
MH	Telephone music on hold
O	Parks, open-air places, pools (mechanical music)
P	Public houses
PV	Passenger vessels
RS	Shops & stores, showrooms, warehouses
RYS	Railway stations
SGS	Sports grounds & stadia, race tracks & courses
SP	Small premises
T	Theatrical presentations
X	Exhibitions & similar functions, trade fairs

planning PRS marketing tests which took the thinking further. A key element in this work was identifying whether copyright music ((recognisable popular commercial recordings) was more effective than non-copyright (eg specially created ambient music, which a shop might prefer because it did not incur a licence fee); in a number of instances that was proved to be true – to a sufficient degree to justify making this idea one plank in the PRS selling pitch. The paper was *The influence of in-store music on win selections*, A C North, D J

Hargreaves, J McKendrick - *Journal of Applied Psychology* 84(2) 271-276

23 Puzzled and resentful users approached both by PRS and PPL to take out licences regularly needed explanation of the distinction between the two bodies. This was most simply put s the difference between a venue which uses copyright music strictly as live performance (PRS licence only) and one which uses music via a juke box, hi-fi, radio etc which all involved commercial recordings (PRS and PPL licences needed)

comprehensive and accurate view of UK premises, and
no certainty that licences issued were correct. There was no
uniformity of licence administration, which led to unnecessary
costs, incomplete data and inefficiencies, as did the largely paper-
based flow of work. Market segmentation was impossible, and
information emerging from the system was insufficient for assisting
royalty distributions or contributing to management information.
This catalogue of deficiencies does, however, need to be set
against the Licensing division's record of continual income growth
in excess of inflation, and of no distribution ever being delayed
or missed. The ability of experienced licensing staff to use the
old (commissioned from 1977) inflexible LiVT system, and coax
from it co-operation and output beyond reasonable expectations,
led to an internal respect akin to that accorded to minor shamans
in some cultures.

Developed in partnership with consultants Cap Gemini, PuPSS is
able both to manage licensing business information, and to exploit
it, for example by determining when licence renewal notices
should be sent out. The next phase of its development as planned
in 2003 would allow cross-matching of the licensed premises
database against external business directory databases to identify
gaps and plan licence marketing campaigns.

Although not all the original projections in terms of licensing
process efficiencies, cost savings and reduction of outstanding debt
have yet been achieved, this was a business transformation. The
combination of the broad marketing and sales approach and the
workflow approach in PuPSS has, Thomas points out, played a
great part in doubling public performance revenues in eight years,
from £50m in1995 to £105m in 2003.

Thomas, with enthusiasm which has only grown over those eight
years, sums up the philosophy: "Music has real value to users, and
if you can show them that value you break down resistance.
Twenty years ago I was a 'music policeman' for PRS and met

resistance all the way. We expected music users to be cheating and
unwilling to pay. But I was convinced that the music user was in
fact a customer, and we were, in fact, selling him something he
actually wanted – not policing him like a shoplifter".

It is reasonable to ask why such an approach was not taken before,
given that the theories, methodology and technology were well
tried and tested in many other business sectors. The answer
relates, as it often does in this society's history, to levels of
awareness of the need to change, and the willingness to do so.

The fact that so many big steps forward, or long-needed changes
in direction, came only after a change in management in one or
another area is not unique to PRS, and it does not necessarily
undermine the ability or contribution of managers at different
times. But the inevitable insularity of an organisation which has
no direct competition in the commercial sense and which is alone
in a highly specialised business sector played its part in patterns of
management thinking and behaviour through the years.

The PRS licensing story is, as Axon and Thomas would stress, one
of evolution rather than revolution. Axon illustrates how far-
reaching that evolution has been by recalling that when he himself
joined PRS in 1983 the body of PRS Licensing Inspectors mostly
comprised retired policemen, very suited to "copyright law
enforcement",who took a judiciously measured approach to their
"beats". Early encounters for Axon included one gentlemanly
Inspector who never went into "ladies' boutiques"; and another
who cheerfully admitted that he did not work on wet days, which
was all the more alarming because he was based in frequently
inclement Aberdeen.

PRS licenses public performance according to a range of tariffs.
These are listed on Page 128, and the length of the list has
regularly prompted curiosity and some puzzlement. Surely, many
think, a public performance of a piece of copyright music can

24 Some years later the PRS Chairman Andrew Potter led a project to create a report which
collected widespread examples of how music affects human behaviour, as a free resource
for anyone who could benefit from the information. *The Power of Music* report, edited by
Professor Sue Hallam of the Institure of Educations, Lonodn University was launched in
2000 , and was accessible via the Performing Right Society Foundation website.
25 *see Distribution section for details*

be priced, and so – like a postage stamp perhaps – it will cost the same to everyone, everywhere. This common mistake firstly assumes that PRS licenses the use of individual compositions and secondly that all licensees and their music usage are essentially the same.

PRS issues blanket licences for the public performance of the entire copyright repertoire it controls (its own members' music, and all the music created by members of other societies around the world with which PRS has reciprocal agreements). And the issue of public performance licences falls naturally and sensibly into different types of music use in different business sectors. Put simply, the way music is used and its perceived or actual value to a business vary widely. Contrast, for example, a large restaurant which relies heavily on music to entertain or create atmosphere for its clients with a sole-trader hairdresser who keeps the radio on in the salon as a largely disregarded background sound. In fact the latter was always likely to be far more highly resistant to the idea paying a PRS licence fee than the former. Among the endless anecdotes which Inspectors retold were incidents of small shopkeepers dramatically throwing small transistor radios into the dustbin when told they needed to pay around £50 a year for a licence to have it on in the shop. And that was at the polite end of the range of disgruntled responses: more than one inspector was given an ultimatum along the lines of "pick a window, you're leaving through it", and there were occasional physical assaults to contend with.

Most tariffs therefore needed to be negotiated with, or if no representative body existed, must be be sensibly suited to, the trade or business user. Users steadfastly resisted a *one size fits all* approach, since there are so many variations in the kinds of music used and the means of usage: Karaoke, TV for sport, live rock band, CD player and juke box are all likely to be encountered just

in one large pub, for example. This easily explains why Tariff P for public houses runs to eight pages of rules and explanations. The flexible approach helps PRS as well as music users, offering scope to negotiate and adjust licence rates relatively.

Possibly wider horizons

The strategic plans which began seriously to be developed by PRS in the mid-90s envisaged broadening its licensing remit to offer appropriate services to organisations responsible for licensing other rights. The obvious potential "fit" was between PRS and PPL because both license performance of music by more-or-less the same users. In 2002/3 much effort went into investigating the possibility of PRS taking on PPL licensing, or even an administrative alliance between the two organisations. Studies have confirmed the range of opportunities for collaboration and what these might deliver. This is under consideration at the highest level in both companies. But, moving forward at a practical level will certainly require changes in thinking and licensing approach.

Public performance revenue distribution

However, the complications at the licensing end inevitably and traditionally cause complexity at the royalty distribution end of the process. The "straight line" between licence income and royalty payment to a PRS writer or publisher member was an impossibility. There were no systems which could cope with this, and for many years it was a regrettable fact of life that the succession of assumptions, use of analogies rather than accurate information on performances, calculations and policy decisions which had to intervene in the distribution process allowed (well-intentioned) manipulation of distributions, for example to benefit certain types of repertoire which would otherwise earn very little in royalties for the writers concerned.

Huge steps forward have been taken in this respect in recent years. But the road forward was through a cactus bed of anger and frustration among many PRS members, including a referral to the Office of Fair Trading (notably by members, not licensees) which culminated in a Monopolies and Mergers Commission investigation[26]; a comprehensive review of how PRS obtained its information on public performance and how it then applied that to royalty distributions[27]; a series of rationalising decisions (some of them very far-reaching in their effect and many of them contentious) relating to the rules and practices of PRS royalty distributions[28]; and the House of Commons Select Committee on culture, Media and Sports decision to investigate the impact of the abolition of the classical music subsidy.

One way of illustrating PRS' task of distributing income for public performance of individual musical works is to think of ways to describe a crowd. People in a packed New Year Trafalgar Square crowd, as seen from the roof of an office at the far end of Whitehall, will all appear to be dressed in either blue or red. As the viewer gets closer these solid colours develop gradations, and closer still resolve into a variety of specks of many different colours. But even from very close, it is going to be extremely difficult to distinguish the one person wearing a jacket in a precise shade of orange. Any method which might be used to locate that one person will take resources and cost money.

There are three issues which have always had to be considered by collecting societies dealing with public performance. Firstly, what information is available about some kinds of music performance which can reasonably be used as analogies for other, much harder to identify, performances? For example, is it safe to assume that Radios 1 & 2 sufficiently represent the general taste in popular music to allow licence income from restaurants and hotels to be distributed according to those broadcast logs? Secondly, what do the members want? The answer to that is never a consensus. It varies from composers who would be prepared to pay very high administration fees to have individual

performances of their works identified and a royalty for every individual performance paid, to those who want the most cost effective methods to be used so that royalty totals net of administration costs will be generally much higher, even if some performances will never be individually identified for royalty payments. Thirdly, what is a proper overall level of administrative cost for a collecting society, in terms of business efficiency and in relation to cost levels in other societies?

What has happened to PRS distribution through the process of examination and change in past decade is that the broad and homogeneous approach to PRS distribution has been greatly refined. But, although many members would like to progress further to "individual" treatment, this is as yet impossible in the vast majority of cases: a rare performance of a work in a rarely or never surveyed venue, or on a small radio station which seldom figures in a sample, will almost certainly continue to be missed. But this has to be set in the big picture, which is now far more accurate and fair than ever before.

The Minutes of many PRS Board and Executive Committee meetings through the years illustrate the unavoidable complexity, and at times sheer quirkiness, of the issue and the pragmatic and policy decisions which have had to be made. One small example was the matter of impromptu performances by audiences at pop concerts. Despite some members' objections the decision was positive (consistent with payments already made for other situations such as the chanting of *I'm Forever Blowing Bubbles* at football matches). So a royalty was paid for the ragged but adoring performance of *Happy Birthday* by the vast crowd at a Michael Jackson concert.

The PRS classical music subsidy had been introduced in1966 broadly to recognise a "value" of classical music composition which was not reflected in the Tariff which could be charged. Some composers suggested "rectification" was a better term than subsidy, and the thinking behind that attitude is still current

26 MMC report *Performing Rights: a report on the supply in the UK of the services of administering performing rights* and film synchronisation rights published in February 1996 by HMSO Cm3147. *See MMC Appendix*
27 The PRS Distribution and Data Review was an unprecedented and comprehensive exercise intended to ensure that information about what music was actually being performed in all kinds of venues was greatly improved and continually collected (using a professional market

research and consumer survey company); and that the consequent royalty distributions were more fair, more accurate and easier for members to understand.
28 The review of the distribution process prompted further wide-reaching debate at Board level; as well as adopting PRS management recommendations for simplifying and modernising a number of long-established and hitherto unquestioned practices, the Society's Directors decided to pursue the objectives of fairness and accuracy further still by

among some classical composer and publisher members, three years after the bitterly contested abolition of the subsidy. Back in 1989 the Tariff change in 1988 led the Council to review the subsidy for the first time.

The debate closely previewed the "abolish classical subsidy" discussions about a decade later. A letter to the Council from Lady Walton, widow and trustee of the late composer William Walton, requested "no precipitate action" because of the detrimental effect on foundations and trusts. Classical publishers pleaded special circumstances in view of their investment in writers, but this argument was countered and matched by pop publishers. It was strongly argued that there should be no difference in PRS' treatment of different genres of music; and that classical music should get its subsidies outside PRS. Alternatively, PRS could subsidise all kinds of music to the extent considered necessary (the practicalities of this idea appear not to have been closely questioned, but it was never pursued).

In 1989, the decision was to wait to see the effect of the still to be revised Tariff LC. But the Board agreed it was "desirable to treat music of all genres according to common standards and that current distinctions between classical, light classical and non-classical should be abandoned provided that a satisfactory way could be found of recognising special technical characteristics of certain music" and the society should consider the possibility of using its social and cultural funds provision to a greater extent.

A Live Music Policy Review began the following year.

The simplification of distribution rules and an end to subsidies mooted in the late 80s were to be issues tackled energetically in the mid-90s[29], boosted in importance by the MMC Report.

The PRS Board by then was a very different entity. With its determined, energetic, unsentimental Chief Executive, the Board was ready to face and win arguments with special interest groups within the membership. The balancing factor was that the same more briskly business-minded Board and CEO introduced and delivered a far higher level of communication, explanation and face-to-face discussion with the membership than ever before.

Broadcast Licensing

The licensing of broadcasters is a short and simple story in comparison to that of general public performance licensing. The relationship between PRS and broadcast companies has historically and habitually been good, although there have been a few notable disputes.[30] The relationship was established strongly and workably in the days of the BBC and ITV duopoly, and it continued in similar fashion as the BBC's activities grew and independent radio stations proliferated – the former negotiating on its own behalf and the latter negotiating collectively through their TV and Radio representative bodies.

Licensing the BBC has always been an extremely important issue. The huge importance of broadcasting to music creators was obvious from the beginning – by the 20s radio was the largest user of music – but as a licensee the BBC was unique, and it took several attempts to find a workable licensing formula (and many, including the BBC, would say that process is not over yet). The "how to licence" question was compounded by the "how much" issue. In the pre-independent broadcast network days, it was a case of two monopolies negotiating with each other – a recipe for tough bargaining.

The 1929 licensing agreement was a landmark. It simplified the basis for the licence to the number of wireless licences issued, so linked licence fee to growth in radio's audience and popularity, and greatly increased the actual amount of PRS income (from £39,000 to £45,000). But the limits of revenue were severe because the link was to the part of the radio licence fee paid to the BBC (only 50% of it), and the PRS 5% share was fixed and non-

---

gradually removing subsidies and special compensatory payments for certain types of composition or certain classes of members. The decision to end the subsidy for the performance of classical music (ie the "topping up" of licence income from performance licensed in Tariff LC – Live Classical – encountered strong and prolonged resistance. Appeals to Government fromsome dissatisfied members led to the Select Committee hearing which found that PRS was not to be criticised for its decision, and that the society

was acting in the best interests of its membership as a whole.

29 The 1995-1997 Simplifications Process eliminated Grading of arrangements, Performance Factor weightings such as Featured/Background, Bonus For Length (extra royalties for broadcast of "longer" works) and other calculations and adjustments in preparation for specifying new post-PROMS computer system. The idea behind some of the rule changes was also to stop PRS from being the "policeman" who always checked that the rules were

negotiable. Other tensions included the BBC's tendency to demand that PRS should patriotically avoid demanding too much money from a Government-funded British institution; and its rather lofty attitude to popular music which did nothing for the health and temper of popular publishers.

By 1933 PRS had managed to win abandonment of the 5% ceiling, but had to accept a sliding scale which saw the amount payable per wireless actually falling as the number of licences grew – the fee to PRS dropping slightly with each successive million additional radio licence holders. Unsurprisingly, the new arrangements did nothing to dampen the irritation of the rights owners, and again they won press support (one journalist describing the effect on "the music trade, authors and composers" as "a blinding whack in the eye"). Allied to the fact that the actual sum the BBC was paying was thought too low, was growing objection to the fact that the Government was taking half the wireless licence fee income. A Government Committee investigated, recommended that the BBC be given more of a share of the wireless licence revenue and that payments to music creators should be "generous". The Government conceded the first proposal and that gave PRS the chance to pursue the second.

Predictably, the process was neither quick nor easy, and at times both PRS and BBC handled the public relations side of the matter badly. But despite the attitude of some of its backward-looking members who regarded broadcasting as a modern evil, PRS kept in mind that radio was essentially a great development for music copyright owners, provided they could earn a fair fee from it. However carefully and reluctantly, the society accepted that things were changing and it had to change with them. Largely thanks to the diplomacy of PRS Chairman Leslie Boosey, that crucial 1937 battle with the BBC went to arbitration, and the result was wholly positive for PRS members.

The link between BBC licence payment and the number of radio (and then also television) licences issued to its audience persisted for decades, as did the low tariffs which the BBC for various reasons won from PRS in a series of negotiations. As a result, PRS revenue from the national broadcaster fell steadily further behind inflation and the perceived value of the performing right as reflected in tariffs for other kinds of usage, a situation only partly masked by several long periods of low inflation.

The 60s explosion in music use across all kinds of premises and through broadcasting should have given great power to the PRS elbow in tackling the poor BBC licence deal. But in 1962 the society was about to start negotiation with the new independent television companies, and felt it could not cope with another row with the BBC at the same time. And it hoped that the BBC would soon be better off because the cost of radio and TV licences to the public would rise (as they did).

In 1966 PRS finally took a very deep breath and demanded a 40% rise in the BBC tariff (worth an additional £0.5m a year). It was no surprise that the BBC absolutely refused to pay this and went to the Performing Right Tribunal with its case. With a flourish, it added its own demand that the tariff should actually be lowered.

Battle positions were closest on the issue that life had changed since the 1937 deal, but they rapidly diverged from there: the BBC claimed its audiences were smaller because of competition from UK independents and loss of the Empire and colonies and their BBC listening habits, while PRS said that public licence evasion meant that the true size of the BBC audience was unknown but in fact very much bigger than estimated because, even in households which had a licence, one licence now covered several radios including the transistors which had facilitated a huge youth market for broadcast music outside the home.

PRS also contended that as inflation rose the cost of living had to be taken into account. And, despite the Tribunal's already established reluctance to take the tariff situation abroad

---

being followed, and to put the onus of the monitoring back onto the membership. 1996-1998 Distribution and Data Review eliminated the Classical Music Subsidy, the Significant Venues system (which had tried to ensure 100% receipt of detailed programmes from what had originally been intended as a representative selection of music venues) to improve the quality of royalty distribution for live music performance income and some allowances claimable by members on proof of performances not reported to PRS, indiscriminate use

of sales charts to represent performance usage etc. It also brought in, after the MMC Report, concepts such as Revenue Weighted Sampling and Straight lining between licence income and distribution instead of "pooling" licence revenue and distributing it according to rules often disconnected from the income source. 2001-2003 began phasing out Earning Equalisation Allowance, which topped up earnings for some members on a sliding scale, to smooth out decline in income; and started charging administration deductions on US and

A visit to PRS in 1987 from students of copyright administration sponsored by WIPO (World Intellectual Property Organisation) with a young manager who went on to become first Director of Membership for PRS and is currently Executive Director Membership for the MCPS-PRS Alliance – John Sweeney (left)

into account in UK decisions, the arrival of ITV, supported by paid advertising, indicated a "value" for broadcast entertainment in Britain with which the value of music to the BBC could be compared.

These were worthwhile arguments, but in 1967 the Tribunal awarded PRS an extra 3d (1.25p) per receiving licence – one third of the requested rise – with no back payments. Adding insult to injury, it fixed this position until 1971, so that PRS members got no benefit from the late 60s arrival of new BBC services and the rise in the public's licence fee. PRS members protested bitterly in public, and to PRS which many felt had not been tough enough.

While not exactly tearing off its jacket and tie and snarling "OK, no more Mr Nice Guy", PRS did toughen its approach. The soon-

to-retire but still tireless General Manager Royce Whale teamed with his lawyer colleague Denis de Freitas in setting out the PRS case again. Their crystal-clear and forcibly worded document went to the Government, denouncing the Tribunal's "misconceptions which threaten permanently to deny justice in our country to the music creators". The Government responded positively by replacing the Tribunal Chairman.

In the 1971 BBC negotiations the Corporation was looking only for small inflation adjustments, but PRS wanted delayed justice. It wanted much bigger fees, and it wanted to tear up the old rule book in getting them. The new licence was to be calculated on a percentage of BBC revenue, or its expenditure. The Tribunal was the obvious next stop on this very bumpy road. But the Tribunal had since 1966 changed its attitude and its Chairmanship. The result in 1978 was entirely in PRS' favour: a percentage of the BBC's revenue plus its grant-in-aid.

Then the crucial battle to alter the hitherto lump sum licence for commercial television to a potentially much more rewarding percentage of net advertising revenue was lost when the Tribunal rejected the PRS case in 1983. However in practical terms PRS won a substantial increase in fee, which raised the platform for subsequent fee negotiations.

Then came the early skirmishes with the rival satellite broadcasters Sky and BSB (British Satellite Broadcasting), which both objected to PRS proposals that their licence fees should be based on a percentage of net advertising revenue. Media tycoon Rupert Murdoch's Sky operation won the war of attrition in a still small market, swallowing BSB to form BSkyB, but the tussle over licensing terms continued and led eventually to a Tribunal hearing in 1997. This resulted in introduction of a new form of lump sum payment, while rejecting any percentage of BSkyB revenue except in the case of music channels. In the view of John Axon it constrained PRS' future income growth from TV, in a static market for "viewer hours" (ie the proliferation of television

EU royalties, which had long been exempt.
30 see Distribution explanation and diagram

channels and the increase in hours of programming offered is not resulting in an increase in the amount of time viewers each spend watching television).

International Revenue

From the beginning, the collection of royalties from overseas has been one of the main priorities of PRS. Foreign royalties gradually became a vital part of the total income, especially after the global success of The Beatles and other pop artists in the 1960s (receipts from affiliated societies went from £0.66m in 1960 to £1.7 million in 1965 and kept on climbing in value until they settled, proportionately at about one-third of all PRS collections).

The first agency in a British Empire territory was established in South Africa in 1925 and the following year PRS was a founder member of CISAC, so as well as its bilateral agreements with fellow CISAC members, PRS had an income flow from its agencies in former or current British colonies in the Mediterranean, Caribbean, Africa and the Far East. Local conditions were taken in true colonial stride: one PRS Annual Report stated that "Hurricane Hugo posed difficulties inAntigua, Montserrat and elsewhere but nonetheless the Windward and Leeward Islands showed an advance in general and broadcasting licensing work."

In 1977, a subsidiary company, MCOS (Music Copyright (Overseas) Services Limited) was set up to co-ordinate collections in these countries through UK-appointed agents. Even though PRS provided most of the funding and was by far the more active partner, MCOS was a joint venture with MCPS. Its board included six directors appointed by PRS and four from MCPS.

Those appointed as MCOS agents came from a range of backgrounds. Some were lawyers or accountants, but the part-time agent in Gibraltar was also an undertaker. The agents had to be tough and committed to the cause of copyright as they often operated in an environment inhospitable to the idea of paying for the use of music. Diana Derrick, the international director of PRS from 1994 to 1999, was the agent for Trinidad and Tobago between 1981 and 1985, and was once chased from a music-using rum shop by its machete-wielding owner.

MCOS also encouraged the formation of national societies, supporting and advising newly-formed societies. Agents could also play a role in lobbying for copyright reform and establishing new societies. In Trinidad and Tobago, Derrick was given a lift by the attorney general shortly after the second reading of a new Copyright Act. He told her that if she wanted to see the law passed, a copyright society would have to be set up. COTT (Copyright Organisation of Trinidad and Tobago) was founded in the following year. MCOS, the agents and local members were the driving force in the launch of other national societies in the Caribbean, south-east Asia and Africa in the years after 1977. A special case in Europe was the Republic of Ireland where IMRO, the Irish Music Rights Organisation, achieved independence from PRS only in 1995 after several years of sometimes acrimonious negotiations with the PRS Board in London, and only after an overwhelming majority (96%) of PRS members resident in the Republic voted for it.

Although foreign earnings were an ever more important component of PRS income, there was for many years only one junior manager with specific responsibility for foreign relations, while senior managers often handled links to sister societies in a relatively informal "old boys' network" way.

The year 1992 was a turning-point in the international strategy of PRS in that a decision was taken to set up a separate international department with its own director and managers. This was the result of a growing disquiet among the PRS Board and members about some practices of some foreign societies that they felt were inimical to the interests of PRS and its members – most notably the "social and cultural" deductions which funded wide ranging benefits such as pensions, subsidies for concerts and recordings, and training schemes for musicians.

Unlike domestic public performance and broadcast income, international revenues are not, of course, the direct result of PRS licensing and negotiation. So the prime concerns of the international team are to maintain the greatest and most up-to-date knowledge of overseas societies' activities, rules and practices; and to ensure in every possible way that money due to PRS members is properly calculated, properly apportioned and rapidly remitted to the UK society. There had been visits by senior management to foreign societies before 1992 and in some cases critical points were made strongly by the PRS management to their overseas counterparts. However, these were never systematic, nor were they followed up to see whether PRS criticisms had been acted upon.

In contrast, the technical visits introduced at the end of 1991 with visits to SACEM (France) and GEMA (Germany) were minutely organised investigations of everything from the governance of a society and its membership rules to methods of collection and distribution. In determining where visits should be made, the top priority was to check on the societies that remitted the greatest amounts to PRS, followed by societies where PRS was already aware of problems concerning the treatment of its members' works. In particular, PRS officials were on the lookout for cases where foreign music was treated less favourably by a national society than the music of its own members; for instance, where music written for television by a local composer was paid for at a higher rate than television scores composed by foreign writers.

Usually PRS investigators were received very cordially but sometimes the cordiality issued thinly through gritted teeth, notably when auditors from BBDO Stoy Hayward accompanied PRS officials to Germany, and when officials of the Greek society AEPI had to deal with the open incredulity of their UK visitors

when they were told that "virtually no British music" was heard in the holiday resorts of the Greek islands.

In 1994 MCOS ceased operations, although its acronym would be used again a few years later for a quite different purpose: as Music Copyright Operational Services Ltd, the first name in 1997 of the jointly-owned operating company set up by MCPS and PRS.

In 1999 there was another rethink on international activities, and a new company, PRS Overseas, was formed, with Derrick as Managing Director, to supervise and support the agencies of which 12 were active in 2003, eight in the Caribbean, three in the Mediterranean and one (Brunei) in the Far East. International relations with all affiliated CISAC societies remained a major revenue function within PRS, with its own director within PRS Executive Director John Axon's team.

Distribution rules and systems

The distribution of licence income to PRS members as royalties was always a greater dilemma and a bigger task than bringing in the licence money, which was difficult enough in itself.

If licensing the performing right always required dogged determination, a particular set of resources and often courage (licensing inspectors over many years reported regular verbal and occasionally physical assaults in the course of their daily work), then for a long time distribution of the revenue collected apparently required ingenuity and a crystal ball . The former is still very useful but the latter has been properly replaced by improved collection of information, better procedures and IT.[31]

Having got the money in PRS had to decide who to give it to, and efforts to arrive at the right answer to that question have always been limited by the expense of doing so. Appreciation of what the

31 see Distribution explanation and diagram

"right answer" might be has changed over time. Originally the practical but admittedly inaccurate and never popular solution was to allocate and pay royalties according to some judgement of "value" of a member's works linked to the perceived popularity and commercial success of the writer.

This was arguably consistent with the founding concept of the performing right society as a collective, acting for the collective rather than individual good of composers and authors, as well as offering collective administration of their right. The right was being upheld through licensing activity, and licence revenue was being passed to copyright owners. There was no way of knowing who should get what precisely, but almost everyone got something.

Today the favoured "right answer" is that performance royalty distributions should come as close as possible to translating a single use of a work into a single payment. This is closely analogous to the mechanical rights "line by line" distribution model which can link a royalty payment directly to the recordings of that work which have been created and the number of copies manufactured.

Through its history, PRS has been moving from one extreme towards the other via a variety of distribution models. The rules and methods have been altered many times, steadily improving although never to the satisfaction of all at any given point. Because there is as yet no precise and automatic way to link every penny of licence income to a particular musical work which has been used, policy decisions need to be taken and reviewed by the elected Directors. Former PRS Secretary George Neighbour summed up the responsibility when he stated that it was incumbent on every generation of Directors to examine and review distribution policy.

This they did regularly over the years, and comprehensively in the mid-90s. Traditionally, distribution policy and rules were decided by the PRS Distribution Committee, which needed to be, but was

not always, acutely and constantly aware of the propriety issues relating to decisions on distributions of monies being made by potential beneficiaries of shifts in policy and practice. The Directors were relieved of this burdensome responsibility when better data and simplified, more transparent, distribution rules were put in place in the mid-to-late 90s[32]. That work included the key decisions on analogies (use of one kind of available performance information as a basis for distribution of licence income from usage for which performance information could not be gathered). Choice of analogies could obviously have considerable impact on who got paid. The available analogies were and are limited: radio performance logs and record sales information (including the weekly sales charts). Their use to distribute licence revenue from pubs, clubs, village halls, aircraft, ships, hotels, restaurants, exhibitions, shops, offices, factories, doctors' and dentists' waiting rooms, and many other venues was acknowledged to be "rough justice", and attempts were regularly made to refine and improve the process.

Over the years many members felt hard done by and the process was extremely complicated, seldom explained and rarely understood. The PRS Board was made increasingly aware of this in the past decade, and some members' dissatisfaction led in 1994/5 to complaints to the Office of Fair Trading, which in turn led to the MMC Enquiry in 1995 and its report in 1996. Prompted by its own wish to do things better, boosted by the MMC report, between 1996 and 1998 PRS undertook the most detailed and extensive review in its history of distributions and the amount and quality of the information on which they are calculated. The MMC's calls for greater fairness, accuracy and transparency in royalty distribution were taken to heart, and were the springboard for far-reaching change.

Agreeing, communicating and implementing that change required frankness and determination on the part of Board Directors and managers of a quality which it is unlikely PRS could have mustered at other crucial junctures in its past, and which probably

32 The PRS Distribution Committee ceased to exist.

could not have been produced at *this* juncture but for the impetus and external authority of the MMC Report. Its recommendations genuinely dispelled some of the clouds obscuring the road into the future, inspiring enthusiasm for change which was now more clearly indicated. They also inevitably carried an implied threat from the Office of Fair Trading, and unity in the face of a common threat is a time-honoured human reflex.

The Distribution and Data Review was an enormous project, in which the Board was closely involved and continually informed and consulted. As a result, significant changes were defined, explained and recommended by management, and adopted by the Board. This achieved major improvement to distribution policies; in the process (and anything but lightly) it involved the slaughtering of a number of "sacred cows", a possibly irreverent but highly descriptive verbal shorthand used by everyone involved. These took the form of long-established diversions of revenue to fund special schemes to assist certain types of repertoire or certain classes of members, the most significant being the Classical Music Subsidy.

More importantly, the D&DR (as it rapidly became known in an organisation which yields to no other in its ability to invent acronyms, economics and whimsical jargon) resulted in a revolutionary approach to gathering and using data about performances. This included the introduction of revenue weighted sampling and the concept of "straightlining" revenue from its source to its distribution, and removing the traditional use of analogous, often inappropriate, data for distributing money for which there was no available or reliable performance information. All this has been followed through into methodology now firmly embedded in the way PRS works.

D&DR began with a clear set of needs: to run an independent study of music use, then create a statistically valid and reliable model for collecting and analysing performance data, *and doing this in an affordable way*. There was an equally clear set of guiding

principles: revenues distributed should relate as closely as practicable to performances; cost should be allocated as closely as practicable to revenues; the basis of all revenue apportionment should be made explicit to members.

It was the first time a project even remotely like this had been undertaken by PRS, and no closely similar project had ever been undertaken by any other collecting society. PRS used Coopers and Lybrand (now IBM Consulting) as lead consultants on setting up the project; the vital independent statistical advice came from Professor Frank Kelly of Cambridge University; and market research company Millward Brown was engaged to do the fieldwork. A strong internal structure involving some Board members, managers and teams of staff ran the project. Invaluable help also came from an advisory group made up of PRS members and some invited outsiders who had specialist practical knowledge about the performance of all the various genres of music – in what sort of venues, by whom, how – and how data about these performances could best be gathered. The task, expressed very simply, was to define a statistically reliable formula for fieldworkers literally to go out into all kinds of places all over the country where music (live, recorded, broadcast) was being used and note titles, times of day, types of usage and types of venues, which was the key factor in determining which tariff was being used to license the usage, and therefore to which revenue stream the data should be applied.

The scope of the initial review can be illustrated by a few figures. In 1996 the total PRS revenue which was affected by the D&DR was £122.5m (out of the then total of £186.7m) and proportions are similar today. Premises checked represented every kind of music user: Millward Brown[33] team members shivered in skating rinks; were rained on at festivals; inhaled detrimental amounts of cigarette smoke and beer fumes in pubs and clubs; enviously watched diners in hotels and restaurants and fought terminal boredom in hairdressers and supermarkets. About 1400 visits to premises were made involving over 8000 hours of market research

---

33 Millward Brown's efforts in this unique project earned recognition within its own business
    sector when its report won the Best Paper accolade at the 1998 Marker Research Society
    annual conference

(researchers spent up to six hours at each premises), plus 7000 research phone calls. Resulting details of 350,000 performances were analysed, yielding 9250 titles of works. Specially detailed "focus studies" were aimed at the performance of dance and folk music, or music played in village halls, for example. The review also covered what data was collected about the use of music in broadcasting, and how that data was applied to distributions, and it tested the validity of analogies which were then currently in use. This last issue raised some interesting questions: one example was why part of the income from Tariff P for public houses was distributed across radio logs which included BBC Radio 3. The market research came up with the fact that this uncompromisingly highbrow classical network was not, oddly enough, being played to customers in pubs.

Two years of ingenuity, hard-won understanding of new information and changing operation landscapes, thoughtful decision making, meticulous hard work and careful communication to members resulted in the closest affordable approach to the MMC-inspired ideal of fairness, accuracy and transparency in royalty distributions. A permanent special unit within PRS was set up to continue the work and ensure that the quality of distribution data is constantly refreshed.

Today performance data is drawn in directly from licensees – concerts, theatres, cinemas, and broadcasters – and via third parties such as background music suppliers, airlines, MCPS, and the continual field survey conducted by market research company Maritz of sample venues selected off the PRS Public Performance system (PuPSS). The importance of this core distribution and data activity means that it is constantly being reviewed, extended and improved. Plans agreed by the Board in 2003 included revising the survey to focus more effort on identifying the use of original repertoire, launching a full "gig reporting " scheme for writer members who are also performers, renewed efforts to source information directly from karaoke operators and piloting a better scheme for DJs to report on music use in clubs and discos.

The launch of the new PRS computer in 1969 with CEO Michael Freegard (*left*) and Chairman composer Alan Frank (*second from right*)

PRS Public Performance Royalties (before the Distribution and Data Review)

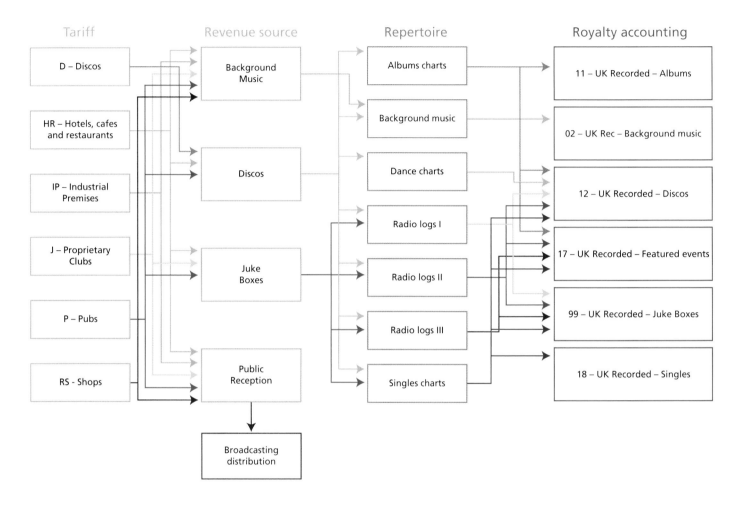

The graphic is a simplified example of how royalties collected under a small selection of tariffs is allocated to members. This graphic broadly looks at performed recorded music.
Six tariffs are shown out of 52. The revenue from the tariffs is allocated to four revenue sources, as shown above, but also to a number of revenue sources not included in this sample graphic. The four revenue sources are also allocated further royalties from tariffs not included in the graphic.

Similarly, royalties allocated to the four revenue sources are distributed over the seven repertoires (i.e. sources of programme information) included as shown, and also over other repertoires not shown, together with royalties from other revenue sources not included. For example, income from the Discos tariff is allocated entirely to the Discos revenue source, which is also allocated royalties from other tariffs in respect of disco performances, and the revenue source is distributed against programme information from a large range of performance sources, including various radio channels and as well as others.

Source: The MCPS-PRS Alliance

PRS Public Performance Royalties today

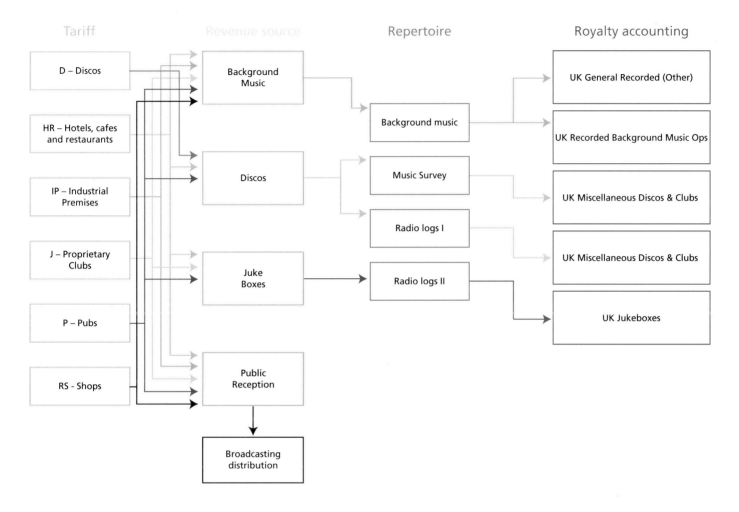

How PRS makes distributions

The work of distributing PRS revenues (less administrative cost) as writers' and publishers' royalties essentially involves bringing together three streams of information: copyright works, performances and money.

Information about works and their ownership are the starting point. Under the terms of the PRS Membership Agreement the society must be provided, in the appropriate form, with information about works when they are created (writers assign the performing right in all existing and future works to PRS, for the life of their membership). At the time a work is registered it these days acquires a unique identifying number (International Standard Works Code, ISWC) applied to it by PRS. It is usually the case

that the writer has a contract with a publisher, through which a proportion of the writer's royalty income is due to that publisher. A publisher claiming a share of performing right income must therefore demonstrate that there is an agreement to this effect, so must lodge a copy of the agreement with PRS. Originally the entire paper agreement was provided, but now the format is an electronic file claiming a share and referring to a previously registered agreement.

All parties should be aware of this information as held by PRS, and online access to PRS (and MCPS) data by members is being developed and improved to make it possible for members to check and correct their own entries (see IT section).

The PRS Data Preparation Department in 1984

IT advances have been incorporated in a continuous programme of hardware and software updates for Alliance offices since the mid-90s. By 2003 the PCs on desks had become the powerful workstations and information hubs necessary for running the societies' wide variety of processes, and maintaining internal and external communications at the speed demanded by the world of business in general, and increasingly demanded by the members and licensees of MCPS and PRS. All were linked to each other via a powerful local area network, which offered access to the Alliance intranet - the instant information source for management and staff; to the internet; to all the normal office applications; and to the specialist systems and applications which serve the performing and mechanical rights businesses.

Building and maintaining an up-to-date and accurate works and agreements database has always been difficult, even just for information relating to PRS' own members. The problems are larger where the works and agreements information originates with a UK sub-publisher for a writer published abroad, or with an overseas collecting society.

Performance information comes in from a variety of sources. Radio broadcasting is the best of these, now supplying PRS via tape, e-mail or electronic file transfer with reliable data about title, usage and duration of music which is broadcast. This may be a full list (from BBC and independent networks and certain very large or specialist stations) or a sample of certain days for small stations, as required.

Television is similar in theory, but the steady increase in provision of programme material from independent production companies has led to a tendency for data from TV channels and networks to be minimal (though happily this is not the only information source available to PRS) on the assumption that PRS will acquire more detailed cue sheet information from the production company. Film music performance information is similar in nature and origin.

In public performance the licence agreement also lays an obligation on the licensee to provide information about works performed if required to do so by PRS. It is accepted that in many types of music usage this is not easy; and demands from the society have at various times provoked angry protests from licensees. The most obviously reasonable sources of public performance information are businesses which have music performance as their primary commercial purpose: concert venues and promoters, theatres, variety shows and to some extent discos. The proportion of public performance revenue which can be distributed using these information sources is small.

The blanket licences for public performance cover three identifiably different kinds of music use: live music, where performers can be expected to know what they performed and provide PRS with this information if asked, although this is open to fraud ; commercially compiled background music, provided on tape or CD to restaurants, shops, hotels etc by companies which can then supply PRS with information on the works used; and mechanical performance, tape and CD players and jukeboxes used by the licensee or his customers. There is also the secondary use (rediffusion) of radio and TV programmes as a source of music performance.

Detailed information about the works used under these blanket licences is still extremely difficult to obtain, and if obtained and used in distributions would increase complexity and cost of data processing and produce per performance payments of minute amounts. For these distributions analogies have long been used as the only way to make these distributions at reasonable administrative cost.

Eventually, the works and agreements, performance and licence income data are brought together in a distribution accounting system to calculate royalties. The principle is that copyright owners receive a share of the appropriate types of revenue; there is no defined payment for the use of a musical work (a commonly-held public and media misconception). The performances, matched to works and agreement data, and translated into a points system for the purposes of calculation, are divided into the appropriate section of licence income to produce the royalties payable to individual copyright owners.

IT: The core job of handling data and turning it into information

For PRS and MCPS the basic practicality of their work, and the function on which depends everything else they may be asked or may choose to do, is handling data. This has been true from the time of handwritten ledgers to present day Information Technology and all the sophistication (and frustration) that implies. That data informs the work of the societies, and much of it becomes information which goes out from the society to members, licensees and other societies. This core function within both organisations deserves a particular focus in their respective histories. It also has an important place in the story of the Alliance: the significant, though far from total, overlap between both organisations' data and the systems needed to handle it, was the basis for building the joint operation which later went on to amalgamate other departmental functions.

For MCPS and PRS data means a huge amount of ever-changing and ever-increasing detail about the copyright musical works administered; about recordings; about types of licences, licences issued and licensees; about members. In PRS' case, there is data about the writer/publisher agreements according to which their performing right royalty distributions are made; about performances; and about everything else relating to running the business. In MCPS' case the list is the same, but with information about recordings substituting for that relating to performances.

At PRS the IT story has several distinct stages. Between 1914 and the 1960s information was held on paper in one form or another. This did not mean it was not handled with some degree of automation. In a 1964 issue of the membership magazine Performing Right (amid reports of celebrations of the society's Golden Jubilee) the PRS General Manager Royce Whale announced an important development in what he might have called IT if the acronym had been in common use then. He

pointed out with pride that between 1931 and 1935 PRS had been the first collecting society to introduce electrical Powers-Sames and Hollerith accounting machines to produce distribution accounts. However, being a pioneer had penalties attached to it, and PRS had inevitably fallen behind as later starters installed newer and better equipment. The society's office move from Margaret Street to Copyright House in Berners Street had allowed staff to start the huge task of transferring details from 250,000 handwritten or typed "master cards" to hand-punched cards for the society's first generation of data processors. Stating a fact which would again be stressed almost 30 years later when a major computer project failed, Whale noted that distributions ad continued uninterrupted despite all the upheaval.

Two years later the first PRS computer was ceremoniously inaugurated, with a sort of charming whimsicality which is glaringly absent from IT projects today. Eminent PRS member A P Herbert wrote an ode to the awesome machine (which occupied an entire floor of the building but had the computing power of one of today's desktops, and far less memory); his poem began: "Welcome, you wonderful unnatural toy, to this Society's august employ".

Chief Executive Michael Freegard was less lyrical when in 1969 he remarked that the "abundant benefits" promised in Herbert's poem were "a bold prophecy, having regard to the many horror stories now circulating about the plagues and tribulations affecting computer users in all types of business" – words which again were a pre-echo of the problems to be experienced in the early 90s.

Admitting that the computer had thrown a few fits, such as sending a rural pub a PRS licence invoice for £34,000, Freegard was able to report that in its first three years it had delivered cost savings of £15,000 a year, and had made it possible to reduce staff by eight even while the amount of revenue being handled had risen by 34%.

Electronic storage of information and automation of PRS business processes developed over the following three decades: "visual display units" and keyboards became a familiar adornment to desks in an increasing variety of departments. But the regiments of filing cabinets containing indexed handwritten cards and voluminous files of typed (later word processed) paper proliferated as fast as the VDUs. This parallel and imperfectly integrated development of data storage and handling allowed complexity of processes to persist. Keeping track of what exactly was stored and where, and checking the quality of the data were difficult, and individuals or departments remained to a large extent the keepers and users of sections of data which they interpreted as their function demanded. This situation would later be a major factor in what came to be known as "the PROMS disaster".

It became obvious that gradual and piecemeal development and expansion of computing was not going adequately to serve PRS' rapidly growing business needs. In the late 80s it was decided to upgrade the mainframe operating system (called DME). It was running well enough but was obsolescent. It was no longer supported by ICL which created it, and the number of people familiar with it was dwindling, so it would have to be replaced at some point fairly soon. One obvious decision taken was to upgrade the operating system (to a system called VME). This was a large but not particularly difficult or very expensive job.

Sensibly, PRS also checked what other collecting societies were doing with their computer systems. This revealed that PRS was trailing well behind its key affiliates in this area, prompting the decision (not uncommon in many other kinds of business) to anticipate further necessary developmental steps in the near and medium term future by taking one big stride immediately.

So the relatively simple systems upgrade was shelved and a project was set up to create a single database which would bring together all the separate member areas of computerisation. Since old software was becoming costly to maintain and staffing levels had climbed, a cost-cutting business plan could be developed; it estimated a 25% annual saving on PRS administration costs.

The PROMS project

The project became known as the Performing Right On-line Membership System (PROMS). It was "to be built in 4GL (fourth-generation language) accessing a Relational Database Management System both running under a Unix operating system". This impenetrable-to-most description could colloquially be translated as "a pretty tall order", considering where the project was starting from. Work began in earnest in 1988 with external consultants, a dedicated in-house team and a steering committee of top managers and members of the Board. It also involved substantial organisational change.

As CEO, Michael Freegard was a member of that steering committee. He recalls that PROMS at the time seemed to hold out the prospect of automating much manual work. He was sceptical, but "early demonstrations were very impressive" and fears diminished. But it was a very big project. PROMS would have combined existing data files on all aspects of Membership Services, including admission to membership, registration of works and agreements, posting of performances, distribution of royalties and handling distribution queries. The main direct benefits to members would have included reduced administration cost (including a major reduction in staff costs) of about £3m a year at 1993 values.

Three years later an independent consultants report on the project, and soon after that a chapter in the computer disasters book *Crash*[34] by *Computer Weekly* journalist Tony Collins, would assert that PROMS started to go wrong very quickly, but this was

---

34 Published in 1997 by Simon and Schuster this book is now out of print but still available from some public libraries

at first not perceived and later not acknowledged quickly or fully enough to save it at economical cost.

Collins quite fairly summed up the outsiders' view in his book, which put the PRS problems in perspective by also telling the stories of other far more spectacular computer project failures of the time, costing many multiples of PRS' £8m estimated loss. These included the Stock Exchange's Taurus system which was abandoned after some £50m was spent on development and the failure of a major computer project for the London Ambulance Service which had the potential to cost lives.

Although in accordance with journalistic tradition he never revealed his sources, Collins almost certainly had the advantage of access to the confidential and never-published full report of the independent assessor commissioned by PRS. The following extracts from *Crash* contain his analysis of the PROMS project failure.

> Once the decision to start [PROMS] has been taken there is no provision for turning back. Tacitly, reputations are staked on the project's success. However, the PRS is blighted by its unfamiliarity with failure, so it doesn't plan for one. Most noticeably, the project lacks any individual who has a notice on his desk saying 'the buck stops here'.

> With any major computer project a single person is needed to take charge who has a profound grasp of the business and the technology, and who is empowered to take major decisions – otherwise group responsibility prevails… everyone hands over responsibility for his or her individual actions to the group… the project starts to control its own destiny….. and everyone works for the sake of the project and not the business.

> At this stage the project managers do not appear to realise that the society's administrative processes are not in a fit state to be computerised. These processes are all too arcane, too complex,

too little understood by even the staff, let alone outside suppliers and programmers. The best maxim at this stage would have been *simplify* before *computerising*….a mastery of the business rather than technical problems prior to the computerisation could have made the difference between success and failure.

> Everyone seems to assume that computerisation and improvement will go hand in hand. Worse, a 'Big Bang' tends to become the preferred plan – an all-encompassing rather than a step-by-step approach to computerisation.

> Tests show that the project is fundamentally flawed, though this is not obvious at the time because all the immense problems that surface during the tests are deemed surmountable.

> None of the project team should feel under pressure to suppress bad news to save their skins. They should always feel they can express the view to the chief executive that the project is going nowhere. In most failures, staff who knew there were major problems kept quiet to avoid jeopardising their jobs…another factor common to almost all computer disasters [is] that systems are built to artificially tight deadlines.

In the summer of 1991 a 10-week delay in the PROMS timetable had to be announced, and the following February, just six weeks before the revised go-live date, deadlines had to be abandoned and the project effectively replanned. In August 1992 the mounting problems already acknowledged by PRS management and Council became public through the press. The Council ordered a technical assessment of the project, and that prompted a further revision of project plans, moving the target go-live date to September 1994 (two years after the original date) and predicting additional cost of £6m. Another internal report was delivered by the new PROMS Technical Co-ordinator appointed in July 92, John Rathbone. The PROMS project was suspended. It was then shut down after an investigation and report commissioned from Ewen Fletcher of consultants Context Systems. Soon afterwards Michael Freegard resigned as CEO.

This was seen by the Board as fitting and necessary, but that was not the universal view among staff or even members, and in his book Collins asserts: "There is no evidence that he is to blame. Indeed one wonders if he and other executives who left after PROMS was suspended had offered themselves as scapegoats."

Conscious as always of the fact that it is not only a company (commercial though non-profit) but also a membership society, PRS went to great lengths to explain to its members what had happened and why, what the cost to them was, and what would be done to repair the situation.

A Members Meeting at Church House Westminster on 2 June 1993 was very fully reported in a special edition of *PRS News*[35], sent to every member. Chairman Wayne Bickerton opened by describing PROMS as "the largest single exercise ever undertaken by PRS" with up to 60 staff working on it at any one time. He stressed "we still have capable technical staff who are not the object of any censure in the PROMS assessment report."

Summarising the Context Systems report, the Chairman explained "PROMS failed because PRS information is not fully understood and there is no clear view of how it all fits together; and because the methods used in the project were inappropriate….What went wrong was not the result of fraud or malice, but the report indicates that there was a lack of understanding. There was a lack of experience. There was also negligence. And, I'm afraid to say, the PRS Council [Board] was misled again and again on the project's lack of progress." The PROMS system was incomplete and would cost too much to finish.

Members heard that disciplinary action had been taken; a full business processes review had begun and would inform future planning; a searching review of the Board itself and matters of corporate governance had been set up; a major exercise had started to clean up existing data and improve its quality, and the first PRS-MCPS joint scheme for registering works had started to run, ensuring that the data held on the systems of both societies had been double checked.

Bickerton added that valuable lessons had been learnt: "In future we will take smaller steps, and ensure that we take our time to produce the right results…to ensure that a mistake like this never happens again."

At the meeting some members held that culpability for the PROMS disaster rested with the Board n its decision-making role and it should consider resigning *en bloc*: calls for a vote of confidence or a full referendum were made but neither was conceded. Others present asked for an ombudsman to represent members, independent of board and management, but this was not pursued. Asked why the information which was to have been put into PROMS was "not good enough" Ewen Fletcher replied: "It was not good enough for an integrated system [PROMS] but it was good enough for current outdated systems. The main difference is that current systems…rely on interrelationships of people at each stage to check input and output". That "people input" could not be automated and put into the computer system to compensate for poor or missing data.

The PROMS project and its demise never had any direct effect on the administration of PRS members' rights and never caused a royalty distribution to be delayed or missed. These facts were a matter of pride for the society's managers at a time when many were demoralised by what had happened.

---

35 PRS News No 17, June 1993- which had a circulation restricted to PRS members only.

One positive note, however, was that a carefully-prepared and aggressively-pursued argument with the project consultancy LBMS led to the recovery of £2.3m of the fees paid to them.

A new approach to information systems

A new IS strategy had to be developed at a time of great soul-searching within PRS, and levels of anger and concern among Board Directors and some members which were greater than the situation warranted, particularly since out of the £11m spent some £3m worth of work was of continued use and value to the society, and over 25% of the £8m write-off was recovered. In comparison with what many other companies went through in a time when IT development was charging ahead in every business sector, and three out of every four IT projects failed, the PRS experience was at the benign end of the scale. But the distress to an organisation like PRS should not be glossed over.

The Board was shaken by events, by the public denting of its image, by the possibility of litigation and by the prospect of the difficult changes which would have to be initiated to retrieve the situation. Middle managers resented the barrage of criticism which ignored all the good work they had tried to do and laid all the blame on them and on the PROMS project suppliers but exonerated the highest-level decision makers. For all concerned, but most extensively for the management and staff, this event would have a cathartic and eventually broadly positive effect. But a rift between the Board and the management opened up which took several years to heal: a situation not helped by the fact that they were very eventful and stressful years. PRS had been weakened in the estimation of the "rights industry", and particularly so where affiliated collecting societies overseas were concerned. The term *schadenfreude* recurs in PRS managers' descriptions of the attitude of the MPA and MCPS Boards, comprising mostly publishers, and of other societies overseas.

The wider potential implications of this were certainly not lost on the MCPS Board and management, and would soon lead to moves to bring some aspects of the administrative work of PRS and MCPS into a joint venture in which MCPS systems would, it was assumed, play a key part. The thinking on this joint "ServiceCo" developed separately in PRS and MCPS before and even while negotiations intended to lead to making it happen were in progress. Although a joint venture did not go forward at the first attempt, it was later reincarnated in a better-planned and structured development which became the MCPS-PRS Alliance. This very important part of collective history is therefore told from appropriate but different angles in the MCPS and Alliance chapters as well as in this one.

On the PRS IT front, it was agreed that the only way to move was forward, PROMS had diverted resources to itself and halted other IT work. The need to overhaul and improve existing systems was more urgent than ever, but the painful PROMS experience led management to offer, and the Board to seize on, a new "best practice" approach to any further IT developments. The prudence, planning and reporting were essentially good things, but unavoidably exerted a heavier controlling, reviewing and continually evaluating hand of caution than might have been warranted in a project and a company of this size.

John Rathbone had been brought into PRS on a year's contract because Michael Freegard and other Top Team members wanted a fresh mind to assess the issues. Rathbone's expertise and his favoured step-by-step approach to IT development won him the permanent role of PRS Information Systems Director in October 1993. In *Crash* Tony Collins described Rathbone as a manager who "understands that calamity and over-ambition are inseparable twins" and this is a fair if journalistically dramatic description of his consistent approach.

His first task was to draw a line under PROMS and help PRS to put behind it what he describes as a "spinning wheel project" – much creativity and energy expended to produce little, but very difficult for the individuals to stop. He planned the route ahead with an Information Services management team which knew change (and *what kind* of change) was needed, but lacked technical expertise and experience in any business other than PRS, and as a result were naïve in business terms. It is a tribute to Rathbone and to the quality of those middle management PROMS survivors that most are still with the company, better-trained, more experienced and in more senior positions.

Priorities were to stabilise the obsolescent DME systems by completing the previously shelved upgrade to VME; to rebuild the IT department with better ways of working, and take forward the good ideas which managers had into a new IT strategy built on small, manageable, incremental projects; and to rebuild confidence generally – *in* IS and *within* IS. This process was in its very early stages when the MMC enquiry into PRS[36] was formally initiated in November 1994, and the PRS Council decided to commission an external Corporate Governance review[37] because it was genuinely interested in the developmental benefits which it might bring to the governing layer of the organisation but also because it could be a positive pre-emptive move in anticipation of the MMC's findings.

The role of full time permanent Chief Executive had been vacant since the resignation of Michael Freegard. In November 1995 that role was filled by the appointment of John Hutchinson, whose professional background in financial services also included a contemporary grasp of IT issues which PRS had not had before at this most senior level.

The MMC Report was published in February 1996 and criticised aspects of PRS royalty distribution practices and the information they were based on. This prompted the commissioning of what the then Chairman Andrew Potter described to PRS members as " the largest independent study of the public use of music ever performed", providing "an ideal opportunity to take a fresh look at all of our distribution procedures and processes and to assess

how we can improve in these areas" . This was the Distribution and Data Review described earlier.

All these events influenced the PRS IT strategy and the amount and type of work the developing systems would have to accommodate. ServiceCo, the 1993 attempt to set up a "back office" and IT joint venture with MCPS for both societies would of course also have a major impact.

As one of the largest societies in the world, in terms of membership, strength of repertoire and revenue collected, PRS has long had an important voice in the international collecting societies' umbrella organisation CISAC, and has played a very active part in its work. In the 90s the IT aspect of CISAC involvement strongly increased.

Alongside the need for each collecting society to provide itself with IT, which will help it to run its own business efficiently, sits the need for societies to communicate and work with counterparts around the globe. Music copyright administration is and must be an international activity, although traditionally and to the present day (with the recently-developed exception of the licensing of certain on-line music usage) the performing right is licensed strictly on national lines.

Reciprocal agreements between CISAC member societies ensure that writers and publishers receive payment for the use of their copyrights outside their own country. Information about copyright works and their ownership, and to some extent about their performance, has for well over a century needed to pass between societies which then identify where payment is due to another society's members. The last vital pieces of the international reciprocal jigsaw are the transfer of revenues, onward distribution to each society's members, and a perpetual flow of enquiries and responses which check and audit accuracy. As with so many businesses, these processes began with the exchange of paper: millions of letters, telexes, faxes, the time-consuming yet never-efficient system of *fiches internationales*- file cards which endlessly flitted between societies

---

36 Title – *A Report on the supply in the UK of the services of administering performing rights and film synchronisation rights.* See MMC Appendix

37 Professor Tom Clarke's review is reported elsewhere in this chapter.

supposedly to alert them to other societies' repertoire which might be performed in their country – and much more.

A major issue in the IT development in the 90s and beyond has been the accuracy of international mutually essential information and conformity to data standards which will ensure efficient use of that information. Under the auspices of CISAC, but with very active UK involvement from the beginning, a demanding initiative named the Common Information System (CIS) was launched in 1994. Again, the general issue of unique identifiers for works and agreements and the technology tools needed by collecting societies and the specific issue of CIS are common to the recent histories of MCPS and PRS, and so are dealt with in the Alliance chapter.

Most companies are driven by cost efficiency, and it was and is always important for PRS to save its members' money. This foundation stone in thinking and practice has in recent years had built on it a structure which more overtly than in the past provides an answer to the question "what does the member need from us to make their business better (applicable to writers as well as publishers) and their lives easier?"

PRS in the 90s strongly embraced the language, methodology, style, systems and operating structures of commercial business. Many believed that baby and bathwater were to an extent sluiced out together. But Rathbone would maintain that the commercial thinking has eventually been a route back to the member-focused ethos, harnessing good business practice and technology for a range of member benefits.

In this PRS would not claim to be leading the pack; it is successfully catching up with what has been happening in other businesses (whose efficiencies raise the expectations of PRS members who are also customers of banks, insurance companies, retailers, travel agents etc etc) in terms of service, and particularly in respect of internet-based service. The society recognises that if it cannot meet those expectations it quite probably will not

survive, although the embracing of this truth is evident throughout The Alliance organisation and is certainly not confined to information systems and services.

The PRS website is at www.prs.co.uk

Pictured early in their long individual terms of service as PRS Board Directors are three former Chairmen *left to right* Dr Donald Mitchell, Richard Toeman and Roger Greenaway

Chairmen

1914	William Boosey	publisher	Chappell Ltd
1929	Leslie Boosey	publisher	Boosey and Hawkes
1967	J.G.O. Roberts	songwriter	(Paddy Roberts)
1968	Laurence Swinyard	publisher	Novello & Co. Ltd
1975	Alan Frank	writer	
1979	Richard Toeman	publisher	Josef Weinberger Ltd
1983	Roger Greenaway	writer	
1987	Ron White	publisher	EMI Music Publishing Ltd
1990	Donald Mitchell	publisher	Faber Music
1993	Wayne Bickerton	writer	
1996	Andrew Potter	publisher	Oxford University Press
2002	David Bedford	writer	

Presidents

1954	Sir Arthur Bliss
1955	Sir Lennox Berkeley
1976	Vivian Ellis

Leslie Boosey

Sir Arthur Bliss

Songwriter Wayne Bickerton, long-serving member and former Chairman of the PRS Board, who was also required act as CEO during two periods during his term of office

Vivian Ellis, at his investiture as Hon GSM (Guildhall School of Music and Drama) while President of PRS

The PRS Members' Fund

Founding of the Fund

In the early 30s the PRS Board, particularly publishers, discussed the fact that they were regularly asked to give financial help to society members who had fallen on hard times through age, illness and severe reduction in their income. A Members' Assistance Fund was established in 1932 – with a £100 credit from the society - for urgent payments to "members of at least 10 years membership who are in need". Only writers could benefit – publishers could make contributions but could not receive payments.

The Board decided to deal in a formal and organised way with this issue, and in 1934 they did so generously by setting up The PRS Benevolent Fund with a contribution of 0.5 % of distributed fees. A Committee of Management was appointed under the first Fund Chairman, Leslie Boosey, and the Fund was originally established under the provisions of a Trust Deed. Funding increased to 1% in 1935 and 2% in 1938.

John Pinfold became secretary in 1952, Leslie Britton in 1974. John Logan has been full-time General Secretary from 1991 to the present.

In June 1962 The PRS Benevolent Fund changed its name to The PRS Members Fund and became a registered charity in September of that year, but its stated purpose remained, and remains today, what it was from the outset: "To assist necessitous Members and ex-Members of the Society and their dependents who for the time being may be in straitened circumstances".

Creating financial strength

The Members Fund grew in value through investment, and as time went on and the Fund became widely recognised as a good cause, it regularly increases through legacies in the form of single bequests and through assignment of late composers' royalty income.

Legacies to the Fund are very important for its work, and John Logan has frequently demonstrated that in this good cause he had no qualms in breaking the very British taboo about mentioning death. In the interests of ensuring future income for the Fund to go on doing its work, he has regularly reminded living PRS members about the need for them to consider including the Fund in their wills. His efforts led to occasional accusations of "ambulance chasing" (though the fact is that the Members Fund has always been more likely to provide an ambulance than chase one). A measure of Logan's success is that the Fund has consistently added new bequests to its sources of income every year. All are welcome, and many are significant in value – one such being 50% of both the performing and mechanical royalties of the late songwriter and Glam Rock icon Marc Bolan. Another very recent example was Stella Morgan, a former writer member of PRS, who left the Fund £31,628, the value of her residuary estate. Mrs Morgan died in 2001 but her membership had been terminated by the Society due to lack of earnings some 20 years earlier, in accordance with PRS policy at that time. She never forgot the Fund's generous support and made the charity the main beneficiary of her will. A sociological footnote is that this Fund, like many charities, also regularly benefits from the late 20th century trend for benefactors to wish that donations should be sent to a chosen good cause in lieu of funeral flowers.

The growth in Fund value led to the need to register as a charity in order to take advantage of tax relief.

During the 90s the continued growth in Fund reserves led to a realisation that the Members Fund was very much making its own way financially and no longer needed the level of annual donation it had been receiving from the PRS distributions. This annual contribution was progressively reduced over the years to £5,000. The deed of covenant between the society and the Fund expired in June 2002. The amounts disbursed by the Fund in the year 2002 totalled £196,082 and loans outstanding at the year end amounted to £128,343.

In February 2003 the Committee received the excellent news that the PRS Board had generously agreed to increase the annual payment to the Fund to £20,000.

Using the Fund's money to help PRS members when they are in need.

Between 300 and 500 grants are made every year, from as little as £15 (for example, a saucepan with a specially-adapted handle for an elderly arthritis sufferer) to several thousand pounds (such as payment towards emergency heart surgery performed in the USA). There are special cases where the Fund itself perceives a need. One such was when the devastating volcanic eruption on the West Indian island of Montserrat led to many near destitute families being relocated elsewhere. Among those who came to the UK were West Indian PRS members, and the Members Fund decided to add its own resettlement grants to the assistance they were receiving from the British Government.

The General Secretary has the power to make emergency grants on his own authority, but rarely has this proved necessary. All applications for PRS Members Fund grants are decided by the Committee of Management comprising Chairman and Deputy Chairman, the three Trustees – a composer, an author (lyricist) and a music publisher – and 12 other members, six of whom are appointed by the PRS Board and six by the members of the society in General Meeting. They take responsibility for running what John Logan puts in context as "a £5m business".

While this is a selective process, the aim is to give the right amount of help to the right applicants in a timely, helpful and considerate way. While carefully obeying the law which governs the conduct of registered charities, and its own clearly defined rules, the Fund aims to use money, not hold on to it. Applications which are clearly outside the Fund's remit are turned down, and these have over the years included some requests which could be described as bizarre, or as the General Secretary more tactfully puts it "very optimistic" but on these everyone is too discreet to go into detail.

One very worthy request which the Fund had to turn down was notably taken up by PRS itself, resulting in a unique event – the placing of a memorial to Marc Bolan near the site of the road accident in which he was killed.

The Fund Chairman annually makes a full and always interesting report to the PRS AGM[1]. The specific anecdotes vary but the main story has always the same: a number of around 100, mostly elderly, PRS members or their dependents receive monthly grants while comforts such as rented televisions and necessities like telephones, home insurance and personal alarms are also provided to many . As well as such regular help for many, the Fund is also there to offer immediate and urgent assistance in emergencies arising from acute or chronic illness or serious accidents. In January 1998 for example the Fund heard that a PRS member was seriously ill in Brazil, in need of a liver transplant, and through the good offices of one of the Brazilian rights societies it arranged for his medication costs to be paid during the period of acute need.

The PRS Members' Fund also liaises with other musical charities such as the Musicians Benevolent Fund and The Royal Society of Musicians to ensure that if a combined approach can be of benefit it is accordingly organised.

---

1 The Chairman's reports are to be found in the Fund Annual Report which until 2002 was part of the *PRS Yearbook*, but since then has been published as a separate document

The Fund in the future

While there is no foreseeable reason for the Fund to change its constitution or its activities and there are no plans that it will, the future is never certain. Logan pointed out that as people tend to live longer, they are less likely to leave sizeable estates and the number and value of charitable bequests will probably fall. That trend is sadly likely to be complemented by the fact that as more PRS members live to very old age and income from their musical works disappears there will be greater call for the Fund's help. Another trend is the ever-increasing and broadening PRS membership and every PRS member, regardless of length of membership or residency in any part of the world, is eligible to apply for Fund help if in genuine need. Yet another recent trend has been the growing number of younger PRS members seeking, and receiving, Fund help. But a history of good management and success in consistently achieving its objectives should ensure that the PRS Members Fund is ready to cross all its own bridges as it comes to them, while continuing to help PRS members to cross theirs.

Fund Chairmen

Year	Name
1934	Leslie Boosey
1957	Robert Elkin
1964	Bill Ward
1981	Hubert David
1987	Geoffrey Bush
1998	Len Thorpe
2003	Ray Davies

At the dedication of the memorial to Marc Bolan, whose bequest greatly benefits the Fund (*left to right*) Bolan's PR Keith Altham, PRS Board Director Nicky Graham, Rolan Bolan, family friend Eric Hall and Bolan's manager Tony Howard.

John Logan, PRS Members Fund General Secretary

The Performing Right Society Foundation

Now established as one of the most respected and forward-thinking UK funding organisations supporting music creation and performance, as well as being the largest independent funder purely for new music of any genre, the PRS Foundation was launched at Abbey Road Studios in March 2000.

However, that happy and newsworthy occasion was not the Society's debut in providing funds for the propagation and development of new music. PRS had been considering and supporting applications for monetary aid since 1953, judging each one on its own merits. By the late 1960s, there were so many requests that a Donations and Awards Committee was established for this task which by the late 90s was distributing about £250,000 per year, with the Communications department taking care of all the administration.

Among the awards and schemes supported by PRS in the past two increasingly active decades of the Donations and Awards Committee were a number founded by the society itself. Pre-dating the existence of the committee in fact ,the Leslie Boosey Award, founded on his death (in honour of one of the leading and most influential figures in the society's early years), is presented biennially to individuals who are considered similarly influential contemporary figures. The death of John Lennon, whose songwriting with his fellow Beatle, Paul McCartney, was acknowledged to have changed pop music and changed the UK music business, was marked by the founding of the John Lennon Award. This went through a variety of forms, but was always associated with popular music courses in universities; it was for example awarded to a student at Salford College, Manchester for a number of years, and later was used to endow facilities at Liverpool University's Institute for Popular Music.

Founded to mark the PRS 75th Anniversary in 1989 the PRS Composers in Education scheme came to be a useful and much-appreciated catalyst for projects which took professional creators of every possible musical genre into schools and colleges, from nursery to sixth form college. Under the particular care of Board director and later two-term PRS Chairman Andrew Potter, who had proposed the scheme, Composers in Education not only brought the fun and learning of composition to children, but linked the society in a very active way with some of its writer members.

To celebrate the 80th birthday of PRS President Vivian Ellis[1] awards to aspiring writers of stage musicals were set up in 1985. With sometime advice and involvement by Andrew Lloyd-Webber[2], and the annual participation of the students of the Guildhall School of Music and Drama, these awards possibly attracted the most public and media attention. The performances of the finalists' work at the School came to be one of the highlights of the year.

In association with the National Federation of Music Societies (NFMS), the Enterprise Awards were set up in the late 80s for choirs and orchestras showing innovation in performing contemporary amateur works.

As well as the set-piece awards the Donations and Awards Committee annually responded to scores of small requests for funding from organisations, bands, orchestras, choirs, drama companies and other sources of music creativity and performance. However, it was noticeable that the great majority of applications came year after year from people and organisations involved in classical music. It was realised that the way pop music was created and performed did not lend itself easily to the established norms of seeking formal funding, and this meant in effect that the

1 Composer of several hit musicals including *Bless the Bride*
2 An enthusiastic admirer of Vivian Ellis, and a successor in terms of composing hit stage musicals, including *Jesus Christ Superstar*, *Cats*, *Starlight Express* and *Aspects of Love*

Tomorrow's Warriors, supported under The PRS Foundation's 'Awards to Organisations' scheme.

musical genres which were actually represented by much the larger portion of the PRS membership were the least likely to seek or get funding. This was one of the factors which contributed to the setting up of the Foundation and to the way it functions.

It is also important to record where the money which PRS applied to donations and awards came from. The society's constitution allowed for up to 1% of revenue to be applied to such activity, although the sums involved never in fact reached that level, and were in most years far below it. The money was taken from the Non Licence Revenue – the money earned by PRS as interest on

bank deposits of revenue awaiting distribution as royalties. And-most importantly for an organisation which was in the 90s to launch a campaign against the "social and cultural" deductions made from its income by overseas affiliated societies in accordance with the CISAC standard reciprocal agreement – the money came only from that part of NLR which would have been paid to PRS' UK writer members.

The "bigger thinking", more businesslike and objective-related, mood of the 90s led to fresh thinking about this PRS activity, as it did about every other. Increasing awareness of the vastly greater variety of music being created by a rapidly growing and diversifying PRS membership, combined with a determination to communicate better with all that membership, were also important factors.

In 1999, the PRS Board designated a task force of PRS staff and Board members to determine the best way of consolidating and continuing its practical campaign and support for new music in the UK. Their research resulted in the advent of an independent charitable foundation for new music of any genre, the Performing Right Society Foundation. With the encouragement of Chief Executive John Hutchinson the Board agreed to fund the charity with a far greater sum than had ever been allocated to donations and awards in the past; it was set up with £1m, and that annual sum was later raised.

The Foundation is now the largest independent source of funds purely for new music in the UK. Its primary functions are to encourage, promote and stimulate the creation and performance of all genres of new music and to enable people to have a positive experience of it. During the three and a half years of its existence it has supported over 800 organisations to the tune of nearly £4 million, facilitating a diverse and frequently pioneering range of new music projects and activities. In the process, it has won an enviable reputation for its culture of efficiency, easy access and fast decision-making and for its free expert advice service for potential applicants.

Its open-door policy and flexibility have extended the breadth of the PRSF's scope. Statistics disclosed at the 2002 PRS AGM showed that the Foundation is successfully communicating with and supporting a wide geographic spread of projects and an impressively diverse range of genres.

Two examples of the differing recipients of its support are demonstrated by the Special Project Award to the City of Birmingham Symphony Orchestra for its extensive new audience development programme inspired by Birmingham's multi-cultural communities and the funding for the Half Moon Young People's Theatre through its Music Creators in Residence scheme, which has provided opportunities for young people to create original music for a specially commissioned play about inner city life and music, utilising the knowledge and experience of the music creator in residence, respected disc jockey Steve Bicknell.

The Foundation now runs the Composers in Education scheme, while other beneficiaries include performance groups involved in promoting and performing new music; festivals that showcase a significant amount of new music; promoters of all genres of new music, and, through the Bliss Trust/PRS Foundation Composer Bursaries, funding of composers in aid of their professional development in the field of classical music.

Details of the wide range of new music activities supported by the Foundation, along with information about its funding schemes and application procedures, are continually updated on its website www.prsfoundation.co.uk.

The CBSO Cultural Harmony Project, supported under The PRS Foundation's Special Projects scheme. Source – Adrian Burrows

PRS Revenue and costs – 1989 to 2003

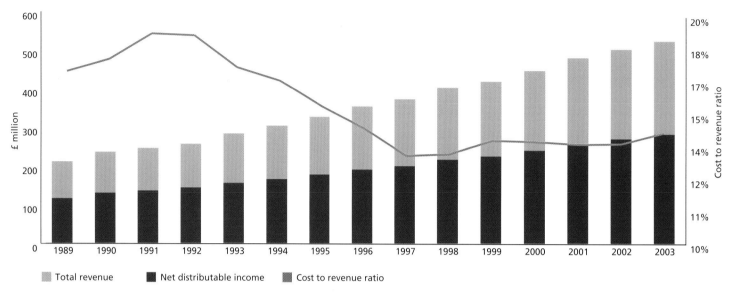

Total revenue   Net distributable income   Cost to revenue ratio

This chart brings together information in £m about total PRS revenue and distributable revenue (which is the amount available in any year for distribution to members a royalties

after all administrative and other cost deductions have been made) and superimposes the ratio of cost-to-revenue expressed as a percentage of total revenue.

PRS Revenue 1988–2002

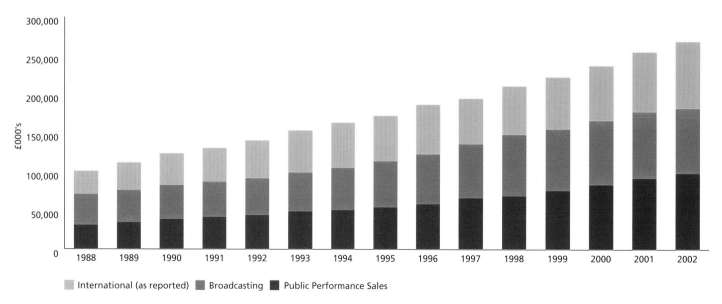

International (as reported)   Broadcasting   Public Performance Sales

This graph illustrates the steady growth of income from all the PRS revenue streams, and the fact that in the past 15 years each has consistently represented about 33% of the total.

PRS Revenue Trends

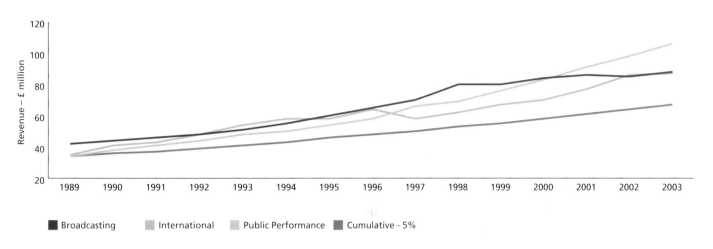

The consistent and continuos growth in public performance licensing income shown in this graph was, on evidence available in 2003, expected to be difficult to maintain in subsequent years. Broadcast income, which dipped below public performance in around 1996 can bee seen levelling off, and was likely to fall below both public performance and international at some point after 2003.

Source: The MCPS-PRS Alliance

A rare picture of four PRS composer members together, in the orchestra pit at the Royal Opera House, Covent Garden during rehearsals for the ballet Les Noles - (*left to right*) are John Gardner, who served as a PRS Consultant Director, choreographer Bronislava Nijinska, Malcolm Williamson, Richard Rodney Bennet, Edmund Rubbra (at piano) and conductor John Lanchbery.

PRS members at the annual British Academy of Composers and Songwriters IVOR Novello awards, sponsored by PRS:

1. Dido and Sting
2. Elton John

3. Don Black, with fellow lyricist - ASCAP member and International Ivor recipient Hal David
4. Annie Lennox and Dave Stewart

Very much an operating company

The MCPS-PRS Alliance is the engine room, not the bridge. It is an operational alliance, and so has clear boundaries as to what its practical (not policy-making) function is. Because it is a very different entity to the societies which brought it into existence and which jointly own it, this company has a different kind of story: one which is about systems, management, workload, business agendas and planning, performance measurement, cost efficiency, service standards and operational improvements. While the story is anything but uneventful, it is fair to say that it is not awash with the kind of colourful anecdote and equally colourful (sometimes maverick) characters of the pioneering days of MCPS and PRS, the latter probably most of all.

The purpose of the operating company is to do the work, leaving the Board Directors of the parent societies free to concentrate on policy and strategy. The licensing of their members' rights is the reserved remit of the two societies, as owners of the income streams and guardians of their separate memberships' rights. This is why the licensing and distribution stories of these music rights are told in the separate MCPS and PRS chapters. However, a very significant pointer to the future is the fact that joint licensing of the performing and mechanical rights has since 2000 been accepted – at least in terms of online music use – as inevitable and found to be practicable by collecting societies, ending many decades of adherence to a principle that the rights must be licensed separately as the only certain way of maintaining their individual values. Equally significant in explaining the MCPS-PRS Alliance structure is the fact that this truly groundbreaking joint online licence is not issued by the Alliance, but by MCPS and PRS. The job of the Alliance is to administer that licence on behalf of the two rights societies.

The Boards also have policy responsibility for relationships with their members, and with external constituencies such as the wider music industry. For the two societies those relationships are still different in character and in their priorities, so could not appropriately be fronted by the operating company. The political (Government relations) activities, which were for a long time the responsibility of the two societies' managements, have been successfully hived off to British Music Rights, and so are not directly part of the Alliance's work.

Therefore the joint operating company concentrates on consolidation and efficiency, and this is a story of work being done in the "back office", however highly visible that back office may be at home and abroad at times. Inevitably it is largely to do with business processes, management and staff rationalisation and development, and above all systems.

Computer dating, but no instant match

The Alliance is the "today" of MCPS and PRS operational history. It is also by far the most likely long-term future. Its own history so far is very short but busy. The story of how its long-established and distinctly different parent societies moved, at first hesitantly and finally with uncharacteristic speed, towards the creation of the Alliance is an interesting starting point.

As already mentioned, the possibility of PRS and MCPS working together has been seriously considered at least three times. Each time the main motivation was the prospect of using the same computer systems to store and process data which was required by both organisations but was held and handled on entirely separate systems in separate companies. A consistent factor on each occasion was a view that the MCPS systems were better than the PRS systems at each of those points in time, and therefore offered the advantage of a "ready-made" solution to IT problems. That is a brief and very simplified description of an always complex set of technical and organisational circumstances. Those most closely involved at a practical level held, and still hold, differing views on many points. But roundly it can be said that computers were what brought PRS and MCPS together in 1997, and computers had been the reason they had twice previously considered some form of joint enterprise.

The first possibility of a joint operation in the early 70s could have been the purchase of MCPS by PRS (*see MCPS Chapter*). This was not pursued and in 1976 MCPS was bought by the MPA, largely to ensure the administration of performing and mechanical rights remained in different hands and the latter came more closely under the control of the music publishers. Collaboration with PRS was definitely not on their agenda at that time: former MPA Board member and first Chairman of MCPS after the MPA takeover in 1976, Bob Kingston, remembers that during his 10-year duty in the chair, "MCPS, with the new and highly efficient computer system, made many endeavours to convince the publishing industry that there should be a point at which PRS and MCPS could merge some of their activities. But this was strongly resisted by the publishers". The lack of agreement did not reflect on the attitudes of the two main protagonists, PRS Chief Executive Michael Freegard and MCPS Managing Director Robert Montgomery. However, the good relationship between these two top executives was not put to work in bringing the two societies together at an operational level. Both had left their organisations before the first practical collaboration attempt in the early 90s.

The fundamental difference in the character and funding of the two UK music copyright owners' societies was a feature from the beginning of both, and has never altered. Twenty years after the MPA purchase of MCPS this was one of the issues that challenged those who had the task of finally bringing MCPS and PRS organisations together into a single operating company, owned by and serving the needs of the two ever-separate societies. That challenge has been met through the MCPS-PRS Alliance, to the approval of today's music publishing industry leaders. From retirement Kingston also signalled his approval: "I am delighted

PRS CEO Michael Freegard (*left*) and MCPS MD Robert Montgomery (pictured here at the opening of the PRS office in Dublin in 1977) discussed the possibility of administrative co-working by their societies, but the idea did not successfully go ahead until the birth of the MCPS-PRS Alliance as a jointly-owned operating company in 1997.

now to have seen that such a merger (sic) has been achieved, to the great advantage of the industry."[1]

But it was a bumpy road. In 1992 there was considerable support and enthusiasm first for a long-overdue piece of co-working and then for a joint venture on a much greater scale than previously mooted. At that time Wayne Bickerton was about to take over the Chairmanship of PRS (and would the following year become acting CEO on the resignation of Michael Freegard); his counterpart as MCPS Chairman was Terry Foster-Key of EMI Music Publishing.

---

1 Full amalgamation or merger of the two companies is not, in fact, possible because although both are *de facto* monopolies in the UK and both administer certain copyrights in music, one is a membership society with a constitution subject to the voting membership's sanction and approval, which takes an assignment of its members' performing right; the other is a commission-based agency wholly-owned by the music publishers' trade association. The constitution of one, or both, would need to be fundamentally changed to allow for a merger in the business sense.

In January 1993 the MCPS and PRS Boards sanctioned what was announced as the first phase of closer collaboration between the two societies, and described as "the first electronic link between the organisations' databases".

The 1993 announcement of collaboration between MCPS and PRS on the task for registration of copyright works was welcomed by the members of both organisations. Pictured here (*left to right*) are PRS Chairman Wayne Bickerton, MCPS MD Frans de Wit, MCPS Database Manager Godfrey Rust and PRS Head of Repertoire, now Alliance IS Director, Chris Gardner

The need for works and claims (to copyright) to be registered twice, separately with PRS and MCPS, and then entered on separate systems was tackled by the setting-up of a joint works notification scheme. All registration forms were to be sent once only, to MCPS, which would then pass data files to PRS daily. The aim was eventually to ensure that both organisations held identical basic information on works, claims and amendments. Since the number of such data entries each year was then about 200,000, the potential cost saving from this joint scheme was high. Further steps intended "to avoid the current costly duplication of effort" were promised. Inevitably there were delays, complications and frustrations. But the joint scheme eventually bedded down and

played its part in the long and somewhat jerky process of bringing the administration of the performing and mechanical rights under one roof.

In November that year, MCPS and PRS announced their intention to set up a much more ambitious joint venture. The stated aim was "within a maximum of five years, to achieve one database of works linked to one database of agreements, products and recordings, maintained by one workforce, within a jointly-owned venture for use of both societies as a common resource for separate distributions to their members". The planned outcome was again stated to be reduction in duplication of work, with simplification of the royalty distribution process of each company and consequent cost reductions, mainly in terms of reducing staff numbers. The means to that end was to be the creation of a joint venture which would "adopt the best of both existing systems".

Within the promised five-year period, something fairly close to what was promised would indeed be delivered, although this carefully-worded 1993 objective would be achieved in a different form and by a different route to that originally anticipated.

The magnitude of the step then being contemplated is emphasised by the fact that in January 1994 the first joint press release from the two societies announced that a meeting of writer and publisher members, including officers of the then separate three writers' Guilds, had been held. It had "affirmed their political will that collaboration between their performing and mechanical rights societies should go ahead". The meeting had been led by Bickerton, Foster-Key, MPA President and independent publisher Andy Heath, and the Chairmen of the writers' Guilds. They had stated that two possible ways forward would be investigated: one would involve amalgamation of the core functions (primarily the databases) of PRS and MCPS in a new joint venture service company; the other would be a bigger version of that plan, with the service company also taking on "certain support functions". The working title for the joint venture was ServiceCo.

A steering group of Board members and senior management teams went to work; the *PRS News* of Spring 1994 reported to members that the steering group had "unanimously agreed at its first meeting in April that a collaboration would have to begin with the examination of one common database [with] the MCPS database as a starting point".

External consultants' reports (Price Waterhouse for PRS and Logica for MCPS) were sufficiently positive for both Boards. The management teams had set out five options for the joint venture structure. As explained to members, four of the options were varying degrees of joint working in varying organisational structures, all retaining the existing controlling Boards with two (or in one option, three) Chief Executives. The fifth possibility was a complete merger of operational activities either under one "MCPRS" Board or under three Boards – those of the two societies plus a joint venture board – but with only one Chief Executive. Interestingly, this option was not at that time examined in detail because it actually lay outside the terms of reference for the management teams. It would, however, be the template for the MCPS-PRS Alliance three years later. But that outcome was not in the minds of Boards and management when they started their cautious progress towards collaboration. If it was, nobody was saying so then, at least not for the record.

ServiceCo was a very important step, but for a while it looked as though it had almost immediately led to a dead end. In late November 1994, the societies' Chairmen regretfully informed their members that the planned collaboration between MCPS and PRS was "suspended". The differing views of the two societies as to the remit of the joint service company had proved irreconcilable. In essence this was because MCPS wanted the remit to be larger than originally envisaged (embracing several operational areas and so requiring greater systems development) while PRS believed that a more restricted remit, focused on databases and IS support functions, was more prudent and should be adhered to. The joint press release in December stated that

"separate but concurring decisions" by both Boards had halted the collaboration plans. It added: "After a year of diverting resources to these negotiations, both [societies] are felt to be putting at risk their ability to shape their future strategies [and they can] now concentrate on developing their own businesses". Co-operation on activities such as the joint registration scheme would continue, it was stressed, and just over a year later this intention was proved sincere with the announcement of their collaborative contribution to "the global project for giving musical works a unique identity within a worldwide virtual database": the International Standard Work Code (ISWC) which was the first "deliverable" in the planned Common Information System (CIS) under the auspices of CISAC.[2]

Picking up (not quite) where everyone had been before

Looking back today, as one of the senior managers then whose area of activity was central to the ServiceCo idea, Chief Information Officer John Rathbone's assessment is that ServiceCo had a significant effect on PRS. As with the PROMS project development and subsequent failure, the impact on PRS IT development was that, again, progress with the "steady advancement" plans had been halted while a more radical idea was investigated and worked on. A condition attached to the ServiceCo negotiations had been a "no further development" rule for both PRS & MCPS IT for the sensible reason that negotiation and planning had to be from a fixed point. It was also felt that the abandonment of ServiceCo exacerbated any existing writer/publisher tensions and prolonged the post-PROMS rift between the PRS Board and management.

From the PRS perspective, the drive towards ServiceCo came mainly from the music publishers: the MPA, MCPS and those on the PRS Board. PRS was perceived to be on its knees after the cancellation of the PROMS project. Revival of the much earlier

---

2 The CIS project had been launched by CISAC in the early 90s as a long-term project (the term originally envisaged was about five years, but that was to stretch past eight years and into the present). See CIS section in this chapter.

idea of MCPS-PRS "merger" seemed to many a logical, pragmatic step. While never mooted in any public statement, there was another strong perception, which enthused some and put others on their guard. It was that this time the operational collaboration would effectively be an MCPS "take-over" because it was in the stronger position, and cost effectiveness would come from using the MCPS IT system which would naturally give MCPS Board and management an edge in terms of controlling the business. In the event, some PRS Board Directors withdrew their support from the ServiceCo idea and led (or just supported – accounts differ) moves to halt the project.

On the PRS side, Rathbone had become convinced that the MCPS system was not in fact suitable for running PRS business in the way proposed. During the many meetings between those charged with making ServiceCo happen, concern grew in the PRS negotiating team that the nature of the joint venture was being pushed by MCPS too far beyond the original proposed remit. Rathbone's MCPS opposite number at the time, Godfrey Rust, accepts today that buoyant self-confidence and possibly rather sweeping assumptions on the MCPS side did little to create comfortable middle ground, but he still firmly maintains that the negative PRS view was overblown and the ServiceCo idea had great business potential for both societies. These choppy waters may now be a decade down-river of the (never completed) ServiceCo bridge, but they seem still to have some strong, chilly undercurrents.

What was an annoying setback for MCPS management proved, perhaps surprisingly, an experience which helped to unite the PRS management team, building their confidence in their own judgement and fighting the post-PROMS perception that they were weak and ineffectual. The view of MCPS Chairman Jonathan Simon is that the abandonment of the never-comfortable ServiceCo plan also came as something of a relief to the MCPS Board. While they had felt that setting up a joint

"back office" was a sensible move, they had come to recognise that, given some key personalities involved at the time, it was not going to succeed. Simon, as a director of both societies, was in a position also to note that the PRS Board felt similarly relieved, although there were differences in emphasis and areas of anxiety due to the difference in Board structures and relative representation levels of publishers and writers. "Intellectually most people agreed ServiceCo was a good idea, but there was deep mistrust about possibly creating a monster which might try to run its masters; and there were big questions about who would run the joint venture – whichever side that person came from was going to give that side supremacy over the other," Simon sums up.

The relief now recalled by Board members was much less evident at the time to MCPS and PRS managers who carried responsibility for making the joint venture work. Most of them have clear memories of their own sense of wasted effort and emotional involvement. The MCPS side was characterised as rather arrogant, assuming that the recent PROMS failure put PRS in the position of quiescently needing superior MCPS expertise: the PRS side was collectively perceived to be rather obstructive and inflexible, and unwilling to accept that what they needed was effectively to be taken over by the lean and efficient MCPS. As always, broad appearances were belied by the efforts of sincere and positive individuals much of the time, but circumstances did not help the situation. A tricky set of negotiations had been largely left to management when policy and strategy should ideally have been hammered out at Board and Chief Executive level – with managers working to a clear brief on operational details only *after* these were fully agreed. In the event, managers felt the weight of what they construed as Board-level disapproval (believed to come more from publishers than writers) for a "management failure"; they believed, at least for a short but anxious period, that having worked on the ServiceCo project deserved the euphemistic label of "not career enhancing".

As many current and past managers in both organisations now reflect, ServiceCo was one example of a "people problem" (personality and culture clashes at the top and senior management levels in the two organisations, plus traditional differences and tensions between writers and publishers). The ServiceCo concept was a very good idea, which was why when it was approached again and differently in 1996/97 in order to create the MCPS-PRS Alliance it went ahead successfully. The essential problem in this and other major initiatives was the "who" and the details of the "how", not the "what".

Broad opinion is that this kind of problem has been a root cause of big and sometimes insurmountable difficulties which affected worthy but complex projects over the years. A thumbnail description in these cases might have been "a very good idea which had some (or most) of its planning well in place, and on which many people sincerely worked very hard, but which was not at crucial points directed/run/delivered by the right people at the right level in the right way". Such a description sums up the retrospective judgement of many who were involved in ServiceCo, and also those who worked on the PRS PROMS project before it and on the Alliance International Music Joint Venture (IMJV) project after it (*described later in this chapter*). Problems with knitting together all the collaborative elements, including people, ways of working, styles of communication, differing aspirations and levels of understanding seem to be the constant. And these elements regularly appear in case studies of all kinds of business projects, collaborations or mergers which run aground. In every case much is stated to have been usefully learnt. Some (but often less than claimed) really useful learning actually takes place.

Whatever the feelings and perceptions, the outcome for ServiceCo was that it officially "went off the agenda" for both PRS and MCPS (and its parent the MPA). However, the common sense view, that some kind of operational collaboration between the two organisations was an obvious way forward, remained very much alive.

Collaboration returns to the agenda – and stays there

So it was no great surprise when it reappeared. The issue of two different CEOs having to work together – and possibly compete – had dissolved in June 1996 when MCPS Chief Executive Frans de Wit left the company. That prompted a rapid initiative from the recently-appointed PRS Chief Executive John Hutchinson. He quickly assembled, set out and then suggested a framework for joint working arrangements which, in all essentials, was eventually to be embodied in the MCPS-PRS Alliance. Directors recall an immediate recognition by both society Boards that the time, the circumstances and the key people were now right. The feeling was as positive as it had previously been negative about ServiceCo. Inevitably there were degrees of positive view, but those who most strongly believed in and wanted the joint operation pushed the idea hard and in every way possible. In particular, both the MCPS and PRS Chairmen were shoulder-to-shoulder with Hutchinson in forging ahead at the fastest safe pace.

There were many reasons for going ahead, and one of them was that MCPS, in a nutshell, needed a partner. The commission rates which funded the work of the society had been held down for several years by a Chief Executive who was understandably complying with Board wishes and a Board which genuinely was unaware of the problems being accumulated as a result. MCPS had in early 1996 won its first ECL deal (*see MCPS chapter*) and now had to administer it, but the question arose as to whether it actually had the resources to do that sustainably. Apart from the mutual desirability and solid good sense of a PRS –MCPS joint operating company, for MCPS alliance with another rights society could offset some of the risk and cost of taking on the new workload.

The launch of the the Music Alliance at London's Wigmore Hall in 1997, with (*left to right*) MPA Chairman Stephen James, PRS Chairman Andrew Potter, MCPS Chairman Jonathan Simon and MPA Board member Andrew Heath

PRS had, under Hutchinson's leadership, already begun the job of bringing its cost-to-income ratio down through increased efficiency; it had embarked on fresh approaches to governance at Board level and to internal structure and quality at management level. An operational alliance with MCPS, if done properly, could drive that change forward.

A number of directors from both Boards now accept, without retrospective reservations or regret, that the deal was approached more in the spirit of determination to get it done than in any detached mood of evaluation of the detailed pros and cons. In negotiations and calculations, MCPS apples and PRS pears were sometimes compared and mutually agreed to be the same in order to move the process forward. If either side "did better" out of one or another aspect of this creation (a jointly and equally owned company holding all the assets of the separate societies), this appears not to be an issue for the Boards now. Quite the reverse:

the success of the deal is heartily applauded by the MCPS, PRS and MPA directors and memberships, also by the British Academy of Composers and Songwriters and by the record business organisations BPI and PPL. As it approached its seventh anniversary in 2004 the Alliance's clear and measurable success, particularly in the area of cutting administrative cost, was taken as proof that the (always legitimate, if sometimes imaginative and highly flexible) means had been fully justified by the ends.

The announcement in late 1996 of the revived intention for the two societies to collaborate hinted both at a much wider scope than before and at the reasons why such collaboration had suddenly become timely and more feasible than it had been in 1993-94. The MCPS and PRS Boards stated jointly that they had decided that the two organisations "should consider the formation of an operational alliance under one Chief Executive and one top management team". They stressed from the outset however that ownership and control of the two different sets of rights would remain separate and fully protected; the composition and responsibilities of the two Boards would remain unchanged.

Both Chairmen at the time – Andrew Potter at PRS and Jonathan Simon at MCPS, both music publishers – warmly welcomed their Boards' decisions. Simon referred to his Board's increasing conviction that such an alliance "could make sound economic sense" and could bring benefits to members and international affiliates. Potter stated: "Only a very short-sighted view would fail to see the opportunities presented by the common sense move [with its] potential for offering both savings and strengths". He allowed an echo of the reasons for the failure of the ServiceCo to sound when he added that his Board "believes that a prudent step-by-step approach" was the correct approach to such change.

Hutchinson, who had made a major career change to take up the post of PRS Chief Executive less than a year before, expressed both enthusiasm and caution when he said: "I am conscious of the trust being placed in me and the management team by the two

3 The first strategic business plan set out by PRS after Hutchinson's appointment had identified alliances – with other appropriate UK organisations and internationally – as business goals; MCPS plans also pointed to collaborations and co-working. Both societies had cost sharing and cost cutting in mind as essential to delivering their services and, in fact, to survival. Hutchinson was well aware that the crucial issues as the operational alliance idea began to move tentatively forward were whether the Boards would really be prepared to give one Chief Executive full operational control, and whether they (effectively MCPS rather than PRS) then would give that role to "a PRS man". His invited informal attendance at MCPS Board meetings allowed him to observe Board and management styles and tensions. His own belief that all the management of a joint or allied operation must be led by one Chief Executive was strengthened, but with that came the equally strong realisation that both sides needed to move carefully and at their own pace to that conclusion. "I knew that if

Boards. I greatly appreciate this opportunity, which was foreseen in our business planning[3] and I know that I have the full and enthusiastic backing of all senior managers in the major work programme ahead. None of us underestimates the size of the task."

Realising that reservations, concerns and conflicting agendas were inevitably going to complicate progress, Hutchinson felt that there was nothing to lose from a "suck it and see" approach, offering to take a full year to reach a final decision. So he took a softly, softly approach, "which I admit went a bit against the grain for me."

It was in mid-1997 that fresh and generally favourable consultants' reports (from Ernst and Young for PRS and Logica for MCPS) were delivered. Most of those involved in the major change decisions agreed with then MPA President Andy Heath: "This is an opportunity to take us all into the 21st century and put us in a position to direct and protect our industry in a way we could never have hoped for a few years back". The urge to move forward was strong enough to overcome any bureaucratic inertia, as remarked on by many, including the then Composers Guild Chairman Martin Dalby: "We watch from the side a process happening with great speed. Blink and yet another piece is in place. The pace is admirable. So is the air of certainty which surrounds the creation of the alliance."

Nevertheless, the MCPS and PRS Board papers of late 1996 and through 1997 attest the care with which the alliance was approached. The proposal was carefully worded as intending "co-management of MCPS and PRS while the different rights remain under the control of the two companies" with promised substantial savings for both societies as a result of combining management teams, rationalising staffing structures and sharing a single Information Systems architecture.

It was pointed out that horizon planning at PRS had revealed a shared vision between writers and publishers of "progressive establishment of a world class rights administration organisation

based in the UK". It was also mooted that successful completion of a co-management project for MCPS and PRS could open up further opportunities for collaboration with PPL and non-music rights organisations in the future.

It was stressed that the corporate structure would be built to fulfil the objective of unifying completely the operations of PRS and MCPS, while allowing the owners of the rights to retain total control of the way in which they are protected and administered. Service level agreements between MPA, MCPS, PRS and the operating company were completed in September 1997. The fact that PRS and MCPS were separately tasked with granting licences and collecting and distributing royalties was clearly stated with the observation that "the operation of such businesses involves duplication which PRS and MCPS wish to eliminate in the interests of their respective members [and] in order to achieve this PRS and MCPS have decided to create a joint venture company, the shares in which will be owned by them equally, and which will manage, administer, operate and perform for both societies certain activities previously carried out by both Societies." It is later stated: "The business of the [joint venture] Company shall be to provide management, administration, collection and other services to MCPS and PRS". However, the remit of the joint venture company and its Board would not include policy in relation to the societies' respective businesses; the parties to whom licences are granted or not granted; decision on new licensing schemes/agreements or codes of practice, and on the terms and conditions of these; terms of membership for the two societies; distribution dates for royalties to their separate memberships; and the societies' commission or other charges payable by their members. Alongside the service level agreements were asset transfer agreements and shareholder agreements.

Avoiding potentially distracting discussion on a name for the joint operating company, Hutchinson quickly won support for the practical and descriptive Music Copyright Operational Services Limited (MCOS). From the outset the clearly stated plan for

MCPS appointed a new CEO the operating alliance would never happen, and I believed the MCPS Board knew that too". He also deduced that they had little appetite for a prolonged search for a new CEO. Perhaps surprisingly, perhaps not, he sensed that the PRS Board was more sceptical at the time than the MCPS Board.

corporate governance was that each parent company (society) would have a separate and completely autonomous Board (and appropriate Board committees) to direct policy and to oversee the administration of rights and licences within its existing Constitution. There would be an "Admin Board" (later named the Alliance Board) to exercise day-to-day control of operations and administration. Parent Boards would be able to monitor progress through service level agreements. The resources of the two companies would be combined under one Chief Executive and one management team. Wherever possible, administration overheads would be removed in the early stages of the co-management development project, but "it would be essential for the management top team to be fully motivated and to work as one from inception [and through progressive rather than abrupt rationalisation] a streamlined [management] structure will have to evolve gradually if the business of the two societies is to continue without disruption". The road to common systems architecture was indicated but at that stage could not be realistically mapped. The broad view was that "a coherent IS strategy for PRS together with the existing MCPS work and dataflow models and new CIS standards [could/would] provide management with a blueprint for combination of MCPS and PRS computer systems".

A step by step approach covers a lot of ground in seven years

Almost seven years later it can be said that these objectives, intentions and outline plans can in all their essentials be seen in the structure, governance and operation of the MCPS-PRS Alliance, although the detailed outworking of the plans for a common IS architecture has proved distinctly different from that first envisaged. This can justifiably be listed as the latest and one of the greatest Alliance milestones, in Hutchinson's view at the time this book went to press.

As the Boards gave their step-by-step approval to the stages of creating the Alliance, the same step-by-step, minimal initial change approach was adopted by Hutchinson in bringing the senior management teams of the two societies together. Both needed reassurance. Having been, virtually from his arrival at PRS, very keen to pursue the idea of working jointly with MCPS in collaboration or any other arrangement up to full merger, Hutchinson had in early 1996 noted that the PRS managers were not then nearly as keen as he was about it (he diagnosed a form of battle fatigue). So he had been prepared to wait, and the PRS planning process soon required that management should wholeheartedly and professionally attempt to fulfil the Board's agreed strategy, whether they liked it or not. MCPS managers had been much keener about an operating alliance and had therefore felt the rejection of ServiceCo more sharply as a rebuttal of their own ideas and aspirations – only to be faced a couple of years later with the renewed prospect of a single operating company, but now to be led by a PRS Chief Executive.

The UK societies had avoided an alliance like this for scores of years after so many of their counterparts, particularly in Europe, had taken the joint operation or fully-merged route. The UK approach to it in 1997 was meticulous, carefully communicated, and the result of Board level deliberation and decision. This was rightly seen as the only proper and certain way to assure success.

The issue of remaining separate while being together

Inevitably there were concerns, some going very deep in the minds of some Directors on both Boards. These related to the need to keep the two societies separate and distinct as they always had been, so that the separate identities and values of their rights and licences should not be diluted in the perception or negotiating stances of music users. The issues of the societies' distinct and different characters, styles, ethos, cultural attitudes and ways of relating to their membership, which neither society wanted to blend with the other's, were wrapped up within that business concern. It was a constant theme, and occasionally cause for real agitation and friction. One such occasion was when (rather suddenly and unexpectedly, from the management standpoint) the modest approach to an identity for the joint operating company MCOS proved to be a flashpoint. It had been agreed that the alliance of the societies would be presented very simply. Both existing logos in their existing colours were incorporated in a minimally-designed joint logo; the PRS tag "giving music its due" was relinquished, and the new joint logo incorporated the wording suggested by a PRS Board member, *The Music Alliance*. For all applications relating only to one society or the other, the separate logos continued to be used. However, "The Music Alliance" tag proved attractive to staff whenever they were referring to the joint operation rather than one of the societies. Its brevity also made it particularly attractive to the media and other external contacts. It rapidly came to be used in the manner of a company name. In a business world where the establishment of a new "brand" usually required determined and expensive marketing this one had established itself. This was probably because it was the only simple, single phrase on offer in an otherwise complicated description of an inevitably complex arrangement. But it was not in fact the operating company's name, and there were Board-level concerns that its use in place of the agreed nomenclature might imply that business could be done with a non-existent company. Furthermore it might be construed to imply that the "music alliance" was some kind of merger of the two societies. All these arguments were perfectly understandable. Yet the real company name Music Copyright Operational Services Ltd was not, in fact, the name by which the organisation was officially to be known anyway. While that name appeared on stationery for suppliers, only the two MCPS and PRS logos and The Music Alliance tag appeared on the operating company's general stationery, press releases and so on. A "false brand" had easily established itself largely because no coherent "true brand" had been defined. After protest and some recrimination from Board members it was agreed that a new naming policy would be applied with the utmost firmness; the company should always and only be referred to as The MCPS-PRS Alliance, and managers and staff whose work was clearly concerned only with the business of one society (most significantly in the licensing and membership-serving areas) should identify themselves only with that society. It was not an intuitively simple rule to follow: it resulted for a time in the need stringently to police written material, and in many hesitant and quickly corrected responses to incoming phone calls (sometimes accompanied by muffled giggling).

Privately many of those insisting on this protocol agreed that things would change as time went on. But this was an unequivocal signal that such a time had not yet come; and that the operating company would have to work hard to make the society Boards feel comfortable with any progress towards merged non-IS functions internally and any alliance-focused identity externally.

To highlight the fulfilment of the "things will evolve" prophecy, MCOS was before too long officially reregistered as The MCPS-PRS Alliance Limited, and by mid 2003 there were merged responsibilities in departments dealing with copyright, repertoire, member communications and members' queries, as well as IT and the core business functions such finance, corporate communications and human resources which had been merged at the outset. Even more significantly there is joint licensing for online music use, under the terms of recent international agreements, and very recently the first joint licence for a television broadcast service. Lastly and most recently has come Board agreement to the gradual introduction of *The Music Alliance* as a trading name for the operating company.

171

Communicating change

Although not always immediately successful in making things completely clear to the societies' members, or to the press who would have preferred a simpler concept such as merger or takeover, every attempt was made to inform members of how the structure of separate societies and a jointly-owned operating company would work, and the benefits it would bring.

In a leaflet issued in July 1997 to members, the media and other contacts, John Hutchinson as Chief Executive of both societies and of the joint operating company, stated: "MCPS and PRS are, and remain, separate societies in terms of income, constitution, membership and guardianship of different rights. To make the best use of their individual strengths they are now an alliance, which we feel proud and confident enough to think of as *The Music Alliance*."

Stressing the main features of a necessarily rather complicated structure and corporate governance, he pointed to the fact that, although the two top management teams had been merged to run the operation, provision was made for the appointment of two divisional directors each charged with protecting exclusively the interests of one society. "If there is a single Chief Executive and combined management team, there needs to be a 'management conscience' for each society, with a close and direct relationship with the respective Boards". At that time this special role was given to the PRS Membership Director John Sweeney and to the MCPS Business Affairs Director Chris Martin.

After very brief descriptions and histories of the two societies, the leaflet sets out the core issue and the initial vision and understanding of how the MCPS-PRS Alliance would tackle that issue: "Between them the societies have a wealth of data, including details of approaching three million works written or owned by their members or affiliated societies, linked to agreements data which enable [each society] to identify copyright owners in the UK and around the world. In addition the societies have built some unique repertoire databases. PRS manages the international Audio Visual Index (AVI) which is the key for societies to acquire details of television programmes and films, and MCPS has an unrivalled database of two million recordings (known as "National Discography") which is a major asset for mechanical licensing and performance identification. The Alliance "core systems" development plan draws all this data and processing together into an integrated "common" system, based on the existing MCPS platform, to support PRS as well as MCPS licensing and distribution."

The vision of an operational alliance of two societies together providing efficient administration, lowered costs (commission for mechanical rights and administration charge for performing rights), greater negotiating power and enhanced protection of members' rights, has never changed and has been unwaveringly pursued. Inevitably, there have been considerable changes to the details of how this vision, and its related data processing plans as described at the outset, have been carried through.

However the ringing endorsements of the formation of the Alliance with which the leaflet closed, from the Chairmen of PRS, MCPS , the then still three separate writers guilds and the Chairman of the MPA, would not be significantly modified by any of them if they were asked to offer their comments again almost seven years later.

Perhaps all the views were summed up in the comment by the songwriter who then headed his own Guild and would go on to be Chairman of the combined British Academy of Composers and Songwriters, Guy Fletcher: "We are constantly seeking improvements in the speed and accuracy with which collection societies deal with our royalties. I believe that the MCPS-PRS Alliance will provide us with the finest collective administration system in the world, giving us the efficiency we require by reducing duplication of effort, thus increasing our income and reducing our cost".

The importance of bringing the staff of the two societies into a single workforce was recognised. Just one example was the fact that MCPS Legal Affairs chief David Lester was attending PRS Board meetings even before the official alliance date of 1 January 1997, and had moved into the PRS offices in Berners St, and amalgamated both legal teams, by February; another was the fact that Hutchinson was writing leaders in both staff magazines by December 1996, when he acknowledged: "I think it is important to say clearly, from the very beginning of what will be a very big project for all of us, that the teamwork will need to happen at a number of levels in both organisations." He ensured that anyone who thought that the first round of big changes might comfortably be expected to be the last was put firmly in the picture of the "interesting times" which would continue. "We are thinking and planning; we will press ahead at the best possible pace but we'll be looking at every angle afresh."

Stressing unity, the first issue of the single staff magazine *FYI* appeared in September 1997 – opportunely featuring a front page picture of the first MCPS-PRS Alliance team to run "under the same colours" in a charity race.

Getting down to working together

The first formal Alliance budget was approved in December 1997. Proposals for the Alliance IS organisation and corporate change programme followed. In June 1998 a business process review for the Copyright and Repertoire functions (at the core of the duplication of work issue) was begun as part of the plan for "alliance migration" of separate systems into one system. In October that year came the first warnings of the potentially huge disruptions to computer systems and the businesses depending on them, via the year 2000 "millennium bug". Alliance operational resources were applied to dealing with that, with complete success. Alliance business planning procedures were developed, with their allied management performance reports. In March 1998 the Alliance business model and associated architecture (the first key piece of work in applying the Alliance IS strategy) defined the scope of the business in terms of individual processes which had to be carried out and which needed to be supported by IT systems. This was based on the vision laid down in the first joint operating company three-year plan and was used to provide information to support systems development, and to assess the impact of change.

Less than two years from his announced retirement date, and from his place in 2003 at the head of a well-established single operating company with increasingly merged management and departments, Hutchinson unstintingly gave credit to everyone in the first MCPS-PRS Alliance top team (when he was confirmed Chief Executive of the *de facto* operating company in March 1997). He clearly continued to admire and appreciate them all as individuals and professionals, both those who remained and those who had left, sooner or later, either voluntarily or involuntarily because he had progressively eliminated their roles.

Looking at the formation and progress of the Alliance, it is fair to say that, as might be expected, the view much closer to the coalface was always more complex than that from the Olympian heights occupied by the Boards' elected, external and executive Directors. Management and staff opinion remains tempered by the fact that they have needed to adjust to the problems of merging two very different business cultures on a workaday level, and they have been involved in an intentionally never-ending programme of change, restructuring, adjustment of plans and processes, sometimes competing priorities and shifting internal balances of power and resource, arrivals, departures and blending of people and jobs. But the inevitability and business sense of creating the Alliance were the drumhead peace terms, agreed by all from the beginning and never recanted since.

The maxim that "those who will not learn from history are doomed to repeat it" is easy to quote but very hard to apply practically in the thick of activity, and hardest of all where very recent history is concerned. So it is not surprising that mistakes were made as well as objectives reached, as most of those involved were ready to reflect several years on. Jonathan Simon remembered that one initial problem was a failure to understand the enormous size of the task of amalgamating the two organisations' databases. Though the similarities and perceived overlap in the data which both had to store and use were the foundation stones of the cost-efficient edifice everyone wanted built, turning plans and perceptions into reality was a huge job with a longer than anticipated time frame. The organisational alignment of seemingly not-too-different activities similarly proved complicated, as did the blending (or at least juxtaposing) of two cultures.

A preoccupied management, which itself had yet to coalesce into something resembling a single team, also failed properly to address the concerns which quite soon developed at Board level in both societies, but decidedly more so on the MCPS side. These chiefly related to delivery of demanding service standards, particularly in relation to the speed and accuracy of works registrations, and

dealing with backlogs in these. Directors grew impatient with what they saw as poor explanation of why problems persisted and why they did not appear to be addressed. So communication with and reporting to the three Boards was another learning process for the Alliance operating company to go through.

The progress in half a dozen years is, however, generally approved. MPA Chairman and former two-term PRS Chairman Andrew Potter succinctly judges that each of the three Boards – MCPS, PRS and the Alliance – "would give it eight out of 10". He adds that they have appreciated, if frequently crossed swords with, John Hutchinson as "a fresh mind from another business, who brought lots of new skills and then became fascinated by this business, where he is now a strong supporter for creators". The Alliance is broadly agreed to be delivering what it promised, and Simon as an independent publisher notes particularly that it is working "at grass roots level". The members of both societies are getting tangible benefits from the operational alliance, and there are more in the pipeline. For example, the view of the MCPS Chairman on the new online member services which were being introduced in late 2003 was that it epitomises the best that was hoped for from a joint operation. "This sort of quality of innovation is worth a five-year wait. It is what we wanted: we just did not know at the beginning how long it would take to get there".

PRS Chairman David Bedford gladly remembered: "The second opportunity for a large-scale MCPS and PRS Alliance was grasped very quickly when the MCPS CEO left in 1996. The speed of planning and action was driven successfully by John Hutchinson, supported by the Board. There were doubts and concerns, particularly among writers, about the governance of such an organisation, but our worries were allayed by the shareholders' and service level agreements and the three-Board structure. That is still in place and seen as working well. I feel that the early doubts have been completely answered. As far as the Alliance has gone so far it is good – useful cost savings have been made – but for the time being at least it cannot go any further because of the major difference in governance between PRS as a membership organisation with an elected Board, and an agency owned by a trade association which appoints its Board."

This point is often made – sometimes by those who would very much like to see the Alliance go further, even to a complete merger between the two societies; and sometimes by those who are content with things as far as they have gone. Jonathan Simon and MPA Chief Executive Sarah Faulder are among the former and sum up their view as "if we can make this amount of progress just by being under one roof, there must be more we can do by taking the Alliance further". David Bedford is among the latter and, summing up the views of the "contented" sector, he says: "Some European organisations successfully combine administration of both rights in a single, or virtually merged, body. But in the UK separate societies are probably the best idea. Despite online convergence of use of the two rights, we must avoid too much blurring of the distinction between them. Also MCPS and PRS have two different cultures which it would be hard to merge. And writers certainly would not want to lose the more caring, involved and communicative traditional culture of PRS, with its membership orientation and consultation".

Business Change and Innovation.

There would have been little point in creating the Alliance if change and innovation were not primary objectives. They are not only corporate objectives but are the personal and consistent aims of John Hutchinson as leading management architect. His innovative thinking and determination to pursue good ideas and learn from them, whether they do or do not succeed in stated terms, have had a tremendous impact on the UK way of doing copyright administration business. He also set out to make a significant impression on the international copyright administration business. As a result, the story of the Alliance

John Hutchinson, by then Chief Executive of PRS, MCPS and the MCPS-PRS Alliance, was in 1998 the first UK collecting society head to be invited to address the record industry at the BPI AGM.

is very much a tale of relentless, fast-paced development and unceasing activity on many fronts at any given time, and the fairly brief accounts which follow attempt to illustrate the different facets of that ongoing story.

As the first Chief Executive of the Alliance, his list of milestones passed by the company in less than seven years covers its entire short history to-date. An early and important one was the formation of British Music Rights. As is usually the case with any development which qualifies for the "milestone" label, it was not a fully-formed idea at its conception, neither was it brought effortlessly to a peak of efficiency and success. It was born out of dissatisfaction. The music publishers, with then MPA Chairman Andrew Heath as chief activist, had justifiably become impatient with the way their UK collecting societies were handling Government relations, lobbying and general presentation of the causes concerning their side of the music industry. This activity was then the remit of the Music Copyright Reform Group, which had been set up in the mid-80s to lobby in preparation for the 1988 Copyright Designs and Patents Act. It had continued to work, very much at a level of monitoring and commentating on relevant UK and EC legal issues, but during the mid-90s had apparently lost its coherence and was plainly out of step with the kind of thinking and action needed in a changing business and legislative environment. In 1997 the writers representing the three separate Guilds of the time were easily recruited to the publishers' view that an entirely new approach was needed, via an entirely new jointly-directed body.

They were possibly unaware that this view was shared just as vehemently by Hutchinson at the head of the collecting societies. He realised that the publishers' and writers' wish to sideline the societies, while understandable given the dithering and inactivity of the previous few years, was potentially dangerous to the cause they wanted to promote. Confrontation on the issue was not a good idea, so Hutchinson took a diplomatic approach of suggesting that the Alliance become the "third man". Diplomacy, and the fact that the new organisation would require funding which could only be supplied by MCPS and PRS, won the day. After a brief incarnation with a different name (and an unpronounceable acronym), British Music Rights was rechristened with the name suggested by Hutchinson, and its story is told in its own chapter in this history.

Again, as Hutchinson would stress, strength and effectiveness were achieved through turning what might have been a fight for control into a properly structured alliance of those who should anyway have been natural allies.

In turn British Music Rights was part of another significant development, described by Hutchinson as "a realignment of entities", which included the coming together of the writers' Guilds as the British Academy of Composers and Songwriters and a change of MPA attitude in the latter part of Heath's chairmanship from confrontation and insistence on its supremacy as the owner of MCPS to collaborative co-working. And all this helped to establish the MCPS-PRS Alliance itself as a settled reality and the way of the future.

The sum of all these parts was, in Hutchinson's view, a great sea change: "All of a sudden what had been a very fractious part of the music industry became well-organised, prepared to work together towards shared aims." At the same time the separate and, by long preference, self-contained parts of this industry sector decided that they could and should make up their minds in a positive way about Hutchinson, who was aware that they had not known what to make of him initially and had responded with a mixture of tough self-assertion and enthusiastic co-operation (usually when it was least expected). Above all, in his recollection: "There were forces there in the industry waiting to make things change, and it all came together. If I was a catalyst, that's good. It would all have happened sooner or later anyway, though there might have been more pain."

He can also reflect on the fact that the founding and development of the MCPS-PRS Alliance has drawn approval from all sides. That includes the UK societies' CISAC peer group, but the very fact that this approval is sometimes qualified is seen as a different kind of evidence of success. Firstly, MCPS and PRS under one Chief Executive and with the combined Alliance management and staff structure could adopt a new approach to pursuing international revenue. The technical visits to affiliated societies could now check simultaneously on both PRS and MCPS income streams and issues. This inevitably strengthened the UK hand and constrained any preference an overseas society might have for dealing separately with the two UK organisations.

Much higher in profile and greater in political and presentational impact was the "business of creativity" issue. This is a piece of author's licence because the phrase was coined some years later, as title and theme chosen by the Alliance when it hosted the CISAC World Congress in London in 2002. It is appropriate to use here because it encapsulates the attitude which John Hutchinson brought to, and demanded from, PRS on his arrival, and then took into the Alliance. For rights organisations which, particularly in Europe, were entrenched in a view of themselves primarily as cultural entities serving creativity, the challenging idea was that these societies actually were and must behave like businesses and financial services. This was, and to some extent still is, perceived in traditionally-minded and traditionally-organised CISAC societies as running counter to their ethos. Some individuals in the UK had similar concerns: former MCPS executive and music publisher Ray Ellis summed up the minority feelings of those who prefer the old to the new as "what used to be personality led and inspired is now just a nuts and bolts operation for collecting and distributing money." Many might respond that this is akin to complaining that a railway is just a nuts and bolts operation for getting trains to and from destinations (that is, exactly what it is supposed to be). But the Alliance would point to the very significant and growing resources which it also put into membership communication and service, above and beyond licensing their rights and paying their royalties as efficiently as possible.

A reorganised Alliance top management team was another milestone in Hutchinson's view (*and is dealt with in detail later in this chapter*). But the first of several reductions in the team's size, accompanied by the rationalisation of top management roles, concluded in 1998 with the creation of a New Technology Division. This was a specialised service division equivalent to the R&D (research and development) function of companies in other industry sectors. With Mark Isherwood as director, a small team of managers who were highly technologically literate focused on new technologies and their applications which were being developed which might impact on creators' rights and their administration. Their remit was intentionally wide to research legitimate and pirate activity via the internet and what digital distribution developments were likely to be taken up most enthusiastically by consumers. They also looked at new entertainment hardware and software which would use music and need licensing. They were asked to peer into the likely futures for creation, administration, distribution and usage of intellectual property, so that the Alliance could be as well-informed as possible about a range of possibilities, and bring that information into their strategic planning as appropriate. Hutchinson believed that a talented team which had come into the Alliance from MCPS would be able to do some ground-breaking work in this area at a time when such work was most needed, and their contribution proved valuable.

One example was the 90-day trial of an online music licensing application called MusicTrial.com, launched by the Alliance in autumn 1998. The prototype integrated licensing system for the trial was developed within MCPS and PRS, and at that time it could claim to be the first such initiative from any collecting society. It was a potential first step to building an infrastructure for automated licensing and creating a framework for legal trading of copyright music via the internet. Partner in MusicTrial .com was the then leading US-based developer of secure online music delivery systems, Liquid Audio. Isherwood stressed that the aim was to find a "user friendly solution for those wishing to operate legally" alongside the industry's efforts to prevent piracy. MusicTrial.com was intended to provide information which could contribute to developing an online licensing system for the future. The MusicTrial.com prototype was able to demonstrate that it was possible for societies to continue effectively to offer their members collective administration of their rights in an online environment. The trial offered 44 digital recordings from which "customers" could choose their downloads. The trial website was accessed 5636 times in the 90-day period and the most popular musical work was Bach's *Air on a G String*.

Five years later the global music industry is still embroiled in an anti-piracy battle which is steadily increasing in scope and bitterness. But it is also working hard, if belatedly, on improving user-friendly access to legal and licensed music. While MusicTrial.com was not continued directly into a full-scale online licensing system for rights societies, it made its contribution to improved understanding of the issues and practicalities involved. For one thing, it indicated that online delivery and usage would be more like broadcasting, offering interactive entertainment, not item-by-item licensing.

A footnote to the story of the relatively short-lived but groundbreaking New Technology Division was the fact that the managers who had been involved in it all became part of interesting and innovative organisations after they left: Rightscom – the digital content strategic consultants; Musically, a technology information, analysis and newsletter provider; and MusicIndie, an R&D company set up by the UK Association of Independent Music (AIM) to participate in a series of innovative projects designed to increase the market share and business potential of British independent record companies.

Not all milestones are on the main highway. Some potentially important ones are on diverging paths which had to be explored as possible ways forward. One such for the Alliance was Musiclicensing.com. Hutchinson describes it as "a good technology trial" and an attempt to find a commercial application on the back of MusicTrial.com, the difference being that the licensing would be item by item, or work by work. Originally it was going to be a "one-stop shop" for various rights, including those owned and controlled by record companies, but a protracted international round of presentations and negotiations by MCPS Executive Director Chris Martin indicated that the record business was not ready to embark on such a development. Meanwhile other strands of work concerning online licensing (including some of the work contributed by the New Technology team a few years earlier) had led the Alliance to believe that a joint MCPS/PRS blanket licence was more attractive to licensees and would be far easier to administer, so MCPS and PRS began moving forward towards a single performing and mechanical online licence on a blanket basis. Such licensing cannot be anything but international, crossing – actually denying the existence of – territorial boundaries. The details are therefore in the International section later in this chapter.

At home

For an organisation whose existence was prompted by a need to rationalise work duplication by combining computer systems, the home front has inevitably been preoccupied with IT.

As stated before, a key reason why PRS and MCPS wanted and needed to work as an alliance was to develop core systems which would serve both businesses. Expectations were high at the outset that this could be accomplished relatively easily (allowing for the fact that any major IT project in any business can be confidently relied on to confound any optimistic expectations of speed and simplicity). Inevitably, but to a much greater extent than anticipated, the Alliance efforts to achieve a single core system handling data which is used both in performing and mechanical rights administration met many difficulties and delays. These are set out in great detail in reports to the Boards over six years, but they cannot be condensed into a readable narrative here.

One valuable outcome of all this work has been a much clearer understanding of where the business processes of MCPS and PRS are the same, or are very similar, or can be made so; these all being pre-requisite for a common, single system. Equally, in six years it has been possible to reach a much clearer idea of where the MCPS and PRS business processes are not the same. In fact there are many very significant differences – more so than there are similarities. Support systems such as e-mail, financial and human resources are shared, as are copyright (works and agreements). Member Services is a common area, with common systems being built. It would be possible to have a common system to process usage returns from broadcasters, but a solid business case would need to be assessed for doing this work. However, large parts of the licensing and distribution operations and their ancillary software are fundamentally different.

This simply summarised collected IS wisdom belies effort which went into the thinking, planning, negotiating, trying, testing, repeated investigation, re-examination and review, planning and re-planning which has been necessary to learn a fundamental fact. In the view of John Rathbone this fact was that the original and perhaps glib concept of, in effect, producing one systems solution to all the operational needs of two societies was the wrong pre-emptive answer to many detailed questions, which had at that point yet to be formulated. The view is that the goal of a single common MCPS and PRS system is not unobtainable, but it is not necessary in order to achieve the equally important goal of a single efficient and effective organisation.

The briefest account of the effect on IS strategy of the business and technical circumstances, events and problems can be drawn from the IT director Chris Gardner's "state of the nation" report to the Boards in mid-2003. This compared the initial plans, assumptions and targets with the actual achievements. In 1997 the MCPS "common system" was running, and enhancements for operating the recently-acquired European Central Licensing deal with PolyGram, and their even more recent data-supply deal with PPL were being developed. The PRS IS strategy was superseded by Alliance imminence, although the major PRS Public Performance Sales System (PuPSS) was being planned. That year the first Alliance IS strategy envisaged common business models supported by common core systems based on MCPS systems. The following year saw foundation work, completion of the business architecture documentation, and plans for enhanced Membership systems. In 1999 the two societies' Copyright and Repertoire migration of data onto one system began, but the Alliance Distribution and Membership system was reduced in scope to serve PRS only because of heavy workload, and IMJV (*detailed later in this chapter*) systems requirements specifications began. In 2000 Repertoire data migration was abandoned because IMJV was intended to provide that functionality, but the vital transfer of works and agreements data onto a single Copyright system proceeded. There were plans for a centralised, systems-supported Alliance Customer Service Centre and an e-Business programme – and these continued as projects in 2001. This was also the year when the IMJV shared

service centre concept was abandoned, but the year when the common Copyright System successfully went live, thus fulfilling one of the major aims at the start of the Alliance five years before.

Improving service levels: Alliance Online Services

Useful separate developments for both PRS and MCPS businesses were steadily achieved throughout this period, and the aims of enhancements to service to members made steady progress. 2003 saw the successful launch of the Alliance Online Services pilot project and late in that year its first phase was ready for implementation.

There are several levels of significance in this initiative. It is a useful and very attractive technical development similar to those which many commercial companies have been using successfully for years, but which for the Alliance represented a very big step forward in "joined-up thinking" and presentation to the customer. And it can be said to mark a point where the internally-focused planning and workload has succeeded sufficiently to allow information systems to "look outwards". Having reached a point where combined society-specific data was of a requisite quality, and was being handled by systems in the requisite manner, the opportunity was seized to make this improvement visible and accessible beyond the operating company, for much wider benefit. The positive response from members who were involved in the pilot is the best testimony to its success.

As described to the Boards, the Alliance Online Services are a prime example of how the concept of "e-business" has moved, from an investigative and technical project in its own right into a way of working embedded in the normal business of the operating company. The project was described as "the Alliance 'e-enabling' its data and processes". The reasons for this development were to

179

provide improved functionality, "making it easier to get at or use our data", and to provide a more secure way for members and others to do the same, while extending the range of data available to them, thereby making it easier for the Alliance to handle a growing demand for access to that data. Other important benefits were that processes could be speeded up and thereby be more cost effective for the Alliance, members and others; and that a platform could be built for future "e–trading" (for example, having copyright usage returns from licensees compiled using Alliance data and identifiers).

As the pilot trials were beginning conclusively to prove their worth in late 2003, John Rathbone summed up: "This work is an important step in our strategy to change the way the Alliance interacts with members, music users and other third parties. It doesn't allow access by the general public at this stage; this will come later. It is one of the projects to add value through systems investment as opposed to 'replacing the foundations'". The name Alliance On-line Services came into being late in the day and superseded the project's original working title WACD (Web Access to Core Data) It is impossible to resist noting that WACD replaced two other acronyms which, although being easier to pronounce, were equally mystifying until they were explained. The MCPS online access system had been called MOLES and the PRS version adopted the rather grander ROME: these had been replaced with a joint system snappily called Repfinder, offering a way for members to look up repertoire information. The first stage of the WACD work was to replace Repfinder with a new and improved web-based version. Following on from that (and in a number of cases, in parallel with the Repfinder work), functionality was added to allow access to other data such as MCPS Product Licensing Reports or PRS unmatched usage files.

Another level of the project's significance is that it neatly illustrates the point made in the introduction to this Alliance chapter.

The Alliance is first, foremost, essentially, necessarily, by design and intent an operating company. So its story from the outset and into the future is one of fulfilling the strategies and policies and purposes of its parent societies in the most efficient, practical way possible. That, in a 21st century business environment, means efficient and practical technology and systems. That, in the slightly quaint but descriptive international English of legislators in Europe at this time also means "communication and protection in the digital information society". And all that means an ongoing corporate story which frequently reads rather more like a technical specification (albeit with touches of Conan Doyle, radio soap opera script and circus artistes' manual at times) than a wide-horizoned history of political manoeuvring and business adventure.

Creating an Alliance Management Team

Of course, the Alliance "home front" involved much that had to do with people as well as much that had to do with IT. Looking back in 2003 Hutchinson admits that his decision simply to bring two complete teams of senior management into one, thereby giving himself a decidedly non-textbook top team of 13 direct reports, was purely tactical: since he always had every intention of reducing it in size, he also admits that his "reassuring" approach of giving a role to everyone could be described as scheming. However, the managers were experienced enough to know what was happening and work with it while always expecting change. That change would certainly adversely affect some of them, the only questions being "who and when"?

Hutchinson has described the first couple of "alliance years " as a time when he sometimes wondered whether he was in control of a rollercoaster or merely riding one and hoping that the track ahead of it was being laid fast enough. Those who at the time found themselves in the management cars just behind

The MCPS–PRS Alliance
Management Board and Direct Reports
As at March 2004

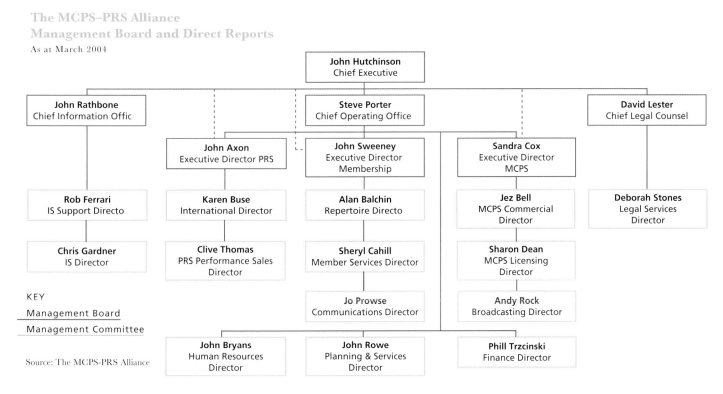

John Hutchinson
Chief Executive

John Rathbone
Chief Information Offic

Steve Porter
Chief Operating Office

David Lester
Chief Legal Counsel

John Axon
Executive Director PRS

John Sweeney
Executive Director
Membership

Sandra Cox
Executive Director
MCPS

Rob Ferrari
IS Support Directo

Karen Buse
International Director

Alan Balchin
Repertoire Directo

Jez Bell
MCPS Commercial
Director

Deborah Stones
Legal Services
Director

Chris Gardner
IS Director

Clive Thomas
PRS Performance Sales
Director

Sheryl Cahill
Member Services Director

Sharon Dean
MCPS Licensing
Director

KEY

Management Board

Management Committee

Jo Prowse
Communications Director

Andy Rock
Broadcasting Director

Source: The MCPS-PRS Alliance

John Bryans
Human Resources
Director

John Rowe
Planning & Services
Director

Phill Trzcinski
Finance Director

his on this ride wondered the same thing, but with understandably greater apprehension.

When the two sets of MCPS and PRS management and staff began the deliberately cautious process of amalgamation in early 1997, the goals were fully understood to be efficiency and cost-effectiveness: that had to mean fewer people. In service companies where a very high percentage of cost related directly to employment of people, headcount reduction had to be a prime objective alongside systems rationalisation. However, the approach was far from the commercial Acquisitions and Mergers norm of swift, swinging cutbacks in a brief initial corporate bloodbath. What was intended in the medium-term future to become, as far as practicable, one company team needed at first simply to

start looking like one team, while reality could be shaped to fit the picture on the lid of the loosely assembled Alliance box. But if change came at a steady pace, it also came relentlessly and unceasingly, affecting several generations of management and departmental structures, managers' roles and titles, and of personnel.

In the "pre-Alliance" year, when Hutchinson combined the activity of pulling the two organisations into a whole (far from seamless but with increasingly strong zip fasteners inserted wherever necessary), with reassurances to the parent Boards that the process was not irreversible, they had the power to reverse it or change it, although common sense indicated that this facility must steadily diminish. His top management team initially embraced all

181

those who had been at the top of their respective PRS and MCPS management trees, all with the equal title of "director". Overlaps in previous functions were finessed out of revised role specifications, more successfully in some cases than in others; organisation charts were redrawn frequently. It was a first step which anyone in their right senses knew would be followed by other and very different arrangements (and given the pace of change which Hutchinson had already showed he favoured, later steps were likely to break into a run or full gallop before too long). The positive and negative impact on individuals over the following few years cannot be dismissed with an airy wave, but the inevitability and business necessity were fully recognised.

Just as finding the "fit" in IT systems took time, creating the joint operational departments (or business units as they were latterly termed) was anything but an overnight transformation. Amalgamation of all the IT managers and staff under one director was necessarily an early move, though it took time to refine. Declaring that the PRS International team would also work on (internationally relatively limited) MCPS issues was similarly swiftly achieved. For understandable reasons, the "customer facing" departments remained separate for several years. The immutable early principle laid down by the parent Boards was that the licensing functions of MCPS and PRS for the different rights would remain totally separate and distinct. The differences in demands, expectations and ways of working between the two memberships in relation to their performing and mechanical rights meant that combined membership services teams were also a long time in arriving.

Internal structures and reporting lines are not of sufficiently general interest for a history such as this, but the broad phases of change can be identified. The first embraced all the management of both societies, ensuring that the Chief Executive would have all possible support from all the senior line directors in both administrations in the very early years of creating a functioning joint operation. The second drew top management power and

responsibility into a much smaller group of Executive Directors handling only the core business functions: finance and operations, information services, the performing and mechanical rights revenue streams, and legal. The third and current structure is tighter still in top management terms, with succession planning for the Chief Executive in mind and (as with the second phase) the intention of focusing Board reporting responsibility and reducing Board and Committee attendance by several managers in many instances where one would suffice.

Working with the writers' organisations

A very important group of people (some 40,000 of them) comprise the members of the UK societies. Their relationship with their rights societies is an important theme throughout this history. In that context, where writers are concerned, the British Academy of Composers and Songwriters (BACS) has played its part in the background (and occasionally pivotally) in this story. PRS and MCPS have both had a close relationship with the bodies representing British composers and songwriters, and PRS played a key role in the 1999 formation of BACS, as an amalgamation of the three original organisations. As mentioned before these were the Composers' Guild of Great Britain (founded in 1944), the British Academy of Songwriters, Composers and Authors (founded as the Songwriters' Guild of Great Britain in 1946) and the Association of Professional Composers, set up in the 1970s as a "breakaway" from the Composers' Guild.

PRS had been in various ways supporting all three and in the early 1990s it provided a common home for them in a building in Hanway Street, close to the PRS offices in Berners Street. By this move, PRS officials hoped to encourage the three bodies to work more closely together.

This they did, founding the Alliance of Composer Organisations to consider the common issues facing all composers and to explore more formal co-operation amongst themselves. Another catalyst for co-operation came in the unlikely form of a Norwegian society, Kopinor. This body had collected royalties for photocopying music by British composers and needed to hand over the money to an organisation serving the whole composer community. Consequently, ACO took receipt of a first payment of £35,000.

The leadership of all three Guilds now favoured amalgamation and a consultant, Chris Green, was hired in 1996 to draw up proposals. Two years later the 2,500 members of the Guilds approved a merger plan with only five votes against. Meanwhile, a strong relationship with the Alliance was formed via the foundation of British Music Rights, as explained in the chapter on that organisation.

Green was appointed Chief Executive of the new Academy, which lost no time in making a new funding agreement with PRS. In order to stress its status as an independent voice for authors' interests, the Academy wished to phase out direct PRS funding but to retain PRS and MCPS sponsorship of Academy events such as the Ivor Novello and Gold Badge Awards. The phasing out took place over a three and a half-year period and since 2002 the Academy has been self-funding.

Green says that relations between BACS and the Alliance – but understandably most closely with PRS – are still very close, not only because the Academy rents office space from the Alliance at an advantageous rate. The Academy collaborates with the Alliance and other industry bodies in campaigning and lobbying through British Music Rights, the Government's Music Business Forum and the Creators Rights Alliance (with literary authors and others). It also lobbies independently on issues of sole concern to composers as well providing its members with access to legal and accountancy advice and general information through seminars and workshops. Green is convinced that, if anything, it is more

important for composers to have an independent voice in Britain than elsewhere in Europe where societies are traditionally more "composer led". BACS' good relationships with the UK societies and the Alliance operating company are much valued.

Improving service levels – Membership communications

Both societies have a requirement to have frequent, timely and two-way communications with their membership communities[4] in order to operate successfully and meet their obligations to their members. There have always been differences in approach – very broadly MCPS members appeared to require more closely business-orientated information aimed at the publishing sector, while PRS members, predominantly writers, were always offered a greater and more frequent flow of information about their society, what it was doing and how, and the people who were working in it on their behalf.

In late 2002 the membership communications functions of the two societies were merged as one management and staff team under one director – as the operating company continued its process of amalgamating departments. The communications requirements were increasingly seen as integral to the objective of delivering ever-improving service levels, although it was finally agreed that the large overlap in MCPS and PRS memberships and in areas of interest could be translated into producing common publications where appropriate.

However PRS has particular requirements, which must regularly be reported on to the Office of Fair Trading (a requirement of the 1996 MMC Report). These include publishing sufficient accounting information for members to be able to see where costs lie; formally setting out in the Members' Handbook the responsibilities it has to members and the standards of service

---

4 The membership of PRS has constantly risen, sometimes dramatically but in recent years very steadily. In 2003 it stood at 38,003 (34,897 writers, 2,982 publishers, and 1,759 successors) MCPS membership also grows, but more slowly. In 2003 it stood at 17,117, of which (possibly to the surprise of many) 12,359 are writers who have joined MCPS directly, while 4,758 are publishing companies.

PRS News

PRS Leaflet

MPA and MCPS Report and Accounts 2000

MCPS-PRS Members Music Magazine

it aims to achieve; publishing clear and up-to-date Rules and Members' Handbook; stating the limitations of the distribution policy in the society's literature; publishing accounting information to include details relating to the members' overseas earnings.

The face-to-face contact between MCPS, PRS and both memberships is an important part of the societies' consultation with their members. As well as its Annual General Meeting, which all full and associate members are invited to attend to exercise their voting powers, there are Open Sessions which visit three regional cities per year and provide an opportunity for relatively informal contact. MCPS has recently followed the PRS lead and in conjunction with the MPA introduced biannual Open Sessions where MCPS management deal with current issues of interest to members.

The Alliance also holds over 40 meetings a year with members and industry representatives to discuss current operations and consult on planned developments. These groups have evolved over the last ten years from previously separate MCPS and PRS groups. The list itself indicates the extent of the efforts to communicate and consult.

- PRS Classical Discussion Group
- MCPS-PRS Copyright Discussion Group
- MCPS Library Publishers Executive Committee
- PRS Major Writer Representatives Group
- MCPS-PRS Media Group
- MCPS-PRS Royalty Group
- Scottish Consultative Committee
- PRS Specialist Music Group (which evolved from the advisory group which assisted with the distribution and data review in the mid 90s)
- PRS/MPA Liaison Group
- PRS/British Academy Liaison Group

Social events for members have become more frequent fronted by both societies and by the Alliance. Similarly, a wide range of information has been offered regularly in an evolutionary series of publications. *PRS News* has a long history of bringing society information to all members, and has been updated and redesigned quite frequently. From the mid-70s it was joined by the very differently "pop" styled *PRS Statement* newsletter which accompanied quarterly royalty distributions – so was only seen by those receiving distributions. The *PRS Yearbook* for many years combined the annual report and accounts with information about the society and the rights business and was sent to all PRS members once a year. While it was widely admired internationally recent research concluded that many members saw it as an unnecessary extravagance with much corporate information that they did not require.

For The Record was a quarterly accompaniment to the MCPS main distributions but towards the end of its life it became an intermittent member newsletter that was event driven, and the *MCPS Report & Accounts* were contained within the MPA Report & Accounts publication provided to MPA members and MCPS members on request.

A review of Member Communications in the late 90s embraced research by Beck Consultancy. Combined with views from members gathered at member meetings this led to a further communications review in 2001. That in turn led to a new single publication from the Alliance, intended to reflect the importance of member communications and the size and importance of the two societies.

M magazine was launched in Autumn 2001 as a quarterly for all PRS members and additional industry contacts. The intention was to establish a quality member communication brand for the Alliance which entertained as well as informed. This was also the first time that an Alliance publication included third party advertising. In December 2002 the coverage of *M magazine* was extended to include the MCPS member audience; it included

a new *MBusiness* section, of particular interest to the publishing community, providing an easy reference point for all policy, procedure, legal and data information. *M annual* was launched in Autumn 2001 to replace the *PRS Yearbook* and broadened its content and audience to include MCPS business and membership.

Other publications include the PRS *Member Information Pack* – a replacement for an annual members handbook which, as policy and administrative change accelerated, could not be updated often enough; the PRS *Music Universe Poster*, which since its creation in 1998 proved extremely popular in offering succinct graphical description of complicated relationships between organisations and individuals in the entire music business; and the *MCPS Handbook*, currently in the process of being split out into separate leaflets. PRS and MCPS both offer distribution information which explains to members exactly what all the entries in the royalty statements mean.

Investors in People (IiP)

INVESTOR IN PEOPLE

Hutchinson and his senior managers recognised the need for better management and staff training, motivation, performance appraisal, matching of remuneration and all the other factors which can weld people into a single corporate entity if done well (the opposite, of course, being equally true).

One initiative which drew people together, both in the attempt and in its eventual success was a bid for Investors in People (IiP) accreditation. PRS had formed an objective of improvement in the wake of the MMC Report, although its TCI (Total Continuous Improvement) initiative had never gathered momentum, lacking the essential highest level commitment at a time of turmoil after the failure of the PROMS system and the departure of almost all the top management team within one year. The IiP accreditation was a fresh goal set for the Alliance as a whole soon after the incorporation of the jointly-owned operating company in 1998.

IiP accreditation recognises specific and regularly assessed levels of achievement in business planning and communication of those plans to employees, who need fully to understand how what they do fits in and aids corporate progress; training and development of people in a way linked to their needs and those of the business; and evaluating the effects and benefits of this training in a comprehensive way. The realisation that the IiP initiative was not just cosmetic, (however slight and grudging that realisation might have been in some for whom the formation of the Alliance was not a happy experience), was probably the true success for the many mixed management teams who worked on earning accreditation. In 2000 the MCPS-PRS Alliance won its IiP certificate, becoming the first major company in the UK music business to do so.

International

The Alliance's relationship with the international umbrella organisations for collecting societies exists at various levels from top level policy to day-to-day co-working on projects and protocols.

The global CISAC embraces societies which administer all kinds of "authors' rights" in their intellectual property (IP) and prefers the term "authors' societies" to collecting societies. Over 90% of its member societies' revenues come from music licensing, and CISAC membership includes performing and mechanical rights administrators (obviously particularly where they are in merged or operationally-allied organisations).

However, the international umbrella organisation specifically for mechanical rights societies, BIEM, has traditionally been of greater relevance and importance to MCPS, whose relationship with BIEM has always been somewhat schizophrenic. As an agent for one of the major repertoires in the world operating in one of the major music markets, MCPS's inclination has always been to seek to provide a strong influence on the activities of BIEM. On the other hand, as one of the few societies not operating its mechanical licensing under the umbrella agreement between BIEM and IFPI, not all the detailed workings of BIEM have seemed of direct relevance. However, things reached something like fever pitch when MCPS entered into its ECL agreement with PolyGram and included direct distribution to PolyGram Music Publishing's local affiliates, which bypassed the local mechanical rights societies (*see MCPS chapter*).

In response to this action BIEM members refused to elect an MCPS representative on to its Management Committee at its Annual Meeting in Scheveningen in the Netherlands in autumn 1996, and Professor Reinhold Kreile of GEMA led the charge against MCPS at the meeting. In the absence of a Chief Executive (Frans de Wit having just left the organisation), David Lester on behalf of MCPS (and to a large extent, its members) was left to throw down the gauntlet to the other BIEM members to reform the central licensing system in a fiery speech which set out MCPS' long standing opposition to the way in which ECL agreements had been operating to the detriment of the rights owners. The speech showed that the direct distribution approach was a way of redressing this balance. Subsequently, the other members of BIEM went as far as calling an Extraordinary Meeting to remove the obligation on the part of BIEM members to enter into reciprocal agreements with each other in so far as this applied to MCPS. Although this had all the signs of leading to a major confrontation, the Cannes Agreement of 1997 (*see MCPS chapter*) included a clause which resolved the position, and as the new Chief Executive of MCPS John Hutchinson was duly re-elected to the Management Committee.

At other levels, MCPS has over the years contributed extensively to BIEM's other activities. Notable among these were the development of a co-ordinated and effective audit and anti-piracy effort across Europe which owed much of its knowledge to MCPS's experience. Similarly, in beginning to address the licensing and administration issues raised by online use of music, MCPS was influential in developing the thinking which led to many of the policies now being taken up across the BIEM societies.

The relationship of John Hutchinson with his peers within the international organisations, particularly CISAC, as Chief Executive first of PRS and then of the Alliance can be regarded as a distinct thread in the Alliance story.

As PRS Chief Executive, Hutchinson's position at the head of one of the biggest societies in the world meant that he automatically merited a seat at every CISAC "top table" (the Executive Bureau and the Administrative Council). He was expected to make a significant contribution to the discussion and direction of the organisation. What was probably not expected was that he would do so in a straight-talking and often confrontational style to which CISAC, with its traditionally elaborate diplomacy and almost rigid requirement for polite consensus, was completely unfamiliar. From his earliest attendance at CISAC meetings Hutchinson believed he saw a need for reform: "What I saw and heard within the organisation as it was then made me feel it was essential to work to make the organisation and secretariat stop living in the past." He questioned the running of the secretariat of that time, and what he judged to be lack of understanding of what was happening in technology which would impact on rights administration. That in

turn led to questions about the lack of progress with the Common Information System (CIS). Attempting to prod forward change and observing that such prodding tended to be absorbed without trace or material reaction, Hutchinson determined in early 1996 to push harder. Realising that he did have like-minded (but far less vocal) allies among major societies he formed a CISAC Reform Group. Quite serious action was planned, but for political reasons none was collectively taken, although Hutchinson's very public criticisms delivered at the CISAC September 1996 World Congress in Paris caused a satisfying stir. While still sure that something had to be done to force change despite inevitable controversy, he admitted later that he had lost the battle that year and had probably been wrong to try to take a lead at CISAC so

A working alliance with the Dutch society Buma:Stemra was one of the strategic steps in international relations plans for the Alliance. Pictured at the signing of the agreement in April 1997 are (*standing left to right*) Buma:Stemra Legal Counsel Cees van Rij and Alliance Director of Legal Affairs David Lester with (*seated left to right*) PRS, MCPS and Alliance CEO John Hutchinson and Buma:Stemra CEO Cees Vervoord

early. He had not been on his own territory, and CISAC was bound to resist robust contributions and tough talking of a kind its long standing customs did not allow for.

However, persistence and a more refined approach brought results over time, he asserted, setting a pattern of straighter talking in international relations whereby unpopular truths could be stated in an atmosphere of respect if not perpetual amity. The CISAC secretariat changed significantly in style, efficiency and effectiveness after the appointment of Eric Baptiste as Secretary General. Other improvements in MCPS and PRS international relations, using the term broadly to mean also the business transactions with affiliated societies, were won as Hutchinson tempered his tactics while sticking to principles. One example was the long-running UK campaign to reduce or eliminate reciprocal social and cultural deductions. By the late 90s Hutchinson and the Alliance held firmly to their view that "social" deductions were completely undesirable, but accepted that their existence helped some societies with their government relations and eased the path to nationally strong licensing tariffs. Hutchinson and his counterparts therefore looked for ways of balancing principles and practice. Gradually new agreements were put in place which address these issues indirectly but with honour being satisfied on both sides.

Hutchinson "learnt as I went along", and part of that learning was the importance of strategic and working alliances with other CISAC societies and with his peers in those societies. An early example was that formed with the Dutch society Buma:Stemra. This gave the Alliance a strong relationship with a medium-sized but influential Continental European society. Another was the set of alliances in the IMJV project. Much information was exchanged and much learnt through that, and although it never came to fruition Hutchinson created personal relationships with the Chief Executives of other important CISAC societies. A third, much looser kind of alliance was illustrated by closer relationship and occasional co-working with the Spanish society SGAE,

sought by Hutchinson because of SGAE's demonstrated superior understanding of how technology could be well used in the cause of rights administration.

The international initiatives need to be described within this section of the Alliance story, and are taken next in chronological order – the first being CISAC initiative, the second a potentially business-changing international project involving the Alliance; and the third being a different international approach to solving data exchange problems and meeting similar objective by a different route – a route which the Alliance has very recently chose to take itself.

The CISAC Common Information System CIS

The arrival of electronic communication improved speed and ease of contact. It also raised (but with monotonous regularity disappointed) public expectations of speed, accuracy, ease of use, access to information and increased "personal" treatment in all business sectors. Collecting society members are part of that public.

Early in 1994 in a letter to some of the panellists in that year's CISAC World Congress in Washington DC, CISAC Chairman and CEO of the Swedish society STIM Gunnar Petri stated:

"Digitisation will lead to an enormous increase in the output of works used. The number of radio and TV channels available will explode. The number of protected works will increase and information regarding ownership will become more complex. All this will take place in a market where licensing revenue will not increase significantly". At the Congress the subject was pursued, and the message summed up by one CISAC speaker was "in the future, the success of our organisations will be determined by their capacity to distribute the money received quickly, efficiently and transparently".

A presentation *Distribution in the Digital Age* by MCPS Database controller Godfrey Rust proposed that by the year 2000 the community of societies should have put in place "a basic, global information infrastructure which will enable us not only to withstand the digital flood which is already breaking, but position us to take advantage of the opportunities which the digital world offers".

His proposed model was The Number Network – the linking of numbers (which would uniquely identify works and other essential rights administration information) in different databases, thereby creating a "virtual global database through which royalties could flow unhindered".

A Common Information System was the proposal from the CISAC Information Systems Steering Committee. The building of this network was stated firmly to be not an option but a necessity.

Work on integrating information between BIEM and CISAC societies had in fact begun in 1987, focusing on building a number of centralised data files, or tools, such as the Compositeurs, Auteurs, Editeurs (CAE) database of composers, lyricists and music publishers, and the World Works List. In 1993 the emphasis changed, in response to a realisation that the approach needed was integration of data when it was first created, not accumulation of data after it already existed in many different places and in many different formats.

The need which CIS was proposed to fill was that "data must be captured once, accurately, as close as possible to its source; it must be uniquely numbered and structured to agreed international standards, and then made generally available and immediately usable in electronic form". The oral shorthand used in his 1994 presentation by Rust was "do it once, do it right".

CIS originally had a five-year timetable for fruition; a decade later work is still in progress. There are a number of reasons for this. Ideas about what "fruition" means have inevitably changed and developed. The marketplace for which CIS was defining standards and creating technology tools has changed, and those tools cannot be developed fast enough through joint working by an international community of organisations which vary widely in their individual approaches, needs and resources. And the good idea of "what" has inevitably and again encountered the booby-trapped maze of the "how", in people and politics terms as well as technical.

Today CISAC's own literature described CIS as its "programme in the field of online intellectual property rights management" which (still) aims to create a worldwide digital rights management system, based on standardised identification of creative works and linked networks of information between CISAC societies. Its means are "two series of tools that provide the building blocks to global digital copyright administration". One features the integration of unique ISO (International Standards Organisation) certified, "standardised international identifiers of works and parties relevant to the creative process". The other is a network of global databases, or sub-systems relying on various technologies, "serving as a repository authoritative information"[5].

PRS and MCPS managers have always been heavily involved in the development of CIS, but experienced growing frustration

5 see the CISAC website – www.cisac.org

with the slowness of pace – largely a function of the CISAC *all for one and one for all* ethos which demanded that the project involved the whole CISAC membership in all its diversity of culture, technical understanding and resources. The pace tended to be that of the slowest. CISAC is described by one seasoned PRS manager who has spent years involved in the CIS working groups as "a bigger version of the old, traditional, intelligent and well-intentioned yet bureaucratic PRS, and therefore prone to putting up old traditional roadblocks in the way of radical joint projects – politics, covert competition, size, culture and (in CISAC's case) language".

However, PRS was an enthusiastic participant in CIS developments, supporting and implementing Common Works Registration (CWR), the International Standard Work Code (ISWC), the audiovisual works AVIndex (which PRS had developed and offered for incorporation in CIS); and contributing to working groups for the Works Information Database (WID) which had grown out of the World Works List, and the Interested Parties Index (IPI) which had grown out of the CAE file[6]. After his arrival to head PRS and then the MCPS-PRS Alliance Hutchinson began, and continued, to put his energetic support behind CIS, largely with the aim of moving it ahead at a more useful pace, and if necessary in a two-speed plan which would give the major societies the data interchange standards and tools they needed urgently, and would have to develop for themselves if CIS could not develop them quickly enough.

Attempting a revolutionary international joint venture

The holy grail of rights administration is total accuracy and seamless linking of all the necessary data, from registration of a work and its ownership through to payment of the correct royalty to every rights owner, every time, nationally and internationally, and with the best achievable cost efficiency.

Within collecting societies' historic paper-based systems, valiant attempts were made over many decades to get as close as possible to this ideal, which was not all that close. Only data processing and communications technology were ever going to provide a satisfactory answer; in recent years several technology-based answers have been explored, with different degrees of success but with general acceptance that there is still a long way to go. Part of the answer had to be international, possibly also inter-IP-genre, co-operation.

A brave international initiative was launched by the MCPS-PRS Alliance in 1998. It built on thinking which was being done by rights administrators in various ways over quite a number of years. For example, at the time that the MCPS "common system" was developed (*see MCPS chapter*) that society felt that it had a system which not only served its own purposes but had potential for taking all music rights and possibly any rights administration closer to the ultimate ideal. Each IP creation, or work, could be uniquely identified and then accurately linked to continually updated information about rights ownership, rights licensed and to whom, type and volumes of usage, agreements between

6 Other tools for non-music rights are ISAN (International Standard Audiovisual Number) and ISTC (International Standard Text Code).

interested parties etc. It was thought such a generic system could manage any kind of creative content administration centrally for a variety of rights-owning clients. And it could be a separate data management company, outside the societies which had guardianship of the rights and did the licensing for their members, protected and promoted their interests and attended to the political agendas of their specific IP sector. It was logical also to assume that such a generic management system could and should operate internationally. The potential achievements in terms of accuracy, efficiency and cost-cutting were believed to be very large.

It is not surprising that this potential became a tempting vision for more than one rights organisation within a short span of years in the mid-90s. But there was no consensus on the way to achieve that vision, and in the event several different approaches were explored by different groupings of organisations, with different outcomes. The basic principle of unique identification of IP creations within what was effectively one database was already driving the CIS development, although the proposed practicalities there were entirely different to the MCPS idea. The same principle drove the development of the co-operation between a number of CISAC music rights societies to develop a differently scaled and devised approach, via the FastTrack project which provides tools and techniques for societies to link and exchange data via network rather than a physical service centre. And the international umbrella organisations for record and publishing sides of the global music industry started to collaborate on developing the Music Industry Integrated identifier Project (which rejoices in the contracted acronym MI3P).

The MCPS ideas about an independent rights data management company were not tested or pursued because the formation of the Alliance made all decisions about the future joint ones with PRS: as one former MCPS manager put it: "There was total friendly disagreement between the two on the feasibility and extent of the idea".

The unprecedented idea of an international joint "back office"

The Alliance did, however, embrace the concept of the centralised "service centre" in its own terms, as the International Music Joint Venture (IMJV). Although that project did not come to fruition, it deserves its place in the recent history of music rights administration. This not least because it was seen as a very good idea – possibly the best idea – for international back office cost effectiveness, and because it is seen as having contributed to the whole debate about the future of IP rights administration in a globalised environment.

Stated simply, the thinking behind IMJV at the beginning of 1998 was built on the premise which had launched the CISAC Common Information System (CIS) project in 1994. This was that the complex web of information streams within and between societies around the world tied up a lot of cost in every society putting more or less the same data through more or less the same processes, with errors and complications abounding as each national database was compiled locally without any way of referring directly to an absolutely (or at least relatively) authoritative original source. A way had to be found to make all this more efficient. The CIS approach was to create a network through which individual databases could be effectively linked to create a "virtual" database in which essential information was stored once, and accurately, for everyone to refer to.

The MCPS-PRS Alliance was not alone in thinking that the CIS project was not moving fast enough to suit the business needs of the world's biggest societies. Allied to this was its own belief that the "network" idea was not actually the best way to tackle the full range of duplication of effort and serially compounded data errors. The Anglo-American repertoire being the largest and most commercially successful in the world it was to be expected that talks about a different solution should initially involve the UK and

American societies, with an important link to continental Europe being provided by involvement of the very "internationally-minded" Netherlands society Buma:Stemra (like the Alliance, a joint operation which served both performing and mechanical rights, though one which has reached a more advanced stage of integration).

In January 1998 talks began between the US performing rights societies ASCAP and BMI and the mechanical rights Harry Fox Agency; Buma:Stemra and the MCPS-PRS Alliance. In March an independent feasibility study was commissioned from Pricewaterhouse Coopers. This was delivered and considered, and led to three (or five, if the UK and Dutch organisations are thought of in terms of the separate societies they represent) of the original potential participants deciding to go ahead, BMI and Harry Fox having dropped out. Detailed planning began in October that year and the IMJV business case was approved by the PRS and MCPS Boards in March 1999. Other societies were approached with the opportunity to be core members or committed early customers. Of these, SOCAN (Society of Composers, Authors and Music Publishers of Canada) decided to come in with co-founder status. BMI later became a leading player in the formation of the FastTrack network (*detailed later in this chapter*).

As there had been among some societies, particularly PRS, within their CIS development work there was an IMJV view that there was "someone missing" from around the discussion table and workbench: the member. Development of CIS did not involve representatives of the societies' memberships, but the conviction that members' views, needs and ideas should be taken into the planning of collecting society developments has been a continually strengthening theme in the planning and activity of PRS and then the Alliance.

IMJV established regular consultation with publishers and writers' groups, setting up policy and practice which created a far greater level of mutual understanding than had ever previously been a characteristic of collecting societies, and thus establishing a huge business and communications benefit which has far outlasted the IMJV project itself.

IMJV was intended to set up a shared service centre, sited in the Netherlands, which would effectively be the back office for all its founder societies (and later for other customers). While maintaining complete independence, the participants would each gain reduced cost and improved efficiency, elimination of work duplication and better service for their members. They would be taking an important initiative which would reflect the globalisation of the rights industry, and to that end would embrace (and share the cost of) technological change. IMJV would maintain positive links with the CISAC community's initiatives by adopting CIS standards when building its systems and tools. The idea that IMJV was a rival to CIS was regularly refuted. The latter was looking at developing data interchange standards and tools, while the former was one specific organisational approach to the use of standards and tools.

Back to late 1998. At that point the implementation plan for IMJV envisaged detailed design and planning being complete by mid-1999; the registration system being built by December 2000 and running live by October 2001, and data matching systems built and live by the end of April 2002. However, by the time that date arrived, IMJV was already several months deceased. A totally objective analysis of "what went wrong" probably needs a more distant perspective: just two years later the who, how and why are still matters for debate. But the facts that the project was informally cancelled in December 2001 and formally interred in January 2002 are absolutely clear.

The view from the UK is that the Alliance had been prepared to take a leadership role in IMJV and to shoulder the workload which always comes with the assumption of such a role in any joint effort. There were "people" problems of various kinds . There were communication and co-working problems across continents and time zones and cultures. The issue of what particular combination of skills were most needed in a CEO could not be satisfactorily resolved. It proved difficult to decide on the extent to which existing individual practices and system requirements could be subsumed into a service centre (different and distinct from a potentially unwieldy amalgam of all participants' needs and preferences). Perhaps most significantly there were, and were perceived to be, different levels of Boards' and managements' commitment to the project. For various reasons it proved difficult for the partners to provide equally the necessary personnel, skills and financial resources in a timely or efficient fashion. There were also inevitably technical problems, which slowed down the timetable: these were solved – yet could not in themselves solve the bigger problems of the project as a whole. However, it is a measure of the conviction and business thinking which was put into the IMJV project that many of those involved in it still believe today that, in the words of one of them, "it was a brilliant idea, and its time maybe is still to come".

An Alliance milestone was inarguably the end of IMJV. The decision to bring the venture to an abrupt close was taken by the Alliance delegation following a project partners' meeting in New York, and immediately supported by the Boards. By his own account, Hutchinson was even then thinking ahead. He saw "no need to go into a shell" and within three months was working to set up group of societies within CISAC to push forward faster and more effectively with development of CIS, another route to a place not too far from where IMJV might have been. His intention was to ensure that the energy of the Alliance was put behind the more rapid development of the CIS project and its practical applications in the CISAC society network. He received the support of Bernard Miyet, CEO of the French society SACEM – which had chosen to become part of the FastTrack initiative rather than IMJV. These two approaches to international collaboration to create more efficient back office functioning for societies had not been in direct competition with each other, and both had been committed to using CIS standards

and tools wherever possible, and whenever such standards and tools should become available. Hutchinson suggested the establishment of a CIS "ginger group" of 10 large societies. Miyet supported this and immediately focused on getting commitment to a date for the first meeting of this grouping, which became known as the G10[7] This was, in Hutchinson's view, a significant personal milestone "because it proved that progress can be made purely because there is an element of mutual respect, even in times of conflict".

After two years as Moderator of the G10 group, Hutchinson was able to report considerable progress at the CISAC Executive Bureau meeting in June 2003; a level of progress which in his view would before long achieve his objective of winding up the group because its work was successfully completed. The G10 reported that the Supervisory Board of FastTrack had agreed to enable societies other than its founder members to join "with a parity of influence and vote" and it added that the societies which had been the IMJV partners were at that point looking at the probability of joining FastTrack under those terms. Additionally, the G10 recommended to the Executive Bureau that all the existing data and document sharing networks or "significant potential nodes" within CISAC should be encouraged to explore the possibility of linking with each other using the FastTrack GDDN (Global Documentation and Distribution Network) protocol as a CISAC standard. Another recommendation was that other CISAC actions should aim at making rapid progress with aspects of CIS through use of FastTrack protocols; and at bringing the CISAC and BIEM (European mechanical rights societies' umbrella organisation) involvement in the MI3P project up to the level already reached by the record industry. For the MCPS-PRS Alliance the prospect of strong working alliances and networks within CISAC aligns well with its own strategic plans and objectives, albeit via a route other than that originally planned and ventured upon.

---

7 G10 societies –ASCAP (USA), BMI (USA) , Buma:Stemra (Netherlands), GEMA (Germany), JASRAC (Japan), MCPS-PRS Alliance (UK), SACEM (France), SGAE (Spain), SOCAN (Canada), STIM (Sweden). Also BIEM and CISAC representation.

Moving forward via FastTrack

After IMJV was closed down the Alliance concentrated on its own IS developments, but never lost touch with CISAC's CIS plans, nor with the other "back office" initiative which had taken the "virtual database" route rather than IMJV's intended physical shared service centre.

FastTrack began as an alliance among five CISAC societies, BMI in the USA, GEMA in Germany, SACEM in France, SGAE in Spain and SIAE in Italy. Others have since joined, and FastTrack has been set up as a separate company with its head office in Paris. The intention was to "collaboratively build a decentralised network to share data and streamline internal operations, based on the adoption of 'best practices' already existing among its members" and the proposal was that the "sharing of technological expertise, development costs and the power of a network computing architecture using the internet will deliver substantial benefits in the near term…" FastTrack also stated at the outset its commitment to the adoption of CIS standards, while it developed its own tools. Put at its simplest, the FastTrack tools are comparable to a typical internet search engine, capable of retrieving data from all and any society databases which make themselves accessible to it. In the event the FastTrack protocols became the best-developed and most pragmatic answer to how the pursuit of the Holy Grail could continue.

The Alliance as operating company recommended to PRS and MCPS as its parent societies and "guardians of the members' rights" that they should join FastTrack, and the Boards agreed late in 2003. FastTrack was judged to have reached critical mass – ie to have achieved the solidity and volume of international support and to be consistently delivering the practical developments needed to make its approach a firm long-term way of doing this vital part of collecting societies' business. So the Alliance came to view it as a key part of its own future way of working. There was a stated view that FastTrack "still has some way to go" in adding business functionality, but the Alliance believes that by becoming a partner it can ensure that its own specific requirements are taken into account as things develop. Alongside consideration of its own business requirements the Alliance happily recognises that this is an important tool to enable affiliated societies to check how it is itself holding and dealing with others' data, and vice versa.

In the same vein of efficient handling and exchange of business data, some milestones look rather small but have significance out of proportion with their size. One was an Alliance achievement to have the second version of the US-originated Common Works Registration accepted as a global standard for collecting societies. Hutchinson concedes that this was in reality forced through by the Alliance because it would be an advantage in the development of IMJV. But its business benefit to societies generally was recognised and it was later adopted by CISAC.

International business change: online music distribution and online licensing

The online "distribution" of music as electronic, digitised sound or audiovisual files is one of the technological and market phenomena of the early 21st century which, in a culture awash with hyperbole, really deserves the description "explosion". *See the Digital Distribution appendix*

Writers and publishers have always been aware that what they control and earn revenue from is intellectual property, the music as an intellectual creation, while those to whom it licenses that music are in the business of selling some commercial product, a physical audio or video recording, or a radio or television programme. The issue of the licensing of rights is habitually uppermost in their minds, and in the minds of their collecting societies. So their reaction to the arrival of the internet file-sharing technology and all its consequences for the record industry was to find a way to license it, rather than finding a way to stop it. The MCPS and PRS involvement in various projects such as RightsWatch (which investigated the means to identify unlicensed providers of copyright music on the internet and warn them that they were infringing copyright) was a demonstration of that wish to create a legitimate, licensed environment for music on the internet rather than a punitive crusade against individuals who were cheerfully flouting copyright in their millions, simply because they could.

Joint global performing and mechanical online licences were the answer, where societies were in a position to offer both rights. And for those who could not, a global licence for one or the other right was needed. So, while it is essential to remember that the performing right is licensed by PRS, and the mechanical rights are licensed by MCPS, the fact that the two societies have agreed to license those rights jointly, and that joint licence is administered by the Alliance, leads to the practical decision to deal with it in the Alliance chapter.

Music service providers (MSPs) who wished to establish legitimate online businesses wanted licences, but a way had to be found to license them. Leaving aside the very different approach taken by the record industry, which in their business sector probably needed to be as stridently litigious as it had become in 2003, the writers' and publishers' rights side of the music business was willing to find a way to offer collective administration for this type of music use as for all others. The main issue was the fact that the reciprocal agreements through which collecting societies ensure that musical works can be licensed, and royalties collected, almost anywhere did not cater for online delivery of music. These agreements were built on the historic fact of territoriality; each society licensed the use of its own national repertoire, and that of the other societies with

which it had agreements, within its own territory. The online environment (the ex-trendy term cyberspace is actually appropriate here – a transcendent "place" which is everywhere and nowhere) is absolutely not territorial. MSPs needed global licences for globally available services. And they needed an easy route to licences for all the different rights which online music distribution uses.

It should be mentioned that it had first to be established *who* should be the licensee. The MSPs were agreed to be the target licensees for the performing and mechanical rights only after much thinking-through of a new market model and (yet another) tussle with the record industry, which would have preferred to roll all the rights into their own licensing for usage of the commercial recording on internet music services. MCPS and PRS stood firmly by a line of reasoning which states that the rights are licensed to the commercial user who is closest in the value chain to the consumer. Significantly, the mechanical right is licensed to the creator of the "product" which is sold to the consumer; thus MCPS' stance was that the record company is licensed directly for the physical recordings it sells, and the MSP is licensed directly for the non-physical product which it sells as a content provider or aggregator (channel through which various types of content from various originators are brought together as an online "package" which the consumer can view or download for an appropriate payment). The online value chain can be very complicated, and MCPS and PRS are determined that the entity they jointly license is one which can be clearly and consistently identified; the one which receives the revenue from the consumer and the one which can consequently be audited.

The licensing model being used is based on gross revenue from a relevant service, taking into account a variety of factors such as how the consumer has access to the content and how it used (all-music downloads onto an electronic storage and play device such as the Apple i-Pod, or subscription services for playing and/or downloading audio and audiovisual files, permanently or temporarily, or free services which have advertising income, or mixed and "bundled" services).

The collecting societies have set up new international agreements to deal with the situation. The Santiago Agreement, launched at the 2000 CISAC World Congress in Santiago, Chile, dealt with the performing right. At its core is a solution to the online licensing problem which allows global licences to be issued to MSPs by the society in the country in which the MSP has economic residence. The Santiago Agreement was finalised and signed by participating societies and went into operation. Its counterpart for global licensing of mechanical rights is the Barcelona Agreement of 2001, approved at a BIEM General Assembly in Barcelona. MCPS was authorised to become a signatory to this agreement in December 2003. These agreements, which may need adjustment as time goes on, are a significant development for collective rights administration; one which could prove historically very important.

The "economic residence" provision means that these licences have so far been (and probably in future will continue to be) issued by the societies in nations where the MSPs are based, which is predominantly the USA –at least in the early years. In the UK the revenue has initially been small; in the 12 months to November 2003 the total income was £160,000, split equally between MCPS and PRS, but licences with major new users looked like having the potential at least to double that figure.

MCPS and PRS took an active role in these developments, and John Hutchinson believes that because the Alliance was from its formation a forward-looking organisation, it had been prepared to undertake R&D as a contribution to "making sure we did not get pushed to one side, as other people did" as digital distribution technology made global changes to the traditional environment in which national music industries have to function, and it was then prepared to move ahead with the practicalities.

Another new source of revenue for both MCPS and PRS, already mentioned in the main Introduction, can be mentioned again here although, as is increasingly the case in the business run by the Alliance as operating company, it could have been placed in both of the separate society chapters; though it appears for convenience here under an International section heading, it is a domestic licensing issue, but for a kind of consumer end usage which frequently crosses territorial boundaries. The use of copyright music as personal ring tones on mobile phones has proved an unexpected but rapidly expanding phenomenon in the market. Often downloaded from internet sites, or distributed via the cell phone networks themselves, the music excerpts offered as ring tones require both performing and mechanical right licences to be issued to the providers of this music download service. There are implications for the record industry because the early tinny monophonic tones are increasingly being replaced by clips from commercial recordings. However, the issue from the collecting societies' point of view is that copyright works are being used. Two rights are involved in this type of usage – PRS charging 5% of income and MCPS charging 10%.

By the end of 2003 the total value of ring tones licensing had reached £3.4m and a total of 125 companies had been licensed (between them responsible for thousands of active URLs or web addresses and brand names which are all registered with MCPS and PRS).Licensees included BBC Worldwide, Carphone Warehouse, Hutchison 3G, InfoMedia Services, Motorola, Orange.co.uk/Orange PCS, Samsung Electronics, Songplayer.com and the Walt Disney Group – simply to name a handful of the major names already known in their respective businesses.

Alliance IT

Chronology demands that the focus here shifts back from the international to the home front. The impact of the cancellation of the IMJV project on the Alliance's IT strategy could have been greater than the impact of the PROMS failure had been on PRS

IT development. It left a gap in the Alliance's medium-term strategy, because IMJV had effectively been the business case for cost reduction through lower staff requirements when major back office functions moved from the Alliance into the shared service centre. The timetable for such cost savings had also been allied closely with the IMJV timetable. But if the proposed solution had proved unachievable in the proposed form at that point, the needs it would have served remained unchanged. A revised, pragmatic IT strategy for the Alliance was an absolute priority as New Year 2002 passed; it had to be one which built on all that had been usefully learnt from IMJV and on the retained benefits of work done.

The most sensible approach at the time was the approach taken: material, ideas, work and experienced people from the IMJV project were applied to setting out a less ambitious, workmanlike domestic plan. Where IMJV had been trying to build a single Copyright and Repertoire system, to use IMJV assets such as plans and specifications to fill the remaining gaps in the Alliance IT armoury.

The importance of the ultimate achievements are highlighted by the society Chairmen who are quoted elsewhere and by a particularly-closely involved Board director below, but one absolutely crucial achievement was possibly stated in the briefest and most heartfelt way by one of the Alliance's very experienced senior managers, who reflected: "With the Alliance integrated copyright database we no longer have to operate two – not very well-managed – copyright and agreements databases, and we have one single point of entry for members' queries; even if the people dealing with them are actually looking up two different usage systems the members do not need to know that, and they get one smooth service. This is fundamental to the improved service the Alliance was set up to give. And it is saving the industry huge amounts of cost".

On the always very closely linked issues of IT, business management and operational efficiency the view of one Board member is particularly relevant here. Malcolm Coster was the first external director[8] appointed by the PRS Board in 1996. His chief focus was and remains PRS, although he has also been a director on the Alliance Board (appointed to that by the PRS Board) since its inception. His main areas of interest, expertise, and activity on the Boards – and the reasons why he had been appointed to the external director role at PRS – were company management and IT, international business, and corporate governance.

He arrived at PRS in the year that the MMC enquiry issued its report, and while John Hutchinson was still a newly-appointed Chief Executive in the process of building his management team. Coster's first impression was of an organisation which was "rather confused and vulnerable" at both Board and management levels as a result of recent major problems and in the face of a comprehensive and fairly critical MMC report. His other observations were that communications between the Board and the management team were "patchy", with the latter often feeling it was not properly briefed; and many members apparently felt they were not getting the service and the benefits they should be getting. Coster was aware that everyone knew things had to change, and the Board knew it had to pull together, writers and publishers, in that time of change.

Perhaps most urgently, in terms of operational improvement, PRS was then achieving a poor return on its IT spend and suffered from "much complexity of processes, which had built up over the years to solve problems as they appeared and it had become hard for people to point to any consistent fundamental rules". He noted "a huge distrust about IT; it was a black art on which a lot of money was spent for seemingly not much return". He has worked closely with John Rathbone and his team throughout his years on the two Boards. He observed over time that the faults and problems were recognised and addressed; the drive for simplification was very successful and helped to justify policies which were useful and throw

8   The term external director was coined in recognition of the traditional structure of the PRS Board; as a membership organisation it had almost throughout its history had a ruling council, later board, comprised entirely of non-executive elected directors. Following the corporate governance review and the MMC Report in the mid 90s, two executive directors were added to the board, and two other directors were appointed for their particular skills and backgrounds. In a normal commercial company with a small board comprising mainly top level executives they would have been simply called "non-executive directors". However, to distinguish them from the majority of the PRS (non-executive) directors and because they came from outside the organisation, they were called external directors. Malcolm Coster was the first to be appointed (he was then with Unisys) and he was soon followed by former diplomat Sir Alistair Hunter.

out those which were not; in PRS the MMC issues have mostly been "ticked" since 1996; but lately the Copyright Tribunal is probably rising in importance for both societies (and therefore the Alliance) as a potentially negative influence.

In Coster's judgement the MCPS-PRS Alliance has "worked from the beginning". Operationally there have been no serious obstacles to achieving measurable benefits, and in governance the Alliance Board has focused on operating issues as it should, and developed an excellent working relationship with what had become a very strong management team. In 2003 he judged the maturing IT skills of the Alliance to have achieved "world class", with application of best practice from good feasibility studies through testing and then manageable, incremental implementation. He stressed that the lesson of avoiding "big bang" approaches had by and large been learnt well, but in that context stressed "IT failure must not be attached to the IMJV project – that came to an end because of governance, management and people problems, not IT problems". It was also, Coster felt, interesting that although the FastTrack initiative had not been held in much regard initially by an Alliance which was focused on the different IMJV approach, subsequent events had again in his view underlined the value of the low-key, evolutionary approach to such developments.

In terms of governance Coster has worked on reviews of first PRS and then Alliance Board and committee structures and roles (but not, he stressed, MCPS, which was embarking on its first comprehensive governance review in late 2003).

Summing up, from his "external" yet closely involved perspective, Coster judged that the Alliance was an organisation which had "learned how to learn". It was generally both doing things right and doing the right things.

The Alliance website is at www.mcps-prs-alliance.co.uk

A Good Idea

BRITISH
MUS|C
RIGHTS:

The belief that the writers' and publishers' side of the music industry was all-but-invisible to Government and Whitehall was raised at the MPA Board table by its Chairman Andrew Heath not long after he began his term of office. A new, higher-profile lobbying and information organisation was needed, and it was agreed that the MPA would request that the Board of MCPS should set aside from its revenue a budget to fund it.

The support and active involvement of the writers' Guilds was seen as essential from the outset. "We knew that the only way it would work was if it was a joint effort," Heath recalls. That aligned closely with a broader objective he was pursuing as MPA Chairman: building better relationships between the MPA and the Guilds – which at that point were still three separate bodies, although they were by the mid-90s already collaborating closely, in anticipation of their eventual amalgamation as the British Academy of Composers and Songwriters in 1999.

Songwriter Guy Fletcher, who would be the first Chairman of the Academy, worked closely with Heath in pursuing the common objective. The MPA and the Guilds were clear in their minds that it was essential for the new organisation to be led and directed by the writers and publishers ("not by the collecting societies, which had their own lobbying issues"). But when plans were made public, Heath was very happy to receive an immediate call from PRS Chief Executive John Hutchinson, who made the true and helpful points that PRS could enhance the necessary budget and broaden representation to encompass all the key rights and rights owners. And so it proved.

There was complete agreement that a new, separate and self-contained body was required. Its initial and core objective as stated by Heath was "to ensure that our voice was heard at Westminster, in Whitehall and in Fleet Street". Looking back in 2003 his view was that "We have succeeded with the first two and to some extent with the third, and our profile is at least as high as we expected".

Giving a good idea a good name

This now very successful and internationally-respected body was originally, briefly, destined to be called the Music Rights Promotion Organisation (giving the not particularly promotional, or pronounceable, acronym MRPO). The choice of the name British Music Rights was a conscious and fairly good-humoured riposte to the UK record industry.

The two sides of the music business had actually worked together in the long march towards copyright law reform in the late 70s and through the 80s. The first independent survey by Annan Impey Morrish of "illegal copying of gramophone records" to determine the level of damage being done by home taping was jointly commissioned by MRS (Mechanical Rights Society) and the record industry trade body the BPI (British Phonographic Industry), soon after the report of the Whitford Committee on copyright reform in 1977. Both PRS and MCPS had allied their 1988 Copyright Act lobbying efforts to those of the record industry wherever possible. However, through the well-directed and consistently successful (if rather high-spending) Government relations efforts fronted by the BPI through the 90s, the record business had become firmly established in the perception of Parliament, Whitehall, the European Commission and the general news media as being "the British music industry". Music business

Pictured at the announcement of the formation of British Music Rights (*left to right*) are composer Martin Dalby, MCPS Chairman Jonathan Simon, British Music Rights Director General Nanette Rigg, then BASCA Chairman Guy Fletcher, Chief Executive John Hutchinson, MPA President at the inception of British Music Rights Andrew Heath, and composer David Stoll.

and record business had become synonymous, and the writing and publishing side was unmentioned and undifferentiated. So, although British Music Rights was set up to work only on behalf of the writers and publishers its name airily ignored the fact that there were British music rights owned by the record business.

As previously explained in the Alliance chapter, the MPA and the writers Guilds had become impatient with the way MCPS and PRS were jointly handling Government relations, lobbying and general presentation of the causes concerning their side of the music industry. That was why they decided to do away with the by-then-moribund Music Copyright Reform Group (MCRG), which had been set up about 15 years earlier in anticipation of the 1988 Copyright Act, and had been a committee of the top management of MCPS and PRS and the MPA with professional legal advisers and Government relations consultants in the UK and Brussels. MCRG's role had been monitoring and responding

to legislative information on behalf of its member organisations and their members.

The view of the MPA and Guilds that a completely different approach was needed had the emphatic support of Hutchinson, who would soon also be CEO of MCPS and the Alliance. His energetic involvement ensured that the collecting societies also had representation on the British Music Rights Board.

So British Music Rights replaced the MCRG, but with a differently-defined role. It was to concentrate full-time on promoting the interests of writers and publishers, both politically in the UK and Europe, and in terms of marketing the importance and value of this side of the music industry.

Education was also a priority, both in terms of educating the law, opinion formers and the public about the value of music copyright, and ensuring that the same messages and information found their way into the education system where possible and appropriate. British Music Rights actively supported continuing development of music talent in Britain by improving music and copyright education in schools. It made very clear its belief that building awareness of intellectual property was something which should happen at the very earliest stages in the education system, even in primary schools. It made a point of contributing to many initiatives, such as the European Music Rights Alliance (EMCA). This represented the interests of collecting societies and worked in 2003 on a pilot project placing composers in schools to offer lessons on intellectual property and copyright awareness, and planned a Copyright Awareness Week in schools across Europe in late 2004.

It also informed UK educators about information websites and teaching tools such as the Patent Office THINK Kit (a resource for teaching design and technology, technology and business studies in senior schools), and the Net Benefit CD ROM developed by the UK's Institute for Citizenship and National Consumer

Council – a project which British Music Rights assisted and helped to fund.

From the beginning British Music Rights liaised and collaborated with the long-standing communications and PR functions of its member organisations, but deliberately did not overlap. Its was from the outset a common voice on all the issues of relevance to all its members, leaving member organisations to voice their own individual concerns on issues which affected them specifically. Fairly recent examples of this way of working included the EU report on collective management of rights, where British Music Rights was expected by its members to speak on their collective behalf: and by contrast the separate handling by PRS and MCPS of their own PR on issues such as the Live Classical Tariff and the Tribunal reference of the DVD licence rate respectively – though both were able to look to British Music Rights for advice and contacts as and when appropriate.

British Music Rights' first brochure in 1997 put down several markers,which remain in place though time and organisational

Frances Lowe, British Music Rights Director General from 1999 to 2003

development have modified and expanded the organisation's thinking and role. Its opening statement asserted: "The British Music Business, which British Music Rights represents, is the most innovative, creative and dynamic in the world. Yet the continuing success of the music business cannot be taken for granted. Today's composers and songwriters are threatened with the erosion of their rights through new forms of music distribution. Tomorrow's talent pool is threatened by a decline of musical opportunities in education. British Music Rights' mission is to counter these threats and to ensure that Britain continues to have a world leading music business". Stated goals were to ensure that "public, policy makers and opinion formers" were aware of the importance of Britain's flourishing music scene and music business; also to ensure that the UK Government and the EC formulated and implemented policies which would enable the music business to retain its worldwide success, "both off-line and on–line"; to seek strong, effectively-enforced copyright law.. Its activities in support of these objectives included monitoring and influencing policy and legislative developments which would affect music creators, undertaking research, public and media relations campaigns, organising and taking part in appropriate trade fairs, conferences and similar events.

Under its first Director General, music industry lawyer Nanette Rigg, British Music Rights set out to make its presence known. The need was to make an impression at Westminster and in Brussels (the latter with the expert help of European lobbyists Cabinet Stewart, headed by Catherine Stewart who had already done excellent work for MCRG) as quickly and effectively as possible.

British Music Rights did succeed in gaining an identity in places where it mattered. At the same time a process by which British Music Rights reported to member Boards was established, with a reciprocal provision for its own Board members, who in time came to include the Chairmen of the MPA and of the British Academy of Composers and Songwriters, to report back to their own Boards.

Rigg was succeeded as Director General by Frances Lowe, who as a senior member of first the PRS and then the Alliance legal team brought great knowledge of the writers and publishers organisations and their business; she also brought a different management and communications style, and a re-focus on what experience so far had indicated should be core activities. These she defined in terms of British Music Rights members: "To represent them, advise them, speak for them and analyse issues for them – in all things to do with Government policy, political developments and the wider music industry – and to be a 'face' for their music industry sector at a PR level".

The analysis she referred to reached a very high degree of sophistication during her tenure as the organisation's Rights Committee reached a peak of effectiveness. Heath is one of many who pay tribute to the collective wisdom on that Committee – of which Alliance Chief Legal Counsel David Lester and MPA CEO Sarah Faulder also were, and remain, members – as having provided its constituent organisations with the "best and most intelligent analysis ever in the UK, or anywhere else".

The British Music Rights Board developed three areas of concern – rights, anti-piracy and communications. The first required British Music Rights constantly to monitor and analyse political developments, feeding back the results of this work to its own Board and those of its members so that their joint and individual strategies and activities were always well-informed. The second was similarly a matter of a very observant watching brief on developments (particularly where increasingly sophisticated online piracy via peer-to-peer (P2P) digital music file sharing was concerned) which needed to be brought to the attention of the policy makers. The third embraced communication with legislators, including research which helped to illustrate the points which needed to be established firmly and clearly in the minds of legislator; with the media; with educators, who needed to be encouraged to bring the importance of copyright and the value of

creativity into the curriculum, and for whom British Music Rights helped to produce teaching aids; and with the public. In that last respect the well-planned and very successful *Respect the Value of Music* campaign was itself valuable. Launched in the autumn of 2000, this campaign was backed by a large number of well-known music creators and it reached out to young people who were those most likely to be ignorant of copyright in the offline world, or to disregard it in their use of online music files.

Active involvement with Government initiatives and groupings, and often leadership through willingness to take responsibility for joint activities with other bodies, strengthened British Music Rights' position, profile, and hand. It was an intelligent, hardworking, steady, consistent and collaborative strategy which was fully in line with objectives. It deserved the positive responses it often achieved.

Its own newsletter to its members in January 2003 illustrated the depth and breadth of its work (and its matured style). This reported on the constructive relationship which had been established with the All Party Music Group of MPs and peers interested in music and regularly looking at key issues for the UK music industry; also on the very active and consistently influential part which British Music Rights continued to play in the creation of the Music Business Forum. This initiative involved all areas of the music business, discussing legislative and other issues and offering authoritative position papers and briefings on proposed legislative developments such, as the Licensing and Communications Bills (2002/3) to Government Departments and contacts in Parliament. The MBF increasingly came to provide the UK music industry with a chance to speak with one voice in the lobbying arena.

The promotional aspect of its work could be illustrated in many ways, but one notable example is its annual high profile presence at the international music industry convention Midem. Support for music creators led to British Music Rights' co-sponsorship with PRS of the 2001 and 2002 "The Song's The Thing" festival, celebrating songwriting. It also worked through participation in the Sound Advice music industry education roadshow, which included a visit to the BRIT school for the performing arts. Delivering ideas and messages internationally has been achieved through the organisation and delivery of a very popular and well-attended panel entitled *The Right Message? –Lobbying and Awareness* at the 2002 CISAC Congress in London.

The increasing problem of worldwide music piracy and counterfeiting (the value of the illegal music market was in 2002 estimated at £2.8 bn) is also within British Music Rights' sphere of concern. Through its Rights and Anti-Piracy Committee it works "to ensure that an appropriate legal system is in place which considers and balances the interests of music creators and consumers alike", and in pursuit of that objective the organisation is a member of the Alliance Against Counterfeiting and Piracy (a coalition of trade and enforcement bodies representing film, music, video, software and other copyright holders).

Shortly before she moved on from British Music Rights Lowe was able to say that the organisation was respected and trusted and listened to, having demonstrated in a little over six years that it had become a body which was taken seriously by Government and the media. Her view was endorsed by all the British Music Rights member organisations. Citing just one achievement Andrew Heath pointed out that the organisation's patient work at informing and communicating with Government and Whitehall had resulted in a distinct improvement in the way the writer/publisher business was able to influence many documents relating to the European Copyright Directive. He, like many, observed a trend for politicians and officials wanting to know about the music business to call British Music Rights as a key source of information. On this Heath commented : "It benefits both sides of our business by ensuring that the official view is based on a balanced, not one-sided, view."

Sir Alistair Hunter reflected on the organisation he has chaired almost since its inception: "It's only seven years since the composers' and songwriters' Guilds, the Music Publishers' Association and the collecting societies created British Music Rights to be their common voice – yet the organisation has long grown to adulthood, and is an established player not only in the music industry but in the political worlds of Westminster and Whitehall, Brussels and Strasbourg.

"During those seven years, we have helped achieve some significant legislative successes. In a long slog over several years we managed substantially to influence the formulation of the EU Copyright Directive (which establishes a legislative framework for copyright in the digital age) and its subsequent implementation, by statutory instrument, into UK law. In 2003, we fought with considerable success to protect the interests of music in two major pieces of UK legislation: the Licensing Act, which affects the performance of live music in pubs, halls and other public places; and the Communications Act, which regulates the merging worlds of broadcasting and telecommunications.

"We've been working ceaselessly, too, to help educate the public, and particularly the young, about the importance of copyright. 'Respect the Value of Music' is a slogan, and logo, which has made a great impact and has plenty of life in it yet: one recent appearance is on covermount CDs on magazines, pointing out to buyers that even though they are getting the music for free, people who have worked to compose it are getting paid for it. We were also proud to contribute to a CD-ROM for schools helping children understand the role of copyright in fostering music creation.

"But perhaps our most important achievement has been to extend the concept of the 'common voice' to other parts of the music business. We were a major influence in the creation of the Music Business Forum, which brings our part of the business together with managers, performers and above all with the record industry, and has got off to a strikingly successful start. Its dialogue with the All-Party Music Group at Westminster has increased interest in, and understanding of, the music world in both Houses of Parliament; and its existence is encouraging Whitehall departments to engage in music issues on a correspondingly 'joined-up' basis. Music is on the political agenda as never before.

"Nevertheless, the war is far from won. The concept of copyright remains under threat, whether from academics who question its continued relevance in its present form or from music lovers who don't see why music shouldn't be free There will still be plenty of work for British Music Rights in the months and years ahead."

Futures

History does not end and the future is always just beginning

This account of the past and present of the UK music rights organisations is the story of very active professional entities. There is obviously no point at which their separate and intertwined stories come to a convenient stopping point. In their increasingly busy and rapidly-evolving corporate lives, every strand in the tale is ongoing. Many of the next steps are clear, planned and already announced or indicated, but thoughts and expectations about the future in general are continually being developed and revised. This final chapter sets out some of these thoughts and expectations.

Change is the new constant. Driven by markets, by legislation and most relentlessly by technology, change for most world industries is the inescapable pattern, the unbuckable trend, the runaway train for the 21st century. Within that fluid, almost fractal, pattern sits the increasingly globalised entertainment industry, and within that is the music industry on which all the factors just mentioned have an effect which is probably proportionately greater, and more easily seen, than in most other businesses. MCPS, PRS and Alliance Chief Executive John Hutchinson observes: "This is the most dangerous period of change in the music industry. There will continue to be a music industry: the public wants it. But all the parts in the play are currently being considered for re-casting. We are grasping for solutions to current and anticipated issues but little is clear yet."

Rights, copyright law and collecting societies

Change is having its impact on traditional, and for so long very robust, music business models based on broadcasting, on continually-growing public demand for live and recorded performance, on manufacture of "pieces of plastic" (the industry's own descriptive shorthand for everything from analogue vinyl records to a proliferation of formats of optical discs with audio and visual and data digital content) and on retail sale. New business models are a continual object of speculation and experimentation.

Intellectual property (IP) rights are the foundation of every type of music use, music product and music market. They are the concern of rights administration organisations: it would appear that they are also the guarantee of a future for the collecting societies. However, people of a sceptical nature would stress that appearances can be deceptive.

So, firstly, a brief look at the rights themselves and the prospects for the two UK collecting societies; followed by some views on the future for collective administration organisations in general.

The Performing Right

The bundle of rights under that heading has over the last few decades increasingly been viewed as unquestionably in the ascendant in terms of future revenue for composers, songwriters and music publishers. Its existence is clearly definable and recognisable in every current method of music use, online or offline, live or recorded. As such the performing right is effectively unassailable, provided there is no radical reversal of the provisions of copyright law – and nothing indicates that that is likely or even remotely being contemplated by the UK Government. This right can with confidence be expected to continue to be a strong source of income for the future.

In the UK the satisfactory settlement in mid-December 2003 of the PRS dispute over Tariff LC for live classical music events pointed to a triumph of good sense, and to better relationships in future. Hutchinson saw the settlement as the last step in a process which he had helped to instigate and had then pursued. He describes this process as moving PRS from a position of subsidising the royalties for one genre of music within its membership to a better licensing tariff for that music which would lead to the higher income which classical writers and publishers wanted. "Promoters, writers, publishers and orchestras have been rather like a family at war, but this closes the classical income issue. We have fulfilled our promise to get the tariff up and we have straightened out the distributions." Broadly, however, he is far from alone in expecting that the task of defending and increasing licensing tariffs in order to realise the value of music rights will get harder, not easier.

PRS' approach to licensing public performance in recent years is one which, it strongly believes, looks to the future rather than the past: marketing and selling the value of the licence rather than majoring on the imposition of the letter of copyright law backed with litigation. PRS Performance Sales director Clive Thomas believes wholeheartedly in the positive line of thinking about music value and selling/marketing it, and in a customer-orientated attitude for collecting societies of all kinds. He foresees development of an approach to the administration of rights which could be led by PRS thinking and activity. "PRS want to be the first resource for music users. However, a broad remit for the PRS Music Advisers[1] needs a move away from historically difficult branding (the "three evils" in the view of the hospitality business sector are PRS, PPL and the local authority public entertainment licence, PEL). One possibility he can see is that PRS and other societies as holders or agents for the rights would be unchanged, but would place their public performance licensing with a neutral third party, with a mandate to expand the market and be a source of information and help to existing and new music users. Its guiding premise would be that music is genuinely desirable, life and business enhancing. He urges that collecting societies should have much greater confidence in what they are licensing, and do business on the basis that people are willing to pay for it because they are convinced of its value to them in a business-to-business relationship.

Looking to the future of the income, PRS Executive Director John Axon makes several points. PRS' traditional business of licensing music in shops, pubs, clubs and concerts – general public performance – has doubled revenue in the nine years 1993 to 2002, at a time of low inflation. Growth will continue but more slowly. There seems no change to the view that (well chosen) music enhances most forms of retail premises, be they boutiques or warehouses, and with service industries continuing to replace manufacturing, use of music in public will not slacken. However, broadcasting is a saturated market, he notes. There will always be niches for new special interest channels and local radio stations but, with relatively full employment and many claims on consumers' money and time, there are only so many hours a day that the people of the UK are going to spend looking at TV or listening to radio. As the viewership falls away from the big duopoly of ITV and BBC, and PRS revenue thereby falls, satellite and cable channels will substitute to some extent. But the revenue to PRS from these new channels has been constrained by the Copyright Tribunal and is from a low base. So PRS broadcasting, once the highest of the three revenue streams, might be relegated to third from 2003 onwards. International revenue is the big unknown. Once a poor relation to the other three this has the prospect of further growth in future, as more of the world's population embraces the UK repertoire. It is the second most important in the world, after that of the US in royalty terms. But that growth in use needs to be pursued vigorously to ensure that foreign collecting societies do send the UK creators their rightful share of local earnings.

From Fran Nevrkla, the CEO of the UK record industry's performing right collecting agency PPL, comes a view which chimes with many of those on the writers' and publishers' side. "Record companies still have to accept voluntarily that in years to come they will be marketing their rights, not products. Performance will become the mainstay of this business. Record companies have to acquire the same discipline of mind and approach to their rights as the music publishers have always had."

---

1   Traditionally PRS operated a field force of Licensing Inspectors, whose role was to find and license premises using music and to deal with them firmly from a position of law enforcement. Under the changed public performance licensing approach the emphasis is on marketing the value of the use of appropriate copyright music to enhance businesses, and the Inspector has become a Territory Manager , backed up by office based Music Service Advisers. Nevertheless, Thomas has established a Copyright Protection Office with two "investigators" to deal with the 1% of customers who attempt performance "piracy" by deliberately putting on music without a licence *See PRS Chapter, Licensing and Distribution section.*

As this book went to press, in February 2004 PRS and PPL were still engaged in considering a future development which would be based on collaboration in licensing the two performing rights (that of the writers in the copyright musical work itself and that of the record companies in the copyright recording of a musical work). It was still open as to whether this might be via full joint venture which would be a separate company, or via some kind of service agreement. But the logic of the principle of marketing and licensing rights to a hugely overlapping market of users via one administrative organisation seemed accepted.

The Mechanical Right

Asked to speculate on the future of phonomechanicals (rather than on their buoyant past and still buoyant but declining present) the Alliance Chief Legal Counsel David Lester is more cautious than those many in the industry and the media who in the early 2000s regularly predicted obsolescence for traditional physical recorded product. He makes no judgement as to whether the production and sale of physical entities (vinyl, CD, DVD and, still in developing countries, cassette tapes) will be entirely replaced by something new. Nor does he guess at what that something new might eventually be, although the digital music file accessed through the internet has to be the current Heir Apparent. The only certainty he sees is that the mechanical right will continue to be needed for new generations of recorded music, in whatever form it reaches the public, as well as for the many other forms of usage which will continue to grow in variety and value – broadcasting, karaoke, video jukebox, novelties from musical greetings cards to musical knickers, toys, copyright ringtones for mobile phones and more.

Lester believes that the right itself is robust enough to take copyright owners into the future with adequate-to-strong protection, even into a future where phonomechanicals disappear altogether. A shift from a market for mechanical reproductions of music to communication of non-physical forms of the music will not negate the right; the mechanical right, as is clear in the 1988 Act, applies to permanent and temporary copies, even though the EC Copyright and Related Rights in the Information Society Directive of May 2001 states that some kinds of temporary copies lack value, and the mechanical licence is traditionally based on the value of the record. Historically the assumption that a copy is something one can pick up – music product, a page of text – is fading as "copies" increasingly appear on a PC screen, are sometimes then stored on that PC (though still not tangible in the "pieces of plastic" sense) but are often not "stored" in any usual meaning of the term.

MCPS Chairman Jonathan Simon is also in the positive-thinking camp where mechanical rights and administration are concerned. Simon is not on the side of those who believe, or at least suspect, that the future for mechanical rights income looks dim. It is true that the traditional record business (the source of the largest section of MCPS income through audio product licensing) currently sees its value slowly declining and any hopes of growth seemingly buried by the combination of online and domestic hardware technology which delivers recorded music directly to consumers. However, he joins Hutchinson, Lester and many others in seeing the opportunities as well as the threats. "These online services are a new use of the copyrights both in the music itself (performing and mechanical rights) and in the copyright commercial recording. The challenge is to establish a licensed environment for this use, as long as there is a consumer demand for recorded music." And Simon finds it very difficult to imagine that demand will ever disappear. Hutchinson amplifies that, asserting that MCPS retains its unassailable place in the process of manufacture and has earned the right to be listened to in that context.

The popularity of the DVD (digital versatile disc) format for music releases appeared to be soaring at the time this chapter was written, and the media commentators were beginning to predict that it would supersede audio-only CDs with its high quality offering of sound, video, still pictures, information and games all in one package. The need for agreement between the two sides of the music industry on a proper mechanical licence rate for this product was high on the agenda of MCPS and of the record companies' trade body the BPI. Negotiations were proceeding in very positive mood in December 2003, but the possibility of the BPI's Copyright Tribunal reference going to hearing remained a real one. However, Hutchinson was firm in predicting that before the end of 2004 (perhaps well before the end) "DVD will be licensed day-to-day by MCPS".

He shares the view that DVD has a good life to look forward to, though part of his reasoning is that an important DVD market is the 35-55 age group which has high disposable income for entertainment products, including music, but which does not want to sit at a PC looking for music and audiovisual product on the internet and downloading it. That age group market will of course gradually become populated by people who are much more inclined to access their entertainment via a PC or a cellphone. He also believes that the new home entertainment hardware with excellent sound and TV screens and a common system for playing all kinds of optical discs will help to build the DVD market. Former MCPS Deputy MD Keith Lowde speculates that there is a very interesting intellectual discussion to be pursued in relation to the future of mechanical rights in terms of "whether or not people will feel the need to make copies and 'own' their music." He proposes that "current mobile phone developments will make it possible to have the world's repertoire available on demand: why should anyone want to store a copy of anything?"

Alongside the administrative issues for MCPS there arose in 2003 issues of governance which were likely to occupy the attention of the MCPS Board for a significant part of 2004, and which could have good and beneficial impact on the structural strength of that society and on the Alliance of which it is a part and joint owner. Hutchinson congratulated the MCPS Board on taking a lead on this issue at this time of great change, when it had not been

thought necessary to address it at any time in the past. "The Board has realised that perhaps now is the time to move governance of the Alliance forward. A governance review, such as this is routine in good businesses. It is a very good move for us to have embarked on it".

Copyright law

The virtually unlimited and worldwide accessibility of copyright material under this new technological, social and (progressively) commercial regime calls logically for some global harmonisation of copyright law. This, Lester believes, will eventually come at the high level of rights definition, but not at the lower levels of national exceptions; and this is as it should be, in his view and that of most creators and operators in the business of music and other intellectual property.

The demise of copyright law in some form of happy online anarchy, as predicted by the "music should be free" camp, is not, Jonathan Simon states, an idea which keeps him awake at night. But he sees no reason for copyright owners to feel relief or contentment even with that solid expectation that copyright protection will never be seriously weakened. He still strongly believes that UK law should embrace the imposing of a royalty on blank recording media or hardware to compensate rights owners for domestic piracy; and he believes that sooner or later the British Government will have to review this issue.

Collecting societies

In the past few years the future for collecting societies has been predicted in terms both of imminent demise and effective immortality, and a number of (much more likely) compromises between those extremes.

The traditional nature of societies is as nationally–based organisations, administering the national repertoire of their own members and the international repertoire through reciprocal agreements with other societies while enjoying complete authority to license within their own territories. It is inevitably being reviewed as the digital distribution of copyright material challenges most, if not all, those administrative criteria.

Waves of opinion have taken the international debate in various directions. These range from those internet enthusiasts who believe that music should be free; through belief that music and audio-visual copyright owners, exploiters and administrators will survive and prosper but only if they can radically alter their business models; to a view that there is complete analogy between the old and new worlds of IP administration, and therefore existing structures and methods can broadly continue to be applied provided the analogy is understood and accepted. CISAC Secretary General Eric Baptiste observes that societies have to re-engineer themselves to adapt still relevant skills to a new context whilst most others, especially content marketers, will have to reinvent themselves to find new business models. The former is of course difficult and requires a lot of hard work, but the latter might simply not be possible, at least not for everyone. Accordingly, music copyright owners' trade organisations and collecting societies have shown a range of reactions to the change in their markets, and have different views about the future.

Swingeing litigation against inventors and suppliers of the file sharing technology[2], which allows copyright material to bypass every traditional checkpoint and control as it bounces around the world's millions of personal computers, is one strategy – it is arguably currently the most appropriate one for the record industry and it has recently been particularly favoured in the US. It has initially been successful in the courts, and in the sense that it has forced some operations to retreat, change their business, sell-up or give up. There have also been setbacks: courts have deemed that some types of defendant are not responsible for the actions of individuals who use their services, or are not required to give copyright organisations information by which individual users might be traced. However, in 2003 the US record industry decided to go a big step further by taking action against private individuals who exchange computer files containing unlicensed copyright music The RIAA's newspaper advertising campaign in that year listed many other rights owners organisations around the world as supporters.

A major issue for collecting societies is digital rights management (DRM). There has been considerable discussion at a political level about this and about the impact it could have on societies. In theory DRM could, some say will, provide for every licensed and appropriately-encoded copyright work to contain information about its owners; and for every usage of that work to be tracked, thereby enabling payment to be made to the copyright owner(s). Since licensing, tracking and royalty payments are the core activities of collecting societies, the speculation is that these will not be needed, at least not in their traditional and current incarnation.

Some observers point to the likelihood that other major players, not specialist DRM companies, will emerge who can do a large part of the copyright management offered by collecting societies. This thinking springs from the development of data management standards which must operate together, because business development in a digital environment demands that they do. This will make it possible for groups and companies which have the technical tools to take the emerging solutions for identification of digitised IP, and to benefit from gradual harmonisation and clarification of the legal position internationally, in order to offer IP rights owners a competitive price for part of the work they now need to have done by collecting societies. Even though these (as yet unidentifiable) new operators would not have the repertoire information which is held by the societies, the belief is that deals would have to be struck; and that the increasing sophistication of connectivity between all kinds of data sources will inexorably erode the traditional exclusive strengths of societies.

---

2 In digital form any kind of creation – literary, graphic, musical, audio-visual, photographic – can be stored as a file on a computer, or some digital device made for the purpose. It can also be sent to another device via the internet, downloaded, played, edited, stored, re-sent endlessly. A variety of programmes and systems have been developed since the mid-90s to enable people to access and exchange these files. Copyright owners are increasingly attempting to offer licensing facilities to legitimate providers of internet services which offer copyright music and other IP, but are also seeking ways to stop the globally pervasive and rapidly growing use of unlicenced websites offering downloads, and the people-to-people sharing of such files bypassing any traceable websites, servers or internet serice providers. *Also see Digital Music Distribution appendix.*

The counter argument is put very strongly, particularly by the music rights administration organisations. David Lester sums it up by pointing to original principles: one of the chief functions of societies is the protection of the creator from abuse by the users of his creations. On that basis alone the relevance of societies is even greater now because of globalisation of users and the means of usage; and because of "convergence" of the formerly quite separate, appropriately licensed and monitored, uses such as broadcasting, making records and videos, and many quite distinct kinds of live or mechanical public performance. Any hope that the individual creator/copyright owner might control and earn revenue from rights in such a diffuseenvironment is non-existent; collective administration is absolutely essential. Noting that CISAC is the societies' main player within international standardisation bodies, Eric Baptiste agrees with that balanced opinion. In his view, authors' societies should give qualified support to DRMs if they can provide efficient, cost-effective, secure and useful tools to assist societies in their operations. But he cautions against relying too much on commercial proprietary schemes so close to the core of the societies' activities. He points out that this is why CISAC is so actively involved in developing DRM components for managing rights and in developing common, interoperable, open and secure DRM standards, either within a joint-venture with record industry organisations IFPI and RIAA (MI3P) or within the International Standards Organisation (MPEG 21).

If collecting societies are essential, the logical next question is whether they are doing this indispensable job properly. The widely (but not unanimously) stated view around the world among *most* copyright owners, Governments and users about *most* societies is that *most of the time* they are – although exceptions could be quoted in every respect. But the issues which societies are dealing with are greater than they ever have been, and the same applies to workload, and the tensions between societies' costs and services are increasing.

It is also argued that while collective licensing is essential and increasingly important for rights owners, collecting societies may lose much of the rest of their remit. It is proposed that they will have to reject the burdensome legacy of non-interoperable systems, national attitudes and histories, poor ability to co-operate and defensive bureaucracies if they are to suceed in the future competitive market for the provision of rights administration and data management. Their competitors, who could emerge from global IT systems or service providers, or from the electronic entertainment giants, or from almost anywhere given the digitised electronic business environment, will be technically superior and structurally unencumbered. A critical factor there could certainly be CIS[3], the CISAC Common Information System. This, as Baptiste acknowledges, proved easier to devise than to implement: "CIS provides to all CISAC members a comprehensive set of standards, rules and supporting databases to eventually fully automate most of the societies' data exchanges worldwide. Bold decisions have recently been taken by CISAC to leapfrog the implementation of this essential tool in the societies 'survival kit' and the time when CIS was known as a 'project' should soon be over."

Another reflection comes from David Ferguson, Chairman of the British Academy of Composers and Songwriters: "The Academy believes that the health of collection societies will become increasingly important to creators in the future. We strongly support a stakeholder owned Alliance which is transparent in all its affairs. We hope that the Alliance will become a model for collection societies around the world where no favour is given to special interest groups or individuals."

Judging the success and "value" of societies by a cost/income ratio and the technical and business efficiences behind good ratios would be easy, and purely commercial solutions could be applied. The special nature of societies as representatives of their nations complicates the issue, as does the broader-than-merely-commercial relationship which they have with their members. Using this yardstick, Baptiste's view is that societies have performed quite

---

well for their members in recent years. Despite the difficult global economic context and deep crises in major industries connected to copyright, CISAC members have consistently exceeded annual collections of 6 billion euros and worldwide collections have grown steadily, sometimes at double digit rates.

These issues may never be entirely resolved to the satisfaction of all concerned, but they have been and are being addressed in the 90s and 2000s in ways which had never previously been proposed or thought necessary. The theme of the 2002 CISAC World Congress, organised and primarily hosted by the Alliance, was *The Business of Creativity*, and the phrase was widely accepted as summing up the function, the complex nature and the new mood of forward-looking collecting societies and their international body CISAC.

From a business technology standpoint comes a view from PRS and Alliance External Director Malcolm Coster: "Where change will come is that the Alliance will lead the way into ever increasing international collaboration, going forward via FastTrack. Worldwide operational collaboration should develop between societies in due course, though there will always be a very strong national element in terms of societies' individual policies. Evolution will be towards doing business online once there is much greater accuracy in the essential data."

Technology will be very important, he asserts. It will inevitably drive further organisational change, driven in turn by the fact that members will have access to technology via the web for their information and transactions. The Alliance organisation will be smaller and different in many ways in five to ten years' time. This is of course very likely to be the case for most or many other societies, but in longer time frames. Coster predicts that there will need to be massive business investment in hardware by societies to support all this, as part of an internationally collaborative philosophy. "It is possible that collective administration as everyone traditionally understands it will go, but it will be a long

time before the data everywhere is accurate enough, so collaboration will be evolutionary via the introduction of global standards etc. Development may be at several different speeds for societies of different sizes and levels of resources. In the UK for example the MCPS, PRS and Alliance organisation has moved ahead onto a new and higher level but many societies are at a much lower level of development in terms of policies and processes."

Hutchinson likewise sees and has joined (often led) the drive towards collaboration. He believes that societies "are being driven together into pragmatic groupings". In that he includes not just the CISAC "authors' rights societies" but organisations operating in the wider rights business – such as PPL. MPA Chairman Andrew Potter adds the thought that there is scope within Europe to remove duplication of costs, while allowing tariffs at local market rates to continue. "But Europe should learn lessons from the US model, where competition between performing right societies causes costs not to be merely duplicated but actually increased because the competition makes them spend more on promotion. There is also room for doubt whether they are competing on behalf of creators to increase value; if they are competing to license a user they may be forced to offer competitive prices which instead reduce the value for the creators."

The future which Jonathan Simon would like to see for the Alliance is for it to move to a position "in the middle of the Anglo-American and Continental European extremes of attitude towards rights and their administration" which would mean a move closer to the European "cultural and pragmatic" approach rather than the Anglo-American "property and business" approach.

PPL's Fran Nevrkla is convinced that "good collecting societies have a bright future; bad ones will disappear". Like Coster, he foresees greater collaboration and co-operation in future, not just technology driven but also in terms of delivering positive messages about rights and creativity to the public and to Governments. He also expects that in due course early efforts to establish the (so far still theoretical) all-purpose one-stop-shop for licensing all kinds of IP rights – to users who want a simple route to legitimate commercial usage for multi-media programmes and products – will bear business fruits, even if not by the originally-planned methods and structures.

CISAC's Baptiste takes a wider view. For historical reasons, the copyright societies' world has long been "Europe-centric". But to him, one of the biggest challenges ahead lies in huge territories like China or India where copyright protection is still minimal: "In the long run, however societies do reorganise themselves, the impact of whatever model China will end up with will be so great that if we get it wrong, the ripple effects will be felt everywhere." So he is pleased that CISAC members, with strong backing from the Alliance, have decided to dedicate more attention to ensuring effective copyright collections and distributions in these two countries.

Online IP distribution and licensing, and doing business online

The IP industry has been trying to nail this blancmange to the wall for years.

This chapter focuses on music rights, but the relevance of this issue to film, computer software, graphic art, and literary copyright should be borne in mind as context.

The online availability of digitised copyright music is having a huge impact on global music industry. It will have potentially even greater significance in future – but how big that will be and how to deal with it are still not clear.

The illegitimate market has to be turned into a legitimate, licensed market, and the tools the rights owners have to hand are litigation, education and persuasion as a complement to, co-operation between agencies and societies for strength and cost effectiveness, and licensing procedures which are attractive, easy to use, and acknowledged to be reasonable in terms of fees and administrative or data requirements. Potter adds the comment that this approach is "pushing the market" but the market is already showing signs of being "pulled" into legitimacy. "Apple i-Tunes is a legitimate, market-friendly business model that obtains value for all – but it is really designed to sell more Apple hardware; also Coca-Cola and McDonalds are now offering music downloading as loss leaders."

It will all take time to develop, but progress is reported in several chapters in this book. A reflection from MCPS Executive Director Sandra Cox is that in the development period collecting societies and users will benefit from a temporary policy of "constructive vagueness". This would allow negotiations on new types of licence and initial tariffs for new usages (online, DVD etc) to proceed, via broad agreements which allow business to be conducted while detailed ways of working for the future of a rights market, for a tangible or intangible product, are arrived at by a process of iteration over a period of time. Short-term renewable agreements, in which little is carved in stone and much depends on the working out of good intentions, will pave the way to new and more solid, long-term deals which are fair to creators and to their licensees.

As director of the Alliance New Technology Division, while it existed, Mark Isherwood ran MusicTrial.com and believes that it was one of several initiatives which signposted the future: "It showed that the process of licensing of musical works could be automated to meet the fast moving environment of online business. As to the nature of licensing that would be applicable there still remains considerable debate. The likelihood is that the current mixed economy of blanket licensing, individual licensing and levies will be maintained in the online environment. What the MusicTrial did make apparent is that there will be increasing pressure, given the ability of the technology, to move more closely towards transactional processing, regardless of the nature of the licence." On this subject John Axon adds his view that "PRS must resist pressure towards transaction processing and must extol to online users, as it does to broadcasters, the advantages and value of a licence for the whole repertoire. The sum of small repertoires licensed never exceeds the sums that can be negotiated for blanket licences".

Malcolm Coster's expectation that the music rights administration business will inevitably be done increasingly online is widely shared. Eric Baptiste adds that "digital convergence" is definitely a reality now and it is here to stay. As people realise they can enjoy their favourite works anywhere, anytime and from any device, all copyright holders and their intermediaries such as societies, will have to show unprecedented flexibility and agility in providing licensing models. Provided they do so, the CISAC Secretary General is bullish about the future: with so much demand for creative content, societies should have a great future as trusted intermediaries between a "content"-hungry world and authors, composers and publishers.

But the concept and perception of "online" being a self-contained, separate and "new" way of doing consumer business does not resonate much with John Hutchinson. "I think that term will disappear. It's just a convenient way to market existing consumer products using interactive techniques. Websites allow producers to experiment with marketing and get information about their product to the world, but there have been very few commercial applications as such online. It's largely a way to sell physical products. Plenty of music is being sent and acquired online, but 'free' music is not music industry commerce, and it's not the market in which those who have real disposable income for buying entertainment are. There is going to be a market transition to the consumer being able to buy anything they want as soon as it is available anywhere in the world, leading to several quite brief product phases – for example a new film could be distributed digitally to cinemas worldwide for the movie-going market, then be released on DVD worldwide to make money quickly, and fairly briefly, from the home entertainment sales market, and then would go into a video on demand (VOD) library accessed through digital TV services. The film companies are already beginning to manage this process. But for their equivalent business development, the record companies are as yet not managing it."

He stresses that what is relevant to collecting societies is licensing the music content of any product streamed, broadcast, sold or digitally distributed online. For example VOD could bring massive performing right income to PRS in future, and to a lesser but probably still significant extent could build MCPS income. The joint online licence with PRS has, Hutchinson points out, set MCPS up as a player in online music distribution. That should ensure transition to MCPS involvement in future configurations where "everything will have a processor in it and so copies of copyright music will come into existence". Simply, mechanical rights will be used in whatever future processes music entertainment goes through, and MCPS will license those rights.

What is this thing called copyright?

By Sarah Faulder, Chief Executive of the Music Publishers' Association

Introduction

The cultural and economic value of creativity is realised in today's society by means of a framework for licensing the use of creative works and so generating income for creators, in short by means of copyright laws developed and refined over centuries. The copyright framework itself incentivises others to invest in the support that creators need whilst they develop their skills and in the promotion and delivery of the results of their creativity to the widest possible audience. In this way the creative industries have developed, providing significant employment(1) and representing an ever increasing percentage of the gross domestic product of those countries with strong copyright laws whilst at the same time encouraging creativity of all kinds and thereby providing consumers with a rich and diverse choice.

Copyright is the lifeblood of composers, songwriters and music publishers. The administration of a large part of their copyright interests is the *raison d'etre* of the collecting societies which are the subject of this book, MCPS and PRS. The scope of this chapter is limited to copyright, principally in the UK but within its international context, insofar as it affects the interests of all these stakeholders and so does not address the related moral(2) and performers'(3) rights. Legal deposit(4), though enshrined in UK copyright law, and the Copyright Tribunal(5) are also beyond the scope of this chapter.

The origins of copyright as we know it today in the UK can be traced back to book publishers in London nearly 300 years ago who claimed that members of the Stationers' Company had exclusive rights to print books by virtue of their tradition of acquiring from authors the perpetual "copy-right" in their books. They were dissatisfied with the remedies available to them at common law and their lobby resulted in the passing in 1709 of the Statute of Anne, the first in a series of statutes seeking to regulate the protection of published works by conferring an exclusive right to print(6). In 1777 Johann Christian Bach brought a case against Longman and established that this exclusive right also protected musical works. In parallel to this was a developing body of common law and subsequent statute law (Bulwer Lytton's Act 1833) on rights in public performances.

The UK was amongst the first signatories in 1886 to the founding international copyright treaty, the Berne Convention, and incorporated most of this(7) into national law the following year. A fundamental principle of Berne, which established minimum levels of copyright protection for literary, artistic and musical works, is that each contracting State agrees to accord the same copyright protection to works by authors of other contracting States as it would to works by its own nationals ("national treatment"). There are now over 130 signatories to the Berne Convention although it is notable that the USA and Russia only joined relatively recently(8), leaving a number of important works with incomplete copyright protection until then.

But it was not until the Copyright Act of 1911 that the blueprint for modern day copyright in the UK was effectively established. It is therefore no coincidence that both MCPS and PRS were established around this time and that the MPA's earlier history centred on the protection of music publishers' interests in printed music, an important area of business but one which today accounts for a mere 10% of the overall turnover of music publishers.

Copyright has continued to evolve and now embraces every form of reproducing and using creative works, whether in the physical or the online (internet and mobile) world. The subsequent Copyright Act of 1956 and the Copyright, Designs and Patents Act of 1988 have been regularly supplemented by secondary legislation. Since 1991 the legislation has had to accommodate no less than six relevant EU Directives(9) as it has tried to catch up with the rapid technological advances of the digital world, keeping all the time to the British tradition of remaining technology neutral in its drafting. All of these Directives have been the subject of intense lobbying by the MPA, MCPS and PRS on behalf of their members, either individually or through the Music Copyright Reform Group and latterly through in effect its replacement, British Music Rights.

A more recent but significant international accord which strengthens copyright protection for British works used abroad has been the 1994 Trade-Related Aspects of Intellectual Property Rights (TRIPS)(10). This imposes international standards of copyright protection as well as obligations for its enforcement in the interests of balancing the need for effective and adequate protection of intellectual property rights against those of legitimate trade.

In response to the issues for copyright raised by the so called Information Super Highway the WIPO Copyright Treaty(11) was adopted in 1996, so extending the Berne Convention and heralding, in legislative terms, the dawn of the digital era. That Treaty was finally incorporated into UK law in 2003(12).

Copyright subsists in a work providing it qualifies for protection and without any formality such as registration, in contrast to patents and trademarks. Although a *de facto* monopoly right, copyright is subject to certain exceptions in recognition of society's desire to balance the right of the creator and investor to be duly rewarded on the one hand against the public interest in having access to protected works for limited purposes on the other.

The tenets for qualifying for copyright protection

What can be protected by copyright?

Music has been protected since well before the 1911 Act through separate copyrights in the music itself and in the words associated with it (literary works). A publisher's investment in the printed edition of a work, whether or not the work itself is still protected, first attracted its own copyright protection under the 1956 Act.

Importantly, there is no copyright in a song *per se* under English law, in contrast to the position in most of Europe where it is regarded as a joint work(13). The House of Lords refused in 1980 even to recognise a song as a collective work in the Redwood litigation(14), brought by music publishers attempting to prevent valuable standard songs in their catalogues from reverting to the songwriters by law after 25 years(15).

A sound recording embodying a song has, since the 1911 Act, attracted separate protection in its own right(16). A CD of a song will therefore enjoy three separate copyrights in addition to the copyright in any artwork on the cover (protected as an artistic work).

Databases, of vital importance to MCPS and PRS as well as to the business of music publishers, were initially eligible for protection as compilations within the definition of literary works under the 1911 Act. Literary works were later interpreted to include computer programmes. Since the EU's Software(17) and Database Directives(18) both computer programmes and databases are protected by copyright in their own right subject to meeting the qualifications for copyright protection(19).

How and when does a work qualify for copyright protection?

The pre-requisites for a work to be protected by copyright have remained largely unchanged since the 1911 Act. These are the requirements for originality (in the sense that its creator invested sufficient skill and labour in its creation, without copying from anyone else, rather than in the sense of being innovative or even artistic), fixation in some material form, whether in writing, on tape or in electronic form, and for the creator to be a British citizen or domiciled or resident in the UK at the time of making the work or, alternatively, for the work to have been first or simultaneously(20) published in the UK.

Similarly, the provisions governing ownership (the creator, or his employer if employed at the time, is the first owner of the copyright) and transferability of ownership (by assignment in writing or by will) have also been consistent throughout. Music publishers have traditionally always taken an assignment of rights so as to enable them to exploit fully and protect the works, with the result that publishing contracts are always in writing(21). Such contracts are always expressed to be subject to the rights of PRS which itself takes an assignment of the performing rights in its membership agreement with all composers and songwriters.

Works are protected for as long as they are within the term of copyright. The Berne Convention recommended a minimum term of the life of the author plus 50 years(22) so as to provide protection for the author and two generations of heirs. This remained the term in the UK until 1996, when it was increased to the author's life plus 70 years following harmonisation of the term of protection throughout the EU(23). One of the effects of this increase was that the copyright in works by anyone who died between 1925 and 1945 was "revived". In the absence of clear guidance in the legislation this raised some very practical problems for publishers and MCPS in relation to those who had taken steps to exploit works in the belief that they were in the public domain. These were largely resolved by compromise agreements.

How does copyright work?

The copyright owner's permission is required to use the whole or a substantial part of a work in certain ways ("restricted acts"). The copyright owner thereby has the opportunity to set the terms on which he is prepared to grant permission and these can include matters such as the type of use permitted, the geographical scope of the licence and charging a fee or royalty. There are primary and secondary restricted acts, the essential difference between the two being that an infringer can only be held liable for secondary acts of infringement if he knew or had reason to believe that he was infringing copyright, there being no such requirement of knowledge for a primary infringer to be held liable. Knowledge is generally conferred by writing a letter putting the infringer on notice of this fact as soon as the copyright owner becomes aware of the suspected infringement.

The primary restricted acts include the right from which copyright takes its name, namely the right to copy, often referred to as the right to reproduce a work in a material form. The 1911 Act spells out the fact that this includes making a "record, perforated roll, cinematograph film, or other contrivance by means of which the work may be mechanically performed or delivered", so giving statutory recognition for the first time to the "mechanical" right for which the MPA had previously fought unsuccessfully(24). This right is also the basis for the synchronisation right, being the right to match music with picture in films, television commercials etc. The scope of the right to copy is vast, ranging from printing a work to downloading it from the internet and even storing it on one's computer. Closely allied to the right to copy is the right to distribute those copies by means of publication, referred to in the 1988 Act as the right to issue copies to the public.

Until the 1988 Act came into force the right to make records was subject to a statutory (compulsory) licence, based on the American model which still prevails today in the US. This allowed anyone to make a recording of a work for retail sale, i.e. distribution, (other than the first recording, for which permission from the copyright owner was required) providing they met certain conditions, essentially notifying the copyright owner and paying a prescribed royalty. A similar approach pertains in practice today but without the statutory compulsion, although the royalty rate has in fact been set by the Copyright Tribunal(25) following MCPS and the BPI failing to agree a rate.

The right of public performance has been a fundamental plank of copyright law since the 1911 Act. It can include "any mode of visual or acoustic presentation" and so extends to both live and recorded performances. This so called "small right" provides the foundation for the work of PRS. Music publishers retain the so called "grand rights", that is the right to licence performances of works with some dramatic element such as musicals, operas and ballets(26).

PRS also owns and administers the rights to broadcast a work and to include it in a cable programme, both introduced at various points under the 1956 Act. The rights handled by PRS are commonly referred to as the performing rights.

A significant amendment to the 1988 Act(27) as a consequence of Copyright Directive(28) has been the introduction of the right of communication to the public by electronic means. This includes a broadcast right, which in effect combines the previous broadcast and cable rights, and an entirely new concept of making works available in such a way that members of the public can choose where and when to access them, i.e. on demand. This vital package of rights equips copyright owners to protect their works from unlicensed use on the increasingly sophisticated digital platforms being developed.

Other rights include making an adaptation of a work (which, in the case of a musical work, means an arrangement or transcription) and the renting and lending of works(29). The adaptation right was introduced into the 1911 Act to make it clear that use of a work in a different medium was as much an infringement of the copyright as a copy made within the same medium as the original, so giving copyright owners more adequate protection as technology developed.

The secondary restricted acts include importing an infringing copy into the UK for non-private use(30); dealing with an infringing copy of a work in the course of business; distributing an infringing copy otherwise than in the course of business to the prejudice of the copyright owner and providing the means for making infringing copies.

Other more recently introduced restricted acts(31) include circumventing technical protection measures designed to prevent a work from being copied, trafficking in devices primarily designed to circumvent such measures and interfering with rights management information attached to a work, a vital tool for effective digital rights management.

Remedies

The copyright owner's remedies against an infringer have remained largely consistent and include the right to apply to the courts for an injunction to stop the infringer from continuing to do unauthorised acts, damages, delivery up of the infringing copies and an account of any profits made. The Copyright Regulations(32) have introduced an effective means for stopping infringements on the internet through a new right to apply for an injunction against service providers even though they may not themselves be liable as infringers but who know that their services are being used to transmit infringing material..

In addition to civil liability, secondary acts of infringement (including trafficking in circumvention devices) are also criminal offences for which the offender may be fined and/or imprisoned. Copyright owners increasingly rely on these as a means of deterring would-be infringers in preference to recovering damages(33).

Fair dealing

It has always been the case that in certain prescribed circumstances a copyright work can be used without needing the prior permission of the copyright owner, subject to not undermining their interests in accordance with the overarching Berne three step test(34). The fair dealing exceptions allow, for example, works to be used for private research and study and, subject to acknowledging the copyright owner, for criticism, review, and the reporting of current events. There are also carefully prescribed exceptions for educational purposes and for librarians.

The public policy time-shifting exception which allows viewers to record broadcasts, and so the works included within those broadcasts, for private viewing at a more convenient time was introduced into the 1988 Act, effectively as an extension of the exception under the 1956 Act which allowed broadcasts (but not the works contained within them) to be copied without infringing copyright. Since the 1956 Act there has also been the so called "ephemeral" exception which permits the temporary copying of a work for the sole purpose of being able to use it in a broadcast for which the broadcaster has a licence, providing it is destroyed within 28 days. This is arguably analogous to the computer-related exception recently introduced into the 1988 Act by virtue of the Copyright Regulations(35) for temporary "machine" copies made in the course of a licensed transmission(36).

Looking ahead

The well established and undoubtedly valid principles of copyright are currently subject to unprecedented challenge from increasing numbers of people who wish to benefit from the fruits of creativity without having to observe the long established formalities of seeking permissions and paying modest licence fees, a challenge which is arguably pivotal to the survival of the music industry if not adequately met by the industry providing viable and attractive alternative means of paying for the music their customers so clearly want to enjoy.

© Sarah Faulder, Music Publishers' Association, 2003

NOTES:

1 Estimated at 6.7% of the workforce in the UK in 2002.
2 Moral rights are personal to the author and cannot be assigned, although they can be waived in the UK, seen as a dilution of the rights by European standards. They have no economic basis, in contrast to copyright, and generally endure for the period of copyright. The moral rights accorded under UK law to authors who died on or after 1 August 1989 include the paternity right (the right to be identified as the author of the work), the integrity right (the right to object to derogatory treatment of the work) and false attribution (the right not to have a work falsely attributed to one).
3 Rights analogous to copyright for performers and the owners of the right to make recordings of a performance (usually the record company) have been recognised under British law since the 1950s but were incorporated into copyright law in the 1988 Act. These so-called neighbouring rights last for 50 years from the end of the year in which the performance takes place or, if a recording of it is released, from the end of the year of release. With the exception of performers' right to equitable remuneration, they are transferable in the same way that copyright is.
4 The statutory obligation imposed on [music] publishers to deposit a copy of every work they publish in print with the British Library (and up to five other deposit libraries), so contributing to the national archive, stems from the 1911 Copyright Act. These provisions have prevailed untouched until the Legal Deposit Libraries Act 2003 which establishes a framework under which new strands of electronic publications can in future be made subject to legal deposit. This is unlikely to affect music publishers until such time as their publications are made available only in electronic form.
5 The Copyright Tribunal, which exists to oversee licensing schemes operated by the collecting societies including MCPS and PRS, is governed by the 1988 Act, with its previous incarnation, the Performing Right Tribunal, having been subject to the 1956 Act.
6 The publisher benefited from protection for 14 years, after which rights reverted to the author for a further 14 years, a precursor of the reversionary rights provisions under the later Copyright Act 1911. See note 15 below.

7 Moral rights were not incorporated into UK law until the Copyright, Designs and Patents Act 1988. See note 2 above.

8 US signed in 1989 and Russia signed in 1996.

9 Software Directive 1991 (see note 17 below); Rental and Lending Directive (see note 29 below); Satellite and Cable Directive 1993 (Council Directive 93/83/EEC of 27 September 1993 on the Coordination of Certain Rules concerning Copyright and Rights related to Copyright applicable to Satellite Broadcasting and Cable Retransmission); Term Directive 1993 (see note 23 below); Database Directive 1996 (see note 18 below) and the Copyright Directive 2001 (see note 28 below).

10 An integral part of the World Trade Organisation Agreement signed in 1994.

11 World Intellectual Property Organisation (WIPO) Copyright Treaty 1996. At the same time the WIPO Performances and Phonograms Treaty was signed, so updating international protection for performers, phonogram producers and broadcasters, previously governed by the 1961 Rome Convention and the 1971 Geneva Convention.

12 Under the Copyright and Related Rights Regulations 2003 implementing the Copyright Directive (see note 28 below) which in turn implemented the WIPO Treaties (see note 11 above).

13 To be distinguished from works created by more than one author, i.e. joint authorship, a concept which is recognised under English law.

14 Chappell & Co Ltd v Redwood Music Ltd [1980] 2 All ER 817

15 Under the 1911 Act the copyright in all but collective works reverted to the creators' heirs 25 years after death, leaving the heirs free to re-negotiate their agreements with the same publishers or to place them with other publishers. This provision, introduced to protect the interests of a creator's heirs against any possibly unwise transfer of his rights made during his lifetime, was abandoned in later statutes although its effect still applies to any transfers made by a creator between the effective dates of the 1911 and the 1956 Acts. See note 6 above.

16 See note 3 above.

17 Council Directive 91/250/EEC of 14 May 1991 on the Legal Protection of Computer Programs.

18 Directive 96/9/EC of the European Parliament and of the Council of 11 March 1996 on the Legal Protection of Databases.

19 Databases which lack the necessary originality to qualify for copyright protection can nevertheless be protected from being copied under a new *sui generis* right established in the Database Directive but provided for outside of UK copyright legislation in the Copyright and Rights in Databases Regulations 1997.

20 i.e. within 30 days of publication elsewhere.

21 Assignments may be subject to reversion. See note 15 above.

22 In the case of a work created by more than one author, the term is calculated by reference to the date of death of the survivor.

23 Council Directive 93/98/EEC of 29 October 1993 Harmonising the Term of Copyright and Certain Related Rights.

24 See Introduction and Beginnings chapter

25 British Phonographic Industry v MCPS (1992) 22 IPR.

26 I.e. dramatico-musical works, a term dating back to the Berne Convention but not found in subsequent UK statutes.

27 Copyright and Related Rights Regulations 2003.

28 Council Directive 2001/29/EC of the European Parliament and of the Council of 22 May 2001 on the Harmonisation of Certain Aspects of Copyright and Related Acts in the Information Society.

29 Council Directive 92/100/EEC of 19 November 1992 on Rental Right and Lending Right and on Certain Rights Relating to Copyright in the Field of Intellectual Property.

30 A copy imported from another part of the EU when it has been lawfully circulated in the EU is not infringing for these purposes.

31 See note 27 above.

32 See note 27 above.

33 The penalties were increased in the the Copyright, etc. and Trade Marks (Offences and Enforcement) Act 2002, making the criminal provisions an even more effective tool.

34 The three step test contained within Article 9(2) of the Berne Convention stipulates that any permitted exploitation must be limited to "the reproduction of such works in certain special cases, provided such reproduction does not conflict with a normal exploitation of the work and does not unreasonably prejudice the legitimate interests" of the copyright owner. The Copyright and Related Rights Regulations 2003 clarify some exceptions by stipulating that they must be strictly for non-commercial purposes only.

35 See note 27 above.

36 Transient and incidental copies are those which are "an integral and essential part of the technological process" involved in (i) transmitting a work or (ii) the lawful use of a work, providing they have no independent economic value.

The Performing Right and Copyright Tribunal – An Overview

By Michael Freegard

Michael Freegard is the longest-serving former Chief Executive of The Performing Right Society Ltd (1969-93). This article is based in part on a book entitled The Decisions of the UK Performing Right and Copyright Tribunal *by Michael Freegard and Jack Black (Butterworths, 1997; ISBN 0 406 89549 X), and on an article by Michael Freegard entitled Forty years on; an appraisal of the United Kingdom Copyright Tribunal 1957-1997 and published in* Revue Internationale du Droit d'Auteur *No. 177 in July 1998*

Origin And Development of the Tribunal

1) Origin

The Performing Right Tribunal, which was set up under the Copyright Act 1956, and which, under the Copyright, Designs and Patents Act 1988, became The Copyright Tribunal, had its origins in the report of a Parliamentary Select Committee published as long ago as 1930. During the preceding decade, the PRS had grown in strength to the extent that it controlled and exercised the performing rights in virtually all "popular" music as well as representing the composers and publishers of a large repertoire of more serious works. Despite a level of fees charged by the PRS which was described by a Board of Trade official of that time as "futilely small", an alliance of commercial music users had campaigned against that society for several years and the Musical Copyright Bill, introduced into Parliament in 1929, was the high-water mark of their efforts. Known as the "Tuppenny Bill" because it proposed a compulsory licence with a maximum

fee of 2d which the owner of the performing right in any musical work could demand, the Bill was furiously opposed by many leading figures in the world of the arts and was widely ridiculed in the press before being dropped. However the Select Committee's Report on the Bill, while wholly accepting the usefulness of an association such as the PRS, feared that it could abuse its powers by imposing unreasonable terms on those requiring its licence and that it should be open to them to have recourse to arbitration or to "some other tribunal".

That more than a quarter of a century elapsed before this proposal was enacted may be attributed in part to the extreme moderation (described by some as excessive caution) on the part of the PRS, against which no charge of actual abuse of monopoly had been substantiated, and in part to doubts as to whether legislation of this kind would have been in conflict with the United Kingdom's obligations under the Berne Convention. It was not until 1948, when the Berne Convention (1) was revised at Brussels, that the United Kingdom made the following declaration:

"The United Kingdom delegation accepts the provisions of Article 11 of the Convention on the understanding that His Majesty's Government remains free to enact such legislation as they may consider necessary in the public interest to prevent or deal with any abuse of the monopoly rights conferred upon owners of copyright by the law of the United Kingdom."

In 1951 a Board of Trade Committee (the Gregory Committee) was appointed to reappraise the law of copyright in the light of technological developments since 1911 and the revised Berne Convention. The President of the Board of Trade at that time was the future Prime Minister, Harold Wilson, who a few years earlier had gone on record as characterising the policy of the PRS as being, in his view, "of the very highest national interest"(2).

In its report, published in 1952 , the Committee took account not only of the near monopoly position of the PRS but also of that of

Phonographic Performance Ltd (PPL) which had been established by the record industry in 1934 to exploit the performing right in its members' recordings. The Committee's recommendation was the establishment of a standing Tribunal with binding powers of determination in cases where conditions of monopoly or quasi-monopoly obtained.

2) The Performing Right Tribunal

This recommendation was in due course enacted in the Copyright Act 1956 which established the Performing Right Tribunal (PRT) to determine disputes arising between "licensing bodies" such as the PRS or PPL and those requiring licences from them for the public performance, broadcasting or cable diffusion of literary, dramatic or musical works and sound recordings... References to the Tribunal could be made by organisations representative of those requiring licences, and other organisations or persons having a substantial interest in the matter in dispute could also, at the Tribunal's discretion, be made a party to the reference.

The task of the Tribunal was, after hearing the parties in dispute, to make whatever order it "may determine to be reasonable in the circumstances" (3).

3) The Copyright Tribunal

The Berne Convention was further revised in Stockholm in 1967 and in Paris in 1971. In the light of this, and of further technological changes affecting copyright which had taken place since 1956, a fresh departmental committee (the Whitford Committee) was set up by the Secretary of State for Trade in 1974. Its report, published in March 1977 (4), recommended that the jurisdiction of the PRT should be extended to cover all situations in which any body or organisation effectively controlled the "going rate" for a number of works, and that it should be given general jurisdiction in respect of licences granted by organisations who issued "blanket" licences as part of their

activities. This recommendation was echoed by the Government in both a Green Paper published in 1981 (5) and a White Paper published in 1986 (6). The latter also signalled some changes in the composition and operation of the Tribunal, and most of its recommendations were incorporated in the Copyright, Designs and Patents Act 1988.

Under the 1988 Act the PRT was renamed The Copyright Tribunal and was given jurisdiction over licences and licensing schemes operated by licensing bodies in relation to the copyright in a much wider range of works and uses than under the 1956 Act, including the copying of musical works, thus bringing, for the first time, the terms of licences and tariffs offered by MCPS within its purview. More recently secondary legislation to implement several European Council Directives on copyright and related rights has added further to the Tribunal's jurisdiction, including licences for new rental, lending, publication and performers' rights.

In addition to broadening the jurisdiction of the Tribunal, the 1988 Act included measures designed to improve its functioning. The 1956 Act did not specify any factors which the PRT should take into account in making its determinations. The test was simply what was "reasonable in the circumstances". While retaining this criterion, the 1988 Act helpfully specified certain factors to be taken into account by the Tribunal. In particular it is required to have regard to the availability and the terms of licences to others in similar circumstances and to ensure that there is no unreasonable discrimination between different categories of licensee (7).

4) References and Decisions (1957–2003)

In the 32 years from the establishment of the PRT until its replacement in 1989 by the Copyright Tribunal there were 46 references and applications to it, of which, however, a considerable number was withdrawn and several others were the subject of a consent order following agreement between the parties; the Tribunal was called upon to reach a decision in only 19 cases (15 of which concerned licences or tariffs of the PRS and four of PPL). Under the 1988 Act, which came into force in 1989, there have to-date (8) been 79 references or applications to the Copyright Tribunal, of which however the great majority were withdrawn after the parties reached agreement. Only 20 have become the subject of interim and/or final decisions of the Tribunal, including several consent orders in cases where the parties eventually came to an agreement. Of these 20 cases, seven have concerned PPL, five the PRS, three the MCPS and the remaining five other parties.

The Tribunal's Decisions: its Principles and Criteria

The task of a tribunal charged by statute with determining what is "reasonable in the circumstances", and with very little else to guide it, must be far from easy Although the avowed purpose of establishing the PRT had been "to prevent or deal with ... abuse of ... monopoly rights", the 1956 legislation in fact contained no reference to abuse of monopoly rights as such, nor did it provide the Tribunal with any specific criteria to assist it in its determination of what is reasonable. This defect was to some extent rectified in the 1988 legislation, but, as the learned judge remarked when giving judgment on an appeal on points of law arising from the Tribunal's first decision under the 1988 Act, the Tribunal has, by and large, found itself "engaged in an exercise in which it was notoriously easier to be right than to explain why" (9). For the most part therefore the Tribunal has had to find its own criteria of reasonableness, having regard always to the circumstances of the particular case before it. Many of those criteria have been peculiar to the case concerned and could not by their nature constitute guidance to be drawn on future cases. However, there have emerged over the years a number of

common threads in the principles and criteria which the Tribunal has considered relevant or not. The most important of these are the following: (10)

1) Previous agreements between the parties

Initially the PRT attached far more importance to the terms of agreements previously reached between the parties before it than to any other factor or consideration, but as time went on it began to accept that there was nothing which was necessarily unreasonable in a party's saying that it had made a bad bargain on the previous occasion and seeking to rectify the error when negotiating the terms of a new licence. It also began to take the view that guidelines more helpful than previous agreements were to be found in the proposals made by the respective parties to the dispute.

On the whole, the Tribunal's position, leaving aside the early days of the PRT when this factor assumed a predominance later abandoned, can be summarised as attaching importance to past agreements while to some extent looking behind them to special considerations which may have led to them and, more importantly, considering relevant changes in circumstances which had since taken place.

2) Past Decisions of the Tribunal

In a reference back to the PRT of a PRS tariff on which it had last adjudicated some 20 years earlier, the Tribunal was clear that "its task was simply to consider all the facts and matters placed before it and to decide what was reasonable in all the circumstances". It said previous decisions of the Tribunal "should be read as of their date and were persuasive and not binding, as to both fact and principle" (11).

In another case, this time concerning PPL, where there had been a previous reference involving the same parties some years earlier, the Copyright Tribunal was urged by the licensing body to treat the PRT's earlier decision "as a springboard". The Tribunal declined to do so because, it said, that that approach would have required it to take a considerable measure of guidance from the previous decision, which in materially changed circumstances it was not prepared to do (12).

3) Licence Fee or Royalty as a Percentage of the Licensees' Receipts

Strong objections to this have been raised by licensees before the Tribunal in a number of cases, and although such a formula has been accepted by it where it had been agreed between the parties, its general approach has been to reject it as unreasonable. Broadly speaking, the Tribunal has accepted as reasonable a licence fee or royalty based on the licensees' receipts only (a) where that has been the formula agreed between the parties, or (b) where it has been satisfied that there is a close causal relationship between the use of the copyright material being licensed and the generation of the receipts on which the royalty has to be based.

4) Foreign Evidence

In a number of cases one or other of the parties has urged upon the Tribunal, as a relevant comparator, the basis and/or amount of licence fees paid in other countries for the same uses of copyright material as were in issue before it. Unlike some of its overseas counterparts (13) the Tribunal has consistently approached such evidence with great caution and in almost all cases has concluded that it was of little assistance to it. In most cases in which such evidence was placed before it the Tribunal found it of "little help" either because "conditions" or the legal position were different.

5) Comparisons between different Users

In view of the requirement of the 1988 Act that the Tribunal must have regard, in considering the reasonableness of a licence or licensing scheme, to the terms of other schemes or licences offered by the same licensing body, and that it must ensure that there is no unreasonable discrimination between licensees, it might be expected that comparison of the terms offered by a licensing body to various categories of users requiring licences would play a central role in the Tribunal's thinking. However, in practice the Tribunal has consistently shown extreme caution in accepting such comparisons, and more often than not has found reasons for discounting them.

Criticisms And Conclusions

1) Criticisms

Apart from criticisms of the Tribunal published from time to time by the licensing body most affected by its decisions – the PRS – and from some of those users of copyright works who have had recourse to it, there have also over the years been recorded various criticisms from more objective sources. As regards criticisms made publicly by the PRS, in the early years of the PRT these included reasoned attacks on the Tribunal's claimed incompetence to carry out properly the terms of reference laid down for it by Parliament; in more recent times the PRS has limited its criticisms mainly to complaints about those very terms of reference and about the Tribunal's reluctance (a) to take foreign comparisons into account and (b) to approve rates of royalty based on a proportion of its licensees' revenues. It has also consistently criticised the composition of the Tribunal's membership, deploring the lack (with only a few exceptions) of persons with knowledge of artistic matters or intellectual property, and has pleaded in vain for its Chairman to be accorded the seniority and status of a High Court judge.

As regards criticisms by users of copyright works, these have for the most part tended to focus on the Tribunal's procedures, the cost of appearing before it, and the length of time it has generally taken for it to reach its decisions.

The most objective source of public criticism in recent years has been another statutory body – The Monopolies and Mergers Commission – which on two occasions has been called upon to examine issues relating to the collective administration of rights. In 1988 it was required to investigate practices relating to the collective licensing of sound recordings for broadcasting and public performance – in practice an investigation into the functioning of Phonographic Performance Ltd (PPL) – and in 1994 it was called upon to examine the supply of the services of administering performing rights and film synchronisation rights in copyright music – in other words to investigate the functioning of the PRS as the only organisation in the UK administering those rights. On both occasions, although the operations of the Tribunal were not matters which it was officially required to consider, inevitably a certain amount of evidence was given about them during its proceedings, and in both its reports the Commission made its own comments and recommendations concerning the Tribunal (14).

In its 1988 report, the Commission's observations and recommendations chiefly concerned procedural matters, recommending various measures to ensure that the Tribunal's proceedings became more accessible and expeditious. Several, though not all, of its suggestions were subsequently acted upon, useful changes to the Tribunal Rules being made which are generally considered to have brought about improvements to the speed with which references are dealt with and hence a reduction in the cost of proceedings to the parties. One of its recommendations – that the authority of the Tribunal – and hence the acceptability of its decisions to the parties – would be enhanced if some of its members were drawn from nominees of the collective licensing bodies and the leading users' associations, was not accepted by the Government.

In its 1996 report on musical performing and broadcasting rights, the Commission's most important observation was that the way in which music was transmitted was becoming increasingly universal, and in a wider and more integrated market with satellite transmissions and the internet, and erosion of national boundaries in Europe, international comparisons may be of greater relevance than before, so that neither users nor authors in the UK were disadvantaged by inappropriate tariff levels, referring in this connection to a decision of the European Court of Justice (15) that such comparisons were relevant in at least some cases.

2) Conclusions

What conclusions can be drawn from the way the Tribunal has functioned since it was first established nearly half a century ago? On the positive side it can be said at the outset that, in providing machinery for the resolution of disputes between a licensing body administering rights collectively and those users requiring that body's licence, the Tribunal has carried out a useful and indeed necessary function. Nor should its usefulness be thought of as being confined to the relatively small number of cases in which it has adjudicated. The very existence of such a Tribunal has been in itself a strong incentive, both to licensing bodies and users, to settle their differences by negotiation leading to agreement, the alternative – namely recourse to the Tribunal's jurisdiction – being perceived by both sides as so costly in terms of expenditure of both time and money as to be regarded as very much a last resort.

The fact that, judging by their evidence to the Monopolies and Mergers Commission in 1995, both users and licensing bodies had certain reservations about the way in which the Tribunal functions, despite acknowledged earlier improvements in its procedures, should not of itself be seen as negating a positive assessment. Nevertheless, from the perspective of the copyright owners, there are certain factors, referred to above, which, on balance, lead inescapably to the conclusion that there are still some fundamental defects in both the jurisdiction of the Tribunal, as established by Parliament, and in the manner in which it has carried out its task, and it is these which explain and justify a serious lack of confidence in it on the part of those whose rights are subject to its jurisdiction.

The charge that, at least as regards Article 11 of the Berne Convention, the powers given to the Tribunal conflict with the obligations of the United Kingdom under that treaty, has, to the present writer's mind, never been satisfactorily answered. The Report of the Whitford Committee, established by the UK Government in 1974 to review the law on Copyright and Designs in the wake of the Paris revision conference of 1971, noted in this connection the provisions of Article 17 of the Convention, usually understood as intended to ensure that governments are free to use such measures as they judge necessary to maintain public order, and admitted that this was "not intended to permit any general system of compulsory licences" (16), but went on to refer to the statement in the unanimously approved report of the Stockholm revision conference of 1967 (inserted at the instance of the United Kingdom) that "questions of public policy should always be a matter for domestic legislation and that the countries of the Union would therefore be able to take all necessary measures to restrict possible abuse of monopolies"(17). However when Parliament debated the Bill which became the 1988 Act, a proposal that the powers of the Copyright Tribunal be expressly limited to the purpose of preventing abuse of monopoly, in line with both the Stockholm statement and the reservation to Article 11 of the Berne Convention made by the United Kingdom at the Brussels revision conference in 1948, was rejected by the Government spokesman in the House of Lords, who accepted that "in general terms the system of Tribunal control over collective licensing was primarily designed to prevent abuse of monopoly power", but went on to say that it did not follow from this that the Tribunal

should be able to vary terms only where there was clear abuse of a monopoly position (18). There could hardly be a clearer admission than this that the jurisdiction given to the Tribunal goes beyond the restriction of abuse, and that the derogation in the UK legislation from the exclusive rights granted to authors under Article 11 of the Convention has exceeded its proper bounds.

Turning to the manner in which the Tribunal has exercised its mandate, any impartial observer could not but help being struck by its extreme reluctance to take guidance from many of the *prima facie* helpful comparisons which have been offered to it as evidence by licensing bodies in support of their claims. These have included evidence of, firstly, the terms on which individual copyright owners not subject to its jurisdiction have licensed their rights by agreement with users in open market conditions; secondly, terms freely negotiated by the same licensing bodies with other (in some cases even similar) categories of users; and, lastly – and perhaps most strikingly – of agreements between licensing organisations and users' organisations in other jurisdictions for uses identical with those which, in the UK, have been the subject of the dispute before it. In all three instances, the Tribunal's first instinct seems consistently to have been to search for reasons why those comparisons should be regarded as, at best, of limited value to it and, all too often, of little or no relevance to its task. In consequence, the Tribunal has left itself little alternative to relying for the most part chiefly, or even only, on previous agreements between the parties to the dispute before it. On its own analysis, agreements entered into before it had come into existence could not have been the subject of "real negotiations" (19), and yet in its own early years the old Performing Right Tribunal relied for guidance on little else. It is this above all that has fuelled a deep-seated sense of injustice on the part of the PRS and its members which has endured to the present day.

The reluctance of the PRT in its early years to take into account or, at any rate, accord much, if any, weight to "foreign evidence" is perhaps understandable, when we recall that it was at the very time that it was established under the Copyright Act 1956 that the United Kingdom was turning its back on participation in the newly established European Community. Now, however, after 30 years in which the aim of the UK has been, in the words of its own politicians, to be "at the heart of Europe" and during which it has been a leading advocate of the Single European Market, it is disappointing to find, even in some of the Tribunal's most recent decisions, such strong traces of the insularity which has marked its entire history. It is true that the Tribunal has in recent years begun, under pressure, as we have seen, from the MMC, to pay at least some lip service to the possible usefulness of European, and even some other "foreign" comparisons, though it is noteworthy that in the only two cases in which it has gone so far as to accord them sufficient weight to influence its decision to any notable extent, the foreign evidence in question has tended to be helpful to the interests of the users in the UK rather than to those of the copyright owners (20).

As national boundaries within the European Union are gradually assuming less and less significance it can only be a matter of time before it will be generally recognised as intolerable that the collective exercise of increasingly harmonised rights should be subject to controls in one part of the Single Market which are unknown in others (21). It is, in the present writer's opinion, to be hoped that the necessary harmonisation measures will include a system of widely acceptable European Union measures providing for arbitration and/or mediation to resolve disputes between organisations such as the PRS and MCPS on the one hand and those requiring their licence on the other. Sadly, the conclusion has to be drawn that the UK Copyright Tribunal does not, in many respects, furnish an acceptable model on which to base such a system.

NOTES:

(1) Paragraph (1) of Article 11 (Brussels Act) provided that the authors of dramatic, dramatico-musical or musical works should enjoy "the exclusive right of authorising ... the public presentation and public performance of their works ...".

(2) In this statement, made at the Society's annual luncheon in 1948, he added: "You have sought to protect the rightful interests of those ... who have the right to get the earnings from their work, but you have not abused the position of monopoly which you hold". (Ehrlich, *Harmonious Alliance*, OUP 1989, p 119).

(3) Copyright Act 1956, ss 25(5) and 27(5).

(4) Report of the Committee to consider the Law on Copyright and Designs (Cmnd 6732).

(5) Reform of the Law relating to Copyright, Designs and Performers' Protection (Cmnd 8302).

(6) Intellectual Property and Innovation (Cmnd 9712).

(7) CDPA 1988, s 129.

(8) As at 18th November 2003.

(9) BEDA v PRS [PRT.44/87].

(10) For a wider and deeper examination of the Tribunal's practices, see Freegard & Black *The Decisions of the UK Performing Right and Copyright Tribunal* (op cit at introductory note supra) at Chapter 2.

(11) PRS v Theatres' National Committee [PRT.42 and 43/86].

(12) AIRC v PPL [CT.9/91].

(13) For example, the Australian Copyright Tribunal in APRA v ABC 1985 [5 IPR 449] and the Singapore Copyright Tribunal in SBC v PRS and COMPASS [CRT No 1 of 1990 (unreported)].

(14) Collective Licensing: a Report on Certain Practices in the Collective Licensing of Public Performance and Broadcasting Rights in Sound Recordings, HMSO 1988 (Cm 530) and Performing Rights: a Report on the Supply in the UK of the Services of Administering Performing Rights and Film Synchronisation Rights, HMSO 1996 (Cm 3147).

(15) Ministère Public v. Tournier (Case 395/87 [1989]).

(16) Report of the Committee to consider the Law on Copyright and Designs (HMSO 1977 Cmnd.6732) atpara.762

(17) Ibid at para 763. See also Records of the Intellectual Property Conference of Stockholm 1967 (WIPO1971), Report of Main Committee I, para.263 (p.1175).

(18) Hansard HL487-504 (14 December 1987).

(19) BACTA v. PPL [CT4/89].

(20) NewsGroup Newspapers Ltd v Independent Television Publications Ltd and BBC Enterprises Ltd [CT.8/91] and British Airways PLC v PRS [CT.45/97].

(21) For a survey of measures of this type which have been taken in various countries within and beyond the European Union, see Freegard *Quis Custodiet? The Role of Copyright Tribunals* (European Intellectual Property Review 16.7, 1994) and Freegard and Black *The Decisions of the UK Performing Right and Copyright Tribunal*, op cit supra, at Chapter 4.

The Monopolies and Mergers Commission Enquiry and Report 1994–1996.

Introduction

In the early 90s discontent from individuals and certain sections of the PRS membership had been signalled publicly at several successive PRS AGMs and through complaints to the Office of Fair Trading (initially leading to a statement from the OFT that no action was required). The complaints varied, but in essence had to do with the way money was distributed, the information used to distribute it (seen by many to disadvantage certain musical genres), and the lack of information to members.

The number and nature of renewed complaints to the OFT prompted an announcement in November 1994 from Sir Bryan Carsberg, Director General of Fair Trading, that he had referred "the supply in the UK of the services of administering performing rights and film synchronisation rights" to the Monopolies and Mergers Commission.

Understandably (and in fact more accurately) this lengthy enquiry title was soon colloquially shortened into "the MMC enquiry into PRS" although the original title appeared on the final Report.

The members' complaints which had prompted the reference were summed up by the Office of Fair Trading as being that

• they were receiving inadequate payments from PRS

• under the society's rules they lacked sufficient representation to be able to pursue their interests effectively

• the revenue distribution policies adopted by the society unduly favoured the writers and publishers of "more popular" forms of music.

The OFT added that it had "subsequently [become] aware of misgivings among the society's members about the exclusive nature of their assignment of performing rights to PRS and the restrictions that apply for members who wish to leave". This was a reference to the major and very public disagreement between PRS and the group U2, which is dealt with elsewhere.

Lastly the OFT pointed to the fact that complaints had been made both by members and licensees "about the proportion of expenditure devoted by the society to administration and to claims of managerial inefficiency".

The MMC enquiry, under the Chairmanship of Mr Dan Goyder, extended through much of 1995, and PRS mobilised an internal Board, management and legal team assisted by external legal advisers and other consultants to respond to the Commission throughout that period. The Commission considered evidence from overseas societies, music users, writers and publishers and others, as well as a painstakingly-assembled dossier of information from PRS. The Commission's report was published in February 1996. The lengthy list of recommendations for change and improvement which it contained were interpreted by some as very damning, but by others as a recognition that a well-established and reputable organisation had deserved scrutiny, and now needed to take constructive action.

The view of the PRS Board members and managers who were in place at the time of the MMC Enquiry was, and remains, that this investigation was one of the most useful things which could have happened to PRS. The senior manager who led the PRS team during the enquiry also made the point, often missed, that the management team's ideas and views were very much taken on board by the MMC panel during the enquiry. As a result these management views of what was wrong and how best it might be put right are reflected to a significant extent in the report itself. So there was every reason for the report to be particularly welcomed by PRS management. They believed that it could be taken as strong support for further management proposals which they thought would be for the common good, to improve communication and shared thinking.

The report also helped those on the Board who wanted wide-ranging changes, and it further proved to be an excellent basis for the newly appointed Chief Executive John Hutchinson to deal firmly and swiftly with necessary situational change.

The MMC Report
A report on the supply in the UK of the services of administering performing rights and film synchronisation rights
London HMSO Cm 3147

Under its terms of reference the MMC was required formally to determine whether "a monopoly situation" existed and in whose favour, although there was no question at any time that PRS was, as it remains today, a *de facto* monopoly in the area of licensing the performing right in music in the UK.

The core of the enquiry therefore related to how this monopoly was operating, and whether such a monopoly situation was working for or against the interests of copyright owners and licensees[1] The first paragraph of the Report Summary was a good fingerpost to the MMC's view. It concluded: "It would be far beyond the majority of copyright owners to negotiate and collect their own royalties for performing rights including both public performance and broadcasting. For this reason, they arrange for a collecting society, in the UK PRS, to do the job for them."

Unsurprisingly, the MMC found that a monopoly situation existed in favour of PRS. It also found that this situation was, in fact, working generally to the benefit of both members and music users. "We are well aware of the very considerable role which PRS has played in the musical life of this country since its formation.

Writers and publishers as well as users have benefited greatly from its operations and from the skilled service of employees and directors over the years." The significant *caveat* however was: "There is always a risk that a monopoly institution may give priority to policies which primarily protect the *status quo* rather than looking to the interests of is members in a rapidly changing environment".

The report referred to "tensions between writers and publishers and between those who are involved in different musical genres" and concluded that these tensions had "contributed to the development of a corporate organisation and a way of working which are cumbersome by modern standards. [There is] evidence of inefficiency, arising from deficiencies in the corporate structure and management practices of the PRS. The division of activities between the General Council (*as the Board was then known*) and the executive is inappropriate…this is not conducive to the making of clear policy decisions; nor is the lack of a clearly defined set of objectives and a long-term strategy". There was specific reference to the need to link business and IT strategy, and a comment that there had been far too little progress in remedying deficiencies in essential databases which had been identified several years before. The report also stated that the failure to appoint a Chief Executive for almost two years had had a prejudicial effect on the way in which the society was managed; it noted that this had been very recently remedied.

Thus, in a single paragraph of a report running to over 350 pages, the MMC condensed a view of an organisation which was fulfilling an essential function largely to the benefit of its members and the market, but which was in need of change and improvement in structure, practices, governance and business technology.

The lengthy and comprehensive Background and Evidence section of the MMC Report included written views submitted to the Enquiry from a variety of groups and individuals – music users, overseas societies, writers, publishers, miscellaneous others and

---

1 Technically the relevant interest is "the public interest" but to all practical intents and "purposes owners and licensees" is correct

PRS itself; and there was an equally comprehensive presentation of information in the nine appendices and their sub-sections

The Commission's Recommendations

The MMC made a total of 44 recommendations for action. These included:

The PRS General Council to step back from the day-to-day management of the society to concentrate on key policy issues and supervision of the development of the PRS' future strategy. This linked to a recommendation that the number of meetings of the full Council should be reduced (1) ;

Formal delegation by the General Council of responsibility for the day-to-day management of the Society to a new Executive Committee comprising the Chief Executive, Chairman, both external directors(2), a second Executive Director(3) and no more than two other director members of the General Council(4). This was linked to a recommendation that the existing Executive Committee should be disbanded;

(1) Both recommendations were followed specifically, with for the first time a clear written definition of the distinct and respective roles of the General Council (Board), the Executive Committee and the Management

(2) As a result of the Corporate Governance report commissioned in 1994 the Board had already extended its own membership from entirely elected non-executive to include two appointed "external Directors" selected for skill and experience outside the area of music rights

(3) The choice was the Director of Membership, although some time after the formation of the MCPS-PRS Alliance this executive directorship on the PRS Board was allocated to the overall PRS Executive Director

(4) It was eventually decided – and reported to the OFT, who accepted the position that such a small Executive Committee was not desirable.

Reduction in the number of Committees and groups (5);

Increase in the amount of formal management representation on the remaining committees and groups (5);

(5) initial reductions were effected, but the requirements of PRS (and later of MCPS, within The Alliance) were over time believed to demand the creation of new Committees (some, such as the Audit Committee, required by Governance rules, others particular to these organisations). The practice of setting up task forces and working groups which combined Board directors and managers also grew, although these groups were not permanent and disbanded after their particular projects were completed.

Clear differentiation between the roles of Chairman and Chief Executive (6);

(6) The required clear and separate definitions were agreed, set down and announced, and remain in place.

A group of recommendations related to the development of a formal and improved process for strategic planning, corporate objective setting, the linking of IT strategy to, and synchronisation of its implementation with strategic business plans (7);

Development of an IT strategy which took into account the need to streamline processes and integrate all major administrative systems. This linked to a recommendation that a high priority be given to improvement of data (7);

Setting out of all key steps necessary to improve efficiency, with target dates for completion (7);

(7) These pragmatic recommendations for business process and IT improvement in line with widely accepted "best practice" were accepted and acted upon (some already being planned or actually in train by the time the MMC Report was published).

A group of recommendations related to management of cost and better information about cost – through evaluation, using cost–benefit analysis, of all future major proposals for change; achievement of improved cost appraisal to determine which costs are direct and which are indirect; implementation of systems to provide the necessary information for more equitable cost allocation to be made; publication of a new cost allocation system and publication of sufficient accounting information for members to see where costs lay. Also targets to be published for reducing administrative costs (8);

(8) These and other recommendations which were clearly intended to ensure better management of costs, to ensure greater fairness and accuracy in the way administration costs were allocated to members' income and to improve the quality and quantity of information provided to members as regards income and costs, were embraced by the society in a wholehearted approach to improving not only fairness and accuracy but also transparency of Society practices and a continually improving flow of well–presented and detailed information for members

Impose separate annual membership fees for writers and publishers of around £25 (plus VAT) and £125 (plus VAT) respectively (9);

(9) imposition of an annual membership fee was rejected and to date no such fee has ever been charged to PRS members although in the light of the MMC's recommendation the Board did take the precaution of reserving the right to require members to pay such a fee (PRS Article 11B)

PRS formally to set out in the Members Handbook the responsibilities it has to members and the standards of service it aims to achieve. Also a recommendation to establish an Appeals Board to resolve the disputes which members may have from time to time with the society about their personal rights (10);

(10) Again, recommendations which were complied with in the letter and the spirit, as part of a gradual and very great improvement in member service and member communications. The Board was required to establish a complaints and appeals procedure under the Articles (Article 54B); the rules governing the Appeals Panel's jurisdiction are contained in PRS Rule 6A.

PRS to work toward accreditation under an approved quality standard (11);

(11) PRS had already set up a Total Continuous Improvement initiative embracing all managers and staff, but it had failed to reach its objectives. Later the MCPS-PRS Alliance would successfully achieve Investors in People (IiP) accreditation.

Rules relating to termination of membership to reflect the flexibility inherent in current practices and set out the changes clearly for members in the published Rules and Members Handbook (12);

(12) Recommendation adopted – (see PRS Articles 9(f)(ii) and 9(f)(iii)

A group of recommendations related to royalty distribution and the data used for such distribution:professional advice to be taken about the measurement and sampling of public performances with benchmarks to be drawn up for all major areas of public performance and regular and statistically valid sampling to take place thereafter; establishment of a committee including representatives of a range of minority musical genres to oversee sampling work; putting in place of a financial model to assess rapidly the effect of changes in distribution policies – all supported plans which were formulated before the Report was published, and actions which developed from these over the following few years. *The Distribution and Data Review, and its contribution to improving the accuracy and fairness of royalty distribution is dealt with the PRS main chapter.*

The amendment of voting rules to allow writer member to send representatives to speak and vote for them at PRS general meetings (13);

(13) Recommendation adopted (and subsequently extended to successor members) (see PRS Article 34A)

The society's Articles of Association to be amended to make it clear that members already had the right to self-administration of their live public performance right (14), and to withdraw or reserve to themselves the categories/forms of utilisation of the performing right (15) as set out in the GEMA decision of the European Commission (16); and for PRS to publicise the changes.

(14) Recommendation adopted (see PRS Article 7(g) and PRS Rule 11A

(15) Recommendations adopted –(see PRS Articles 7(cc), (cd), 9(f)(i) and (iii).

(16) GEMA Decision (No 2) (Commission Decision 72/268 OJL166. The society was required to transplant the English translation of the Decisions straight into its Articles.

The Development of Digital Music Distribution

by Paul Brindley

Director of MusicAlly, research and analysis consultancy

Amongst the many and varied landmarks to date in the technological revolution facing the global music business, there have been four key developments which have impacted on distinct elements of the digital music distribution chain.

First came digitisation, the process by which all information – text, audio, graphics, film – can be converted into binary code. Having appeared to be the saviour of the music business, combating stagnating vinyl sales at the end of the 70s and through the early 80s with very rapid early sales growth of the CD, digitisation also let the genie out of the bottle by allowing recordings to be effectively 'cloned' when they were copied as digital files. But for a considerable time the music files were too big to be transferred easily from computer to computer. Then what began as a research project at the Fraunhofer Institute in Germany in 1987 resulted in the creation of a European-backed standard for audio compression called MPEG[1]-Layer3 in 1992 (which came to be commonly known as MP3). The third element was the growth of the internet itself, as millions of computers were able to link to each other and the worldwide web grew and spread immeasurably through the 90s. But the final catalyst to the real digital music revolution was the invention by an American teenage music fan, Shawn Fanning, of a piece of software called Napster which allowed individual users to find and share those MP3 audio files at the click of a mouse. The fury, fear and (ultimately successful) defensive/retaliatory pressure from the global music industry led Napster (as it had other early MP3 audio file distributors) to step away from its anarchic beginnings and seek legitimacy by putting its technology in the hands of a company working in or alongside the music business.

The fact that in mid-2003 Napster was relaunched as the rebranded name for Pressplay – the ex-major record label backed service (originally developed by Universal and Sony) which was sold to the CD-burning company Roxio – shows just what a challenging business the digital music scene is proving to be. Whilst the collecting societies have gathered increasingly significant revenues from ringtones, the unforeseen technological success of the mobile platform, the music business as a whole has been struggling to turn online music from a threat into an opportunity.

After the legal success against the original Napster in the US, the current generation of unlicensed decentralised file sharing services have so far evaded most legal attempts to have them shut down – Grokster and Morpheus in the US and KaZaA in the Netherlands. 2001–3 saw a new generation of services that aim to preserve user anonymity (Blubster, Piolet, Freenet et al) that could turn the recent American deterrent of suing individual users into an idle threat, making it impossible to track down individual file sharers. But compelling legal alternatives are finally beginning to give consumers what they want.

In early 2004, services like Apple's iTunes Music Store (which sold about 25m downloads between its Mac-only launch in April 2003 through the introduction of a Windows version in October, up to December that year) and Rhapsody (which claimed to be delivering millions of streams' of songs a month to over 250,000 subscribers) were leading the way in the US, and plenty was happening on this side of the ocean too. The UK collecting societies have now licensed over 75 services under their joint online licensing scheme administered by the MCPS-PRS Alliance, including the likes of OD2, writer/performer Peter Gabriel's digital distribution company which is powering so many of Europe's leading online music outlets; Playlouder ISP, a pioneering

1 A stream involves the music being streamed, ie transmitted, to the end user without being permanently downloaded.

peer-to-peer (from one individual to another rather than a
commercially and centrally provided service); and O2, the first
over-the-air mobile download service; and PlayLouder MSP, the
internet service provider which allows its users to share music over
a closed network And with big consumer brands such as Coca
Cola (in the UK) following hot on the heels of Pepsi, McDonalds,
Walmart and HP (in the US) all launching download initiatives,
there's every reason to believe that online music is finally set to hit
the mainstream consumer market in 2004.

Timeline

1881	Music Publishers' Association (MPA) founded.
1882	Copyright (Musical Performance) Act passed, requiring right owner to print a notice reserving the public performance right on each sheet music copy.
1884	MPA offers £10 reward for information leading to the conviction of sheet music pirates.
1888	New Copyright (Musical Performance) Act passed.
1891	The American Copyright Act grants protection to UK works in the United States for the first time.
1899	Appeal Court in England rules that reproduction of music works by means of sound recording did not infringe authors' rights.
1902	Music (Summary Proceedings) Act becomes law.
1905	Musical Defence League founded by publishers and composers to lobby for action against sheet music piracy.
1906	Music Copyright Act becomes law.
1908	Revised Berne Convention agreed in Berlin.
1909	Gorell Committee on copyright established by Parliament.
1910	Mecolico (Mechanical Copyright Licences Company) founded. Formation of British Composers' Society. MPA officials attend the International Congress of Music Publishers.
1911	Passage of Copyright Act. Copyright Protection Society (Mechanical Rights) Ltd formed.
1914	Performing Right Society formed.
1915	Death of PRS general manager Pierre Sarpy. His successor is H S J Booth.
1916	PRS membership reaches 234.

1917	First PRS distribution, totalling £11,000 for three years' collections.
1919	Popular music publishers resign from PRS.
1920	Gross collections of PRS are £22,468.
1921	PRS wins case against Bradford Corporation confirming that venue owners are liable for copyright payments.
1922	First broadcasts by the British Broadcasting Company (BBC). PRS launches *Performing Right Gazette* for members.
1923	PRS issues first broadcasting licence to the BBC.
1924	New composer members of PRS include Frederick Delius, Arnold Bax and John Ireland. MCPS (Mechanical Copyright Protection Society) formed by the amalgamation of Mecolico and Copyright Protection Society.
1925	Copyright Protection Society (Mechanical Rights) transfers its members to MCPS and ceases to exist. MPA gives evidence to the Crawford Committee on the future of broadcasting. First PRS agency established in South Africa.
1926	CISAC formed in Paris with PRS as a founder member. Popular music publishers rejoin PRS.
1927	Music Copyright Defence Association requests inquiry into mechanical royalty rate. International Council of Music Users Ltd formed to lobby for maximum PRS royalty of two pence.
1928	Copyright Royalty (Mechanical Musical Instruments) inquiry by Parliamentary committee. Berne Convention revised at Rome.
1929	PRS signs landmark agreement with the BBC. BIEM (international bureau for mechanical rights organisations) founded in Paris. Tuppenny Bill introduced in the House of Commons.

1930 PRS membership is now over 1,000.
Parliamentary report on musical copyright helps to defeat the Tuppenny Bill.

1931 Heirs of deceased members permitted to join PRS.

1932 PRS Members Assistance Fund established.

1933 PRS introduces category of Associate Member.
New PRS composer members include Bud Flanagan and Havergal Brian.

1934 Phonographic Performance Ltd (PPL) formed.
PRS wins case against Hammonds Bradford Brewery concerning public performance by radio receivers.

1935 PRS royalty income reaches £346,329.

1936 New publisher members of PRS include Oxford University Press and Novello.

1937 PRS royalties from the BBC are increased by an arbitration decision.
MPA joins the Radio Defence Committee in support of Radio Luxembourg and other commercial stations.
New PRS composer members include Bela Bartok and Zoltan Kodaly.

1938 The Patents, Designs, Copyright and Trade Marks (Emergency) Act establishes that PRS can continue to collect royalties due for foreign works during wartime.

1940 BBC launches *Music While You Work* programme.

1943 PRS v Gillette Industries establishes that piped music in factories is a public performance.

1944 Composers' Guild formed.

1945 PRS membership passes 2,000 and its income is £857,986.

1946 Leslie Boosey elected president of CISAC.

1947 British Songwriters' Protective Association (later the Songwriters'
Guild of Great Britain) formed.
PRS hosts the first post-war CISAC Congress.

1948 Berne Convention revised at Brussels.

1949 First Top Twenty sheet music chart published by the Popular Music Committee of the MPA.
MPA signs agreement with BBC over radio programme content and plug money.
New PRS members include Steve Race.

1950 PRS revenues are £1.5 million and membership is 2,416.

1952 Universal Copyright Convention adopted.
Gregory Committee recommends the formation of a copyright tribunal.

1953 Formation of British Joint Copyright Council (renamed the British Copyright Council in 1965).

1954 Sir Arthur Bliss is elected president of PRS.

1955 PRS revenues are £2.4 million and membership is 2,835.
Mechanical Rights Society (MRS) established by MPA.
First issue of Performing Right, the PRS membership magazine.
Launch of independent television in the UK.

1956 Copyright Act adopted by Parliament.
Ivor Novello Awards founded.

1957 Performing Right Tribunal (PRT) set up.
New PRS composer members include Lionel Bart, George Martin and Wilfred Josephs.

1959 PRT reduces PRS tariff for commercial dance halls.

1960 PRS moves to its current location in Berners Street, London W1.
Its revenues are £3.3 million and membership is 3,370.

1961 New PRS composer members include Tony Hatch and Benny Hill.

1963   PRT approves PRS tariff for music used at bingo sessions in cinemas and ballrooms.
New PRS composer members include John Lennon and Paul McCartney.

1964   PRS hosts the CISAC Congress.
Royce Whale appointed PRS general manager.
New PRS composer members include Ray Davies and Mick Jagger.

1965   PRS revenues are £5.6 million and membership is 3,715.
Number of licenses issued by PRS passes 100,000 and income passes £5 million.
New PRS composer members include Roger Greenaway and Harrison Birtwistle.

1966   Songwriter Paddy Roberts succeeds Leslie Boosey as PRS chairman.
PRS installs its first computer.

1967   Berne Convention revised at Stockholm.
New PRS composer members include David Bedford and David Bowie.

1968   New PRS members include Wayne Bickerton, Tim Rice, Andrew Lloyd Webber and 'proprietors of Hymns Ancient and Modern'.

1969   Michael Freegard succeeds Royce Whale as PRS general manager.

1970   PRS membership passes 5,000 and PRS income reaches £9,127,395.

1971   PRS receives the Queen's Award for Export Achievement.
Berne Convention revised at Paris.

1972   PRT rules that BBC payments to PRS should be based on a percentage of the BBC's income.

1973   British Phonographic Industry (BPI) founded.
New PRS members include Virgin Music Publishing and Gilbert O'Sullivan.

1974   Leslie Britton becomes secretary of the PRS Members' Fund.
First BASCA Gold Badge Awards presented.

1975   PRS revenues are £17.2 million and membership is 8,697.
Sir Lennox Berkeley is elected president of PRS.

1976
Record Royalty Review begins.
CISAC awards its gold medal to Leslie Boosey.
PRS begins publication of Performing Right News.

1977
MCPS revenues pass £5 million.
Publication of Whitford Committee report on copyright.
Music Copyright (Overseas) Services Ltd formed by PRS.

1978
First edition of the *Performing Right Yearbook* published by PRS.

1979
PRS wins Harlequin Records case in the High Court.
New PRS members include Judith Weir and Mick Hucknall (Simply Red) .

1980
PRS revenues are £39.3 million and membership is 13,462.
PRS delegation makes fact-finding visit to JASRAC (Japan).
MCPS withdraws its home recording licence.
UK record companies abolish Recommended Retail Price (RRP).
New PRS members include Paul Hewson (Bono).

1981
Stemra (the Netherlands) and CBS Records sign first European central licensing contract.

1982
New agreement signed by MRS and MCPS with the BPI (British Phonographic Industry).
New PRS members include Steve Martland.

1983
Roger Greenaway elected Chairman and Vivian Ellis appointed President of PRS.
New PRS members include Debbie Wiseman and Sade.

1984
First PRS regional office established in Edinburgh.
New PRS members include Courtney Pine.

1985
PRS membership passes 20,000 and its income is £74,487,000.
New PRS members include Neil Tennant (Pet Shop Boys).

1987
Ron White is elected chairman of PRS and Geoffrey Bush becomes Chairman of the PRS Members' Fund.
MCPS launches the National Discography project.
Warner Communications bid for Chappell Music is referred to the Monopolies Commission.

1988	PRS logo redesigned by The Jenkins Group. Monopolies and Mergers Commission publishes report on the licensing of sound recordings. BPI and MCPS sign their first Music Videogram Agreement.
1989	Publication of *Harmonious Alliance* by Professor Cyril Ehrlich to mark the 75th anniversary of the founding of PRS. PRS Composers in Education scheme launched. New PRS members include Norman Cook (Fatboy Slim).
1990	PRS revenues are £131 million and member ship is 23,984. MCPS distributions are £281 million. PROMS information technology project launched by PRS. New PRS members include Thomas Ades.
1991	Groupement Europeén de Societes des Auteurs et Compositeurs (GESAC) formed as European Economic Interest Grouping. Copyright Tribunal adjudicates in mechanical royalty dispute between MCPS and BPI. MPA publishes the 500th edition of *MPA News*. New PRS members include Polly Jean Harvey (P J Harvey) and Damon Albarn (Blur).
1992	Wayne Bickerton succeeds Dr Donald Mitchell as PRS chairman. PRS sets up an international department. PRS suspends PROMS project. MCPS publishes its Manufactuers' Code of Practice. First UK National Music Day (June 28).
1993	MCPS revenues top £100 million for the first time. Michael Freegard resigns as PRS Chief Executive. New PRS members include Thom Yorke (Radiohead).
1994	Publication of *Playing In Tune*, a corporate governance review of PRS by Professor Tom Clarke. Bureau Europeen de Licences (BEL), comprising MCPS, SDRM (France) and GEMA (Germany), signs European central licensing contract with EMI Records. MCPS establishes its Anti Piracy Unit.
1995	PRS revenues reach £178.5 million and membership is 29,510. John Hutchinson appointed PRS chief executive. Irish Music Rights Organisation (IMRO) becomes an independent collection society.

1996

Andrew Potter succeeds Wayne Bickerton as PRS chairman.
Publication of British Invisibles report *Overseas Earnings of the UK Music Industry*.

Publication of Monopolies and Mergers Commission report on PRS.
Resignation of Frans de Wit, the last MCPS chief executive.
Death of Vivian Ellis, life President of PRS.
MCPS signs European central licensing (ECL) contract with PolyGram Records.
PRS announces plan to abolish classical music subsidy.
PRS Distribution and Data Review launched.
WIPO (World Intellectual Property Organisation) Copyright and Performances and Phonograms treaties adopted at Geneva.
European Union 'Rental' Directive adopted by UK Government.
ServiceCo project to link MCPS and PRS.
British Music Rights formed.
New PRS members include the Spice Girls.

1997

MCPS-PRS Alliance formed. MCPS total royalty collection is £197.4 million and PRS income is £201 million.
Cannes Agreement signed by European mechanical right societies and major music publishers.
Sarah Faulder appointed MPA Chief Executive.
New PRS members include Robbie Williams, Liam Gallagher (Oasis) and Eliza Carthy.

1998

International Music Joint Venture (IMJV) launched by the MCPS-PRS Alliance, ASCAP (US) and Buma/Stemra (Netherlands).

1999

PRS Overseas formed to supervise agency territories.
British Academy of Composers and Songwriters (BACS) formed.
New PRS members include Chris Martin (Coldplay).

2000

PRS Foundation launched.
Santiago Agreement provides the basis for national societies to give international.
Performing right licences to online music companies.

2001

PRS total revenues are £260.5 million and membership is over 37,000.
International Music Joint Venture (IMJV) project cancelled.
The mechanical rights counterpart of the Santiago Agreement is launched as the Barcelona Agreement.
New PRS members include Keisha Buchanan (Sugababes).

2002

PRS total revenues are £272.4 million and MCPS distributions are £221.4 million.
David Bedford begins his term as Chairman of PRS.
All Party Music Group founded at House of Commons with 170 members.
The MCPS-PRS Alliance is chief host and organiser in London of the biennial CISAC World Congress.

2003

UK Government implements the European Directive on Copyright in the Information Society
through the Copyright and related Rights Regulations.
Launch of BACS British Composer Awards in association with BBC Radio 3.
PRS licenses London Transport for performances by buskers in underground stations.
The MCPS–PRS Alliance joins the FastTrack digital copyright network.
New PRS members include Jamie Cullum and Dylan Mills (Dizzee Rascal).

Index

Terri Anderson joined PRS in December 1990 as Public Affairs Controller, running the department responsible for PR and media relations, for the entire range of the society's printed publications for press, public, members, and licensees, for events and awards, and for internal communications. She also very actively represented PRS on the Communications Group of the international rights societies' organisation CISAC. She came to PRS after a career in journalism, as newpaper and news agency reporter and feature writer and then for 10 years as a writer and Features Editor for the UK music business paper *Music Week*, and a further career in corporate PR and communications, first with the UK record industry trade body the BPI and then with EMI Music and EMI Records. Her record industry experience was also put to use during a short-term placement in 1990 as Vocational Studies Director advising the educational team which set up the curriculum for the Brit performing arts school (run by the British Record Industry Trust).

She became a member of the PRS management top team, as Director of Planning and Corporate Communications, in early 1996 after John Hutchinson had joined the company as Chief Executive. Her role then included setting up and developing a business planning and management performance reporting process, creating a marketing function for the first time, and raising the public affairs activity to a strategic corporate communications level. These played their part in the creation and identity of the MCPS-PRS Alliance. Business and structural change led again to exclusive focus on communications issues, and her final project for the Alliance was a Project Director for the CISAC World Congress 2002, which took place in London and for which the Alliance was the chief host and the organiser.

Since January 2003 Terri Anderson has been running Big Red Kite, her own PR and communications consultancy.